Cognitive Behavior Therapies

A GUIDEBOOK FOR PRACTITIONERS

edited by
Ann Vernon and Kristene A. Doyle

AMERICAN COUNSELING
ASSOCIATION

6101 Stevenson Avenue, Suite 600
Alexandria, VA 22304
www.counseling.org

Cognitive Behavior Therapies

A GUIDEBOOK FOR PRACTITIONERS

American Counseling Association
6101 Stevenson Avenue, Suite 600, Alexandria, VA 22304

Associate Publisher
Carolyn C. Baker

Digital and Print Development Editor
Nancy Driver

Senior Production Manager
Bonny E. Gaston

Production Coordinator
Karen Thompson

Copy Editor
Beth Ciha

Cover and text design by Bonny E. Gaston.

Library of Congress Cataloging-in-Publication Data
Names: Vernon, Ann, editor. | Doyle, Kristene A., editor. | American Counseling Association, issuing body.
Title: Cognitive behavior therapies : a guidebook for practitioners / Ann Vernon, Kristene A. Doyle, editors.
Description: Alexandria, VA: American Counseling Association, [2017] | Includes bibliographical references and index.
Identifiers: LCCN 2017003943 | ISBN 9781556203671 (pbk. : alk. paper)
Subjects: | MESH: Cognitive Therapy–methods
Classification: LCC RC489.C63 | NLM WM 425.5.C6 | DDC 616.89/1425—dc23
LC record available at https://lccn.loc.gov/2017003943

Dedication

We dedicate this work to the key theorists of the cognitive behavior therapies discussed in this book. Each pioneer has had a profound impact on the foundation and evolution of evidence-based counseling approaches. As a result of their innovative work, countless numbers of people of all ages are able to apply the principles to themselves to enhance their emotional well-being.

Table of Contents

Preface

The term *cognitive behavior therapy* (CBT) is familiar to most mental health practitioners throughout the world. As you will read in the first chapter, CBT is a generic term that describes a wide range of approaches, despite the misconception that there is one type of CBT. As O'Kelly (2010) noted, CBT is "like a river" with many tributaries, including classical and operant conditioning and learning theory, among other influences, and the premise that cognitions trigger emotional and behavioral reactions (p. 10). Albert Ellis and Aaron Beck were at the forefront of the cognitive revolution, which has steadily gained momentum and popularity over the years in part because the various CBT approaches have wide applicability and have been shown to be effective with many different types of presenting problems. Furthermore, CBT readily lends itself to a broad array of interventions that are practical in nature and have been proven to effect change.

The authors of these chapters are experts in this field, both as practitioners and as scholars. They provide a comprehensive overview of the following theories: behavior therapy, cognitive therapy, rational emotive behavior therapy, multimodal behavior therapy, acceptance and commitment therapy, dialectical behavior therapy, and mindfulness. They address pertinent information pertaining to the key theorist or theorists associated with the theory as well as give an overview of the basic principles of that theory. In addition, they describe the therapeutic process, with an emphasis on the process of change and specific interventions associated with the theory. Applications and efficacy are also addressed. At the end of each chapter, the authors include a verbatim transcript of an actual counseling session so that you will have a better idea of how the theory works in practice. These transcripts are from a fourth session, with some background about the client and issues addressed in previous sessions. Each author also provides a short critique of why the theory is effective in addressing the problem and what went well or could have been done differently. Clients' names and identifying information for these transcripts have been modified to protect their identities. The final chapter considers the case of Marcos, contributed by Anthony Pantaleno, who coauthors the chapter on mindfulness. After a description of the case, the authors who discussed each respective theory describe how they would conceptualize this case, including the establishment of the therapeutic alliance, goal setting, the process of change, and interventions to address the targeted issues.

As coeditors and contributing authors, we hope that this book enlightens students and practitioners about the various forms of CBT, dispelling myths and misconceptions. We hope that the emphasis on practical information, further illustrated through the verbatim case examples and the case of Marcos, contributes to a broader understanding of the "what's" and "how to's" of the seven theories addressed in this book.

References

O'Kelly, M. (2010). *CBT in action: A practitioner's toolkit.* Melbourne, Australia: CBT Australia.

About the Editors

Ann Vernon, PhD, ScD, LPC, is president of the Albert Ellis Board of Trustees, one of the first diplomates of the Albert Ellis Institute, a member of the International Training Standards and Review Committee of the Albert Ellis Institute, a member of the Board of Consulting Advisors for the *Journal of Rational-Emotive & Cognitive-Behavior Therapy*, and former director of the Midwest Center for rational emotive behavior therapy. In addition, she was selected by the American Psychological Association to do a counseling video demonstration titled *Rational Emotive Behavior Therapy Over Time: Psychotherapy in Six Sessions*. Dr. Vernon is recognized as the leading international expert in applications of rational emotive and cognitive behavior therapy (RE&CBT) with children and adolescents and has written numerous books, chapters, and articles about counseling this population, including *Thinking, Feeling, Behaving: An Emotional Education Curriculum*; *What Works When With Children and Adolescents: A Handbook of Individual Counseling Techniques*; *The Passport Program*; and *More What Works When With Children and Adolescents*. Dr. Vernon is a professor emerita of the University of Northern Iowa, where she served as coordinator of the school and mental health counseling programs for many years. In addition to her university appointment, Dr. Vernon was in private practice for many years, applying RE&CBT with children and adolescents as well as with couples and individuals. She has been a frequent presenter at national conferences and has presented RE&CBT workshops throughout the United States, Canada, Australia, and several countries in Europe and South America. Currently she is a visiting professor at the University of Oradea in Romania, where she teaches courses in school and mental health counseling and continues to do RE&CBT trainings around the world.

Kristene A. Doyle, PhD, ScD, is the director of the Albert Ellis Institute (AEI). Dr. Doyle is also director of clinical services, founding director of the Eating Disorders Treatment and Research Center, and a licensed psychologist at AEI. She is also a founding diplomate in rational emotive and cognitive behavior therapy and serves on the Diplomate Board. In addition to training and supervising AEI's fellows and staff therapists, Dr. Doyle conducts numerous workshops and professional trainings throughout the world. With a distinguished international presence, Dr. Doyle has influenced the growth and practice of rational emotive and cognitive behavior therapy in countries spanning several continents, including South America, Europe, Asia, and Africa.

Dr. Doyle is coauthor of *A Practitioner's Guide to Rational Emotive Behavior Therapy* (3rd ed.). She is coeditor of the *Journal of Rational-Emotive & Cognitive-Behavior Therapy.* She has contributed numerous book chapters on topics such as the treatment of eating disorders, attention-deficit/hyperactivity disorder, and coping with loss. She has presented her research at several national and international conventions, including those of the American Psychological Association, Association for Behavioral and Cognitive Therapies, and World Congress of Behavioral and Cognitive Therapies. In addition, Dr. Doyle has published in numerous scientific journals and has been quoted in prestigious publications, including the *New York Times, U.S. News & World Report,* and the *Wall Street Journal.* In addition to her work at AEI, Dr. Doyle is appointed as full adjunct professor at St. John's University in both the clinical psychology and school psychology doctoral programs, where she has taught for 16 years.

About the Authors

Michal Barnea, PsyD, is a fourth-year doctoral student in the school psychology program at St. John's University. She is a psychology extern at Columbia University's Children's Day Unit and a doctoral fellow at St. John's Center for Counseling and Consultation. She received her bachelor's degree in neuroscience from the Hebrew University in Jerusalem and her master's degree in school psychology from St. John's University. She is also a New York State certified bilingual school psychologist. Michal's research interests include cross-cultural research, especially as it pertains to emotional experiences.

Daniel David, PhD, is an Aaron T. Beck Professor of clinical cognitive sciences at Babeş-Bolyai University (BBU), Cluj-Napoca, Romania, and the pro-rector for research at BBU. Dr. David is also an adjunct professor at Icahn School of Medicine at Mount Sinai, the head of the research program at the Albert Ellis Institute in New York, and the director of the International Institute for the Advanced Studies of Psychotherapy and Applied Mental Health at BBU. He has contributed extensively via randomized controlled clinical trials to the development of the theory and practice of rational emotive and cognitive behavior therapies. As founding editor of the *Journal of Evidence-Based Psychotherapies,* he has supported the evidence-based approach in the clinical field. Dr. David has authored and coauthored numerous highly cited articles, books, and book chapters.

Raymond DiGiuseppe, PhD, received his bachelor's degree from Villanova University (1971) and his doctorate from Hofstra University (1975). He has served as president of the Association for Behavioral and Cognitive Therapies (2006) and the Society for the Advancement of Psychotherapy (2014). He has coauthored six books, including *Understanding Anger Disorders* and *A Practitioner's Guide to Rational Emotive Behavior Therapy.* He has also developed two psychological tests, the Anger Disorders Scale for adults and the Anger Regulation and Expression Scale for youth. He is a professor of psychology at St. John's University and Director of Education at the Albert Ellis Institute in New York. Dr. DiGiuseppe regularly conducts rational emotive and cognitive behavior therapy trainings at the Albert Ellis Institute and its affiliated training centers around the world.

Nora Gerardi, MS, is an advanced doctoral candidate in school psychology at St. John's University in New York City. She earned her undergraduate degree in psychology from the University of Connecticut and her master's degree in school psychology from St. John's University. Nora completed a school psychology externship in the Ardsley Union Free School District in Ardsley, New York, and she is currently a psychology extern at Cognitive and Behavioral Consultants in White Plains, New York. Nora is an active member of the Association for Behavior and Cognitive Therapies, where she has presented research on suicidal behaviors, nonsuicidal self-injury, and dialectical behavior therapy.

Roseanne Gotterbarn, PhD, earned her doctorate in clinical-school psychology from Hofstra University and her bachelor's degree in philosophy from Fordham University. She works as a cognitive behavior therapist in private practice and also as a school psychologist where she applies the principles of rational emotive and cognitive behavior therapy with children, adolescents, and families.

Michael Hickey, PhD, is the director of the Center for Psychological Evaluation and the Obsessive-Compulsive & Related Disorders Treatment and Research Center at the Albert Ellis Institute in New York. In addition, he is a licensed psychologist, fellow, and certified supervisor at the Albert Ellis Institute. Dr. Hickey has trained numerous students and mental health professionals in the method and application of rational emotive and cognitive behavior therapy. He has conducted public lectures and professional workshops on a variety of topics ranging from eating and body image issues to empirically supported cognitive–behavioral treatment for anxiety disorders, body dysmorphic disorder, and obsessive-compulsive disorder. Dr. Hickey also serves on the editorial review board of the *Journal of Rational-Emotive & Cognitive-Behavior Therapy*.

Gary B. Kelley, PhD, is a counseling psychologist in private practice at the Multimodal Therapy Institute in the Cleveland, Ohio, area. He is on staff at several local hospitals and has worked on both an inpatient and outpatient basis in both psychiatric and chemical dependency facilities. He is a member of several professional societies, is an approved consultant with the American Society for Clinical Hypnosis, and is certified as a trainer in Ericksonian hypnosis and brief psychotherapy by the American Hypnosis Training Academy. Dr. Kelley is certified by Arnold Lazarus as a trainer in multimodal therapy and has a Certificate of Proficiency in the Treatment of Alcohol and Other Psychoactive Substance Use Disorders by the American Psychological Association Practice Organization, College of Professional Psychology. In his private practice, he treats individuals, couples, and children using multimodal therapy.

Chris Kelly, MA, received her bachelor's degree in psychology from the University of Virginia and her master's degree in clinical psychology from Fordham University, where she is currently an advanced doctoral student in clinical psychology. Her research focuses on biological and psychological factors that interfere with treatment response in major depressive disorders. Ms. Kelly has clinical experience with adults in school/community and intensive outpatient settings. Her clinical interests include treatment for depression, suicidality, self-harm, and addiction.

Silviu A. Matu, PhD, is a senior assistant professor in the Department of Clinical Psychology and Psychotherapy at Babeş-Bolyai University in Cluj-Napoca, Romania. His research interests are related to evidence-based psychological interventions and the integration of psychological services (e.g., assessment, treatment) with new technological tools (the Internet, virtual reality, robotics). He has also worked on fundamental research focused on the cognitive processes (cognitive emotional regulation) relevant to the development of psychopathology. He is a clinical psychologist certified by the Romanian Board of Psychologists.

Cristina Mogoaşe, PhD, is a clinical psychologist and cognitive–behavioral psychotherapist certified by the Romanian National Board of Psychologists and by the Albert Ellis Institute, New York. She is a fellow of the International Institute for the Advanced Studies of Psychotherapy and Applied Mental Health at Babeş-Bolyai University, Romania. Dr. Mogoaşe is involved in national and international clinical trials of the efficacy of cognitive–behavioral interventions for treating emotional problems in children, adolescents, and adults. Her research interests are focused on clinical cognitive sciences and new developments in cognitive–behavioral interventions.

Victoria Nicosia, BS, is a first-year graduate student at St. John's University, where she is working toward her doctorate in school psychology. Prior to attending St. John's, Victoria earned her bachelor's degree in psychology from Muhlenberg College in Allentown, Pennsylvania. Victoria has presented research at regional and national conferences and is interested in working with children who have autism spectrum disorder and other developmental and behavioral disorders.

Anthony Pantaleno, PhD, is a recently retired school psychologist, having worked for 38 years in the Elwood School District in Long Island. He is the recipient of several awards, including the National Association of School Psychologists 2013 School Psychologist of the Year, the New York Association of School Psychologists 2011 Leadership Award in School Psychology, and the 2008 Suffolk County Psychological Association Psychologist of the Year. He has developed peer helping models, developed applications of mindfulness-based interventions in school settings and the workplace, and most recently created the Long Island School Practitioner Action Network as a model for coordinating regional crisis response efforts in schools.

Ioana R. Podina, PhD, is a senior assistant professor affiliated with the University of Bucharest and a scientific researcher at Babeş-Bolyai University. Dr. Podina is a licensed clinical psychologist and psychotherapist with a background in cognitive–behavioral psychotherapy. She is certified by the Romanian National Board of Psychologists and by the Albert Ellis Institute, New York. For the past 5 years her clinical practice and research activities have been dedicated to advancing knowledge in the field of e-CBT (i.e., technology-mediated cognitive behavior therapy). She is currently the principal investigator of a research project focused on using e-CBT to treat emotional eating problems in adults at risk for obesity, a project that intertwines second-wave and third-wave CBT techniques. Dr. Podina's orientation toward scientific excellence in the clinical field is demonstrated by the number of articles for which she is first author that have been published in top journals such as *Behavior Therapy*.

Diana M. Robinson, MD, has a bachelor's degree in neurobehavioral biology from Emory University and a medical degree from Texas A&M University. She is a psychiatry resident in adult general psychiatry at the University of Virginia and primarily treats patients with mood and psychotic disorders. As a trained practitioner of dialectical behavior therapy, Dr. Robinson applies this approach in group therapy, primarily with clients with borderline personality disorder. She is an American Psychiatric Association Leadership Fellow (2016–2018).

Tara Rooney, PhD, is the director of the St. John's University Center for Psychological Services, the training center for the graduate programs in school and clinical psychology at St. John's University. Dr. Rooney earned her doctorate in clinical psychology from St. John's University. Prior to serving in her current position, Dr. Rooney served as the coordinator of training and a staff psychologist at the St. John's University Center for Counseling and Consultation. Her clinical interests include internalizing disorders in children, the emerging adult population, and training.

Mark Sisti, PhD, is a psychologist and the founder/director of the Suffolk Cognitive–Behavioral Group Treatment and Training Center. He is an adjunct clinical supervisor at Yeshiva-Ferkauf University and a founding fellow, diplomat, and certified trainer with the Academy of Cognitive Therapy. Dr. Sisti is a past president of the New York chapter of the Association of Contextual Behavioral Science and has trained and supervised students and practitioners in third-generation cognitive behavior therapy approaches.

Mark Terjesen, PhD, is an associate professor of psychology at St. John's University and program director of the school psychology programs. He earned his doctorate in clinical and school psychology from Hofstra University. Dr. Terjesen has studied, published, and presented at numerous national and international conferences on rational emotive and cognitive behavior therapy as well as the assessment and treatment of attention-deficit/hyperactivity disorder and cultural issues. Dr. Terjesen has trained many professionals internationally in the use of cognitive–behavioral practices with children and families. He has served as president of Division 52 of the American Psychological Association, of which he is also a fellow; president of the School Division of the New York State Psychological Association; and president of the Trainers of School Psychologists.

Rachel Venezia, MA, received her bachelor's degree from the University of Chicago. She is currently a clinical psychology doctoral student and a doctoral fellow at St. John's University. Rachel has presented at national conferences on the measurement of anger and the impact of psychiatric and medical conditions on neuropsychological functioning, including at the Association for Behavioral and Cognitive Therapies, the International Neuropsychological Society, and the American Academy of Clinical Neuropsychology.

Chapter 1

What Is Cognitive Behavior Therapy?

Raymond DiGiuseppe, Rachel Venezia,
and Roseanne Gotterbarn

Cognitive behavior therapy (CBT) represents a form of psychotherapy that solves current problems, disturbed emotions, and dysfunctional behavior by acknowledging the role of human learning as well as the effects of the environment, cognitions, and language in disturbance. It has become the overriding, generic term used to describe a wide range of approaches to counseling and psychotherapy that represent three distinct yet overlapping therapeutic approaches: behavior therapy (BT), cognitive therapies, and mindfulness and acceptance therapies. These approaches are similar but conceptualize the mediation of dysfunctional behavior differently.

CBT originated in BT and remains committed to many of its values and traditions. The main organization that represents the professional and scientific advancement of these therapies was originally known as the Association for the Advancement of Behavior Therapy; in 2004 this group added the term *Cognitive* to its name, thus becoming the Association for Behavioral and Cognitive Therapies.

This chapter provides an overview of CBT and orients you to general concepts that are described more specifically in the chapters of this book. Although there are many varieties of CBT, this book focuses on BT, cognitive therapy (CT), rational emotive behavior therapy (REBT), multimodal therapy (MMT), acceptance and commitment therapy (ACT), dialectical behavior therapy (DBT), and mindfulness. The editors selected these models because they each have good empirical support, are widely accepted, and appear to be growing in popularity.

Variation in CBT

Despite its popularity, CBT does not represent a monolithic paradigm. Some theorists have used the metaphor of three waves to understand the differences among the forms of CBT. The first wave of CBT started with the behavioral tradition, based on the work of B. F. Skinner and Ivan Pavlov and the clinical areas of applied behavior analysis (Martin & Pear, 2015) and pragmatic behavior therapy (Fishman, Rotgers, & Franks, 1988). Learning principles formed the basis of this initial approach, and interventions included relaxation training, exposure, operant interventions, and the rehearsal of new adaptive responses to problems.

The second wave emerged because of some dissatisfaction with the behavioral model. Behavior therapists recognized that human thoughts and language played a more central role in disturbed behavior than the behavioral model recognized. As the cognitive revolution occurred in BT, the number of approaches increased very quickly. This group of therapies included Albert Ellis's REBT, Aaron Beck's CT, Don Meichenbaum's (1993) self-instructional training, and problem-solving skills training (Nezu, Maguth Nezu, & D'Zurilla, 2013).

The third wave included techniques based on mindfulness and a new approach to language and cognition called *relational frame theory,* which represents a new approach to Skinner's learning theory applied to language. Relational frame theory differs from previous schools of thought insofar as it does not recommend trying to change the content of a belief or thought but instead attempts to break the connections between thoughts and rigid behavior actions. It relies on teaching acceptance of negative thoughts and training flexible behavioral reactions in response to their occurrence.

The metaphor of the three waves might not be the best way to conceptualize these differences in CBT. Waves come in an order, and new waves overtake previous waves, which recede back to the ocean unnoticed. The three waves of CBT did not occur in three different points in time; each has ancient roots in philosophy and psychology. Also, the first two waves have not run out of energy and fallen back into the undertow of science or clinical practice; they still exist and are going strong. A better metaphor would be three branches on an evolutionary bush, such as three groups of apes: gorillas, chimpanzees, and bonobos. Each model has common ancestors in psychology and philosophy and continues to evolve on its own. None of the models has driven the others into extinction.

Even in these three major groups there continues to be diversification and expansion. As early as 1993, Kuehlwein identified 10 schools of CBT. Since that time, more variants of CBT have appeared. Table 1.1 represents an inexhaustive list of types of CBT theories that we uncovered in a recent search.

As noted, this book describes only a few variants of CBT but includes representatives from all three branches or waves. The chapter on BT represents the first branch and includes the basic skills of CBT. The chapters on

Table 1.1

Models of CBT and Their Founders

Form of Counseling	Founder and Reference
Acceptance and commitment therapy	Hayes et al. (2011)
Applied behavior analysis	Martin & Pear (2015)
Behavior therapy	Wolpe (1969)
Cognitive therapy	A. T. Beck (1976)
Cognitive analytic therapy	Ryle (2005)
Constructivist cognitive psychotherapy	Neimeyer (2009)
Dialectical behavior therapy	Linehan (1993)
Fixed role therapy	Kelly (1955)
Functional analytic psychotherapy	Kohlenberg & Tsai (1991)
Meta-cognitive therapy	Wells (2008)
Mindfulness cognitive therapy	Sigel, et al. (2013)
Mindfulness-based interventions	Kabat-Zinn (2013)
Multimodal therapy	A. A. Lazarus (1981)
Parent training	Forgatch & Patterson (2010)
Pragmatic behavior therapy	Fishman et al. (1988)
Problem-solving therapy	Nezu et al. (2013)
Rational emotive behavior therapy	Ellis (1962)
Rumination-focused CBT	Watkins et al. (2007)
Schema-focused cognitive therapy	Young et al. (2003)
Self-instructional training	Meichenbaum (1977)
Trauma-focused CBT (TF-CBT)	Cohen (2006)
Trial-based cognitive therapy	de Oliveira (2016)
Wellness therapy	Fava (2016)

Note. CBT = Cognitive behavior therapy.

REBT (Ellis, 1962), CT (A. T. Beck, 1970, 1976), and MMT (A. A. Lazarus, 1981) represent the second branch. The chapters on ACT (Hayes, Villatte, Levin, & Hildebrandt, 2011), DBT (Linehan, 1993), and mindfulness (Kabat-Zinn, 2013) represent the third branch.

Although these models share more similarities than differences, they emphasize different learning, cognitive, and psychological processes as mediating the relationship between environmental stressors and emotional and behavioral disturbances. Furthermore, although they use many different interventions, most of the interventions in each of these models are compatible with the other models. Hofmann, Asmundson, and Beck (2013) described CBT as a theoretically consistent model that focuses on a wide range of clinical problems, each of which might require a different emphasis and intervention. Thus, CBT practitioners might use multiple procedures to accomplish change yet remain theoretically consistent, describing their clients in terms of CBT theoretical constructs that are presented in this book.

Observing a number of professionals delivering CBT sessions might be confusing to the novice because one is likely to see the counselors doing many different things without a consistent pattern. O'Donohue and Fisher (2009) described 74 different CBT interventions. Here is a list of some of the techniques used in CBT:

- Assertiveness training
- Assessing the emotions, thoughts, and behaviors that occurred when the client tried to implement a homework assignment
- Assessing the presence of dysfunctional behaviors or emotions
- Behavioral activation—increasing mastery and pleasuring experiences
- Bibliotherapy
- Challenging the client's irrational beliefs
- Challenging the client's negative automatic thoughts
- Changing the client's underlying schemas
- Decentering
- Defusion
- Diagnostic interviewing
- Distress tolerance
- Exploring the adaptability of the client's belief system
- Exploring the adaptability of the client's emotions and behaviors
- Flooding
- Graduate exposure
- Habit reversal training
- Harm reduction
- Imaginal exposure
- Mindfulness exercises
- Modeling and role-playing new skills
- Negotiating homework
- Offering alternative rational beliefs or schemas to replace the client's irrational beliefs or dysfunctional schemas
- Operant strategies
- Opposite action
- Parent training
- Performing a comprehensive multimodal assessment of behaviors, affect, sensations, imagery, cognitions, interpersonal relationships, drugs, or biological influences
- Performing an ABC analysis of thoughts: activating event, beliefs, and emotional consequences
- Performing an ABC functional analysis of behavior: antecedents, behaviors, and consequences
- Relapse prevention
- Relaxation procedures
- Response chaining
- Response prevention and exposure
- Reviewing homework
- Self-control procedures
- Self-instructional training
- Shaping

- Social problem solving
  - Helping the client generate alternative solutions to problems
  - Helping the client evaluate the consequences and effectiveness of alternative solutions
- Social skills training
- Stimulus control procedures
- Teaching the B → C connection
- Teaching the difference between irrational and rational beliefs
- Token economies
- Validating the client's emotions
- Values and goals clarification

It is important to note that although CBT is eclectic in techniques, it is consistent in its theory. And although many therapists consider themselves eclectic, eclecticism can be a confusing and difficult path to follow. A. A. Lazarus (1967; A. A. Lazarus & Beutler, 1993) pointed out that therapists who practice as theoretically eclectic must inevitably use contradictory ideas, which begs the question of how one chooses or justifies using one theory with one case and a different theoretical approach with another case. However, CBT practitioners can and do use many different interventions while remaining theoretically consistent. A. A. Lazarus (1967) coined the term *technical eclecticism* to describe clinical practice that remains theoretically consistent yet uses a variety of methods that target the theoretical mechanism identified by one's orientation.

Assumptions and Core Principles of CBT

Given all of these variations on CBT, you might wonder what they have in common. In this section, we review the common assumptions, principles, and histories that unite CBT.

For most CBT therapists, the term *behavior* refers to actions of striated muscles as well as to the reaction of the sympathetic nervous system, thoughts, and emotions. Thus, the definition of *behavior* is broad. CBT started with and remains committed to basing its practice on concepts derived from the field of scientific and experimental psychology. CBT-based interventions evolved from basic scientific learning principles. This is reflected in the field of applied behavior analysis (Martin & Pear, 2015) and Joseph Wolpe's systematic desensitization. Also, there remains a strong behavioral tradition using learning theory principles to inform clinical practice (Fishman, 2016). As CBT grew, its practitioners discovered that other factors besides the scientific laws of learning contributed to effective therapies, which influenced practitioners to shift their emphases to developing therapies based on any scientific principles of human behavior (A. A. Lazarus, 1977). Presently learning, cognitive, social, and system principles all influence the practice of CBT.

CBT began with a commitment to conducting research on the efficacy and effectiveness of its interventions. The gold standard for such research is the randomized clinical trial, but single-subject designs and meta-analytic reviews of interventions and treatments of diagnostic and clinical problems also remain a hallmark of CBT. Adherents to CBT have been responsible for setting the criteria for empirically supported treatments (ESTs). A task force of scientists (American Psychological Association Presidential Task Force on Evidence-Based Practice, 2006) set the criteria for the degree and type of scientific support necessary for an intervention to be classified as an EST. Based on reviews of research, two websites identify the interventions that meet these criteria. ESTs for adults are posted and revised online by the Society of Clinical Psychology (Division 12 of the American Psychological Association), and treatments for children and adolescents appear on a website maintained by the Society for Child and Adolescent Clinical Psychology (Division 53 of the American Psychological Association).

In addition to a commitment to research, the original behavior thera-pists held the following assumptions or values that served as the basis for the field (Fishman, 2016) and are adhered to by the other two branches (DiGiuseppe, David, & Venezia, 2016; Follette & Hazlett-Stevens, 2016). These basic principles included the following:

- All humans learn and maintain normal and abnormal behaviors by the same learning and psychological principles.
- Abnormal behavior can be altered or changed through the scien-tifically established principles of social learning, including operant learning, classical conditioning, cognitive appraisal, and learning new responses to stressors. These principles are discussed in the oth-er chapters of this book.
- Assessment of clients' problems is a continuous process that informs case formulation, diagnosis, and the monitoring of clinical progress.
- Change methods are clearly identified in a manner that can be repli-cated by any other professional and objectively evaluated.
- Outcome measures focus on behavior change in the real world and its generalization across multiple situations and time.
- Treatment plans are individually crafted to the particular characteris-tics of the client after a functional assessment of the problem.
- The client and the counselor jointly decide on the treatment goals and methods.
- The client's goals are described in terms of concrete behaviors and emotions and not by hypothetical or theoretical constructs.
- Practitioners evaluate clients' strengths and try to decrease clients' problems through increasing behaviors that are incompatible with clients' problems.
- Change usually takes place in small steps.
- Flexibility in responses is associated with coping and personal growth, and interventions usually focus on multiple adaptive behaviors.
- The stimuli that precede maladaptive behaviors create connections that need to be changed.

- The consequences of a behavior are a powerful influence on the continuation of the behavior.

CBT practitioners share these assumptions. However, several other theoretical ideas have been added that reflect the contributions of Beck and Ellis via the cognitive revolution in BT. These were clearly identified by Dobson (2010) and DiGiuseppe, Doyle, Dryden, and Backx (2014) as follows:

- Cognitive activity affects behavior.
- Cognitions can be monitored and altered.
- Desired emotional and behavior change can occur through cognitive change.
- The active rehearsal of new incompatible adaptive cognitions to counter maladaptive cognitions affects change. CBT differs from psychodynamic therapy in believing that insight into the relationship between thoughts and emotions or into the irrationality or incorrectness of thoughts is usually not sufficient to bring about desired change.

These last four points represent the most controversial assumptions in the models presented in the following chapters. You are advised to pay close attention to how the models adhere to these assumptions. Some models, such as Ellis's REBT, Beck's CT, and Arnold Lazarus's MMT, adhere to these positions. Steven Hayes's ACT and the mindfulness perspectives see cognitions as stimuli that preceded the disturbed emotions and behaviors. The third-branch therapies of CBT are less concerned with changing the content of clients' thoughts and instead work on breaking the connections between clients' thoughts and behaviors. The goal is to establish new connections between thoughts and a new set of behaviors. BT and DBT change the content of thoughts or the relationship between thoughts and behavior depending on what might work for that client.

The Therapeutic Relationship in CBT

CBT differs from other theoretical orientations in that it does not claim that the therapeutic relationship is a causative factor that helps clients improve. It does not posit that acceptance by the counselor is a curative component of treatment or that an analysis of the client's relationship with the counselor is necessary for change. Because of this lesser emphasis on the therapeutic relationship as a curative factor, many professionals assume that CBT practitioners do not focus on the relationship or work to foster a strong connection between the therapist and client. Nothing can be further from the truth.

The source of this misperception goes back to a debate between Rogers (1950, 1957) and Ellis (1948/2000, 1959, 1962). Rogers (1957), in his client-centered therapy approach, proposed that unconditional acceptance by the therapist was a necessary and sufficient condition for human therapeutic change, a position he held for some time. By *necessary*, Rogers meant that change could not take place without unconditional acceptance; by *sufficient*, Rogers meant that unconditional acceptance alone was all that was required for change. Ellis (1948/2000, 1959, 1962) responded by suggesting that unconditional acceptance was neither necessary nor sufficient for human change. It was not necessary because many people changed without it, often through engaging in bibliotherapy, attending lectures, modeling friends, or numerous other experiences. Ellis contended that unconditional acceptance could not be sufficient because many clients experienced unconditional acceptance from their psychotherapists and still failed to change. It is notable that Ellis (1962) concluded that although he thought that unconditional acceptance by therapists was neither necessary nor sufficient for therapeutic change, it was still important. Without attaining a close relationship, the client would most likely not listen to the therapist and fail to benefit from other therapeutic methods.

Jacques Barber (personal communication, August 20, 2015), a psychodynamic clinician, made an interesting observation about the role of the therapeutic relationship in CBT. He noted that the founders of CBT, theorists such as Aaron Beck, Albert Ellis, George Spivack, Marvin Goldfried, and Walter Mischel, were originally trained in the psychodynamic tradition. They learned how to establish and use the therapeutic relationship. However, they went on to develop new theories and did not write about this aspect of their work in the first generation of textbooks on CBT. The second generation of CBT therapists, people such as Arthur Freeman, Marsh Linehan, and Raymond DiGiuseppe, were trained by the first generation of CBT theorists, who modeled how to form good therapeutic relationships, but still did not lecture or write about the therapeutic relationship. The first and second generations focused on emphasizing how their theories differed from client-centered and psychodynamic approaches. The third generation of CBT practitioners might have failed to learn about forming good therapeutic relationships, as it was not part of the curriculum. This has now changed. Those who write about and demonstrate all forms of CBT explicitly teach the importance of developing a strong therapeutic relationship (DiGiuseppe et al., 2016; Fishman, 2016; Follette & Hazlett-Stevens, 2016). Although CBT believes in the notion of establishing a good relationship, many CBT theorists take the position that a good relationship is necessary but not sufficient for change (J. Beck, 2011; Brady, 1980; DiGiuseppe et al., 2014; Persons, 2008).

Closely tied to the establishment of a good therapeutic relationship is the concept of unconditional self-acceptance, which has become a central tenet of all forms of CBT. Although the importance of unconditionally accepting the client is crucial, it would be quite hypocritical to believe that clients have to accept themselves and others and yet the therapist is not expected to model and display the same acceptance. Thus, it is important that not only clients but also therapists acknowledge the existence of their own faults, negative thoughts, and uncomfortable emotions without condemning themselves.

The active and directive nature of CBT also leads some to believe that CBT does not place importance on the therapeutic relationship. Modern research on the therapeutic relationship refers to the importance of the relationships as the therapeutic alliance. This concept is a multidimensional construct and includes (a) agreement on the goals of therapy, (b) agreement on the tasks of therapy, and (c) an emotional bond between the client and therapist. Research dating back more than 40 years has demonstrated that behavior therapists establish as strong or stronger therapeutic relationships with their clients compared to psychodynamic therapists (Sloan, Staples, Cristol, & Whipple, 1975). However, the myth about the lack of attention paid to the development of the therapeutic alliance has persisted. Using a measure based on Carl Rogers's model of the therapeutic relationship, DiGiuseppe, Leaf, and Linscott (1993) countered this claim. They found that clients receiving REBT/CBT had scores on therapeutic relationship scales that were equal to or greater than those reported by clients in all studies conducted using that instrument.

Factors Affecting the Therapeutic Relationship

It is common for a therapeutic alliance to rupture in CBT when clients are reluctant to engage in identifying or challenging their beliefs. Castonguay, Goldfried, Wiser, Raue, and Hayes (1996) found that attempts to resolve the rupture by persuading clients of the validity of the cognitive rationale were *negatively* correlated with outcome. These interventions worsened the alliance and thus potentially interfered with client change. In contrast, successful strategies to repair the relationship included (a) inviting the client to explore the potential rupture; (b) offering an empathic response by expressing concern about the client's emotional reaction toward the therapist or therapy; and (c) disarming interventions, such as exploring and validating some aspects of the client's perception of the therapist's contribution to the rupture. After discussing the rupture in the alliance, therapists can continue applying CBT techniques.

Clients' motivation is another factor that can affect the therapeutic alliance. Specifically, people seeking counseling have differing attitudes toward change. The stages of change model (Norcross, Krebs, & Prochaska, 2011) identifies attitudes toward change along a continuum from not thinking one needs to change (the precontemplative stage) to thinking one is ready to take concrete action (the action stage). CBT is most useful when clients have reached this action stage of change because by nature CBT represents a set of action stage interventions. Unlike psychodynamic psychotherapy, CBT is not a treatment designed for exploration. Some CBT techniques such as behavioral activation or reinforcement sampling could be used to increase clients' motivation for change and move them to the action stage. However, given CBT's predilection to action, asking clients to actively change their thoughts, feelings, and behaviors could cause a rupture or break in the therapeutic alliance if they have not reached the action stage and are ambivalent about change. Therefore, it is important to first assess clients' attitude motivation to change to prevent the possibility of a rupture in the alliance. Therefore, it is important to first assess clients' attitude motivation to change to prevent the possibility. If clients have not reached the action stage of change, CBT practitioners can first use motivational enhancement intervention until the clients are motivated to change (Miller & Rollnick, 2012).

Transference and countertransference can also impact the therapeutic alliance. *Transference* refers to clients acting toward therapists as they do with significant others in their lives, such as their parents. *Countertransference* refers to therapists' feelings and thoughts about clients that relate to their own personal issues and interfere with therapy. These concepts have been central aspects of psychodynamic therapy. Although CBT therapists do not believe that an analysis of transference is a necessary mechanism of change in psychotherapy, they regularly attend to transference and countertransference issues. Countertransference issues come up regularly in CBT supervision sessions (DiGiuseppe et al., 2014), even though empirical literature exploring the nature of countertransference in CBT does not appear to exist. Ellis (2001) noted that countertransference is almost inevitable and can have both beneficial and destructive effects. He described how CBT practitioners could make good use of countertransference. Several CBT theorists (DiGiuseppe et al., 2014; Leahy, 2012) have speculated that countertransference can arise more often in active, directive psychotherapies, such as CBT. For example, when a client presents an emotionally charged issue, a therapist using a less active approach would perhaps avoid dealing with the issue. However, when following CBT protocol, counselors confront or restructure the upsetting thought, belief, or schema even though they might find this upsetting.

The Status of CBT in Counseling and Psychotherapy

The origins of BT date back to the 1950s with the development of Wolpe's (1958) book *Psychotherapy by Reciprocal Inhibition* and the founding of the University of London's Maudsley Hospital under Hans Eysenck. The first use of the term *CBT* occurred at the First Conference on Cognitive Behavior Therapy in 1976, hosted and funded by the Albert Ellis Institute (Hollon & DiGiuseppe, 2011). Presently CBT has become a major force in counseling and psychotherapy. CBT has many specialty journals dedicated to theory, practice, and research; articles on CBT appear in the most prestigious journals in counseling, clinical and counseling psychology, and psychiatry. Andersson and colleagues (2005) noted that CBT is acknowledged as an effective intervention for almost all psychiatric conditions and numerous somatic conditions and that it is difficult to find a psychological problem for which the efficacy of CBT has not been tested. For many conditions, CBT has become the treatment of choice. The commitment to research has fostered this legacy of CBT as a successful form of psychotherapy.

CBT has evolved into a major and the most popular theoretical orientation to psychotherapy among practitioners and faculty members. A Delphi poll of counseling and psychotherapy experts rated CBT as the most likely form of psychotherapy to increase in popularity by 2022 after eclectic/integrative approaches, which emerged as most likely to increase in popularity (Norcross, Pfund, & Prochaska, 2013). When writing this chapter, we conducted a PsycINFO literature search for the term *CBT* in the abstract. We uncovered 8,562 citations, which is evidence that CBT has attained a predominant position in the field of academic counseling as well as in the psychotherapy literature. This research emphasis garnered the support of CBT in the academic community, particularly among academic scholars who seek university positions and then train new generations of mental health professionals.

Several factors could account for the ascendance of CBT. First, advocates of CBT emerged from BT that strongly valued research. Using randomized clinical trials to test treatments has always been a hallmark of CBT because this type of research has strongly influenced the conversation about the effectiveness of counseling and therapy among academics, practitioners, the public, and governments. The major professional organization for CBT, the Association for Behavioral and Cognitive Therapies, continually provides resources to disseminate knowledge and practice of CBT interventions to all mental health professionals (DiGiuseppe, 2007). The dissemination of CBT has been extended to include training of primary health care providers such as nurses and physicians (Mathieson et al., 2013). Second, CBT theorists stated their hypothetical construct in definitions that promoted the measurement, testing, and falsification of their theories. The hypothetical constructs identified by CBT theories were more easily turned into self-report measures than the constructs of psychodynamic theories. Automatic thoughts, underlying schemas, irrational beliefs, cognitive flexibility, defusion, and social problem-solving skills all spawned self-report measures that assess clients' thinking and test the models of CBT, helping counselors and therapists assess what to target in therapy and how to assess change in these constructs over the course of treatment.

Third, all types of CBT prescribed relatively brief and structured treatments that easily fit into the cost-effective, managed care, and evidence-based zeitgeist of the past several decades. Fourth, the structured nature of CBT theories and the clearly identifiable skills then makes them easy to teach; many treatment manuals are available to guide the training of practitioners and graduate students. CBT interventions are simple enough that live or video demonstrations of sessions can illustrate the techniques to practitioners.

Fifth, CBT has achieved an integration of psychodynamic psychotherapy's focus on the internal experience, early BT's focus on observable behavior, and the focus of client-centered therapies on forming therapeutic relationships. Focusing on clients' present and conscious thoughts, emotions, and behaviors allows counselors to access internal experiences and thoughts about past harmful events while at the same time maintaining the goals of assessing and changing something observable. The focus on both stream-of-consciousness thoughts and tacit, underlying beliefs and schemas provides insights into the deeper aspects of clients' personalities. Attaining a good working alliance with clients allows them to experience a healthy relationship with a helping professional. This integrative aspect of CBT allows practitioners to focus on the best aspects of the psychodynamic, humanistic, and behavioral methods.

Sixth, strong personalities have historically dominated the field of counseling and psychotherapy. Charismatic personalities developed most variants of CBT. Each of them were inspirational speakers and teachers, innovative theorists, compassionate therapists, leaders of professional organizations, and recipients of prestigious awards.

In 2009 Cook, Biyanova, and Coyne surveyed more than 2,400 North American psychotherapists and counselors and asked them to identify the most prominent figures in the field of psychotherapy and counseling. Although Carl Rogers continued to hold the position as the most prominent theorist, the next two of the top 10 represented CBT, with Aaron Beck second and Albert Ellis third. We predict that if that study were replicated now and data collection extended beyond North America, more CBT scholars would be added among the top 10 most influential theorists.

CBT has strongly influenced the professional education of mental health professionals. CBT is the predominant psychotherapy theoretical orientation for faculty teaching in clinical psychology doctoral programs (Levy & Anderson, 2013). The dominance of CBT has not been as extreme among the faculty of counseling psychology doctoral programs. However, most (43%) of the faculty in this field identify with CBT, whereas only 28% identify with the humanistic orientation, 21% identify as systemic theorists, and only 19% report an allegiance to the psychodynamic paradigm (Norcross, Evans, & Ellis, 2010). In the past decade, CBT has also made substantial inroads into psychiatric residency programs because of medicine's commitment to empirically based practice in general and to the larger research literature supporting CBT. However, psychodynamic training remains the most popular orientation in psychiatry (Sudak & Goldberg, 2012). No such data exist for faculty in mental health counseling or social work programs, although given the increased popularity of CBT, it is likely that there is growth in these programs as well.

The History of CBT

When CBT emerged, psychoanalytic therapy dominated the field and Rogerian client-centered therapy was a close second. As noted previously, the first generation of CBT therapists based their work on the learning theories of Pavlov and John Watson (Martin & Pear, 2015). They believed that humans learned maladaptive behavior and emotional reactions from learning experiences. In some sense, there were always two arms or traditions in BT: interventions developed on Pavlov's classical conditioning and those based on Skinner's operant procedures. In classical conditioning, feared stimuli are paired with painful or unpleasant stimuli and replaced by experiencing the stimuli without the presence of painful or unpleasant stimuli or pairing the feared stimulus with a new response, such as relaxation. Work based on Pavlov's classical conditioning enhanced the treatment of fear and anxiety disorders. It has continued to grow, and exposure is still the treatment of choice for these disorders.

The work of Watson and Skinner focused on the operant conditioning paradigm, with an emphasis on the consequence of behavior. In other words, behavioral reactions are strengthened and increased if they are rewarded or reinforced. Reinforcement can be positive when the behavior is followed by something pleasant. However, behavior can also be reinforced followed with the avoidance or removal of a negative stimulus, referred to as *negative reinforcement*. The stimulus that precedes the behavior is also important because people learn that reinforcers for a behavior only occur when a certain stimulus or situation is present. Techniques used by Watson and Skinner involved withholding reinforcers for maladaptive behavior; reinforcing adaptive behavior that was incompatible with the symptomatic behavior; and providing discrimination training, in which reinforcers followed behavior in some situations and not in others. These operant principles were quickly used to create reinforcement systems or token economies that were used to increase on-task academic behaviors in children and help children complete homework as well as to reduce psychotic symptoms and improve self-care and prosocial behavior in psychiatric hospital patients. Teaching clients to increase the number of rewarding activities in their daily activity became an early operant intervention for depression (Lewinsohn, Weinstein, & Alper, 1970) and is still considered the first-line intervention for depression today (Finning et al., 2017).

Operant principles can describe and change interpersonal relationships. Patterson (1975) described the interaction between disruptive children and their families as coercive family process. In such an interaction, one person's tantrums (the child's) are annoying to another person (the parent). As the parent gives in to the child's tantrums, the response positively reinforces the child's tantrums by providing a pleasurable reward and negatively reinforces the parent by removing the unpleasant stimulus—the tantrum. The parent training procedures that developed from this model remain the most effective intervention for many child behavior problems (Skotarczak & Lee, 2015); however, they have been improved with the addition of cognitive procedures to increase the parent's compliance with the treatment (O. David & DiGiuseppe, 2016).

Most of the second branches of CBT can trace their origins to several early works (see Hollon & DiGiuseppe, 2011). First Julian Rotter (1954) published his book *Social Learning and Clinical Psychology*. George Kelly's book *The Psychology of Personal Constructs* appeared in the next year, 1955. Albert

Ellis (1955, 1957) initiated rational psychotherapy the same year and used the ABC model. Here *A* stands for *activating event, B* stands for *beliefs,* and *C* stands for emotional *consequences.* This model specifies that beliefs mediate the relationship between activating events and emotional consequences. However, Ellis's early writings were self-help books, and he did not write for a professional or academic audience until his "Rational Psychotherapy and Individual Psychology" article (Ellis, 1957) and his seminal book *Reason and Emotion in Psychotherapy* (Ellis, 1962). A. T. Beck published his "Thinking and Depression: I. Idiosyncratic Content and Cognitive Distortions" article in 1959 (A. T. Beck & Hurvich, 1959) and his outcome research supporting this therapy in 1975 (Rush, Khatami, & Beck, 1975).

Many mental health practitioners have assumed that a connection exists between cognitive psychology and the applied field of CBT. In the 1950s, some pioneers (e.g., Noam Chomsky, George Miller, Alan Newell, and Herbert Simon) broke with the major behaviorist paradigm of scientific psychology and began a cognitive revolution in psychology that laid the foundation for the field of cognitive psychology (D. David, Miclea, & Opre, 2004). Cognitive psychology did not develop into its modern form until the early 1960s. Among the important milestones cited by historians of psychology are Chomsky's (1972) critique of B. F. Skinner (1957), the creation of the Harvard Center for Cognitive Studies by Jerome Bruner and George Miller in 1960, and the publication of the influential book *Cognitive Psychology* by Ulric Neisser (1967; J. Hogan, personal communication, February 2014). D. David, Lynn, and Ellis (2010), D. David and Hofmann (2013), and D. David and Szentagotai (2006) have provided examples of how the science of cognitive psychology can inform and support CBT.

The first evidence-based paradigm in the counseling and psychotherapy field was BT (D. David et al., 2010), which focuses on how the environment affects learned behaviors. The behaviorist school boasts such influential leaders as Hans Eysenck, Arnold Lazarus, and Joseph Wolpe. Behaviorists sought to understand human behavior using a structured, empirical approach. BT went through a crisis when it faced the fact that many topics (e.g., the role of modeling in learning, the Skinnerian theory of language) could not be explained by behavioral principles. Thus, a new paradigm—a cognitive paradigm—appeared as an exposition of a cognitive revolution (e.g., A. T. Beck, 1976; Ellis, 1957). During this revolution, some behavior therapists challenged the emergence of CBT. They claimed that cognitions were an epiphenomenon that played no role in the mediation of disturbance and that cognitive interventions added nothing to the effectiveness of counseling. The founders of CBT, who came from the behavioral tradition, had to overcome a theoretical bias against even talking about private experiences such as beliefs, thoughts, or language. In the end, however, the new cognitive paradigm assimilated components of the behavioral paradigm, and an integrated paradigm—CBT—emerged (e.g., Ellis, Lazarus, Mahoney, and Meichenbaum; see Hollon & DiGiuseppe, 2011).

Many of the seminal figures in the second branch of CBT were originally trained in the behavioral tradition, including Goldfried and Davison (1976), A. A. Lazarus (1977), Mahoney (1974), and Meichenbaum (1977). Goldfried and Davison's and A. A. Lazarus's seminal books integrated cognitive and behavioral approaches into a coherent practice. These pioneers integrated a cognitive perspective into their BT practices. Most CBT models incorporate behavioral principles, incorporate behavioral techniques, and include behavioral assignments between sessions. Although cognitive theories can explain the effectiveness of behavioral interventions (D. David, 2004), almost no CBT approach uses cognitive interventions alone. This is because cognitions, emotions, and behaviors are interconnected aspects of human experience. Thoughts, emotions, and behaviors have reciprocal relationships with one another; if one component is changed, the others are changed.

Other important seminal figures in CBT came from the psychodynamic field. Ellis (1962) and A. T. Beck (1976) both received their initial training in psychoanalytic therapy. Each of them broke with that approach to found schools of psychotherapy that emphasized the role of cognition in the etiology of distress and the process of change. Ellis (1957, 1962) and A. T. Beck (1970, 1976) had a tremendous impact on this field and on the integrative influences on CBT. Although compared with psychodynamic psychotherapies, CBT includes more activity on the part of the counselor and relies less on insight as a mechanism of change, both approaches are concerned with deep cognitions, such as schemas and assumptions, that are tacit or unconscious (Hollon & DiGiuseppe, 2011).

What the Waves/Branches of CBT Share

Unlike psychodynamic and other insight approaches to psychotherapy, CBT focuses on changing what and how people think, behave, and feel in order to reduce psychopathology and promote human growth. CBT does not focus on identifying unconscious drives or past memories but instead is based on the premise that people's thoughts and language influence their emotions and actions. CBT posits that certain types of cognitions lead to functional emotions and adaptive behaviors, whereas other types of cognitions generate dysfunctional emotions and maladaptive behavior, leading to psychological disorders.

The notion that thoughts connect to emotions, behavior, and disturbance has a long history in Western civilization in both philosophy and literature. The Greek Stoic philosopher Epictetus (trans. 1996) noted in his now famous quote that "people are not disturbed by things, but by the view they take of them" (p. 5). The Roman philosopher-emperor Marcus Aurelius (121–180) wrote, "Very little is needed to make a happy life; it is all within yourself, in your way of thinking" (Rutherford, 1989, p. 168). Michel de Montaigne (1533–1592), an influential author of the French Renaissance and the father of modern skepticism, qualifies as an early CBT practitioner with his quote "My life has been full of terrible misfortunes, most of which never happened" (de Montaigne, 1957, p. 47). CBT theory appears in the writings of the most famous author in the English language, William Shakespeare, whose character Hamlet says, "There is nothing either good or bad, but thinking makes it so" (Shakespeare, 1602/1985, Act 2, Scene 2).

Hamlet's statement alludes to CBT's distinction between knowing and appraising information. People process information by first making observations, extracting a perception, and determining what they perceive is relevant to the achievement of their goals. This final stage involves an evaluation of what they have perceived. Next people make appraisals of the facts that lead to aroused emotions (R. S. Lazarus, 1991). As Hamlet says, the *appraisal* of facts makes things bad or good. CBT focuses on the link between knowledge and appraisal and on the arousal of emotions.

Cognitions

CBT focuses on information processing of the world. Information processing results in cognitions, including knowledge, thoughts, and mental representation, that people experience as beliefs and hold to be true. These cognitions and mental representations can be out of awareness and exist as implicit expectations and associations. CBT proposes that people aim to survive, procreate, and thrive and that humans extract knowledge from their environment concerning the existence of any threats and the presence of resources, as this knowledge facilitates the achieving of life goals. Humans appraise knowledge about the environment for goal significance, thus arousing emotions (R. S. Lazarus, 1991). Most CBT theories focus on this link between the extraction of knowledge and appraisals of this knowledge and the arousal of emotional states.

CBT mostly focuses on articulated, conscious cognitions and automatic thoughts that make up the *stream of consciousness,* a term coined by William James (1890), or *automatic thoughts,* the term used by A. T. Beck (1976). Any taxonomy of cognitions in CBT needs to make this fundamental distinction between knowing and appraising (D. David et al., 2004; D. David & Szentagotai, 2006). Abelson and Rosenberg (1958) originally proposed this distinction and used the terms *hot* and *cold cognitions* to distinguish between appraisals and associations and desired and undesired outcomes (hot cognitions) and knowledge or fact-based thoughts (cold cognitions). Cold cognitions refer to people's representations of relevant circumstances, for example, the negative events that clients predict will happen. Another type of cognition is appraisal or evaluative hot cognitions that determine how people process the cold cognitions in terms of their relevance for personal well-being (R. S. Lazarus, 1991). Hot cognitions are experienced and coded as evaluative automatic thoughts (e.g., self-statements), whereas deep hot cognitions (e.g., irrational beliefs) are schemas and other meaning-based representations. An example of a cold cognition would be awareness of a fact or inference, such as "I am stuck in traffic and will be late for class." The hot cognition evaluation of these events would be experienced as "It is awful to be late for class." Often people experience these hot and cold cognitions almost simultaneously.

Some cognitions, however, are nonconscious or tacit rather than being conscious verbal statements. Cognitive theories on the psychology of emotions propose that many forms of associational connections between stimuli and emotional reactions are cognitive, even if nonconscious thoughts or attitudes are evoked (Harmon-Jones & Mills, 1999). Another level of cognitions, called *schemas*, is less accessible to consciousness and refers to descriptions and inferences (e.g., attributions). These cognitions reflect broad ideas about the state of the world and interpersonal relationships. They are not in conscious experience but can be activated and made conscious by exploration.

Emotions

Emotions mobilize humans to respond to or to cope with environmental threats or a lack of resources (Darwin, 1872). Although emotions are a normal and necessary part of life, many forms of psychological disturbance involve excessive, prolonged, or extended emotional arousal. Alternatively, some forms of psychopathology result from a lack of appropriate emotions or emotions that are too mild in intensity or too short in duration. Disturbed, unhealthy, or dysfunctional emotions are a barrier to adaptation if the high emotional arousal interferes with people's ability to function effectively. Changing beliefs helps people move from disturbed emotions to emotions that are more functional. Some critics of CBT falsely portray it as dismissing emotion or as promoting an emotionless style of functioning. This is not true. Emotions provide internal cues to people signaling that a problem exists in their environment that requires attention. The elimination of emotions would interfere with human adaptation because the absence of emotion would eliminate this important signaling system. CBT attempts to replace dysfunctional cognitions that lead to disturbed emotions with cognitions that lead to more adaptive emotions that promote coping or help people circumvent dysfunctional beliefs and emotions and behave consistently with their goals and values despite the dysfunctional thoughts.

The various forms of CBT view the roles of beliefs and emotions differently. Some theorists would assert that emotions are caused by the appraisal cognitions, which can be either conscious or unconscious (Ellis, 1962, 1994). Others view cognitions, behaviors, and emotions as influencing one another. Essentially, thoughts are only a symptom associated with emotions and behaviors, and changing any one of the three can change the other two. Also, cognitions are easily accessible through human language. Emotions or behaviors cannot be directly affected without the ability to present distress-causing stimuli or to change behaviors without access to reinforcers that are important to the client. However, through language, one can discuss thoughts about the stimuli and reinforcers and the evaluations of those things (CT; A. T. Beck, 1976). For other theories, thoughts are linguistic covert responses that are linked to dysfunctional emotions and behaviors, and therapy is designed to break these connections and help people learn to react flexibly, acting in their own best interest despite the arousal of the thoughts and emotions (ACT [Hayes et al., 2011]) and mindfulness (Kabat-Zinn, 2013). For some of these theories, cognitions are the independent variables that change emotions, the dependent variables. For others, cognitions are the dependent measures that are provided by life experiences and environmental in nature.

Once emotions are generated, humans often evaluate these emotions. These appraisals about one's internal emotional experiences can generate new, more intense and disruptive emotional reactions. These new emotional reactions can create anxiety about anxiety, depression about depression, or any subset of the possible permutations. These types of emotional reactions are often called *metacognitive beliefs,* or *secondary reactions,* because the emotions that elicit them are secondary to the original link that led to the disturbance. What unites them is that they are beliefs about one's internal experiences (Wells, 2008).

A prerequisite for working with emotions in CBT is that clients have some awareness of their emotions. CBT counselors assume that clients have some ability to identify stream-of-consciousness thoughts that co-occur with their emotions. They assume that clients can access and articulate tacit, nonconscious deeper beliefs from these stream-of-consciousness thoughts. They assume that clients can identify which desires are being thwarted to generate these emotions. Finally, they assume that clients want to change the disturbed emotions that interfere with achieving their goals. According to the stages of change model (Norcross et al., 2011), CBT represents an active stage intervention. CBT might fail for clients who are unaware of their emotions, cannot identify which motives are being thwarted, are unable to identify their stream-of-consciousness beliefs, cannot access their deeper tacit schema, or lack a desire to change. In such cases, the practitioner would use other therapeutic strategies that best address these issues before returning to the CBT interventions.

Understanding clients' emotions is crucial to effective CBT. Counselors cannot know which cognitions to target unless they know which emotions relate to their clients' problems. Therapists work to change cognitions that relate to disturbed unhealthy emotions and help clients develop new cognitions that lead to more functional adaptive emotions and coping skills. By focusing on emotions, practitioners can identify which cognitions to target in treatment.

CBT focuses on the knowledge and appraisal processes that are involved in excessive or insufficient emotional arousal. Disturbed emotional arousal or dysfunctional behaviors are hypothesized to occur because of some absent, erroneous, dysfunctional, incorrect, exaggerated, or extremely overevaluative appraisal of environmental threats or rigid reactions that one must behave in a certain way. CBT proposes that practitioners focus on both events and beliefs that are likely to arouse emotions. This emphasis on the information that people extract from the environment to ensure survival and adaptation is the key focus of CBT.

Cognitive Models

Understanding the convergent and distinctive features of the various CBT models will prepare you to understand, practice, and research CBT.

The Cognitive Deficit Model

The first tradition that influenced CBT is known as the cognitive deficit model. This model originated from the behaviorists who became disappointed that their methods, such as token economies, produced poor generalization across time and place (O'Leary & Drabman, 1971). They found that even assertiveness training, which involved clients rehearsing new adaptive skills to express themselves to others, had limited generalizability. In other words, the exigencies of life present clients with many variations of problematic situations, which makes it impossible to rehearse an adaptive response for every potential event that could cue maladaptive behavior. In addition, behavior therapists could not always be present to reinforce adaptive behavior, so they attempted to teach a skill that clients could use to cue the desired behaviors and thus self-reinforce their occurrence. This strategy required language-based rules to generate effective coping across a wide variety of situations and provide the self-reinforcement necessary to internalize or generate the response. Such cognitive interventions involved teaching clients self-control skills and self-instructional statements for responding to stimuli outside of therapy sessions that were similar to those events that elicited maladaptive responses that the client and therapist discussed in session (Kanfer & Goldstein, 1975; Meichenbaum, 1977).

We refer to these approaches as the *cognitive deficit models* of CBT (Crawley, Podell, Beidas, Braswell, & Kendall, 2009). According to the self-instructional training model, well-adjusted people develop cognitive processes and structures that mediate or guide their adaptive behavior when they encounter novel stressful situations, whereas disturbed individuals fail to develop the skills to recall these adaptive cognitive processes. Teaching adaptive skills requires a mechanism that allows clients to recall new learned responses in novel, real-world situations. Cognitive deficit model interventions such as cognitive behavior modification, self-instructional training, stress inoculation methods (Meichenbaum, 1977, 1993), and problem-solving therapy (Spivack, Platt, & Shure, 1976) were originally intended for use with children with externalizing disorders and with seriously disturbed clients.

The Cognitive Dysfunction Model

The second tradition from which CBT emerged is the cognitive dysfunction model. It can be divided into two parts: constructivist attributions models and incorrect beliefs models. Most proponents of CBT point to Kelly's (1955) *The Psychology of Personal Constructs* as the first modern approach to cognitive psychotherapy. Kelly recognized that humans attempt to understand their world and have evolved and survived because of their ability to impose order on a seemingly chaotic universe. Individuals develop a system of dichotomous constructs to help make the world predictable. This system of constructs grows and changes as individuals interact with the world, and this system becomes clients' truth as they understand and experience the world. The extent to which individuals can understand another's construct system represents an important measure of empathy. Counseling from a CBT perspective involves understanding clients' systems of constructs and helping them evaluate whether their constructs help them maneuver the world effectively. Kelly focused on helping clients become flexible (a recurrent theme in CBT), relinquish ineffective constructs, and develop effective ones. The idea that a person's own construction of reality played such an important role in disturbance led to the constructivist methods, which conceptualize therapy as a task of understanding a person's world (Neimeyer, 2009). Compared with the objective reductionist models of the natural sciences, advocates of the constructivist approaches developed and adopted an epistemology and philosophy of science based more on phenomenology.

Differences Among the CBT Theories

Some variants of CBT, such as A. T. Beck's (1976) CT, focus on helping clients examine the truth or veracity of their thoughts. They theorize that the cognitions hypothesized to lead to disturbance are faulty in some way. Thus, variants of CBT are interwoven with epistemology: the philosophical study of how people know things. Different types of CBT posit divergent epistemological positions. This often results in deeper philosophical disagreements between methods than theoretical disagreements or disagreements on clinical techniques. Beck's approach focuses on false or exaggerated beliefs about the existence of threats and resources, which lead to unnecessary emotional upset. This approach differs widely from the position taken by many of the more recent approaches to CBT, which assert that humans are incapable of knowing objective reality and that empirical verification of an idea is unattainable. These approaches argue that the only characteristics of thought to consider are viability and utility. Other forms of CBT, such as REBT (Ellis, 1994), posit that both types of information veracity and viability are important for evaluating a client's beliefs. Debates among adherents to various types of CBT are often reduced to issues concerning the nature of reality, the ability of humans to know it, and criteria for knowing or holding beliefs. Therapists adverse to philosophical debate on the nature of truth might be happier with an orientation other than CBT.

Resolving the Differences Among the Three Waves/Branches

Considerable controversy exists in CBT over the emergence of the third wave of behavior therapies that has challenged the theory and procedures of traditional CBT. The debate between these new approaches and the more traditional forms of CBT led Mennin, Ellard, Fresco, and Gross (2013) to propose common elements that unite the second and third branches. They identified three broad core common principles of CBT. First, CBT therapists explore the content of clients' thoughts, feelings, and behaviors to encourage clients to consider adaptive imagining and performing of new experiences to counter their previous well-rehearsed associations between stimuli and maladaptive responses. Second, therapists encourage clients to change their attention to encourage focusing on the adaptive response. This involves sustaining, shifting, and broadening clients' attention to all aspects of situations, not those they narrowly focused on before therapy. Third, therapists encourage cognitive change that promotes adaptive perspective taking of events that alter linguistic meanings.

Context engagement refers to varying one's responses based on present environmental inputs. It involves teaching clients to refrain from emitting a rigid, inflexible response, previously overlearned automatic behavior, and to respond differently depending on the reinforcement contingencies that confront them presently—that is, determining what behavior is in their best interest. Several common procedures represent context engagement strategies. Alternative solution thinking from problem-solving therapy (Nezu et al., 2013) involves learning to generate new solutions to problems. Exposure interventions for anxiety disorders (Craske et al., 2008) help clients develop new learning about conditioned and unconditioned stimuli that will inhibit fear responses and allow new responses to occur. Learning new responses helps clients become aware of available positive reinforcement, including behavioral activation in the treatment of depression, and aggression replacement training (Glick & Gibbs, 2011). The goal is to teach clients to replace antisocial behaviors with functional alternatives and assertive behaviors.

Attention change teaches clients to flexibly focus their attention based on the present situational demands. Thus, clients learn to improve their focus on a target stimulus, sustain attention on the chosen stimulus, or flexibly shift their attention away from a stimulus, depending on what is good for them. Attention change includes being mindful of emotions in which the client imagines an emotionally provocative situation and observes, allows, and directs attention toward his or her internal emotional experience (Mennin & Fresco, 2010; Roemer & Orsillo, 2009).

Mennin and colleagues (2013) considered radical acceptance and emotional tolerance core attention processes. These procedures train clients to engage in sustained focus on feeling states without focusing on thought processes that promote disengagement and avoidance of feelings. For example, clients maintain attention to visceral sensations of emotions without labeling or judging (Linehan, 1993). Promoting acceptance and tolerance of emotions is a core component of the newer forms of CBT, such as ACT and DBT. In these approaches, clients learn to notice the function of their thoughts and actions; it is important to know whether the experience promotes distraction, attentional constriction, or experiential avoidance (Hayes et al., 2011). Clients can use tolerance skills to allow their difficult emotional experience to occur while broadening their attention to focus on other aspects of their experience that are less negative (Linehan, 1993). These attentional and emotion tolerance skills are compatible with all branches of CBT.

Cognitive change refers to the ability to change one's perspective about an event to alter the linguistic meanings and their emotional significance. Mennin et al. (2013) proposed that all versions of CBT share two types of cognitive change processes: cognitive distancing and cognitive reinterpretation. Cognitive distancing is the ability to observe the contents of mental activities such as thoughts, self-talk, and memories with healthy psychological distance, self-awareness, perspective taking, and the notion that one's thoughts, feelings, and desires are transient subjective states, not inherent, permanent, or identifying characteristics of the self (Fresco et al., 2007).

Cognitive change can also involve reinterpretations of situations or circumstances in life. For example, cognitive reinterpretation could include more realistically reappraising and reevaluating an event in a more accurate, objective, factual manner (Ray, Wilhelm, & Gross, 2008). Such reappraisal and reevaluations of events take into account the possible desirable, rewarding, or beneficial aspects of the event that one previously overlooked (Ray et al., 2008). These activities involve evaluating the accuracy of cold cognitions or reappraising clients' valances of hot cognitions.

Cognitive reframing represents another common intervention in CBT. Therapists promote reframing by encouraging clients to monitor and interpret emotionally provocative events. When they find interpretations of reality that are unrealistic or unhelpful, they collaboratively involve clients in challenging their meaning through engaging in logical questioning; identifying cognitive distortions; and generating new possible meanings that are more rational, heuristic, and realistic. This is commonly referred to as *cognitive restructuring* (A. T. Beck, Rush, Shaw, & Emery, 1979). Behavioral experiments can also demonstrate the dysfunctional and unrealistic meanings associated with thoughts.

Many therapeutic processes in CBT (A. T. Beck et al., 1979; Hayes et al., 2011) promote cognitive defusion, albeit by different means. *Defusion* refers to techniques that change the functional connection between a thought and emotional arousal. The common practice of instructing clients to self-monitor distressing thoughts and emotions and record their experiences encourages them to observe their thoughts and feelings from a distance. Mindfulness and acceptance-based techniques (Hayes et al., 2011; Roemer & Orsillo, 2009) accomplish cognitive distancing through exercises such as mindfully noticing inner experiences or visualizing inner experiences as objects rather than part of one's self.

The idea that defusion and mindfulness help clients become aware of their upsetting thoughts without appraising the truth or usefulness of the thoughts conflicts with some research in cognitive psychology. In a series of experiments concerning the believability of thoughts, Gilbert (1992) failed to find support for the underlying theoretical mechanism of change for defusion and mindfulness interventions. If Gilbert is correct, perhaps people can hold an idea in their mind without evaluating it only after they have appraised whether it is an incorrect or dysfunctional thought. Humans by their nature find it hard to withhold judgment and suspend evaluation of a thought.

CBT practitioners usually incorporate all or most of the processes identified by Mennin and colleagues (2013). It is noteworthy that there is not yet a scientific theory or data that can guide practitioners to choose when it is most advantageous to select each respective cognitive process. In their integrative and multimodal CBT model, D. David and Szentagotai (2006) recently tried to unify these models under a cognitive science and cognitive neuroscience framework to move the field from competing schools of thought to a unified theory (D. David & Freeman, 2015).

Theory of Personality and Psychopathology

Two Pathways to Emotions

All CBT approaches include both cognitive and behavioral interventions. Although they challenge, change, or teach new cognitions, they include behavioral activities in sessions and behavioral assignments between them. Do the behavioral and cognitive interventions use the same neural pathways to connect to our emotions?

This question goes back to a debate between Ellis and Wolpe. In 1974 Joe Wolpe and Al Ellis went to Hofstra University to debate the role of cognition and conditioning in psychopathology and psychotherapy (see Hollon & DiGiuseppe, 2011). Wolpe, who spoke first, drew a human head on the blackboard and identified visual and auditory sensory brain centers, proposing that two pathways lead to anxiety. The first pathway runs from the senses to the lower levels of the brain (around the thalamus) and makes connections from there to the hypothalamus. This pathway, he said, is learned through conditioning. Wolpe stated that this pathway accounts for about 90% of all anxiety disorders. Exposure interventions and systematic desensitization effectively treat disturbed anxiety mediated by this pathway. The second pathway involves information from the senses traveling to connections in the thalamus, then up through the cortex, and then back down the thalamus and into the hypothalamus. The reaction time for this pathway is slower and requires individuals to learn through testing their faulty assumptions. Treating disturbed emotions that form through this pathway involves testing and replacing disturbed thoughts and beliefs.

The audience expected Ellis to challenge Wolpe, but instead Ellis agreed with Wolpe's explanation of the two pathways mediating emotional disturbance. He disagreed, however, with Wolpe's idea of how much emotional disturbance is caused by each pathway. Ellis said that the cognitive pathway mediates 90% of emotional disturbance and the conditioning pathway mediates 10%. This debate demonstrated that CBT and REBT clearly existed in the larger context of BT. CBT holds that there are multiple mechanisms of psychopathology, and different strategies are often required for effective therapy. The dual pathway theory Wolpe and Ellis identified remains an active area of inquiry in CBT (Power & Dalgleish, 2008).

Two Competing Psychological Systems

Nobel Prize–winning psychologist Kahneman (2011) wrote extensively on this aspect of human functioning in his book *Thinking Fast and Slow.* His review of the research in cognitive psychology indicated that humans have two major information-processing systems. System 1 is characterized by processing that is fast, is automatic, and requires little or no effort. It is irrational and impressionistic and executes overlearned responses. It draws inferences and quickly invents causes for events, neglects ambiguity, suppresses doubt in all of these thoughts, and speaks to one in a voice of assurance. System 1 is biased to confirm what one already thinks and overweighs low-probability events. It responds more to losses (threats) than to gains (resources) and evaluates those losses as negative without reservation. Dysfunctional thoughts that lead to emotional disturbance usually have the characteristics of System 1. If there is any possibility that a threat or a danger exists, System 1 thinking reacts to keep one safe no matter how small the chance of the threat.

System 2 is rational and algorithmic. It involves computations. It is characterized by slow cognitive processing and requires sustained attention and effort. These processes are susceptible to energy depletion (Baumeister, Vohs, & Tice, 2007) until they become overlearned. Luckily, System 2 can override System 1. This process of slow, rational thinking overriding fast, irrational thinking has often been presented in TV characters, film, and literature.

Kahneman's description of human cognitions suggests that people have some beliefs and processes related to disturbed emotions and some systems that lead to functional emotions. Humans will always experience some quick, negative, irrational, and impulsive thoughts processed by System 1. Human consciousness includes an internal dialogue between System 2 processes and System 1 processes and beliefs. Counseling teaches clients to use System 2 cognitions to counter or react to System 1 cognitions. The philosopher Spinoza (1677/2000; see also Damasio, 2003) first proposed this idea in his book *Ethics.* Spinoza wrote that people carry their experiences and thoughts, which they adapt by developing and rehearsing a new set of thoughts. Thus, coping is learning to have a longer dialogue or chain of thoughts. The experience of the old maladaptive thoughts can serve as a cue to rehearse more adaptive thoughts. This idea of using maladaptive emotions to cue the internal dialogue with adaptive thoughts to counter maladaptive ones was suggested by Suinn and Richardson (1971) several centuries later.

People without emotional or behavioral disturbance have more positive than negative thoughts. As the ratio of negative thoughts increases, people become more depressed (Schwartz, 1986; Schwartz & Garamoni, 1989). Research on negative automatic thoughts associated with depression has shown that nondepressed people have 1.61803 positive thoughts for every 1 negative thought. This number is *phi*, and it is known as the golden ratio (Livio, 2002), which dates back to classical Greek mathematics. Its applications to architecture and art are well known. Da Vinci's *Mona Lisa* and his picture of a man's body in a pentagram are based on the golden ratio. People's daily lives include many things designed on this ratio: shapes of postcards, wide-screen televisions, photographs, and even the standard American single wall light switch plate. New psychometric data confirm the presence of this mysterious number in domains such as computer science and neuroscience (Roopun et al., 2008; Weiss & Weiss, 2003).

Schwartz (1997) provided a case study showing that the ratio of positive to negative thoughts changed as a client improved through therapy. In an effectiveness study, Garamoni, Reynolds, Thase, Frank, and Fasiczka (1992) treated depressed patients with CBT and measured their positive and negative cognitions both before and after treatment. Clients who responded to CBT shifted the balance of positivity and negativity into the optimal range, whereas nonresponders had a higher ratio of negative thoughts. These results support the idea that clinical responses to CBT reflect a reduction in negativity and an increase in positivity until the client achieves an optimal balance. Regardless of their progress in therapy, clients will continue to experience some recurring negative thoughts. Clients sometimes erroneously infer from such experiences that they are not getting better or that treatment is not working and that they will remain disturbed. It is important to teach clients that negative beliefs are part of the human condition. Everyone has them, but once the thoughts occur, people have a choice as to how to respond to them. They can give in to them or cope with them by challenging them, accepting them, or moving onto activities that are more positive.

Clinical Assessment and Diagnosis

Clinical assessment in CBT usually relies on ideographic approaches to interviewing, which means that the aim is to determine the unique characteristics influencing a particular client's behavior. The first step in assessment is to clearly identify the presenting problem and develop a list that includes specific problems and symptoms. The practitioner will question the client to define these behaviors as concretely as possible so that they can be specific and measurable. Most practitioners will attempt to make a diagnosis, but diagnoses are not as important as identifying clients' specific problems. CBT practitioners also assess the client's psychopathology to ensure the appropriate diagnosis, to understand the client's problems, and to determine the right treatment strategy derived from the psychotherapy outcome literature. CBT practitioners usually include some monitoring of targeted symptom behaviors or the use of self-report measures. The use of such outcome measures helps the therapist and the client evaluate progress and plan new strategies if therapy is not successful.

CBT practitioners usually engage in two types of ABC assessments. The first ABCs explore the components of a functional behavioral analysis, which includes (a) exploring the *antecedent* stimuli that occur before the symptoms, (b) defining the *behavior* as concretely as possible, and (c) exploring the *consequences* after the behavior occurs. The second ABCs include the (a) *activating events* or antecedent events, (b) the *beliefs* or thoughts the person experiences during, preceding, or after the event, and (c) the emotional and behavioral *consequences* after (a) and (b). During the second ABC assessment, clients will reveal stream-of-consciousness or automatic thoughts. Clients can use different strategies to develop awareness of tacit, schematic beliefs.

A number of instruments have been created in CBT to assess the types of cognitions that each of the differing models propose mediate psychopathology, including negative automatic thoughts, dysfunctional attitudes, irrational beliefs, underlying schemas, flexibility versus habitual responding, and problem-solving skills. However, most of these instruments were devised for research purposes. We know of no test of these cognitive constructs that would have a sufficiently large, stratified normative sample that could serve as a clinical instrument. Thus, assessing the beliefs related to clients' problems remains a task practitioners perform throughout interviews. Most of these measures and most interview techniques identify stream-of-consciousness thoughts, but counselors can move from these surface-level thoughts to more tacit beliefs by using several interview or interpretive processes that are discussed in different clinical manuals.

One difficulty with cognitive assessment strategies is that they often rely on the therapist's memory of what the client recalled thinking at the time of emotional symptoms. Therefore, it is best to assess cognitions when clients are feeling their emotions. Imagery exercises that focus on activating events that trigger emotions are effective in helping clients become aware of their thoughts when they experience the emotions.

Future Directions

The amount of evidence supporting the efficacy and effectiveness for CBT is overwhelming. An examination of the Society of Clinical Psychology's (2015) website of research-supported psychological treatments demonstrates the degree to which CBT has produced successful forms of psychotherapy for almost every psychiatric disorder and clinical problem. Clearly, all branches of the CBT tree have strong empirical support and represent empirically based practice. Although the research support for CBT is massive and impressive for each disorder and clinical problem, many clients still fail to respond to this form of psychotherapy. We think that the magnitude of clinical efficacy could be improved with greater theoretical clarity. We often know that CBT can be effective for a clinical problem, but we still are not sure which strategy or combination of techniques will be the most effective for a particular client. In many CBT studies, books, and manuals, the authors describe focusing on dysfunctional cognitions. However, it is often unclear what exactly they mean by "dysfunctional cognitions" because the fact that such cognitions can manifest at different levels is often unacknowledged or unaddressed by cocktail-like CBT, which instead mixes or confounds those levels. Consequently, it is hard to incorporate these results into a coherent, complete, and integrated theory of CBT. Given all of the different types of interventions that reside under the CBT tree, we usually do not know which one will be best for a particular problem. CBT has failed to develop an assessment paradigm that will tell the practitioner whether radical acceptance, assertiveness training, challenging irrational beliefs, or teaching problem solving is the best strategy for a particular client at a particular moment. Perhaps all of the CBT techniques would do equally well, but it would be helpful to have an assessment strategy that leads to prescriptive interventions.

CBT interventions typically focus on the present problems as conceptualized by a cognitive model (e.g., the ABC model). However, when necessary in the therapeutic process, CBT can engage a historical understanding of the present problems (e.g., how irrational beliefs were developed in the client's life history) or even a here-and-now approach (e.g., how irrational beliefs are expressed during the therapy process in relation to the therapist). This can represent a bridge to similar interventions in the dynamic of dynamic psychotherapies.

Therapeutic benefits are likely to occur if a clearer understanding is developed of which types of cognitions mediate which emotional disturbances and which cognitive constructs are influenced by which interventions. For example, J. Beck (2011) suggested that CT conceptualizes the pathway to emotional disturbance as merging from schemas to middle-level cognitions such as assumptions, rules, and evaluations. These middle-level cognitions then activate automatic thoughts that activate emotions. Research has not kept pace with this type of theoretical development, and this model has yet to be tested. Research in the area would require that each construct in the model be carefully defined and that separate scales to measure each construct be carefully designed. Next researchers could administer the measures to nonclinical and clinical samples to test which variables represent the core of the model and which have the most direct influence on the outcome variables of emotional disturbance. Whatever the outcome, a more specific test of this model could suggest which cognitive constructs are operative with different emotions or with different disorders.

Summary

CBT is a multifaceted approach to counseling that has come to dominate the field of mental health. It has a long history that draws on ancient Western and Asian philosophies, scientific learning theories, and new research on cognitive processing. CBT includes a wide variety of interventions that fit most diagnoses and clinical problems. It is well supported by research. However, the most important reason why we have stayed committed to CBT is that CBT is an evolving system that is responsive to external criticism and new research findings. It is still evolving, as you will learn in the following chapters.

If you wish to search for definitions of and support for these CBT interventions or discover new ones, a website describes many of these in a common language. The Common Language of Psychotherapy provides a list of psychotherapy techniques that are described in language that avoids the jargon of psychotherapy orientations (*Common Language for Psychotherapy [CLP] Procedures*, n.d.). One could find that some CBT techniques are known by a different name in other theoretical orientations.

References

Abelson, R. P., & Rosenberg, M. J. (1958). Symbolic psycho-logic: A model of attitudinal cognition. *Behavioral Science, 3*(1), 1–13. doi:10.1002/bs.3830030102

American Psychological Association Presidential Task Force on Evidence-Based Practice. (2006). Evidence-based practice in psychology. *American Psychologist, 61,* 271–285.

Andersson, G., Asmundson, G. G., Carlbring, P., Ghaderi, A., Hofmann, S. G., & Stewart, S. H. (2005). Is CBT already the dominant paradigm in psychotherapy research and practice? *Cognitive Behaviour Therapy, 34*(1), 1–2.

Baumeister, R. F., Vohs, K. D., & Tice, D. M. (2007). The strength model of self-control. *Current Directions in Psychological Science, 16*(6), 351–355. doi:10.1111/j.1467-8721.2007.00534.x

Beck, A. T. (1970). Cognitive therapy: Nature and relation to behavior therapy. *Behavior Therapy, 1,* 184–200.

Beck, A. T. (1976). *Cognitive therapy and the emotional disorders.* New York, NY: Meridian.

Beck, A. T., & Hurvich, M. S. (1959). Psychological correlates of depression: 1. Frequency of "masochistic" dream content in a private practice sample. *Psychosomatic Medicine, 21,* 50–55.

Beck, A. T., Rush, A. J., Shaw, B. F., & Emery, G. (1979). *The cognitive therapy of depression.* New York, NY: Guilford Press.

Beck, J. (2011). *Cognitive behavior therapy: Basics and beyond* (2nd ed.). New York, NY: Guilford Press.

Brady, J. P. (1980). Some views on the effective principles of psychotherapy. *Cognitive Therapy and Research, 4,* 271–306.

Castonguay, L. G., Goldfried, M. R., Wiser, S., Raue, P. J., & Hayes, A. M. (1996). Predicting outcome in cognitive therapy for depression: A comparison of unique and common factors. *Journal of Consulting and Clinical Psychology, 64,* 497–504.

Chomsky, N. (1972). Psychology and ideology. *Cognition, 1*(1), 11–46. doi:10.1016/0010-0277(72)90043-1

Cohen, J. A. (2006). *Treating trauma and traumatic grief in children and adolescents.* New York, NY: Guilford Press.

Common language for psychotherapy (CLP) procedures. (n.d.). Retrieved from http://www.commonlanguagepsychotherapy.org/

Cook, J. M., Biyanova, T., & Coyne, J. C. (2009). Influential psychotherapy figures, authors, and books: An Internet survey of over 2,000 psychotherapists. *Psychotherapy: Theory, Research, Practice, Training, 46*(1), 42–51.

Craske, M. G., Kircanski, K., Zelikowsky, M., Mystkowski, J., Chowdhury, N., & Baker, A. (2008). Optimizing inhibitory learning during exposure therapy. *Behaviour Research and Therapy, 46,* 5–27. doi:10.1016/j.brat. 2007.10.003

Crawley, S. A., Podell, J. L., Beidas, R. S., Braswell, L., & Kendall, P. C. (2009). Cognitive-behavior therapy with youth. In K. Dobson (Ed.), *Handbook of cognitive-behavior therapies* (2nd ed., pp. 390–425). New York, NY: Guilford Press.

Damasio, A. (2003). *Looking for Spinoza: Joy, sorrow, and the feeling brain.* Orlando, FL: Harcourt Books.

Darwin, C. (1872). *The expression of the emotions in man and animals.* London, UK: John Murray.

David, D. (2004). Special issue on the cognitive revolution in clinical psychology: Beyond the behavioral approach—Conclusions: Toward an evidence-based psychology and psychotherapy. *Journal of Clinical Psychology, 60,* 447–451.

David, D., & Freeman, A. (2015). Overview of cognitive behavior therapy of personality disorders. In A. Beck, D. Davis, & A. Freeman (Eds.), *Cognitive therapy of personality disorders* (3rd ed., pp. 3–18). New York, NY: Guilford Press.

David, D., & Hofmann, S. G. (2013). Another error of Descartes? Implications for the "third wave" cognitive-behavioral therapy. *Journal of Cognitive and Behavioral Psychotherapies, 13*(1), 111–121.

David, D., Lynn, S., & Ellis, A. (2010). *Rational and irrational beliefs: Research, theory, and clinical practice.* New York, NY: Oxford University Press.

David, D., Miclea, M., & Opre, A. (2004). The information-processing approach to the human mind: Basics and beyond. *Journal of Clinical Psychology, 60,* 353–368. doi:10.1002/jclp.10250

David, D., & Szentagotai, A. (2006). Cognitions in cognitive-behavioral psychotherapies: Toward an integrative model. *Clinical Psychology Review, 26*(3), 284–298. doi:10.1016/j.cpr.2005.09.003

David, O., & DiGiuseppe, R. (2016). *The rational parenting program.* New York, NY: Springer.

de Montaigne, M. (1957). *Complete works: Essays, travel journal, letters.* Stanford, CA: Stanford University Press.

de Oliveira, I. R. (2016). *Trial-based cognitive therapy: Distinctive features.* New York, NY: Routledge.

DiGiuseppe, R. (2007). Dissemination of CBT research results: Preaching to the uninterested or engaging in scientific debate. *The Behavior Therapist, 30*(6), 117–120.

DiGiuseppe, R., David, D., & Venezia, R. (2016). Cognitive theories. In J. C. Norcross, G. R. VandenBos, & D. F. Freedheim (Series Eds.) & B. O. Olatunji (Vol. Ed.), *The handbook of clinical psychology: Vol. 2. Theory and research* (pp. 145–182). Washington, DC: American Psychological Association.

DiGiuseppe, R. A., Doyle, K. A., Dryden, W., & Backx, W. (2014). *A practitioner's guide to rational emotive behavior therapy* (3rd ed.). New York, NY: Oxford University Press.

DiGiuseppe, R., Leaf, R., & Linscott, J. (1993). The therapeutic relationship in rational-emotive therapy: Some preliminary data. *Journal of Rational-Emotive & Cognitive-Behavior Therapy, 11*(4), 223–233. doi:10.1007/BF01089777

Dobson, K. S. (Ed.). (2010). *Handbook of cognitive behavioral therapies*. New York, NY: Guilford Press.

Ellis, A. (1955). New approaches to psychotherapy techniques. *Journal of Clinical Psychology, 11,* 207–260.

Ellis, A. (1957). Rational psychotherapy and individual psychology. *Journal of Individual Psychology, 13,* 38–44.

Ellis, A. (1959). Requisite conditions for basic personality change. *Journal of Consulting Psychology, 23,* 538–540.

Ellis, A. (1962). *Reason and emotion in psychotherapy*. Secaucus, NJ: Carol.

Ellis, A. (1994). *Reason and emotion in psychotherapy: A comprehensive method of treating human disturbance* (Rev. ed.). New York, NY: Birch Lane Press.

Ellis, A. (2000). A critique of the theoretical contributions of nondirective therapy. *Journal of Clinical Psychology, 56,* 897–905. (Original work published in 1948, *Journal of Clinical Psychology, 4,* pp. 248–255)

Ellis, A. (2001). Rational and irrational aspects of countertransference. *Journal of Clinical Psychology, 57,* 999–1004. doi:10.1002/jclp.1067

Epictetus. (trans. 1996). *The enchiridion*. Raleigh, NC: Alex Catalogue.

Fava, G. A. (2016). *Well-being therapy: Treatment manual and clinical applications*. Buffalo, NY: Karger.

Finning, K., Richards, D. A., Moore, L., Ekers, D., McMillan, D., Farrand, P. A., . . . Wray, F. (2017). Cost and outcome of behavioural activation versus cognitive behavioural therapy for depression (COBRA): A qualitative process evaluation. *BMJ Open, 7*(4), e014161. doi:10.1136/bmjopen-2016-014161

Fishman, D. B. (2016). Behavioral theories. In J. C. Norcross, G. R. VandenBos, & D. F. Freedheim (Series Eds.) & B. O. Olatunji (Vol. Ed.), *The handbook of clinical psychology: Vol. 2. Theory and research* (pp. 79–118). Washington, DC: American Psychological Association.

Fishman, D. B., Rotgers, F., & Franks, C. M. (Eds.). (1988). *Paradigms in behavior therapy: Present and promise*. New York, NY: Springer.

Follette, V. M., & Hazlett-Stevens, H. (2016). Mindfulness and acceptance therapies In J. C. Norcross, G. R. VandenBos, & D. F. Freedheim (Series Eds.) & B. O. Olatunji (Vol. Ed.), *The handbook of clinical psychology: Vol. 2. Theory and research* (pp. 273–302). Washington, DC: American Psychological Association.

Forgatch, M. S., & Patterson, G. R. (2010). Parent management training—Oregon model: An intervention for antisocial behavior in children and adolescents. In J. R. Weisz & A. E. Kazdin (Eds.), *Evidence-based psychotherapies for children and adolescents* (2nd ed., pp. 159–178). New York, NY: Guilford Press.

Fresco, D. M., Moore, M., van Dulmen, M., Segal, Z., Ma, S., Teasdale, J., & Williams, J. (2007). Initial psychometric properties of the Experiences Questionnaire: Validation of a self-report measure of decentering. *Behavior Therapy, 38*, 234–246. doi:10.1016/j.beth.2006.08.003

Garamoni, G. L., Reynolds, C. F., Thase, M. E., Frank, E., & Fasiczka, A. L. (1992). Shifts in affective balance during cognitive therapy of major depression. *Journal of Consulting and Clinical Psychology, 60*(2), 260–266. doi:10.1037/0022-006X.60.2.260

Gilbert, D. T. (1992). Assent of man: Mental representation and the control of belief. In D. M. Wegner & J. Pennebaker (Eds.), *Handbook of mental control* (pp. 57–87). New York, NY: Prentice Hall.

Glick, B., & Gibbs, J. C. (2011). *Aggression replacement training: A comprehensive intervention for aggressive youth* (3rd ed.). Champaign, IL: Research Press.

Goldfried, M., & Davison, G. (1976). *Clinical behavior therapy.* New York, NY: Holt, Rinehart & Winston.

Harmon-Jones, E., & Mills, J. (Eds.). (1999). *Cognitive dissonance: Progress on a pivotal theory in social psychology.* Washington, DC: American Psychological Association.

Hayes, S. C., Villatte, M., Levin, M., & Hildebrandt, M. (2011). Open, aware, and active: Contextual approaches as an emerging trend in the behavioral and cognitive therapies. *Annual Review of Clinical Psychology, 7*, 141–168. doi:10.1146/annurev-clinpsy-032210-104449

Hofmann, S. G., Asmundson, G. G., & Beck, A. T. (2013). The science of cognitive therapy. *Behavior Therapy, 44*(2), 199–212. doi:10.1016/j.beth.2009.01.007

Hollon, S. D., & DiGiuseppe, R. (2011). Cognitive theories of psychotherapy. In J. C. Norcross, G. R. VandenBos, & D. K. Freedheim (Eds.), *History of psychotherapy: Continuity and change* (2nd ed., pp. 203–241). Washington, DC: American Psychological Association. doi:10.1037/12353-007

James, W. (1890). *The principles of psychology.* New York, NY: Holt.

Kabat-Zinn, J. (2013). *Full catastrophe living: How to cope with stress, pain and illness with mindfulness meditation.* Boston, MA: Piatkus Books.

Kahneman, D. (2011). *Thinking fast and slow.* New York, NY: Farrar, Straus & Giroux.

Kanfer, F. H., & Goldstein, A. P. (1975). *Helping people change: A textbook of methods.* Oxford, UK: Pergamon Press.

Kelly, G. (1955). *The psychology of personal constructs* (Vol. 1). New York, NY: Norton.

Kohlenberg, R. J., & Tsai, M. (1991). *Functional analytic psychotherapy: Creating intense and curative therapeutic relationships.* New York, NY: Plenum.

Kuehlwein, K. T. (1993). A survey and update of cognitive therapy systems. In K. T. Kuehlwein & H. Rosen (Eds.), *Cognitive therapies in action: Evolving innovative practice* (pp. 1–32). San Francisco, CA: Jossey-Bass.

Lazarus, A. A. (1967). In support of technical eclecticism. *Psychological Reports, 21,* 415–416.

Lazarus, A. A. (1977). Has behavior therapy outlived its usefulness? *American Psychologist, 32,* 550–554.

Lazarus, A. A. (1981). *The practice of multimodal therapy.* New York, NY: McGraw-Hill.

Lazarus, A. A., & Beutler, L. E. (1993). On technical eclecticism. *Journal of Counseling & Development, 71,* 381–385.

Lazarus, R. S. (1991). *Emotion and adaptation.* London, UK: Oxford University Press.

Leahy, R. (2012). *Overcoming resistance in cognitive therapy.* New York, NY: Guilford Press.

Levy, K. N., & Anderson, T. (2013). Is clinical psychology doctoral training becoming less intellectually diverse? And if so, what can be done? *Clinical Psychology: Science & Practice, 20*(2), 211–220. doi:10.1111/cpsp.12035

Lewinsohn, P. M., Weinstein, M. S., & Alper, T. (1970). A behavioral approach to the group treatment of depressed persons: A methodological contribution. *Journal of Clinical Psychology, 26,* 525–532. doi:10.1002/1097-4679(197010)26:4<525::AID-JCLP2270260441>3.0.CO;2-Y

Linehan, M. (1993). *Skills training manual for treating borderline personality disorder.* New York, NY: Guilford Press.

Livio, M. (2002). *The golden ratio: The story of phi, the world's most astonishing number.* New York, NY: Broadway Books.

Mahoney, M. J. (1974). *Cognition and behavior modification.* Cambridge, MA: Ballinger.

Martin, G., & Pear, J. (2015). *Behavior modification: What it is and how to do it* (10th ed.). New York, NY: Routledge.

Mathieson, F., Collings, S., Dowell, A., Goodyear-Smith, F., Stanley, J., & Hatcher, S. (2013). Collaborative research: A case example of dissemination of CBT in primary care. *The Cognitive Behaviour Therapist, 6.* doi:10.1017/S1754470X13000093

Meichenbaum, D. (1977). *Cognitive behavior modification: An integrative approach.* New York, NY: Plenum.

Meichenbaum, D. (1993). Changing conceptions of cognitive behavior modification: Retrospect and prospect. *Journal of Consulting and Clinical Psychology, 61,* 202–204.

Mennin, D. S., Ellard, K. K., Fresco, D. M., & Gross, J. J. (2013). United we stand: Emphasizing commonalities across cognitive-behavioral therapies. *Behavior Therapy, 44*(2), 234–248. doi:10.1016/j.beth.2013.02.004

Mennin, D. S., & Fresco, D. M. (2010). Emotion regulation as an integrative framework for understanding and treating psychopathology. In A. M. Kring & D. M. Sloan (Eds.), *Emotion regulation and psychopathology: A transdiagnostic approach to etiology and treatment* (pp. 356–379). New York, NY: Guilford Press.

Miller, W. R., & Rollnick, S. (2012). *Motivational interviewing: Helping people change* (3rd ed.). New York, NY: Guilford Press.

Neimeyer, R. A. (2009). *Constructivist psychotherapy: Distinctive features.* New York, NY: Routledge.

Neisser, U. (1967). *Cognitive psychology.* East Norwalk, CT: Appleton-Century-Crofts.

Nezu, A. M., Maguth Nezu, C., & D'Zurilla, T. J. (2013). *Problem-solving therapy: A treatment manual.* New York, NY: Springer.

Norcross, J. C., Evans, K. L., & Ellis, J. L. (2010). The model does matter II: Admissions and training in APA–accredited counseling psychology programs. *The Counseling Psychologist, 38*(2), 257–268. doi:10.1177/0011000009339342

Norcross, J. C., Krebs, P. M., & Prochaska, J. O. (2011). Stages of change. *Journal of Clinical Psychology, 67*(2), 143–154. doi:10.1002/jclp.20758

Norcross, J. C., Pfund, R. A., & Prochaska, J. O. (2013). Psychotherapy in 2022: A Delphi poll on its future. *Professional Psychology: Research and Practice, 44*(5), 363–370. doi:10.1037/a0034633

O'Donohue, W. T., & Fisher, J. E. (2009). *General principles and empirically supported techniques of cognitive behavior therapy.* Hoboken, NJ: Wiley.

O'Leary, K. D., & Drabman, R. (1971). Token reinforcement programs in the classroom: A review. *Psychological Bulletin, 75,* 379–398.

Patterson, G. R. (1975). *Applications of social learning to family life.* Champaign, IL: Research Press.

Persons, J. B. (2008). *Case formulation-approach to cognitive behavior therapy.* New York, NY: Guilford Press.

Power, M. J., & Dalgleish, T. (2008). *Cognition and emotion: From order to disorder* (2nd ed.). New York, NY: Psychology Press.

Ray, R. D., Wilhelm, F. H., & Gross, J. J. (2008). All in the mind's eye? Anger rumination and reappraisal. *Journal of Personality and Social Psychology, 94,* 133–145. doi:10.1037/0022-3514.94.1.133

Roemer, L., & Orsillo, S. M. (2009). *Mindfulness and acceptance based behavioral therapies in practice.* New York, NY: Guilford Press.

Rogers, C. R. (1950). A current formulation of client-centered therapy. *Social Service Review, 24*(1), 442–450.

Rogers, C. R. (1957). The necessary and sufficient conditions of therapeutic personality change. *Journal of Consulting Psychology, 21*(2), 95–103.

Roopun, A. K., Kramer, M. A., Carracedo, L. M., Kaiser, M., Davies, C. H., Traub, R. D., . . . Whittington, M. A. (2008). Temporal interactions between cortical rhythms. *Frontiers in Neuroscience, 2*(2), 145–154. doi:10.3389/neuro.01.034.2008

Rotter, J. B. (1954). *Social learning and clinical psychology.* Englewood Cliffs, NJ: Prentice Hall. doi:10.1037/10788-000

Rush, A. J., Khatami, M. M., & Beck, A. T. (1975). Cognitive and behavior therapy in chronic depression. *Behavior Therapy, 6*(3), 398–404. doi:10.1016/S0005-7894(75)80116-X

Rutherford, R. B. (1989). *The meditations of Marcus Aurelius: A study.* New York, NY: Oxford University Press.

Ryle, A. (2005). Cognitive analytic therapy. In J. C. Norcross & M. R. Gold-fried (Eds.), *Handbook of psychotherapy integration* (2nd ed., pp. 196–217). New York, NY: Oxford University Press.

Schwartz, R. M. (1986). The internal dialogue: On the asymmetry between positive and negative coping thoughts. *Cognitive Therapy and Research, 10,* 591–605.

Schwartz, R. M. (1997). Consider the simple screw: Cognitive science, quality improvement, and psychotherapy. *Journal of Consulting and Clinical Psychology, 65,* 970–983. doi:10.1037/0022-006X.65.6.970

Schwartz, R. M., & Garamoni, G. L. (1989). Cognitive balance and psychopathology: Evaluation of an information processing model of positive and negative states of mind. *Clinical Psychology Review, 9,* 271–294.

Shakespeare, W. (1985). *Hamlet prince of Denmark* (W. Farnham, Ed.). New York, NY: Penguin Books. (Original work published 1602)

Sigel, Z. V., Williams, J. M. C., & Teasdale, J. D. (2013). *Mindfulness-based cognitive therapy for depression* (2nd ed.). New York, NY: Guilford Press.

Skinner, B. F. (1957). *Verbal behavior.* East Norwalk, CT: Appleton-Century-Crofts. doi:10.1037/11256-000

Skotarczak, L., & Lee, G. K. (2015). Effects of parent management training programs on disruptive behavior for children with a developmental disability: A meta-analysis. *Research in Developmental Disabilities, 38,* 272–287. doi:10.1016/j.ridd.2014.12.004

Sloan, R. d., Staples, F. R., Cristol, A. H., & Whipple, K. (1975). *Psychotherapy versus behavior therapy.* Cambridge, MA: Harvard University Press.

Society of Clinical Psychology. (2015). *Research-supported psychological treatments.* Retrieved from http://www.psychologicaltreatments.org/

Spinoza, B. (2000). *Ethics* (E. Parkinson, Trans.). New York, NY: Oxford University Press. (Original work published 1677)

Spivack, G., Platt, J., & Shure, M. (1976). *The social problem solving approach to adjustment.* San Francisco, CA: Jossey-Bass.

Sudak, D. M., & Goldberg, D. A. (2012). Trends in psychotherapy training: A national survey of psychiatry residency training. *Academic Psychiatry, 36*(5), 369–373. doi:10.1176/appi.ap.11030057

Suinn, R. M., & Richardson, F. (1971). Anxiety management training: A nonspecific behavior therapy program for anxiety control. *Behavior Therapy, 2,* 498–510. doi:10.1016/S0005-7894(71)80096-5

Watkins, E., Scott, J., Wingrove, J., Rimes, K., Bathurst, N., Steiner, H., . . . Malliaris, Y. (2007). Rumination-focused cognitive behaviour therapy for residual depression: A case series. *Behaviour Research and Therapy, 45,* 2144–2154.

Weiss, V., & Weiss, H. (2003). The golden mean as clock cycle of brain waves. *Chaos, Solitons & Fractals, 18,* 643–652. doi:10.1016/S0960-0779(03)00026-2

Wells, A. (2008). *Metacognitive therapy for anxiety and depression.* New York, NY: Guilford Press.

Wolpe, J. (1958). *Psychotherapy by reciprocal inhibition.* Palo Alto, CA: Stanford University Press.

Wolpe, J. (1969). *The practice of behavior therapy.* New York, NY: Pergamon.

Young, J. E., Klosko, J. S., & Weishaar, M. (2003). *Schema therapy: A practitioner's guide.* New York, NY: Guilford Press.

Chapter 2

Behavior Therapy

Mark Terjesen, Tara Rooney, Michal Barnea, and Victoria Nicosia

Behavior therapy (BT) is a broad umbrella term that is used to cover a number of techniques that are based on "experimental established principles and paradigms of learning to overcome maladaptive habits" (Wolpe, 1990, p. 3). A BT approach examines the history of reinforcement of undesirable and self-defeating behaviors and targets them for change while attempting to increase the development of positive behaviors. The application and practice of BT are best informed through a review of the theories and basic learning principles behind this clinical approach, which are described in this chapter.

As BT involves the integration of a multitude of techniques influenced by a broad range of theorists and approaches, a complete review of the origins of all behavioral techniques and theorists is beyond the scope of this chapter. However, we present pertinent information about BT, the first cognitive behavior therapy (CBT) approach, discussing theoretical constructs, practical applications, numerous behavioral interventions, and information about two prominent theorists who have had a profound impact on the development of the theory and practice of BT.

B. F. Skinner and Joseph Wolpe: Key Theorists

Two notable theorists had a profound impact on the development of the theory and practice of BT: B. F. Skinner and Joseph Wolpe. We briefly describe their significant contributions here.

Interestingly enough, one of the names linked most often to the practice of BT was not even a clinician. However, the scientific work of B. F. Skinner not only had a lasting impact on behaviorism research but also was quite influential in the field of BT. Skinner was born in Pennsylvania and completed his undergraduate work at Hamilton College before abandoning his plans to become a writer and pursuing studies in psychology at Harvard University (Holland, 1992). Skinner received his doctorate from Harvard in 1931, and after appointments at the University of Minnesota and Indiana University he returned to Harvard in 1948 (Bjork, 1997).

Skinner was influenced by W. J. Crozier, a positivistic biologist, who described the growth of plants as a function of the environment without any consideration of the nervous system or other internal events (Holland, 1992). According to Holland (1992), Skinner dedicated his professional life to the pursuit of the direct observation of causal relations among behavior and, more specifically, the consequences of this behavior. His scientific goals were to control, predict, and explain behavior, as reflected in two of his books, *The Behavior of Organisms* (1991) and *Verbal Behavior* (1992), which are seminal and significant works in understanding behavior. The scientific work that he did with animals in an experimental chamber, the Skinner box, demonstrated how behavior can be predicted in an orderly manner. Although the implications for psychology and the experimental analysis of behavior were profound, it was really not until Skinner applied these principles to understanding human behavior that his work began to have a greater impact on the science and practice of BT. The application of behavior analysis is best seen in his book *Walden Two* (1974), which describes a fictional community based on the principles of behavior analysis and contingent reinforcement. Skinner then extended applications of the science of behavior analysis to explain everyday behaviors in society in *Science and Human Behavior* (1953). His principles of behavior analysis have been applied to a myriad of societal and clinical problems and are discussed in greater detail later in this chapter.

Skinner was married and had two daughters. In fact, some of his applications of behavior analysis came about from his experiences with his children. For example, he developed the air crib to create a better sleeping environment for his daughter Deborah, and he developed teaching machines to correct faulty educational practices that his children were receiving in school (Holland, 1992). Skinner remained active professionally and continued to work until just before his death in 1990.

Another prominent theorist, Joseph Wolpe, was born in 1915 in Johannesburg, South Africa. He obtained his bachelor of medicine and medical degree at the University of Witswatersrand. From 1947 to 1956 he lectured part time at the university and also had a private practice (Rachman, 2000). In 1956 Wolpe spent a year at Stanford University in the Center for Behavioral Sciences, moving permanently to the United States in 1960. He initially held an academic appointment at the University of Virginia and then accepted a position at Temple University, where he continued to work until 1982. He was a distinguished professor at Pepperdine University from 1989 to 1997, and his dedication to psychology was evident in the fact that he continued to be involved professionally at the university right up until his death in 1997 (Rachman, 2000; Wolpe, 1958).

Trained as a psychoanalyst, Wolpe practiced dynamic therapy as a captain in the South African army, working with soldiers who were diagnosed with war neurosis (which is known as posttraumatic stress disorder today). At that time, the predominant treatment was drug therapy, which did not cure the problem. This experience, as well as his disappointment with the poor results he was seeing when he returned to clinical practice, led Wolpe to question his psychoanalytic background and seek more effective treatment options (Rachman, 2000). Wolpe initially returned to experimental designs, and he set out to test the degree to which aversive stimulation could produce neurotic disturbances among animals. By demonstrating this, he was then able to develop a theory of the conditioning of human fears, and by extension how to adapt these approaches to the treatment of human fears and anxiety (Rachman, 2000). This approach became known as systematic desensitization and is described in depth later in this chapter. Wolpe tested the efficacy of this approach, and its support resulted in the development of exposure-based approaches that continue to be among the most widely used and effective clinical approaches in BT (Rachman, 2000).

Two of Wolpe's books, *Psychotherapy by Reciprocal Inhibition* (1958) and *The Practice of Behavior Therapy* (1990), were highly influential in developing the practice and science of BT. The recognition that Wolpe received from many professional organizations for his scientific and practical achievements warrants his status as one of the pioneer theorists in BT.

Theoretical Overview of BT

As noted previously, BT was the first CBT approach. Over the years, BT has undergone a number of significant developments and evolutions, in part in response to some of the controversy this theory has evoked. Behavior therapists have been accused of ignoring the importance of emotion and cognition in human behavior because of the emphasis on observable behavior, and there has also been criticism regarding the mechanical and impersonal nature of the theory (Goldfried & Davison, 1994; Sweet, 1984). However, as you will read in this chapter, BT as practiced today has addressed these criticisms and has proven to be an effective form of therapy that has wide applicability across many CBT approaches.

Historical Perspectives and Core Principles

The term *behavior modification*, which is often associated with BT, predates the use of the term *behavior therapy* and first appeared in *Animal Intelligence* by Edward Thorndike (1911). During the 1970s and 1980s the term *behavior modification* was used somewhat interchangeably with *behavior therapy*, even though the first formal use of the term *behavior therapy* in the literature occurred in a 1953 report in which Lindsley, Skinner, and Solomon described the application of an operant conditioning learning model with patients with psychosis.

Behavior modification was based on studies that sought to modify behavior through the systematic application of social learning principles (O'Donohue & Krasner, 1995) and focused on techniques for increasing positive and desired behaviors through the use of reinforcers (something tangible, edible, social, or symbolic that is used to increase the likelihood of a behavior) while decreasing maladaptive behaviors through withholding of reinforcement (extinction) or punishment. BT applies these principles of learning to change behavior in the context of therapy.

It is important for counselors to be aware of a number of core values or principles of BT and utilize them to guide clinical practice. To begin with, in contrast to psychoanalytic approaches that look for some underlying/unconscious cause of behavior, BT focuses on the behavior itself as it is in the here and now. Attempts to understand the history of the behavior can be helpful, but the focus is on the presentation of the behavior in the current context, which typically includes an analysis of the behavior and the variables that may be maintaining it and interfering with adaptive change. The behavioral approach looks at learning history and its impact on behavior and emotion, so the behavioral counselor will try to understand how the behavior is acquired through learning and work with clients to educate them on how these same paradigms of learning can be used to unlearn the behavior.

A challenge to the principle that maladaptive behaviors are learned is that biological or situational factors may contribute to the behavior, and thus not all of a behavior is an outcome of a prior maladaptive learning history. For example, an individual may be more genetically predisposed to experiencing anxiety in stressful situations, such as when faced with project deadlines or social engagements that may trigger the emotional experience of anxiety and the subsequent anxious pattern of behavior (e.g., avoidance). Therefore, it is important for counselors to conduct a good behavioral assessment in order to understand not only the *function* of a behavior but also the variables that are maintaining it.

Behavioral assessment is another core principle of BT, and data gathered during the assessment can also be used to evaluate the effectiveness of behavioral interventions. In comparison with more traditional assessment batteries, in which inferences are made based on results of testing, behavioral assessment is more direct and tends to focus on specific behaviors. Behavioral assessment approaches help explain the *why* of a behavior by looking for what precedes and follows the behavior that may be influencing its occurrence and are then utilized to inform treatment planning and evaluate progress.

As noted previously, the field and practice of BT is not without controversy. In fact, the terminology used and the approaches applied have not consistently garnered support in the behavioral community. Probably the biggest area of controversy in the BT community involves the use of cognitive strategies in the BT framework. Forsyth (1997) outlined the resistance to the integration of cognitive approaches due to the fact that

(a) cognition is not behavior, (b) behavior principles and theory cannot account for events occurring within the skin, and most important, (c) we therefore need a unique conceptual system to account for how thinking, feeling, and other private events relate to overt human action. (p. 621)

At present, the majority of clinicians who practice BT identify themselves as cognitive behavioral in orientation (Cook, Biyanova, Elhai, Schnurr, & Coyne, 2010), and cognitive approaches are regularly part of BT, as discussed in more depth elsewhere in this book. We thought it important for you to understand that many behaviorists routinely utilize cognitive strategies in their therapeutic work. Learn more about the resistance regarding the integration of cognitive techniques into BT by reading the article by Forsyth (1997).

Pioneering Theories in BT

As a discipline, BT has three main points of origin that diverge somewhat in how they view and treat behavior problems. First, Wolpe and his disciples developed a technique called *reciprocal inhibition* as a way to treat anxiety by identifying behaviors that are functionally opposite of those behaviors that they wish to change. Second, Hans Eysenck (1951) considered the interaction between behavior, environment, and personality characteristics in understanding human behavior. Third, Skinner (1953) sought to explain and change behavior through an operant conditioning focus, implementing reinforcement and behavioral activation (BA). Each of these approaches has a number of behavioral techniques that can be applied in counseling and have been extended to work with clients as discussed in depth in the following paragraphs.

O'Donohue and Krasner (1995) provided a review of the broad spectrum of major theories that have influenced the current practice of BT. Perhaps more important, they highlighted the role of *theory* in BT and how it was critical to the beginnings of BT, emphasizing Wolpe's reciprocal inhibition and Skinner's operant explanation of abnormal behavior. Simply stated, as scientists formulate and test different aspects of learning theory, they give rise to behavioral interventions and therapy.

Reciprocal Inhibition

One of the earliest applications of behavioral principles to clinical work is the concept of *reciprocal inhibition,* which is a label for a physiological phenomenon initially described by Sherrington in 1906. Sherrington argued that the evocation of a response is typically accompanied by the inhibition of functionally related behaviors that are opposite of the one that is being evoked and that this reciprocal inhibition is built into the structure of the nervous system. Wolpe (1990) offered a number of both physiological (e.g., reflexes) and emotional (e.g., laughter being inhibited by sadness) examples of how reciprocal inhibition is seen in everyday life, highlighting how it can have an impact on learning. Wolpe's early work involved a number of research experiments that looked at the role of reciprocal inhibition in changing bad habits in animals. He then extended his work and demonstrated how reciprocal inhibition could be applied to humans, more specifically to help clients overcome maladaptive anxious responses. A number of these interventions, such as assertiveness training, relaxation training, and desensitization, are discussed later in this chapter as they relate to the application of reciprocal inhibition.

Reinforcement

The role of reinforcement in explaining and treating maladaptive behaviors is another core principle of BT with extensive theoretical and empirical support. The early experimental studies by Pavlov (1927) and John B. Watson set the scientific and eventual clinical stage for the application of principles of conditioning and learning to behavior. The well-known work by J. B. Watson and Rayner (1920) on "Little Albert," an 11-month-old boy who was conditioned to become fearful of a white rat by having the rat paired with a loud, aversive noise, is an early example of how learning principles may contribute to the development of unhealthy emotions and behaviors and how emotions are acquired and learned. Although subsequent reviews (Harris, 1979) argued that the degree to which Albert's fear and conditioning led to the development of this emotional response may have been exaggerated, the experiment demonstrated the role of learning and conditioning in the development of an emotional response. An additional example in which these principles were applied is Mary Cover Jones's (1924) work in which she treated children's phobias using reconditioning. Similarly, Wolpe was able to produce comparable changes through conditioning when working with clients with anxiety. Reinforcement principles are discussed in more detail later in this chapter.

As described previously, Skinner built on the role of learning in explaining human behavior and argued that behavior can be explained through a series of reinforcements. He referred to this application of reinforcement to strengthen behavior as *operant conditioning* (Skinner, 1953). Skinner drew a distinction between *respondent* behaviors, which are elicited by stimuli (e.g., Pavlovian conditioning), and *operant* behaviors, which are emitted but not induced by a stimulus. These operant behaviors are strengthened through reinforcement or operant conditioning, in which the occurrence of a behavior leads to a reinforcer.

The major theorists and early history of BT have helped explain how behaviors associated with psychological disorders are developed and maintained through a behavioral mechanism. Having this understanding is important for counselors, as the behavioral interventions they implement may focus on helping clients *un*learn these behaviors, typically by using a number of strategies discussed later in the chapter. It is helpful for counselors to explain to clients how their behaviors may have been reinforced and use this as a way of educating them about the clinical approaches that they will be using to change the undesirable behaviors. To gain practice in recognizing how clients' unhelpful behaviors can be maintained, refer to Sidebar 1.

The Therapeutic Process in BT

Behaviorists consider the degree to which the desired targets of behavior change have a significant and adverse effect on social functioning, occupational functioning, or another important area of functioning. The level of impairment that one may experience may be mild (e.g., test anxiety) or more severe (e.g., an inability to work). Behavior therapists consider the environmental context of the behavior and how it may be setting the stage for the maladaptive behavior or in fact maintaining it. For example, if clients are angry and engage in aggressive behaviors toward others, and they get what they want, then their behavior has been reinforced. A behaviorist would consider the purpose or function of the behavior and then try to change the reinforcers in order to reduce or extinguish the undesirable behavior. This section describes the process of BT with clients and differentiates when there are special considerations as a function of the type of behavior or due to client variables, such as age.

Goal Setting

Goal setting is very important in this theory. To motivate clients to engage in goal setting, the counselor may ask them to consider the advantages and disadvantages of working toward a particular goal. In essence, the process of goal setting is very collaborative in nature and enhances the therapeutic alliance. The goals will often focus on decreasing maladaptive and unhealthy behaviors through increasing clients' participation in positive or socially reinforcing activities, although tasks and goals will differ depending on the specific characteristics of the client and the treatment targets. For instance, clients who are experiencing anxiety disorders may benefit from interventions such as systematic desensitization, graduated exposure, and relaxation (Akin-Little, 2009; T. S. Watson & Gresham, 2013), whereas clients with externalizing disorders might benefit from positive reinforcement, positive attending, and planned ignoring (Flanagan, Allen, & Levine,

Sidebar 1
Theories and Practice of BT

How do the major theorists relate to the practice of BT today?

Describe two clients whose difficulties are or were behaviorally maintained, or think of two people you know whose problems are behaviorally maintained.

How could you or did you address the maintaining factors?

2015). These interventions are discussed later in the chapter. Clients with highly specific goals are likely to benefit from BT, but if clients present with vague or broad goals (e.g., "I don't want to get so upset," "I just want to be happy"), the counselor will work with them to help determine objective and measurable behavioral goals for change.

During the goal-setting process, it is helpful to assess the frequency (e.g., how often it happens), the duration (e.g., how long it lasts), and the intensity (i.e., the strength of the emotion or behavior) of the problematic behavior. Furthermore, the focus will be on increasing adaptive behaviors rather than just reducing unhealthy behaviors. Goals may also be graded in complexity, and the counselor will help the client systematically work through the different steps needed to achieve the overall goal. Ongoing behavioral assessment of goals will also help monitor progress and can serve as an indicator that either the client is moving closer to termination or the goals may need to be revised. If it is necessary to revise the goals, it is important that the counselor not frame this as evidence that they or the client have failed.

Setting goals and assessing progress are critical tasks of the counselor. Practice generating goals by referring to Sidebar 2.

The Role of the Counselor

In BT the relationship between the counselor and client is collaborative, which requires the counselor to be empathic and demonstrate positive regard for the client (Fall, Holden, & Marquis, 2010). Sweet (1984) noted that clients are like cotherapists and the counselor is like a consultant who models appropriate behaviors and teaches clients skills to help them achieve the goals that have been identified as the targets for treatment. Behavioral counselors communicate concern and support to clients by paying close attention to them and by acknowledging and reinforcing their strengths and progress toward identified goals.

The effective behavioral counselor wants to know what is causing clients to behave in a particular way at the present time and what the counselor can do to help change that behavior; the focus is on the present and future instead of on the past (Wilson, 2008). Skillful behavioral counselors are active and directive and are adept at listening to clients discuss their concerns, analyzing the target behaviors, and helping clients identify measurable goals.

Sidebar 2
Goal Setting

A 13-year-old adolescent female is referred to you by her parents in response to depressive symptoms, specifically social isolation and negative self-talk of being worthless. Write down specific, measurable goals and discuss with a peer how you would go about evaluating this client's progress toward those goals and how you would address any barriers or lack of progress.

Not only do behavioral counselors use reinforcement, but they also use confrontation when necessary by pointing out discrepancies and helping clients persist in order to overcome the obstacles that are preventing them from attaining their goals (Fall et al., 2010). Behavioral counselors see their role as helping clients identify specific targets for change and also specific change strategies, because although various techniques can be used for particular problems, a client is more likely to follow through if the strategy is adapted to that individual (Swift & Callahan, 2009).

Providing clients with psychoeducational information about the presenting problem and what behavioral approaches have been shown to be effective in addressing the problem is another task behavioral counselors assume. They also may model some of the desirable client behaviors as well as provide feedback about the behavior. For instance, if clients present with social skills deficits, the counselor may model effective social skills and then offer feedback to the clients when they practice these behaviors.

The Therapeutic Alliance

There has been some debate about the importance of the therapeutic alliance in BT because of the emphasis on the scientific approach. Eysenck (1960) was of the opinion that personal relationships may sometimes be necessary, but not always. Wolpe and others emphasized that the therapeutic relationship is essential, noting that "trust, positive regard, and serious acceptance of the patient are part and parcel of behavior therapy practice" (Wolpe, 1985, p. 127). According to Goldfried and Davison (1994), "A tough-minded approach to conceptualizing human problems in no way precludes a warm, genuine, or empathic interaction with clients" (p. 7). Overall, the consensus seems to be that establishing a strong therapeutic relationship is important in helping clients achieve their goals.

The therapeutic or working alliance consists of three components: agreement on goals, agreement on tasks, and the bond (Horvath & Luborsky, 1993). As the alliance solidifies, counselors can engage in *alliance expectant behaviors*, such as validating feelings, demonstrating patience, and showing an interest in problem solving to further maintain the alliance (Baylis, Collins, & Coleman, 2011). Because behavioral counselors may ask clients to engage in behaviors that clients may find uncomfortable or wish to avoid, it is very important to maintain a strong working alliance.

There are some special considerations when establishing a therapeutic alliance with children as opposed to adults, in part depending on the age or developmental level of the child or adolescent. One important difference is to understand that children and adolescents are not typically self-referred for counseling, and therefore younger clients may not understand why they need counseling or may be resistant to participating in any stage of the process (DiGiuseppe, Linscott, & Jilton, 1996). Thus, behavioral counselors will need to use age-appropriate techniques and take more time to develop a good relationship. This is very important with adolescents in particular because the alliance between the counselor and adolescent client has been shown to be significantly correlated with decreased symptoms, improved family relationships, increased self-esteem, and higher levels of perceived social support and satisfaction with counseling (Hawley & Garland, 2008). In addition, adolescents who were more ready to change rated the alliance with their counselor higher than those who were not ready to change (Fitzpatrick & Irannejad, 2008).

Baylis and colleagues (2011) encouraged using *alliance dependent behaviors,* such as being nice, doing activities, and using active listening, when developing a working alliance with children. In addition, working with children often occurs concomitantly with working with parents, so it is important for the counselor to ascertain parents' perceptions of any behavioral strategies that might be implemented. If parents do not think that these behavioral interventions would be effective, think that the interventions are too difficult to implement, or disagree with the interventions, they will be less likely to implement them. Thus, it is important to build an alliance with parents as well.

The Process of Change

Assessment and intervention are two distinct components of the therapeutic process, with assessment driving the intervention. During the initial counseling session, behavioral counselors aim to accomplish four things: establish the working alliance, develop an understanding of the client's problems and identify target behaviors for change, learn more about what maintains the target behaviors, and orient the client to the BT change process (Spiegler & Guevremont, 1998). In addition, they may want to have the client sign a contract that describes expectations for both the counselor and client.

It is important to note that behavioral assessment differs from more traditional assessment in that it targets specific behaviors rather than one's personality more generally (Spiegler & Guevremont, 2009). As noted previously, it is especially important to identify the frequency, intensity, and duration of the behavior(s) targeted for change, which can be accomplished through direct methods (such as behavioral observation and self-monitoring) as well as the use of permanent products (such as exam performance, the number of homework assignments completed, work attendance records, etc.). A variety of indirect methods are also used, including interviews, rating scales, checklists, and other self-report inventories (Akin-Little, 2009; Flanagan et al., 2015; T. S. Watson & Gresham, 2013). Assessment is ongoing throughout the counseling process as a means of monitoring process and adjusting the change strategies as needed, but the goal of the initial assessment is to develop a specific plan that identifies behavioral goals and how to achieve them (Fall et al., 2010).

An important part of the assessment process is knowing not only exactly what the behavior entails but even more important what the function of the behavior is. This can be determined through a functional behavioral assessment, which is a procedure that focuses on identifying and describing the relationships between an individual, a behavior, and the variables that trigger or reinforce the behavior. Essentially, the counselor conducting the functional behavioral assessment assesses the stimulus or event that occurs immediately before and after the problem behavior and uses that information to determine the function of the behavior (Steege & Watson, 2009). In addition to uncovering the function of problem behaviors, a functional behavioral assessment can be used to design or tailor interventions that will be most effective for the client. The development of an intervention plan should be informed by an analysis of all of the assessment data that have been collected.

Throughout the counseling process the counselor helps clients identify any practical or emotional barriers that may interfere with goal attainment. This may be done at the beginning of each counseling session as well as through the development of homework assignments that should be completed before the next session. In fact, it is good to begin each session with an evaluation of the collaboratively agreed-on homework, with clients describing how successful they were in completing the assignment. If they were successful, the counselor can verbally reinforce this and ask what they did to increase the likelihood of success. If they were not successful, the counselor will work with the clients, discussing the challenges that may have prevented completion of the homework. When establishing subsequent homework assignments, it is a good idea to help clients identify any barriers that could interfere with their ability to successfully complete the assignments.

Following a review of the homework, the counselor and client collaboratively set an agenda for the session. Typically this will involve a discussion of the targeted goals and identification of specific concrete behaviors that may have occurred since the prior session relative to those goals. A review of the implementation of previously learned behavioral strategies will be discussed, and then new skills may be taught and practiced in session as they relate to those goals. Skills may involve both a didactic component (e.g., educating clients about the relationship of behavior to mood) or instruction and practice in a number of behavioral interventions that are discussed later in this chapter.

After the appropriate interventions have been selected and implemented, they should be continually monitored to ensure that behavior change is actually occurring. This can be done by collecting data and comparing them to the baseline that was established during the assessment stage. Analyzing these data will allow the counselor to determine whether the intervention is effectively changing the behavior or whether the plan needs to be altered or even terminated.

The Termination Process

When clients are progressing toward their goals, it is important for the counselor to consider at what point to broach termination of the counseling relationship. The termination process itself can be challenging given that short-term services are frequently characteristic of BT. However, a number of strategies can be used throughout the counseling process to assist with this process. To begin, it is often helpful to discuss termination with clients early on and collaboratively establish that termination is warranted when they make sufficient progress toward achieving their goals. The termination process may also involve collaboration between client and counselor at the end of treatment when they establish the actual termination date and engage in a review of the progress that has been made, the skills that were learned and developed, and what needs to be addressed in the future, if applicable. This review allows for closure in the therapeutic relationship (Davis & Younggren, 2009).

Termination with children and adolescents may be a bit more complex given that these clients may have been unprepared as to what to expect from counseling and perhaps were initially resistant to the idea. They may experience a variety of emotions that could interfere with their progress toward their goals. It is a good idea to regularly review young clients' success in counseling and reinforce them when they are able to manage previously difficult situations independently. At the same time, it is important for the counselor to discuss when a follow-up/check-in appointment would be helpful to revisit old issues or work on new counseling goals. If children and adolescents do return to counseling, the counselor should examine how they attempted to use the previously learned behavioral strategies to manage the problem independently.

BT Interventions

In this section a number of different behavioral intervention strategies that are often used in the context of counseling are described. The choice of strategy depends on the presenting problem and the research demonstrating the efficacy of a specific intervention for the particular problem. Furthermore, it is very common for counselors to use multiple interventions as part of a behavioral treatment package.

Applied Behavior Analysis (ABA)

There is probably no intervention more closely linked with BT than ABA. ABA is based on learning theory principles and their systematic application to change behavior. ABA aims to change behavior by first assessing the functional relationship between the behavior and the environment in which the behavior occurs. The intervention then seeks to develop replacement adaptive behaviors that serve the same function as the target behavior.

A review of the compendium of interventions and methodologies utilized in ABA is beyond the scope of this chapter, but examples include antecedent and consequential manipulation, prompt/fading procedures, motivational operations, joint attention intervention, functional communication training, discrete trial training, pivotal response training, reinforcement, and shaping. All are highly behavioral and are based on principles of learning. You are referred to Fisher, Piazza, and Roane (2011) for a complete review of ABA strategies.

Reinforcement

The use of reinforcement is considered the cornerstone of BT and is an active component of most behavior change programs. A reinforcer is an event or consequence that follows a behavior and increases the probability of that behavior occurring in the future. With the goal being to strengthen specific behaviors, the counselor will work with clients to examine the history of reinforcers that have successfully increased the frequency of the desired behavior. A functional analysis of the behavior may also help practitioners understand what reinforcers are maintaining the behavior so that they can work with clients to actively change these reinforcers. Reinforcers may be activities (e.g., watching a favorite movie), social interactions (e.g., going out with friends), tangibles (e.g., stickers, access to a toy), or sensory stimuli. The use of the reinforcer will depend on the clients' developmental level, history of reinforcement, as well as motivation to work toward the reinforcer. When using reinforcers with children in school settings, counselors often rely on parents and teachers to help identify and implement appropriate reinforcers (Martin & Pear, 2015).

Punishment

Punishment is intended to decrease the occurrence of an undesirable behavior and occurs after the behavior has been performed, whereas it is hoped that reinforcement increases the occurrence of a desirable behavior (Murdock, 2004). Punishment is an approach that parents or teachers may rely on almost instinctively and is not something counselors actively promote. Typically the type of punishment that is utilized with children involves response cost, which is the removal of something desirable. For example, parents may take away computer time when their child engages in a forbidden behavior, or teachers may make a child stay in for recess if he or she misbehaves in the classroom.

It is helpful to teach parents and teachers strategies that can increase children's adaptive/desirable behavior rather than strategies that punish the negative behavior. It is important for parents and teachers to understand that punishment does not teach children what they should be doing, and there is also a risk of overpunishment, which may negatively impact the relationship between the parent/teacher and the child. Punishment may also serve as a maladaptive model for children regarding how to respond to others when they perform behaviors they do not like (Martin & Pear, 2015). Skinner (1971) noted that punishment only suppresses behavior, so it may reoccur if certain conditions are not present. Furthermore, punishment usually results in negative emotions such as anger or frustration that may then be associated with the punisher. For these reasons, other behavioral techniques are preferred.

Extinction

Related to operant conditioning, *extinction* is a term used to describe withholding or discontinuing reinforcement of a previously reinforced behavior. The expectation is that when this reinforcement is withheld there will be a decrease in the behavior. This approach is often applied in time out, when a child is removed from a desirable/reinforcing activity. For example, if attention from the teacher is maintaining a student's acting-out behavior, the counselor may advise the teacher to withhold attention for the purpose of extinguishing the undesirable behavior. Time out is most effective when it is paired with time in, when the child is able to gain reinforcement through positive experiences. If this strategy is to be implemented, it is important to communicate the possibility of an extinction burst, which is a brief but temporary increase in the behavior that is intended to be extinguished. In the aforementioned example, if attention is the function that maintains the acting-out behavior, when the teacher initially attempts to withhold the reinforcer (attention), the child's behavior may initially get worse with the expectation of that behavior being reinforced. Eventually the lack of reinforcement will result in the behavior decreasing in frequency or intensity as it is being extinguished (Martin & Pear, 2015).

Token Economy

Token economy is a commonly used behavioral reinforcement strategy that rewards clients for demonstrating positive behavior with tokens or symbols that can be exchanged for desirable/tangible rewards. In a school setting, counselors may work with teachers to develop a token economy program for individual students or for an entire classroom. When this intervention is implemented, clear procedures are defined at the outset, specific behaviors to target are identified, and rewards are clearly specified. The goal is twofold: (a) to increase the likelihood that the positive behaviors will be performed in the future; and (b) to eventually replace the tokens with less tangible rewards and more natural reinforcers, such as verbal praise, which is more consistent with the type of reinforcement that clients will experience in the real world (Martin & Pear, 2015). For example, if the desired behavior is in-seat/on-task behavior in the classroom, the counselor will clearly define the behavior with the student and collaboratively work with the teacher and the student to develop and implement a token economy program. Each time the student performs the desired behavior (e.g., stays in his or her seat for 15 consecutive minutes or completes a worksheet without speaking to a peer), he or she will receive a sticker or ticket as a token. The tokens are symbolic and have value that can be exchanged for a reward, such as more time on the computer or a small tangible object such as a colorful eraser. Parents can also use a token economy system at home, working with the child to identify targeted desirable behaviors that when exhibited are rewarded with a token that is later exchanged for something tangible, such as going to a movie or spending time at the park with friends.

Although token economy systems are typically used with children, this approach can also be modified for use with older clients. For example, a client whose goal is to lose 10 pounds can monitor her progress by giving herself a penny for each pound she loses. When she has reached the goal, she can trade in the coins for an enjoyable activity, such as a spa treatment.

Modeling

Modeling involves a number of behavioral strategies and was initially introduced by Albert Bandura (1969). Modeling is closely linked with imitation and observational learning and very often considered synonymous with them. The procedures in modeling involve the client engaging in observation of others (e.g., the counselor) performing desired behaviors and the client retaining and reproducing these behaviors in the desired context (Fall et al., 2010). For example, if clients have deficiencies in social skills, the counselor may model appropriate social skills in the session. Then the clients can recall and perform these behaviors both in the session and eventually in the setting where they have difficulty socializing. This process of utilizing skills in one's natural environment is called *generalization* and is an important treatment goal in behavioral approaches.

Shaping

Shaping and graded task assignments are used when the desired behavior is complex in nature and may need to be broken down into simpler steps (Fall et al., 2010). As the counselor systematically works with the client to break down the more complex behavior into smaller, manageable tasks, the ultimate goal is for the client to complete these smaller, successive steps, which it is hoped will result in the more complex behavior. Reinforcement is used throughout this stepwise program. For example, if clients want to develop social skills in order to be in a more intimate relationship with someone of the same or opposite sex, the counselor may suggest that they begin by going to a social setting three times a week and observing others. Next they are instructed to introduce themselves to two people at a given social event. The next step would be to engage in a short conversation with at least one person at a social outing. This shaping process continues to build on previous goal-related behaviors so that the next step might be asking another person to go to a movie or out to eat. This systematic approach of breaking the desired behavior down into smaller steps helps clients see the targeted problem as manageable and the goals as achievable and see that with effort and structure they can achieve more complex tasks and behavior change (Martin & Pear, 2015).

Assertiveness Skills Training

Although the objective of assertiveness training is to teach appropriate assertive as opposed to aggressive verbal and nonverbal behaviors, the counselor will want to determine whether a client's lack of assertiveness is a *skill* deficit or a *performance* deficit (Alberti & Emmons, 2001; O'Donohue, 2003; Weiner & Craighead, 2010). For example, if a client has never had the opportunity to develop appropriate assertive behavior and receive feedback and reinforcement for it, then the counseling approach may be primarily behavioral in nature, addressing the skill deficit. In this situation, the counselor could use modeling, feedback, and reinforcement to increase the desired assertive behaviors. However, the counselor should also consider the role of anxiety when clients have difficulty communicating assertively, because it is oftentimes the case that anxiety and fear may prevent clients from engaging in assertive behaviors; this would imply a performance deficit. If the lack of assertiveness is a function of anxiety, the initial target of assertiveness training would be to decondition maladaptive socially anxious responses. Through the use of behavioral strategies, the counselor would have clients engage in behaviors that inhibit the anxious response and thus increase the likelihood of effective and adaptive behavior.

It is helpful for clients to rehearse assertive messages and behaviors in session so that the counselor can provide feedback and encourage them to try these new behaviors out in the real world. Clients then report back to the counselor about their performance and discuss any variables that may have contributed to the outcome as well as any feedback they received when delivering the assertive message. It is also important that the counselor take into consideration any cultural or familial values that may impact the acceptability and perceived appropriateness of engaging in assertive behavior. Some clients may think, "It would be selfish for me to put my concerns over what others want." The counselor can address this by helping them understand the benefits and appropriateness of behaving in an assertive manner while still respecting cultural and familial values.

Relaxation Training

Relaxation training has an extensive history and has undergone a number of modifications throughout the years, but regardless most approaches are based to some degree on the techniques initially described by Jacobson (1938). Jacobson's approach involved more than 50 sessions of sequential training in the relaxation of various muscle groups, but subsequent research has shown that relaxation training can be done more efficiently (Richardson & Rothstein, 2008) and that there is no specific order in which the muscle groups must be relaxed. In using relaxation training with clients, it is good to begin with an explanation of the purpose of this approach and also demonstrate it. It is helpful to ask clients to identify which parts of the body they wish to start with, preferably an area convenient for demonstration purposes (e.g., the arms or legs). For demonstration purposes, the counselor could ask a client to place his or her left hand on the left arm of a chair and right hand on the right arm and then grip only the left arm of the chair with the left hand to create tension. The counselor would then ask the client whether there were any differences in physiological arousal and any resistance or tension in his or her arms. The counselor would explain that tension is purposely being created and ask the client to note the physiological changes and any changes in muscle relaxation when he or she lets it go. Subsequent to the demonstration and instruction in relaxation training, counselors can work with clients to identify the regions of the body in which they experience the most anxiety or tension, then practice in-session relaxation on various muscle groups for anywhere from 30 seconds to a minute, becoming aware of the sensations they experience. It is also a good idea to develop a method for practicing relaxation outside of the counseling session.

Systematic Desensitization

The purpose of systematic desensitization is to break down the client's anxiety response habits in a structured manner. More specifically, the intervention involves inducing a state of physiological arousal that inhibits anxiety through muscle relaxation. The original model proposed by Wolpe (1961) involved three sets of operations:

1. Training the client in deep muscle relaxation
2. Constructing an anxiety hierarchy of stimuli to which the client experiences an anxious response
3. Engaging the client in relaxation while exposing him or her to anxiety-evoking stimuli from the hierarchy

The process goes like this. The counselor will expose the client to lower level anxiety-arousing stimuli for a few seconds. If the exposure is repeated, the stimulus progressively loses its ability to induce anxiety. The counselor continues the approach by successfully exposing the client to stronger levels of stimuli that may induce anxiety and helping the client manage the anxiety through habituation (i.e., the client stops responding to the feared stimulus) and relaxation training. The counselor will often coach the client to use relaxation skills during the exposure exercise.

Exposure and Response Prevention (ERP)

A behavioral approach that is commonly utilized with clients experiencing anxiety is ERP. In using ERP, the counselor exposes the client to anxiety-provoking stimuli while preventing the historically reinforced occurrence of avoidant behaviors that have maintained the anxiety. It is important for the counselor to thoroughly explain the rationale behind this approach, highlighting the role of avoidance in reinforcing the anxiety. That is, when clients encounter a situation that may be uncomfortable and avoid that situation, they have experienced negative reinforcement of the anxiety because there is no negative direct outcome and they experience physiological relaxation. This reinforces both their anxiety and their likelihood of avoiding that situation in the future. For example, if a client is fearful of public speaking and regularly avoids opportunities to speak publicly, he or she will experience a sense of comfort and relaxation that maintains the avoidant behavior. ERP is a behavioral approach that teaches clients to use relaxation and face the feared stimulus rather than avoid the anxiety. Thus, clients are prevented from engaging in the behavior that would maintain the anxiety.

This approach is somewhat similar to systematic desensitization, in which clients create a hierarchy of situations that they would typically avoid out of fear. Exposing clients to this hierarchy without allowing them to engage in avoidant behavior (and thus extinguishing it) has been shown to be effective in treating a variety of disorders in both children and adults (Richard & Lauterbach, 2011). Research has demonstrated that this is particularly effective with clients with obsessive-compulsive disorder (Foa & McLean, 2016; Van Oppen et al., 1995). The exposure could be direct exposure to the actual feared stimulus (in vivo) or to imaginal versions of it. A number of studies have demonstrated that although both approaches are effective, in vivo exposure tends to have stronger treatment effects (McKay & Ojserkis, 2015).

BA

BA is a technique that is often used in the treatment of depression. In this approach, clients learn to monitor their mood and daily activities and work on increasing the number of pleasant activities they experience. They also aim to increase positive interactions with their environment through activity scheduling, because when clients get depressed they may disengage from routines and withdraw from enjoyable activities, which further exacerbates their depressed mood (Dimidjian, Barrera, Martell, Muñoz, & Lewinsohn, 2011). BA increases the client's contact with potential sources of reward and is an attractive behavioral treatment because it is not overly complicated and does not require complex skills from either the client or the counselor.

Research showed that when BA was compared to cognitive therapy in the treatment of depression, there were no differences between the approaches and the benefits of the treatments were maintained at follow-up (Dimidjian et al., 2011; Dobson et al., 2008; Mazzucchelli, Kane, & Rees, 2009). This method is described in greater detail in "Applications of BT."

Problem Solving

Problem-solving approaches teach clients a variety of potentially effective responses to allow them to handle situations more effectively in the future (D'Zurilla & Goldfried, 1971). The first step is for the counselor and client to collaboratively define what the problem is. D'Zurilla and Nezu (2010) defined a *problem* as "any life situation or task present or anticipated that demands an effective response to achieve a goal or resolve a conflict when no effective response is immediately apparent or available to the person" (p. 199). Once the problem has been defined, the counselor asks the client to brainstorm alternative solutions, encouraging the client to identify as many potential solutions as possible and not to evaluate them so as not to inhibit the brainstorming process. The next step involves deciding which solution may be the most effective—one that targets the problem while also increasing positive emotions and decreasing negative emotions. Next the client implements the identified solution and then is taught how to evaluate the effectiveness of the solution as it relates to the desired outcome.

The goal of problem solving is to change behavior and affect as well as promote client well-being and the ability to make decisions. Counselors work with clients to develop constructive attitudes and problem-solving skills and break down what may seem to be impossible tasks into manageable elements. In addition to teaching strategies to evaluate the problem objectively, the counselor may work on promoting coping strategies to improve the situation and hopefully reduce clients' emotional distress. D'Zurilla and Nezu (2010) stressed the importance of problem solving occurring in the natural social environment and being viewed as a learning process that may increase the probability of adaptive outcomes.

As one of the goals of BT is for clients to experience behavioral and affective change in the real world, behavior therapists often have clients engage in homework between sessions. Homework may be used to self-monitor and record affective and behavioral experiences during the week, engage in exposure exercises during the course of treatment, practice relaxation, and so forth. Monitoring homework compliance is also a good way to start subsequent counseling sessions: "Last week you said you were going to reduce the number of cigarettes you smoked. How did that go?"

All of the aforementioned interventions have merit, but an error that beginning counselors make is assuming that the intervention they choose to implement will resonate with clients. For practice in thinking critically about various behavioral interventions for your clients, refer to Sidebar 3.

Applications of BT

BT can be applied to a wide range of client problems and is supported by research attesting to the efficacy of this approach. In this section we discuss specific applications with anxiety, depression, and externalizing disorders in children.

Sidebar 3
The Selection of Behavioral Strategies

Consider the number of behavioral strategies reviewed.

Which interventions do you think may be more of a challenge for clients to accept as part of their treatment?

Which strategies would you want to consider to help them become more comfortable with these interventions?

Discuss with a partner.

Behavioral Interventions for Anxiety Disorders

Anxiety disorders develop when a client experiences an excessive level of fear of a specified object or situation that may lead to avoidance in the absence of true danger. Anxiety disorders tend to have very high prevalence rates, affecting 18% of the adult population (Kessler, Chiu, Demler, & Walters, 2005). CBT garners the greatest degree of support in meta-analytic reviews for the treatment of anxiety disorders (Hofmann, Asnaani, Vonk, Sawyer, & Fang, 2012; Olatunji, Cisler, & Deacon, 2010).

As CBT includes a combination of behavioral and cognitive interventions, it is difficult to discern exactly which components of CBT lead to therapeutic change that is truly behavioral in nature. However, imaginal and in vivo exposure to the feared stimuli are among the more common techniques for treating anxiety and primarily focus on modifying the antecedents and consequences of the behavior. This may be seen in the use of ERP in the treatment of obsessive-compulsive disorder (Abramowitz, 1997). The basic rationale behind ERP is that as clients begin to confront their fears and not engage in an avoidant response, they may experience a reduction in their level of anxiety and eventually learn that the perceived threat is not actually present. Clients will systematically expose themselves to the various objects, situations, and thoughts that they would typically get anxious about and subsequently avoid. They are prevented from engaging in the compulsive behaviors (e.g., checking, handwashing) that they would normally do as a means of reducing the anxiety. Learning occurs when clients understand that their fear is irrational and they no longer experience anxiety when exposed to the stimulus.

These exposure-based approaches may be used to treat a number of anxiety disorders in addition to obsessive-compulsive disorder, such as specific and social phobias. Adler and Cook-Nobles (2010) described treating a college-age student with specific phobia with in vivo exposure. Treatment components included psychoeducation about the nature of specific phobia in general and also as it pertained to the phobia (fear of elevators) as well as the treatment rationale, behavioral strategies (diaphragmatic breathing), cognitive strategies (evaluating the validity of the fear), and graduated in vivo exposure. At the conclusion of the treatment, the client's self-report on the Anxiety Sensitivity Index decreased from 90 to 59. Qualitative data suggest high treatment acceptability (Adler & Cook-Nobles, 2010).

Group interventions are also an effective means of treating anxiety disorders. According to van Ingen and Novicki (2009), teaching techniques such as exposure, ritual prevention (in which clients are encouraged not to engage in compulsions to reduce anxiety), cognitive restructuring, psychoeducation, diaphragmatic breathing, and social skills training led to significant improvements in generalized anxiety disorder, panic disorder with agoraphobia, social phobia, specific phobia, and obsessive-compulsive disorder (van Ingen & Novicki, 2009). When these strategies are implemented in a group setting, clients benefit from hearing about how others are learning to manage their anxiety, and group members can reinforce one another on their progress.

BA for the Treatment of Depression

BA is often the first line of treatment for depressed individuals and is implemented in order to help clients prevent the downward spiral of depression by negotiating gradual increases in potentially rewarding activities. In using this method, clients first develop a list of reinforcing activities (i.e., things they would enjoy doing) and rank-order them by level of difficulty. As they actually engage in this hierarchy of activities they are rewarded, often with the use of a token. The counselor may suggest that they rate their mood before and after engaging in the designated activity because many depressed individuals make negative predictions that they will not enjoy an activity or that it will not be worth their effort. This type of thinking usually results in a vicious cycle in which the depressed mood leads to reduced activity, which in turn results in further depressed mood. In addition, rating their mood may also help reinforce the rewarding component of engaging in these behaviors, as they may not initially be intrinsically rewarding. In addition, studies have shown that it is helpful for clients to continue to engage in at least two low to moderate levels of physical/recreational activity during the course of therapy (David, Kangas, Schnur, & Montgomery, 2004). Behavioral techniques are especially necessary for those more severely depressed clients who are passive, anhedonic, socially withdrawn, and unable to concentrate for extended periods of time.

Although BA is a fairly straightforward strategy for treating depression, it is important to note that oftentimes clients resist engaging in this approach because of irrational beliefs. Therefore, it is important for the counselor to assess for any barriers and address them. Specifically, the irrational belief of *frustration intolerance* (e.g., "Doing the BA is *too* hard") should be assessed and restructured before the client is asked to do the activities in BA. Restructuring strategies as utilized in rational emotive behavior therapy can prove especially helpful (see Chapter 4 for a more detailed explanation of restructuring irrational beliefs).

Behavioral Interventions for Child Externalizing Behaviors

Principles of behavior theory have been applied in a variety of settings but perhaps none more successful than in work with parents of children with aggressive, noncompliant, and externalizing behaviors (Furlong et al., 2012; Kazdin, 2010). Behavioral parent training targets parenting behaviors that need to change in order to reduce a child's disruptive behavior and improve parent and family functioning (Michelson, Davenport, Dretzke, Barlow, & Day, 2013). The theory behind the application of behavioral principles (operant conditioning) in parent training is that many children's maladaptive behaviors have been learned and maintained through reinforcement. Therefore, if the parenting behavior is changed (e.g., through an increase in the use of reinforcement and setting limits with consequences), the child's behavior will change.

Thus, behavioral parent training focuses on educating parents about how and when to provide positive reinforcement for desired behaviors while also using strategies such as limit setting, extinction of attention, and so forth that address inappropriate behaviors. Although many of the techniques used may appear to be commonsense parenting techniques, the actual application of these principles with children may require careful instruction, modeling, and support to promote consistent use. Children and Adults with Attention-Deficit/Hyperactivity Disorder (n.d.) outlined topics covered in a typical series of parent training sessions:

- Establishing house rules
- Learning to praise appropriate behaviors
- Using appropriate commands (e.g., "Take your dishes to the sink")
- Using "when . . . then" contingencies (withdrawing rewards or privileges in response to inappropriate behavior)
- Planning ahead and working with children in public places
- Using time out from positive reinforcement

As is the case with BA for the treatment of depression, when the counselor is providing parent training, it is important to assess for any emotional and/or practical obstacles that could impede parents' ability to carry out an intervention such as praise, time out, or the use of appropriate commands. Many parents hold irrational beliefs that prevent them from successfully using strategies known to be effective in child management. For this reason, it is important for the counselor to identify and replace any parental beliefs leading to emotional/behavioral disturbance that would thwart parents from utilizing the learned strategies (e.g., demandingness, frustration intolerance, awfulizing, global evaluations of worth).

BT offers a wide range of clinical interventions for use with various types of problems. Refer to Sidebar 4 for practice in determining which interventions are most appropriate for various client problems.

Sidebar 4
The Development of a Treatment Plan

How would you tailor your behavioral treatment plan if working with an anxious college student in a short-term treatment model?

What behavioral approaches would best fit this model?

Support your plan with research that attests to the efficacy of these approaches.

Efficacy of BT

Although a complete review of the efficacy of all behavioral interventions is beyond the scope of this chapter, there is considerable support for BT across a variety of presenting problems with different populations and age groups. Although we highlight some of the specific areas of effectiveness, it can be a challenge to filter out interventions that are purely behavioral from those that integrate allied cognitive–behavioral strategies. Behavioral interventions that utilize principles of reinforcement have demonstrated efficacy in work with clients with anxiety disorders. In a meta-analytic review, operant-based procedures had the largest effect size for training social skills. Also, exposure-based methods and systematic desensitization have received considerable research support in the treatment of anxiety and related disorders. Relaxation training has been shown to be effective in the treatment of insomnia (Morin et al., 2006).

Specific to work with youth, the scientific literature on the treatment of attention-deficit/hyperactivity disorder (ADHD) has shown that BT is the only type of psychosocial treatment that is effective for ADHD (Evans, Sarno-Owens, & Bunford, 2014; Fabiano et al., 2009; Pelham & Fabiano, 2008). In addition, parent management training, which is highly behavioral, has been shown to be effective in the treatment of conduct and oppositional defiant disorders (Eyberg, Nelson, & Boggs, 2008). Family BT has been shown to be effective in the treatment of eating disorders in children and adolescents (Lock, 2015).

There is strong evidence for the efficacy of ABA in the treatment of autism spectrum disorder (Smith & Iadarola, 2015), and BT is considered to be efficacious in the treatment of childhood depression (David-Ferndon & Kaslow, 2008). Habit reversal training is considered to be possibly efficacious in treating tics (Woods & Houghton, 2016).

Verbatim Transcript: BT

The following verbatim transcript of a fourth session is presented in order to illustrate information about the principles and practice of BT as described in this chapter. Here we provide a brief overview of the case, the actual transcript, a short critique of the session, and an explanation as to why we think this theory effectively addressed the problem.

Overview

Jenny was an 18-year-old female college freshman at a large metropolitan private university in the northeastern United States. Jenny was of Korean descent but had been born and raised in Texas. Her older brother attended a public community college near the family home, and she was the first in her family to pursue a degree at a 4-year college. Aside from visits to her grandparents and cousins in Korea, she had never been away from her immediate family until going away to college. Jenny was a biology major and, in addition to taking the universal curriculum that all freshmen took, was taking advanced biology and advanced chemistry. She had a partial scholarship and also a work-study position that provided her with some financial support in addition to student loans.

Jenny went to her initial appointment at the university counseling center in early November, missed the next two appointments, but then began attending with regularity. Jenny reported no previous history of mental health issues but indicated that she regularly experienced stress, particularly about exams. She completed a standard battery of psychological assessments provided at the university counseling center, and through a clinical interview, a discussion of Jenny's history, and a review of results from the assessment battery the counselor concluded that Jenny was experiencing some moderate depression as well as anxiety, which appeared to be a combination of concerns regarding academics, family issues, and fitting in at college.

The initial three sessions focused on interviewing Jenny, reviewing the results of the evaluation, and setting treatment goals. Specific behavioral targets for Jenny were to reduce her physiological arousal through relaxation training, BA for treatment of depression, and contingency contracting to improve social and academic assignments. The transcript of the fourth session follows.

Transcript of the Fourth Session

Therapist: Good to see you again Jenny. How was your weekend?

Client: Pretty good . . . or pretty much the same. No difference from last time.

Therapist: Thanks for coming early and completing the forms again. I only have one of them scored so far, and your overall stress does seem to be lower from the initial weeks but has been fairly stable the last 2 weeks. That is a good thing, and I am hopeful we can speak further about how to continue to build on your progress.

Client: Yeah, when I first came I wouldn't say I was in "crisis mode" but I was definitely struggling more than I am now. But still . . . I don't feel like "me," and I still have this fairly low threshold for having the simplest thing set me off. As an example, I did what we agreed to and went to the soccer game with friends on Friday night and it was actually kind of fun. But I then made the mistake of calling home, and that ruined the rest of the weekend. I had made social and academic plans for Saturday and Sunday and then I just cancelled them both. I was *so* stressed.

Therapist: How long did this experience of stress last? How strong was it in comparison with earlier in the semester where you said you were considering moving back home?

Client: It was bad . . . but not *so* bad. At my worst I was a 10 on a scale of 1 to 10. This was more of a 7 or an 8, but again, it got so bad that I ended up cancelling things and ignoring all the texts and calls from family and friends.

Therapist: I am sorry to hear that you had some difficulty, but as we have previously discussed, counseling is not always a straight path towards getting better. We will make progress and then take a step back. The key is to not let those steps back linger too long and use some of the techniques we have spoken about to assist in moving forward and dealing with these situations better the next time. Before we talk about what it was about your call home that you got upset about, could you tell me what you think you could have done to more effectively deal with this stressor better?

Client: Well, the first thing I could have done is to *not* call my family. I just thought I had a really good day and I wanted to let them know and check in with them. As much as they cause me grief I know they care about and miss me and I miss them.

Therapist: Sure, yes, you could not have called them, but it makes sense to me you would want to share that with them. And like you said, you miss them as well. But you did call and then got upset and ended up cancelling your plans. Is there anything you think you could have done to manage things better after the phone call?

Client: Well, all my friends and roommates were right down the hall and were watching bad reality TV and making fun of it. I have enjoyed that with them in the past and it would not have been so difficult for me to just go spend time with them. At the minimum, it would be a distraction, but it may also have reminded me that there are enjoyable things in life . . . and they are easily within my reach.

Therapist: That's great. And the fact that you are able to express that now means you are aware of this and can choose this option going forward. In the moment, after hanging up the phone with your family, when you say you felt stressed . . . is that more anxiety or more depression?

Client: Initially it was a little bit of anxiety as well as some anger at them. Then over the weekend it moved towards more depression, with me basically concluding that going away to school was a mistake, choosing premed as a major was a mistake, and I am better at home with my family.

Therapist: That shows really good awareness on your part. I imagine that things are clearer now, but in the moment . . . it just feels bad.

Client: Yeah, like a cycle I just can't get out of.

Therapist: Yes, it is common for people who are struggling with anxiety and depression to report that they feel helpless to break this cycle. Do you remember when we spoke about doing some of the relaxation techniques to help you manage some of the anxiety you have about test performance? Do you think you could have applied that here to assist with some of the stress and anxiety you experienced after speaking with your family?

Client: I hadn't thought of that. Actually, a difference here is that the tests are in the future . . . whereas this *just* happened.

Therapist: That is true, but the goal would be similar . . . for you to decrease your level of physiological upset. Actually, I forgot to ask you if there were any physiological changes after the conversation?

Client: Most definitely. My blood was pumping and my mind was racing. I actually had more difficulty falling asleep that night than I had when I first saw you. I just kept replaying this in my head over and over and I felt the pit in my stomach just getting bigger and bigger. I couldn't even eat the next morning when they had a waffle station at breakfast. I made myself sick.

Therapist: Again, I think that is terrific insight. I would like to suggest that you consider using some of the techniques for relaxation for test anxiety that we had spoken about and apply them in almost any situation where you find yourself getting stressed. What do you think? Do you still have the handout we wrote up?

Client: Actually I had typed it so I can open it on my phone at any point.

Therapist: That's terrific and a great idea . . . you make it easily accessible. Do you think you can use that when you experience stress in response to speaking with your family or really any stressors in addition to academic ones?

Client: I guess so. I really hadn't thought of that.

Therapist: We also spoke about you doing this in more of a preventative manner. That is, not waiting until you experience stress, but practicing these skills when you are not stressed. How did you do with that?

Client: Well, I obviously am not going to be your "client of the week" because I didn't do that.

Therapist: Did you forget to do it or choose not to?

Client: I know we agreed on the fact that I would do it four times this week, but the next day I started thinking it was silly and I would only need to do it when I felt upset. I also didn't think I could find a time and place to do it when others would not see me doing it.

Therapist: I appreciate your honesty. Some of the comments you make have both a practical component, the "where" that you just spoke about, as well as a concern about others judging you. I think it would be helpful for you to consider where on or off campus you can practice this and also maybe schedule it like a class and put it in your calendar. As far as your concern about others judging you, the truth is . . . some may. As we spoke about early on, anxiety is the most common problem that college students experience. I think more people may be accepting than you would think.

Client: Yeah, you are probably right and the alternative of checking out like I did last weekend is probably worse than just doing it and seeing what happens. I will try this week, but maybe only three times, okay?

Therapist: That's a great first step. And if you find it helps you on a daily basis you may want to do more. So now, if you are comfortable with it, I would like to hear what about the conversation with your family you got so upset about.

Client: I was so happy to have gone to the game and have friends that I was hopeful that happiness would continue when I spoke to my family. It was pretty predictable and the same issues came up as in the past. One, I miss them . . . a lot. And hearing my younger sister in the background and knowing I won't make it home for Thanksgiving break because of financial reasons makes it even more upsetting. Then my father started asking about my grades and pointed out maybe three times that he didn't take out loans to have me go away and have fun. I could have stayed home like my brother did and go to a public university and save everyone money. He described his paying for my college as "Jenny's $100,000 adventure in the Big City." I know he loves me, but that hurts. It also makes me feel guilty that maybe he is right and I should have stayed home. I didn't argue with him and I let him say his piece and then I spoke to my mother and just cried. She also told me that she would support whatever I wanted and she wishes she could have gone to college but also told me that my room is ready for me when I want to come home. So . . . she seems to think this was a bad idea as well. When I told her I was seeing you to help deal with this, she told me not to tell my father and she never asks me how it is going. I got so upset at both of them and then began looking at other colleges near home that I could apply and transfer to. I also began doubting my academic ability as well as my choice of major. I think because I was good in the sciences in high school my family thought it would be a good idea for me to go premed. I don't think I want to be a doctor, but at the same time, I am not sure what I want to do. So, all these thoughts just overwhelmed me and then I just withdrew from everything this past weekend. With finals coming up, that was not a good idea.

Therapist: Well, that was a lengthy list of things you have addressed, and I can see how when you put them all together that it can be stressful. That is also the first time you mentioned that your mother does not ask about counseling. Do you think that is a family thing or a cultural thing?

Client: For me, I think it is a little bit of both. I watched how my family was so in denial about my brother's ADHD and fought the school on many recommendations they made for him. I also saw how this impacted their relationship with him. But I do think there is some stigma attached to pursuing help for problems that you should be able to handle on your own. Initially that is probably what led me to drag my feet towards pursuing counseling and eventually what led to cancelling a few early appointments, but as you and I have spoken about, the alternative is to feel the way I do now. And I don't like that.

Therapist: Thanks for that, and please let me know where you see familial or cultural values impacting upon what goes on within counseling. Going forward, I want you to know that I will support and help you in whatever decision you make, be it to stay here or to transfer. I do think it would be helpful if we could continue to work on you managing your stress and then getting to a point about making those decisions. What do you think?

Client: Thanks and yes, I know what I want. . . . I *think* I want to stay here. . . . But it is difficult.

Therapist: Sure, that makes sense and I would think if we had to predict early on, knowing all that we know now, we would have predicted that this would be difficult. So why do you think this is where you want to be?

Client: I see that there are many more opportunities for me here to grow as a person and to benefit from the educational opportunities. I regularly Facetime with friends who stayed back home and I see how they all have stayed together and do some of the same things we always did. And I miss that. I really do. But I also have had some experiences and met some people here that I *never* would have had the opportunity to meet if I had stayed home. But, if someone told me you will have these next 3½ years where you will have these great opportunities but not be happy . . . I would buy my ticket home tomorrow.

Therapist: I am glad to hear about all the positive things you think about when staying home. I do wish that you could be guaranteed a stress-free existence for the next 3½ years. We can't do that. But . . . we can work together to teach you skills to manage difficult situations and difficult people, both here and at home, and if you practice them it will increase the opportunity for happiness. What do you think?

Client: You really can't guarantee that? [laughs] Yes, if my goal is to stay here and benefit from this terrific opportunity I do want to learn to make the most of it. So . . . where do we begin?

Therapist: Well, you have already begun. Let's review some of the things that we have spoken about the first few sessions and see how you can continue to apply them. Earlier we spoke about doing relaxation training in preparation for dealing with anxiety in academic as well as other situations. You said you have the materials typed up and on your phone and were going to try and apply them this week three times. You need not think of any specific situation, but rather practice the breathing exercises and muscle tension and relaxation that we spoke about. Are you willing to commit to that?

Client: Yes, if I can find a place I will do this. Now that I am thinking about it, my roommate has an earlier class so I can practice in my room if need be.

Therapist: That's great. The second skill that we spoke about last week and I *think* you did this week but you hadn't really talked about it was *activity scheduling.* You said you had scheduled things to do on the weekend but then cancelled them when you got upset on Friday. Can you talk about that?

Client: Yes, like we spoke about last Monday, I chose three things to do that I thought would be fun and that had a social part to it. I let Monday through Thursday be more about focused on school work and then scheduled three things for the weekend: a soccer game, brunch, and a trip to the city. While the soccer game was fun because we are going to the playoffs, things took a bad turn after speaking with my family. I didn't go to brunch and I cancelled the trip to the city with my suitemates. I didn't have an appetite and didn't think it would be fun. So instead, I stayed in my room and looked up colleges closer to home.

Therapist: I could see how you would think these things would not be enjoyable if you were already in a bad mood. I think a good percentage of people may have also bailed on them. It is probably easier to not think they will be as enjoyable to do as when you made those arrangements when you were in a better mood.

Client: Yes, when I agreed to them earlier I was actually excited. It seems silly now to think that I would not enjoy blueberry waffles because of my mood. I actually got in a worse mood when I heard my suitemates come back and talk about Nutella waffles!

Therapist: I am kind of upset now that I missed those as well! So, do you see how thinking you won't enjoy those activities is contrary to your history of evidence of enjoying them? You know what you enjoy. Let's write some of them down now and have you plan to do them this week whether you are in a good mood or not. Are there events coming up that are fun and productive, that maybe you have not done in a while and would like to? Maybe we reward productivity with a fun activity.

Client: Is exercise a good example of productivity? There is a 5K race that I have thought about signing up for but haven't. I was a good cross-country runner in high school and some of my friends have signed up already. I am not sure why I haven't. Maybe I hear my dad's voice in my head. I would like to sign up for this.

Therapist: Okay, great. So what fun thing will you do to reward yourself for exercising?

Client: I thought the exercise was the reward.

Therapist: Well, it may be something you like to do but you haven't done it. Let's find something else to serve as an additional motivator/reward.

Client: We could all go get waffles after the race? [laughs]

Therapist: I think that might work. But the key is afterwards to not just say, "Well, I don't deserve the reward as I *should* have been exercising anyway." Stick to the reward! How do you think you will feel if you set this goal and accomplish it and then reward yourself?

Client: I would feel pretty good and also very full.

Therapist: Great. What do you think about also identifying two other productive goals and then rewards to receive after you complete them? These can be academic or social goals.

Client: I think two is doable as long as I make them not overly difficult. Could they be as simple as working on my lab paper for 4 hours and then I reward myself with . . . waffles. [laughs]

Therapist: Yes, that would work. I may invest in waffle stock! So, if you could e-mail me those other goals by the end of the day, we can then start up here next week. How does that sound?

Client: Okay, I can do that. So should I spend time this week trying to decide about whether to transfer or not?

Therapist: Well, you had stated before that you wanted to stay here. The activities that we agreed for you to try and work on will hopefully improve your mood and may then put you in a better position to make any important decisions like this. It is probably better to make a decision when we don't let our mood make it for us. What do you think?

Client: Yes, that makes sense.

Therapist: There will probably also be times this week that you will struggle. Those would be the ideal times to practice some of the things that we spoke about.

Client: Yes, but I also plan on doing it each morning when my roommate is out.

Therapist: That sounds like a plan. I appreciate your openness and willingness to try some of these things this week and look forward to working together next week.

Client: Great. Have a nice week!

Therapist: You too and enjoy the waffles!

Session Critique

A common practice in BT and reflected at multiple points in this transcript is the use of reinforcement *in* the session. More specifically, I (Mark Terjesen) reinforced Jenny's completion of the forms, her openness in discussing personal matters, and her insight into her involvement in the therapeutic tasks. Because there is the potential for stigma when one pursues assistance for mental health issues, which initially appeared to be the case with Jenny, reinforcing participation in counseling can help reduce this stigma and make the therapeutic process more rewarding for the client. This also helped foster the therapeutic alliance with Jenny, as she appeared to enjoy working with me. Collaboratively establishing goals and tasks to achieve those goals further enhanced the alliance, as did the use of humor and normalizing some of her experiences. Consistent with BT, rather than treating each session as a unique session, I linked content in the session to what had been discussed in prior sessions. Working with Jenny to recall behavioral techniques that were previously discussed and how they could be applied in the context of the current session helped define the process as fluid, which increased the likelihood that Jenny could take the skills she learned in one session and generalize them to others. In this case, relaxation training was initially applied in relation to academics and then generalized to other areas. It would have been helpful to have Jenny practice relaxation in the session and provide feedback.

Cultural values are an important part of counseling. I did ask Jenny whether the fact that her mother did not ask about the counseling sessions was a cultural or familial issue, and cultural values were addressed both initially when she missed two sessions following her first visit and in subsequent sessions.

Effectiveness of the Theory Relative to This Case

As noted previously, the research supporting the use of behavioral techniques with anxiety and depression is strong, which makes BT a good approach relative to this case. Specifically, scheduling pleasurable activities, exposure, and behavioral rehearsal were used with this client to help her reduce her anxiety, and in subsequent sessions relaxation and exposure were also combined with cognitive restructuring. These techniques are among the more common strategies used to treat anxiety. Learning new skills, taking notes, and keeping behavior logs were other behavioral techniques that proved helpful in this case, as did the problem-focused nature of this theory.

As this case illustrates, BT immediately addressed the problem, which seemed to be a good approach because Jenny needed to be able to do something to help alleviate her problems. The collaborative nature of the counselor–client relationship facilitated the development of a specific plan of action.

Summary

BT and the behavioral approaches to counseling described here have considerable empirical support for changing maladaptive behaviors and affect. The techniques described are often part of a treatment package that includes some of the common factors integral to behavior change. Establishing a good working counseling alliance with clients is important to prepare them for actual behavior change. Recognizing that behavior does not exist in a vacuum, it is important for counselors to consider environmental, cultural, and other client factors that may contribute to the effectiveness of the therapeutic process and those factors that may maintain the maladaptive behaviors.

Suggested Resources and Websites

The following websites may provide you with additional information to develop your knowledge and skills in the delivery of behavioral interventions:

- Association for Behavior Analysis International
  https://www.abainternational.org/welcome.aspx
- Association for Behavioral and Cognitive Therapies
  www.abct.org/Home
- Association for Contextual Behavioral Science
  https://contextualscience.org/
- Center for Collegiate Mental Health
  http://ccmh.psu.edu/

- EffectiveChildTherapy.com
  https://www.clinicalchildpsychology.org/effectivechildtherapycom-0
- Research-supported psychological treatments
  https://www.div12.org/psychological-treatments
- Training for mental health professionals
  http://behavioraltech.org/index.cfm

There are also a number of treatment manuals that may be helpful for practitioners:

Bernstein, D. A., Borkovec, T. D., & Hazlett-Stevens, H. (2000). *New directions in progressive relaxation training: A guidebook for helping professionals.* Westport, CT: Praeger.

Foa, E. B., Yadin, E., & Lichner, T. K. (2012). *Exposure and response (ritual) prevention for obsessive-compulsive disorder: Therapist guide* (2nd ed.). New York, NY: Oxford University Press.

Martell, C. R., Dimidjian, S., Herman-Dunn, R., & Lewinsohn, P. M. (2013). *Behavioral activation for depression: A clinician's guide.* New York, NY: Guilford Press.

Paterson, R. J. (2000). *The assertiveness workbook: How to express your ideas and stand up for yourself at work and in relationships.* Oakland, CA: New Harbinger.

Petry, N. M. (2011). *Contingency management for substance abuse treatment: A guide to implementing this evidence-based practice.* New York, NY: Routledge.

References

Abramowitz, J. (1997). Effectiveness of psychological and pharmacological treatments for obsessive-compulsive disorder: A quantitative review. *Journal of Consulting and Clinical Psychology, 65*(1), 44–52. doi:10.1037/0022-006X.65

Adler, J. M., & Cook-Nobles, R. (2010). The successful treatment of specific phobia in a college counseling center. *Journal of College Student Psychotherapy, 25,* 56–66. doi:10.1080/87568225.2011.532669

Akin-Little, A. (2009). *Behavioral interventions in schools: Evidence-based positive strategies.* Washington, DC: American Psychological Association.

Alberti, R. E., & Emmons, M. L. (2001). *Your perfect right: Assertiveness and equality in your life and relationships* (8th ed.). Atascadero, CA: Impact.

Bandura, A. (1969). Social learning of moral judgments. *Journal of Personality and Social Psychology, 11*(3), 275–279. doi:10.1037/h0026998

Baylis, P. J., Collins, D., & Coleman, H. (2011). Child alliance process theory: A qualitative study of a child centered therapeutic alliance. *Child & Adolescent Social Work Journal, 28*(2), 79–95. doi:10.1007/s10560-011-0224-2

Bjork, D. W. (1997). *B. F. Skinner: A life.* Washington, DC: American Psychological Association.

Children and Adults with Attention-Deficit/Hyperactivity Disorder. (n.d.). *Parent training and education.* Retrieved from http://www.chadd.org/Understanding-ADHD/For-Parents-caregivers/Treatment-Overview/Psychosocial-Treatments/Parent-Training-and-Education.aspx

Cook, J. M., Biyanova, T., Elhai, J., Schnurr, P. P., & Coyne, J. C. (2010). What do psychotherapists really do in practice? An Internet study of over 2,000 practitioners. *Psychotherapy, 47*(2), 260–267. doi.org:10.1037/a0019788

David, D., Kangas, M., Schnur, J. B., & Montgomery, G. H. (2004). *REBT depression manual: Managing depression using rational emotive behavior therapy.* Retrieved from http://albertellis.org/pdf_files/rebt_depression.pdf

David-Ferndon, C., & Kaslow, N. J. (2008). Evidence-based psychosocial treatments for child and adolescent depression. *Journal of Clinical Child & Adolescent Psychology, 37,* 62–104. doi:10.1080/15374410701817865

Davis, D. D., & Younggren, J. N. (2009). Ethical competence in psychotherapy termination. *Professional Psychology: Research and Practice, 40,* 572–578. doi:10.1037/a0017699

DiGiuseppe, R., Linscott, J., & Jilton, R. (1996). Developing the therapeutic alliance in child–adolescent psychotherapy. *Applied & Preventive Psychology, 5*(2), 85–100. doi:10.1016/S0962-1849(96)80002-3

Dimidjian, S., Barrera, M., Jr., Martell, C., Muñoz, R. F., & Lewinsohn, P. M. (2011). The origins and current status of behavioral activation treatments for depression. *Annual Review of Clinical Psychology, 7,* 1–38. doi:10.1146/annurev-clinpsy-032210-104535

Dobson, K. S., Hollon, S. D., Dimidjian, S., Schmaling, K. B., Kohlenberg, R. J., Gallop, R. J., . . . Jacobson, N. S. (2008). Randomized trial of behavioral activation, cognitive therapy, and antidepressant medication in the prevention of relapse and recurrence in major depression. *Journal of Consulting and Clinical Psychology, 76,* 468–477. doi:10.1037/0022-006X.76.3.468

D'Zurilla, T. J., & Goldfried, M. R. (1971). Problem solving and behavior modification. *Journal of Abnormal Psychology, 78*(1), 107–126. doi:10.1037/h0031360

D'Zurilla, T. J., & Nezu, A. M. (2010). Problem-solving therapy. In K. S. Dobson (Ed.), *Handbook of cognitive–behavioral therapies* (3rd ed., pp. 197–225). New York, NY: Guilford Press.

Evans, S. W., Sarno-Owens, J., & Bunford, N. (2014). Evidence-based psychosocial treatments for children and adolescents with attention-deficit/hyperactivity disorder. *Journal of Clinical Child & Adolescent Psychology, 43,* 527–521. doi:10.1080/15374416.2013.850700

Eyberg, S. M., Nelson, M. M., & Boggs, S. R. (2008). Evidence-based psychosocial treatments for child and adolescent with disruptive behavior. *Journal of Clinical Child & Adolescent Psychology, 37,* 215–237. doi:10.1080/15374410701820117

Eysenck, H. J. (1951). The organization of personality. *Journal of Personality*, *20*(1), 101–117. doi:10.1111/1467-6494.ep8930274

Eysenck, H. J. (1960). Learning theory and behavior therapy. In H. J. Eysenck (Ed.), *Behavior therapy and the neuroses* (pp. 4–21). New York, NY: Macmillan.

Fabiano, G., Pelham, W. E., Coles, R., Gnagy, E., Chronis, A., & O'Connor, B. (2009). A meta-analysis of behavioral treatments for attention-deficit/hyperactivity disorder. *Clinical Psychology Review*, *29*, 129–140. doi:10.1016/j.cpr.2008.11.001

Fall, K. A., Holden, J. M., & Marquis, A. (2010). *Theoretical models of counseling and psychotherapy* (2nd ed.). New York, NY: Routledge.

Fisher, W. W., Piazza, C. C., & Roane, H. S. (2011). *Handbook of applied behavior analysis*. New York, NY: Guilford Press.

Fitzpatrick, M. R., & Irannejad, S. (2008). Adolescent readiness for change and the working alliance in counseling. *Journal of Counseling & Development*, *86*, 438–445. doi:10.1002/j.1556-6678.2008.tb00532.x

Flanagan, R., Allen, K., & Levine, E. (Eds.). (2015). *Cognitive and behavioral interventions in the schools*. New York, NY: Springer.

Foa, E. B., & McLean, C. P. (2016). The efficacy of exposure therapy for anxiety-related disorders and its underlying mechanisms: The case of OCD and PTSD. *Annual Review of Clinical Psychology*, *12*, 1–28. doi:10.1146/annurev-clinpsy-021815-093533

Forsyth, J. P. (1997). In the name of the "advancement" of behavior therapy: Is it all in a name? *Behavior Therapy*, *28*, 615–627.

Furlong, M., McGilloway, S., Bywater, T., Hutchings, J., Smith, S. M., & Donnelly, M. (2012). Behavioural and cognitive–behavioural group-based parenting programmes for early-onset conduct problems in children aged 3 to 12 years. *Cochrane Database of Systematic Reviews*, Issue 2, Article No. CD008225. doi:10.1002/14651858.CD008225.pub2

Goldfried, M. R., & Davison, G. C. (1994). *Clinical behavior therapy*. New York, NY: Wiley.

Harris, B. (1979). Whatever happened to little Albert? *American Psychologist*, *34*(2), 151–160. doi:10.1037/0003-066X.34.2.151

Hawley, K. M., & Garland, A. F. (2008). Working alliance in adolescent outpatient therapy: Youth, parent and therapist reports and associations with therapy outcomes. *Child & Youth Care Forum*, *37*(2), 59–74. doi:10.1007/s10566-008-9050-x

Hofmann, S. G., Asnaani, A., Vonk, I. J. J., Sawyer, A. T., & Fang, A. (2012). The efficacy of cognitive behavioral therapy: A review of meta-analyses. *Cognitive Therapy and Research*, *36*, 427–440. doi:10.1007/s10608-012-9476-1

Holland, J. G. (1992). B. F. Skinner (1904–1990): Obituary. *American Psychologist*, *47*, 665–667. doi:10.1037/0003-066X.47.5.665

Horvath, A. O., & Luborsky, L. (1993). The role of the therapeutic alliance in psychotherapy. *Journal of Consulting and Clinical Psychology*, *61*, 561–573. doi:10.1037/0022-006X.61.4.561

Jacobson, E. (1938). *Progressive relaxation* (2nd ed.). Oxford, UK: Oxford University Press.

Jones, M. C. (1924). A laboratory study of fear: The case of Peter. *Journal of Genetic Psychology, 152,* 462–469.

Kazdin, A. E. (2010). Problem-solving skills training and parent management training for oppositional defiant disorder and conduct disorder. In J. R. Weisz & A. E. Kazdin (Eds.), *Evidence-based psychotherapies for children and adolescents* (2nd ed., pp. 211–226). New York, NY: Guilford Press.

Kessler, R. C., Chiu, W. T., Demler, O., & Walters, E. E. (2005). Prevalence, severity, and comorbidity of twelve-month *DSM-IV* disorders in the National Comorbidity Survey Replication (NCS-R). *Archives of General Psychiatry, 62,* 617–627.

Lindsley, O., Skinner, B. F., & Solomon, H. C. (1953, November). *Studies in behavior therapy (Status Report I).* Waltham, MA: Metropolitan State Hospital.

Lock, J. (2015). An update on evidence-based psychosocial treatments for eating disorders in children and adolescents. *Journal of Clinical Child & Adolescent Psychology, 44,* 707–721. doi:10.1080/15374416.2014.971458

Martin, G., & Pear, J. J. (2015). *Behavior modification: What it is and how to do it* (10th ed.). New York, NY: Routledge.

Mazzucchelli, T., Kane, R., & Rees, C. (2009). Behavioral activation treatments for depression in adults: A meta-analysis and review. *Clinical Psychology: Science & Practice, 16*(4), 383–411. doi:10.1111/j.1468-2850.2009.01178.x

McKay, D., & Ojserkis, R. (2015). Exposure in experiential context: Imaginal and in vivo approaches. In N. C. Thoma & D. McKay (Eds.), *Working with emotion in cognitive–behavioral therapy: Techniques for clinical practice* (pp. 83–104). New York, NY: Guilford Press.

Michelson, D., Davenport, C., Dretzke, J., Barlow, J., & Day, C. (2013). Do evidence-based interventions work when tested in the "real world?" A systematic review and meta-analysis of parent management training for the treatment of child disruptive behavior. *Clinical Child Family Psychology Review, 16*(1), 18–34. doi:10.1007/s10567-013-0128-0

Morin, C., Bootzin, R., Buysse, D., Edinger, J., Espie, C., & Lichstein, K. (2006). Psychological and behavioral treatment of insomnia: Update of the recent evidence (1998–2004). *Sleep, 29,* 1398–1414.

Murdock, N. L. (2004). *Theories of counseling and psychotherapy: A case approach.* Upper Saddle River, NJ: Pearson.

O'Donohue, W. (2003). Psychological skills training: Issues and controversies. *The Behavior Analyst Today, 4*(3), 331–335. doi:10.1037/h0100021

O'Donohue, W. T., & Krasner, L. (Eds.). (1995). *Theories of behavior therapy: Exploring behavior change.* Washington, DC: American Psychological Association. doi:10.1037/10169-000

Olatunji, B. O., Cisler, J. M., & Deacon, B. J. (2010). Efficacy of cognitive behavioral therapy for anxiety disorders: A review of meta-analytic findings. *Psychiatric Clinics of North America, 33,* 557–577.

Pavlov, I. P. (1927). *Conditioned reflexes: An investigation of the physiological activity of the cerebral cortex.* Oxford, UK: Oxford University Press.

Pelham, W. E., & Fabiano, G. A. (2008). Evidence-based psychosocial treatment for attention deficit/hyperactivity disorder: An update. *Journal of Clinical Child & Adolescent Psychology, 37,* 185–214. doi:10.1080/15374410701818681

Rachman, S. (2000). Joseph Wolpe (1915–1997): Obituary. *American Psychologist, 55,* 431–432. doi:10.1037/0003-066X.55.4.431

Richard, D. C. S., & Lauterbach, D. (2011). *Handbook of exposure therapies.* Cambridge, MA: Academic Press.

Richardson, K. M., & Rothstein, H. R. (2008). Effects of occupational stress management intervention programs: A meta-analysis. *Journal of Occupational Health Psychology, 13*(1), 69–93. doi:10.1037/1076-8998.13.1.69

Sherrington, S. C. S. (1906). *The integrative action of the nervous system.* New Haven, CT: Yale University Press.

Skinner, B. F. (1953). *Science and human behavior.* New York NY: Simon & Schuster.

Skinner, B. F. (1971). *Beyond freedom and dignity.* New York, NY: Bantam/Vintage.

Skinner, B. F. (1974). *Walden two.* Indianapolis, IN: Hackett.

Skinner, B. F. (1991). *The behavior of organisms: An experimental analysis.* Cambridge, MA: B. F. Skinner Foundation.

Skinner, B. F. (1992). *Verbal behavior.* Cambridge, MA: B. F. Skinner Foundation.

Smith, T., & Iadarola, S. (2015). Evidence base update for autism spectrum disorder. *Journal of Clinical Child & Adolescent Psychology, 44,* 897–922. doi:10.1080/15374416.2015.1077448

Spiegler, M. D., & Guevremont, D. C. (1998). *Contemporary behavior therapy* (3rd ed.). Pacific Grove, CA: Brooks/Cole.

Spiegler, M. D., & Guevremont, D. C. (2009). *Contemporary behavior therapy.* Independence, MO: Wadsworth.

Steege, M. W., & Watson, T. S. (2009). *Conducting school-based functional behavioral assessments: A practitioner's guide* (2nd ed.). New York, NY: Guilford Press.

Sweet, A. A. (1984). The therapeutic relationship in behavior therapy. *Clinical Psychology Review, 4,* 253–272.

Swift, J. K., & Callahan, J. L. (2009). The impact of client treatment preference on outcome: A meta-analysis. *Journal of Clinical Psychology, 65,* 368–381.

Thorndike, E. L. (1911). *Animal intelligence.* New York, NY: Macmillan.

van Ingen, D. J., & Novicki, D. J. (2009). An effectiveness study of group therapy for anxiety disorders. *International Journal of Group Psychotherapy, 59,* 243–251. doi:10.1521/ijgp.2009.59.2.243

Van Oppen, P., De Haan, E., Van Balkom, A. J. L. M., Spinhoven, P., Hoogduin, K., & Van Dyck, R. (1995). Cognitive therapy and exposure in vivo in the treatment of obsessive compulsive disorder. *Behaviour Research and Therapy, 33*(4), 379–390. doi:10.1016/0005-7967(94)00052-L

Watson, J. B., & Rayner, R. (1920). Conditioned emotional reactions. *Journal of Experimental Psychology, 3*(1), 1–14. doi:10.1037/h0069608

Watson, T. S., & Gresham, F. M. (2013). *Handbook of child behavior therapy.* New York, NY: Springer.

Weiner, I. B., & Craighead, W. E. (2010). *The Corsini encyclopedia of psychology and behavioral science* (4th ed.). New York, NY: Wiley.

Wilson, G. T. (2008). Behavior therapy. In R. J. Corsini & D. Wedding (Eds.), *Current psychotherapies* (8th ed., pp. 223–262). Belmont, CA: Thomson Higher Education.

Wolpe, J. (1958). *Psychotherapy by reciprocal inhibition.* Palo Alto, CA: Stanford University Press.

Wolpe, J. (1961). The systematic desensitization treatment of neuroses. *Journal of Nervous and Mental Disease, 132,* 189–203.

Wolpe, J. (1985). Existential problems and behavior therapy. *The Behavior Therapist, 8,* 126–127.

Wolpe, J. (1990). *The practice of behavior therapy* (4th ed.). New York, NY: Pergamon Press.

Woods, D. W., & Houghton, D. C. (2016). Evidence-based psychosocial treatments for pediatric body-focused repetitive behavior disorders. *Journal of Clinical Child & Adolescent Psychology, 45*(3), 227–240. doi:10.1080/15374416.2015.1055860

Chapter 3

Cognitive Therapy

Silviu A. Matu

Cognitive therapy (CT), developed by Aaron T. Beck (1976), is one of the main pillars of cognitive behavior therapy (CBT). CT and rational emotive behavior therapy (Ellis, 1962) form the foundation of modern CBT and were the first therapeutic approaches used to treat mental disorders from a cognitive processing perspective. CT has at its core the cognitive mediation hypothesis, which states that emotional and behavioral responses are consequences of processing information from the environment. Specifically, the human mind works as a meaning-making machine, and mental disorders emerge when the normal cognitive structures used to make sense of the world distort reality to an extent that is no longer adaptive. These meaning-making structures are called *cognitive schemas* (Alford & Beck, 1997) and are discussed in more detail later in this chapter.

As a therapeutic approach, CT has had a strong commitment to empiricism and science since its inception. More specific models based on the general theory were developed for particular disorders, treatment strategies were designed to target the cognitive factors in these models, and clinical protocols were then tested in efficacy studies and randomized clinical trials (A. T. Beck & Dozois, 2011; J. S. Beck, 2011; D. A. Clark & Beck, 2010; Padesky & Beck, 2003). The fact that CBT is now regarded as the therapeutic approach with the most empirical support is due at least in part to the scientific commitment of CT, one of the most influential theories and therapeutic approaches under the umbrella of CBT.

It is beyond the scope of this chapter to cover all of the developments in CT theory and practice. However, an overview of the theory and practice of this approach, including an emphasis on a variety of CT interventions and specific applications, is presented. Empirical support for this theory is addressed, and you will have an opportunity to learn more about how the theory works by reading the verbatim case transcript illustrating the therapeutic process of CT.

Aaron T. Beck: Key Theorist

Aaron T. Beck was born July 18, 1921, in Rhode Island. He attended Brown University as an undergraduate and received his medical degree from Yale in 1946. In 1954 he joined the Department of Psychiatry at the University of Pennsylvania where he is a professor emeritus. Beck is the father of four children. His daughter Judith is also a renowned CT trainer and president of the Beck Institute for Cognitive Behavior Therapy, which her father founded (*Aaron T. Beck*, n.d.).

Beck started developing a cognitive approach to mental disorders in the 1950s while he was working as a psychiatrist and researcher and testing the psychoanalytic theory of depression, namely, that depression is an expression of an unconscious anger toward the self. As the predictions proved to be unsupported, Beck began to have doubts about the scientific status of this theory and instead started to work on the idea that depression might in fact be a form of thought disorder reflecting erroneous patterns of thinking (J. S. Beck, 2011; Padesky, 2004). During the 1960s and 1970s he developed a scale for measuring depressive symptoms, the Beck Depression Inventory (A. T. Beck, Ward, Mendelson, Mock, & Erbaugh, 1961), and published his first books describing the cognitive theory of depression and emotional disorders (A. T. Beck, 1967, 1972, 1976). Also during this period he published the first treatment protocol for depression (A. T. Beck, Rush, Shaw, & Emery, 1979) and conducted the first clinical trial testing the efficacy of his new approach (Rush, Beck, Kovacs, & Hollon, 1977). In fact, this was the first clinical trial comparing in a rigorous scientific manner the efficacy of a psychological intervention with that of medication (Padesky, 2004; Wills, 2009). This was a cornerstone in the evolution of modern psychotherapy and has become a model for the evidence-based approach of psychological interventions. During the same period, Beck also made significant contributions to the scientific study of suicide, introducing the concept of hopelessness and publishing several relevant scales for measuring suicide risk (Padesky, 2004). In the 1980s and 1990s he expanded his research from depression to anxiety disorders, addiction, and even personality disorders. For each of these psychological problems, his approach was to first describe the cognitive model that would explain the symptoms and then develop a treatment and test it in outcome studies (A. T. Beck, Davis, & Freeman, 2004; D. A. Clark & Beck, 2010; Padesky, 2004; Wills, 2009). Toward the second millennium he extended CT theory to the understanding and treatment of schizophrenia (A. T. Beck & Rector, 2000, 2005).

Beck, considered to be the father of CT, is one of the five most influential psychotherapists of all time. He is the honorary president of the Academy of Cognitive Therapy and president emeritus of the Beck Institute for Cognitive Behavioral Psychotherapy. Throughout his professional career he has received numerous honors and awards for his landmark contributions to the advancement of psychotherapy (Padesky, 2004). He has contributed extensively to the field, having written more than 600 journal articles and published 25 books. As one can easily see, Beck has invested extensive effort in developing and expanding both the theory and the practice of CT across more than six decades. CT is now a scientifically grounded and effective psychological intervention for a wide range of mental disorders (for a time perspective on the evolution of CT, see A. T. Beck, 2005; A. T. Beck & Dozois, 2011; Butler, Chapman, Forman, & Beck, 2006). However, this progress is also due to the strong professional collaboration that Beck has managed to develop with scholars across the world, testing and expanding his work on the cognitive model and CT. His daughter and close collaborator, Judith, is now continuing to expand the theory and practice of CT and disseminate CT treatments to practitioners (J. S. Beck, 2011; Padesky, 2004; Wills, 2009).

Theoretical Overview of CT

The practice of CT has many elements in common with other CBT approaches but also with other schools of psychotherapy, such as behavioral and humanistic approaches. Client problems are conceptualized under the ABC model developed initially by Albert Ellis (1962). (In the ABC model, A = activating events; B = beliefs; and C = consequences, such as emotions, behaviors, and psychophysiological reactions.) The therapeutic alliance is characterized by warmth and genuine empathy toward client problems, similar to Carl Rogers's (2012) approach, but sessions are more structured, follow specific goals, and are centered mostly on the present problems and the therapist acts proactively to engage clients in identifying and changing dysfunctional thinking patterns (J. S. Beck, 2011). The therapeutic process includes a plethora of techniques, some of which are derived from other therapeutic approaches, including behavioral activation, Socratic questioning, behavioral experiments, and exposure. CT scholars describe this therapeutic approach as *collaborative empiricism*, which means that the counselor and client work together to test the validity of the client's beliefs, and if these beliefs prove to be unrealistic, they develop better, more adaptive alternatives (J. S. Beck, 2011; Padesky & Beck, 2003).

At the core of the CT theory, as with any of the other cognitive–behavioral approaches, is the idea that emotional and behavioral responses are the result of the cognitive processing of an activating event (A. T. Beck et al., 1979). Psychophysiological responses that are associated with behavioral and emotional reactions (e.g., changes in heart rate when feeling fear) are also caused by cognitive processing. CT theory acknowledges that both external life events and internal stimuli such as a physical sensation, an emotional state, or a thought might constitute activating events that are cognitively processed. Also, cognitive processing might lead to new cognitions that are concomitant to emotional and behavioral responses, which in turn might become activating events for further processing. The theoretical model of CT considers the idea that cognition can be represented in the human mind as both conscious and unconscious processes (Alford & Beck, 1997; A. T. Beck & Dozois, 2011; A. T. Beck & Haigh, 2014). All symptoms of mental disorders are composed of dysfunctional responses due to distorted cognitive processing (conscious and/or unconscious) of activating events. Thus, the target of the CT treatment for alleviating symptoms is faulty cognitive processing.

CT theory has evolved over time in part because of its commitment to empirical evidence (Padesky & Beck, 2003) and consequently has changed to integrate new findings and developments, such as results related to different biases in cognitive processing. It can be said that CT is not only a conceptual therapeutic model but also an integrative cognitive model of mental disorders. In the current CT model of practice, cognition is organized on three levels. The first level reflects the automatic thoughts that individuals experience when confronted with different internal or external events. Automatic thoughts are generated by the interaction between the events and the third, deepest level of the information-processing system, namely, schemas. Schemas are the cognitive meaning-making structures of the mind and are mostly unconscious. In between automatic thoughts and schemas is the second level, composed of intermediate beliefs: rules, assumptions, and attitudes in relation to self or others that guide individuals in dealing with the schemas they hold (J. S. Beck, 2011; Dozois & Beck, 2008).

Automatic Thoughts

Automatic thoughts appear as a rapid stream of thoughts that are generated unintentionally in a given context. In fact, people are often unaware of them, but during the course of therapy they are encouraged to monitor them in order to become aware of their existence. Although these thoughts have a direct impact on emotional and behavioral responses, it is important to remember that they are not a direct consequence of activating events. Rather, they are the product of a deeper cognitive processing of the activating events, namely, the schemas or core beliefs (Alford & Beck, 1997; A. T. Beck & Dozois, 2011).

Schemas

A schema represents a mental structure that selects information and processes it following a specific pattern that has been repeatedly shaped during the development of an individual and reflects the particular way the individual makes sense of the world. Schemas develop based on genetic predispositions and early life experiences and are further shaped by experiences during later life stages. A dysfunctional schema regularly contains negative beliefs about the self and the world around the self and is rigid, absolutistic, and generalized (A. T. Beck & Dozois, 2011; Dozois & Beck, 2008). A dysfunctional schema does not necessarily lead to mental health problems, but once it is activated by a specific life event, individuals see the world through the lens of the schema. When activated, a schema acts as a self-enhancing, self-consistent structure by searching for information that is congruent with the belief it comprises, discarding or distorting any other information that is incongruent. In other words, individuals only attend to the information that confirms the schema. Any mental disorder can be conceptualized as an interaction between a life stressor and a dysfunctional schema, which in turn generates a certain pattern of thinking in specific situations and which will most likely be dysfunctional. Later, the thinking pattern will generate maladaptive emotional, behavioral, and psychophysiological consequences (A. T. Beck & Alford, 2009; A. T. Beck et al., 1979).

The content of a cognitive schema can be described as a core belief (J. S. Beck, 2011). For example, individuals who select and process information congruent with the idea that they cannot have a close relationship with others or will always be rejected are likely to have a core belief about being unworthy of being loved. Thus, if others act disapprovingly toward them in daily life interactions, they might experience automatic thoughts related to being unlovable and may interpret positive affection from others as being disingenuous. However, these thoughts result from looking at the event through the lens of the schema that holds at its core the belief that they are unlovable. Individuals might also have positive schemas about themselves. It is also important to point out that different life events activate specific schemas.

CT theory considers that mental disorders have at their core dysfunctional schemas that are activated by different stressors. Although the core belief that is being contained by a schema might reflect a distortion of reality, other characteristics of the schema are also relevant, such as permeability, density, and flexibility. Such characteristics describe the degree to which a schema can be modified by new experiences that are incongruent with the belief it comprises (A. T. Beck & Alford, 2009). Dysfunctional schemas associated with various mental disorders are frequently global, represent an overgeneralization of reality, and are absolutistic. CT theorists argue that core beliefs can generally be divided in two main types: helpless and unlovable (J. S. Beck, 2011).

Intermediate Beliefs

Although schemas and core beliefs can be regarded as the source of faulty cognitive processing, their impact on automatic thoughts is mediated by an intermediate level of cognitions called *intermediate beliefs*. As individuals develop a negative dysfunctional schema about themselves or the world around them, they will struggle against the predictions from the core belief. Such efforts will be reflected in a set of assumptions, rules, and attitudes that can help them cope with the schema (J. S. Beck, 2011; Dozois & Beck, 2008). Individuals with an unlovable core belief might think that it is awful to be rejected by others (an assumption) and develop the rule that if they do not please others they will be rejected. This is translated into a rule stating that they must always please others. The content of these intermediate beliefs is often translated into behavioral strategies to cope with the schema. However, in the long run, these behaviors prevent these individuals from confronting the schema with discrepant information (Dozois & Beck, 2008).

Cognitive Errors

Across all levels of processing, including surface processing (automatic thoughts), intermediate beliefs (attitudes, rules, and assumptions), and deeper processing (schemas and core beliefs), CT theory signals the presence of several cognitive errors that are common across mental disorders. These errors reflect particular types of flaws in logic that people make when interpreting life events. Such errors include the following: (a) overgeneralization, characterized by rules the individual constructs about the self, others, or life based on one or only a few examples; (b) dichotomous thinking, which involves judging things as if they belong to one of two exclusive categories (e.g., good or bad) rather than on a continuum (metaphorically speaking, it means to see things as black or white, dismissing all shades of gray); (c) selective abstraction, which involves focusing attention on only one particular characteristic of a complex event (usually a negative one) and omitting all other characteristics; (d) maximization or minimization, which involves either exaggerating the significance of some events (often for negative events) or reducing the relevance of others (frequently for positive events); (e) emotional reasoning, in which things are judged as true or not true based on emotion; and (f) personalization, in which people think that they are the cause of something that is in fact controlled by other factors. You are encouraged to read more about other cognitive errors in Dozois and Beck (2008) or Freeman, Pretzer, Fleming, and Simon (2004).

In addition to this generic architecture of the cognitive system, CT theory has developed specific models for different mental disorders highlighting the most relevant beliefs and distortions that are expected to be found in clients suffering from these specific mental health problems. These are discussed further in "Applications of CT."

The Therapeutic Process in CT

The therapeutic process in CT is collaborative, with the goal being to identify and test underlying dysfunctional beliefs/cognitions so that clients can overcome psychological problems (J. S. Beck, 2011). Clients are trained to view their beliefs as hypotheses and not as facts, using guided discovery to test these hypotheses through empirical validation, much like a scientist who is testing the predictions of a certain theory. After testing their hypotheses, clients decide whether they are adequate or more realistic perspectives should be adopted. This approach allows clients to distance themselves from the targeted beliefs and start to engage in a more objective examination. The goal of treatment is not only to change dysfunctional beliefs but also to teach clients the rationale and techniques so that they can become experts in identifying, testing, and challenging their own dysfunctional thinking patterns (A. T. Beck & Dozois, 2011; A. T. Beck et al., 1979; J. S. Beck, 2011; DeRubeis, Webb, Tang, & Beck, 2010). What follows is a description of the structure of therapy, followed by information about critical aspects of the therapeutic process.

Structure of the Therapy

After the initial assessment, the first session of the treatment is dedicated to (a) discussing with the client the diagnostic and other relevant results of the assessment, (b) socializing the client to the cognitive model of CT and providing psychoeducation about the treatment (which also helps establish realistic expectations and is especially important for clients who are new to CT or who are seeing a therapist for the first time), and (c) establishing the goals of therapy and the list of problems to work on (J. S. Beck, 2011). Psychoeducation is also used to inform clients about the type of work that will be required (e.g., monitoring mood, completing homework assignments, the frequency of the sessions). Clients will receive a homework assignment starting with the first session that will most likely include thought monitoring as well as other strategies, depending on the case. If clients have severe depression, the initial phase might be prolonged until they get involved in more activities and are more optimistic about the possible outcome of therapy (DeRubeis et al., 2010).

In the middle phase of the treatment clients are actively engaged in learning cognitive and behavioral skills that will help them identify and change dysfunctional cognitions. The process starts with more easily accessible cognitions (namely, automatic thoughts) and moves progressively to deeper level processing (the intermediate and core beliefs). There is also a progressive approach from identifying dysfunctional cognitions; to learning how to respond to them; to developing and reinforcing new, more adaptive alternatives. As more and more data are gathered, case conceptualization will also evolve throughout treatment from general and hypothetical to a specific conceptualization that accurately reflects clients' automatic thoughts, intermediate beliefs, and core beliefs (J. S. Beck, 2011; Dobson & Dobson, 2009; Freeman et al., 2004). The final phase of the treatment will prepare clients for termination, including discussion about possible relapses and the development of a plan to prevent them.

Despite the fact that the actual content will probably differ, in all phases of treatment a regular CT session has the following structure: (a) setting the agenda for the session, (b) evaluating the client's status (e.g., mood, important problems that have arisen during the past week), (c), reviewing homework, (d) going through the points on the agenda, (e) establishing new homework, (f) summarizing, and (g) generating feedback (J. S. Beck, 2011).

The Therapeutic Relationship

A key component of the CT therapeutic process is the therapeutic relationship, which can be characterized as a collaboration between the therapist and clients in order to help clients overcome their problems and attain their goals. J. S. Beck (2011) described the therapeutic relationship as a team approach in which both client and counselor share their expertise. The therapist is an expert in the cognitive model as well as interpersonal skills, and the client is an expert in his or her own life problems. This does not preclude the idea that the therapist is in some kind of power position given that he or she is the one who establishes the formal matters of therapy, such as the session schedule, duration, costs, and so forth. The assumption is that although most clients see the therapist as an authority figure, this does not imply that they should not be actively engaged in the course of treatment by helping set the agenda, providing feedback to the therapist, and identifying and challenging their own distorted beliefs, for example.

Perhaps even more important for the collaborative nature of the CT process is the fact that the therapist is not the only one deciding whether a belief, behavior, or other psychological process is dysfunctional and should be revised. Instead, such decisions are made as a team in which the therapist shares knowledge about psychological problems and effective treatment options and the client applies this to his or her life history and context, goals, and values (A. T. Beck et al., 1979; J. S. Beck, 2011; Dobson & Dobson, 2009; Wills, 2009).

Besides this generic perspective, developing a good therapeutic alliance in CT depends on some key characteristics and strategies that should be exhibited by the therapist and used appropriately to foster and maintain a strong alliance. In a seminal work, A. T. Beck and colleagues (1979) described a good CT therapist as one who shows adequate levels of warmth, empathy, and genuineness, taking into account the client's perspective and showing acceptance while being genuine. These characteristics are still considered mandatory for any CT practitioner. Making empathetic reflections and maintaining a balance between letting clients express their emotions and perspectives of the problem while at the same time keeping the session focused is critical.

Appropriate self-disclosure and other basic counseling skills are also required for effective CT therapists (J. S. Beck, 2011; Dobson & Dobson, 2009). A CT therapist should, however, make judicious use of these characteristics depending on the client's problems and beliefs. For example, showing too much empathy and concern toward depressive clients who think they are unworthy of such consideration might lead to negative consequences for the therapeutic relationship and the treatment outcome because clients might interpret the therapist's warmth as a lack of genuineness (A. T. Beck et al., 1979). In other cases, an expression of warmth and consideration during the first sessions might generate anxiety, as a client may fear that the therapist will get angry or upset when he or she discovers that the client is really defective and worthless (A. T. Beck, 2005).

Self-disclosure can enhance the therapeutic relationship if it is used for modeling adjustment to life problems but might be harmful if clients believe that it is wasting their time or if the counselor appears as a flawless model. If the therapist realizes that he or she has made some mistakes in relating to the client through self-disclosure or other approaches, it is best to openly admit this and correct the behavior if necessary (A. T. Beck, 2005; Dobson & Dobson, 2009).

If the barriers to building a therapeutic alliance steam from some of the client's unrealistic beliefs about the therapist, the practitioner might decide to tackle them directly and openly discuss them with the client. Subtle changes in emotional states and nonverbal cues might offer insight into the activations of such beliefs (J. S. Beck, 2011). However, if the difficulties in building the alliance are related to some general dysfunctional beliefs about interpersonal relationships, such as in the case of personality disorders (e.g., the suspicious beliefs of a paranoid client), the counselor might decide to address them later in therapy, as openly approaching them at the beginning of the therapeutic process might prove unproductive (A. T. Beck, 2005).

In order to build and maintain the therapeutic alliance, CT therapists are encouraged to explicitly ask for feedback during each session. Such feedback might be related to the work conducted in the session, the general progress, or even the relationship between the client and the therapist. Feedback should also be requested regarding the case conceptualization so that both the counselor and client are on the same page regarding the direction of therapy, which also enhances the sense of collaboration. If the therapist does not request such feedback, he or she might end up approaching the problems in a manner that is not relevant to the client, which could have a negative effect on the outcome. Requesting feedback might also help in identifying and solving the problems that emerge in the alliance at much more incipient stages than at the point when these problems interfere with progress in treatment (A. T. Beck, 2005; J. S. Beck, 2011).

Finally, CT practice relies on the idea that a good therapeutic alliance will emerge as the counselor shows competence and helps the client reduce the burden of the psychological problems. Helping the client feel better and function more effectively in daily life enhances the perception that the therapist is effective (A. T. Beck, 2005). The relationship between showing competence, relieving distress, and enhancing the therapeutic alliance is sustained by empirical evidence showing that therapists who are effective in providing CT-specific strategies in the first session will impact the early evolution of symptoms, which in turn will enhance the helping alliance as experienced by the client (DeRubeis & Feeley, 1990). Without a good relationship the treatment will most likely not be as effective because clients could feel misunderstood or judged, which might result in clients failing to follow through with the treatment plan or terminating sessions before goals have been accomplished (A. T. Beck et al., 1979; J. S. Beck, 2011). And although a good therapeutic relationship is a must for successful CT treatment, it is not sufficient to achieve therapeutic goals.

Problem Assessment

Assessment is another critical aspect of the therapeutic process and shares many features with the clinical assessment conducted in other forms of CBT or even other therapeutic approaches. A wide spectrum of assessment instruments and interview strategies exist to help the therapist and client evaluate problematic symptoms and other relevant psychological features and decide on the course of treatment and ways to assess progress. These assessment tools vary in terms of their purpose, their level of standardization, and the source of the information. There are many good descriptions of the typologies and instruments that can be used in clinical assessment in general and in CT in particular, including descriptions of scales that are designed to assess symptoms and mechanisms relevant to specific symptoms. It is beyond the scope of this chapter to discuss in detail all of the possible assessment instruments, but you are encouraged to consult the following sources for further information: D. A. Clark and Beck (2010), Dobson and Dobson (2009), Dunkley, Blankstein, and Segal (2010), and Wells (2013).

CT assessment is conducted at the beginning of the treatment in order to make a diagnosis and to help develop a conceptualization of the case. However, assessment does not end here; rather, it is a continuous process and is used as a main source of data for understanding clients' problems and monitoring treatment progress. It is also used after the treatment has ended to establish the degree of success and to monitor client status over time to determine whether relapse has occurred (J. S. Beck, 2011). A clinical diagnosis is necessary in order to develop a general conceptualization of the case and to decide on treatment options (e.g., CT has specific conceptualizations of different mental disorders, and the treatment plan will be developed around this conceptualization). CT practitioners are encouraged to rely on standardized and structured interviews such as the Structured Clinical Interview for *DSM-5* Disorders—Clinician Version (First, Williams, Karg, & Spitzer, 2016), as they prove to be more reliable and cost effective, even though they require that more time be spent on conducting such an interview (Dobson & Dobson, 2009). The practitioner should strive to gather information from as many sources as possible, and clinical interviews might be complemented with standardized scales that assess the severity or the frequency of general symptoms (e.g., depression or anxiety) and scales that assess more specific symptoms (e.g., suicidal ideation, panic attacks).

Some illustrative scales, such as the Beck Depression Inventory–II (A. T. Beck, Steer, & Brown, 1996), can be used to assess depressive symptoms when this is the main diagnosis but also when they appear as a comorbid problem with other disorders. The Beck Anxiety Inventory (A. T. Beck & Steer, 1993) or the State–Trait Anxiety Inventory (Spielberger, Gorsuch, Lushene, Vagg,

& Jacobs, 1983) could be used as general measures of anxiety, and more specific instruments such as the Social Phobia Scale (Mattick & Clarke, 1998) or the Fear Questionnaire (Marks & Mathews, 1979) can be used to assess symptoms of social anxiety and symptoms of phobias. Information from clinical interviews and self-report scales can also be correlated with information from family members if clients agree to this (J. S. Beck, 2011).

The assessment procedure should not be limited to clinical symptoms only. Other factors, such as the history of the problems and other treatments, level of social support, and coping strategies, offer relevant information for developing an accurate picture of clients' problems and strengths that could later be used in the conceptualization of the case (J. S. Beck, 2011; Dobson & Dobson, 2009).

CT practitioners could also use a wide range of measures to assess relevant general and specific cognitive factors. It can be useful to use self-report scales, such as the Automatic Thoughts Questionnaire (Hollon & Kendall, 1980), which assesses negative thoughts common in depressed clients. Practitioners often want specific, individualized information regarding the thinking patterns of the client in relevant contexts. A daily record of triggers (also called *activating events*), thoughts, and consequences (emotional or behavioral) can be used to get more insight into what the client finds distressing as well as the emotional reactions and thoughts that support the negative emotional states and dysfunctional behaviors. Other more or less standardized procedures, such as the think-aloud technique and the articulated thoughts in simulated situations procedures, in which the client is exposed to stressful situations by being asked to imagine such situations or by viewing video recordings of stressful situations, can be used to elicit specific thoughts the client is experiencing during these moments. The thoughts can be recorded and used in the therapeutic process. Such procedures might be especially useful when the client has difficulty recalling his or her stream of thoughts in real-life situations (Davison, Robins, & Johnson, 1983; Dobson & Dobson, 2009). Refer to Sidebar 1 for practice monitoring your own thoughts and feelings.

The CT initial assessment should offer sufficient information to formulate a general conceptualization of the case following the stress-diathesis model (A. T. Beck & Dozois, 2011). However, assessment will continue

Sidebar 1
Monitoring Thoughts and Feelings

For 1 week, carry a small notebook with you. Monitor your emotional state, and every time you feel distressed, use the notebook to record the situation you are in, how you feel, the degree of intensity of the feeling, and the automatic thoughts that go through your mind. After 1 week, read all of the information you wrote down. Do you see any patterns? Can you identify any schema?

throughout the treatment to monitor progress or to obtain other relevant information about the targeted problems.

Case Conceptualization

Case conceptualization is a critical phase in the CT therapeutic process because it provides the general framework for understanding clients' current mental health problems, how they developed, and why they are maintained. It also helps direct the intervention phase.

CT therapists begin working on a cognitive conceptualization starting with the first session (J. S. Beck, 2011). The information gathered in the assessment will form the basis for the initial case formulation. Using the generic model of CT and more specific models of the disorder or disorders that have been diagnosed, the therapist can formulate a hypothesis about the cognitive factors that might be relevant to a client's problems. However, this hypothesis should be further tested and reviewed during the next sessions to verify that it is appropriate and adjusted as needed to more accurately describe the symptoms and problems. Although the case formulation hypothesis might include possible schemas, as well as assumptions and rules, it is not effective to begin asking questions about such cognitive structures because the client is most likely unaware of their existence. The case formulation will be developed further based on the analysis of specific problems, the client's emotional and behavioral responses, and the underlying automatic thoughts that emerge when the client is confronted with negative activating events. Monitoring automatic dysfunctional thinking will help counselor and the client identify common patterns that repeat themselves across situations and that are likely to reflect deeper beliefs and schemas (J. S. Beck, 2011; Freeman et al., 2004; Wenzel, 2012).

It is important for the therapist to explicitly present the case formulation to the client as it evolves and ask for feedback. Presenting the conceptualization to the client will help him or her to better understand the problems and will provide a rationale for the therapeutic strategies and for doing homework assignments. Also, sharing this information and asking for the client's input can help prevent misinterpretation and misunderstanding.

Homework Assignments

Homework assignments are given after each session, starting with the first one, and should relate to what was addressed in the session. Developing the homework assignments is a collaborative process. Problems must be clearly defined before the homework is assigned, the homework assignment should be achievable given the client's abilities, and clients should clearly understand the rationale for completing the homework (Freeman et al., 2004).

Termination and Relapse Prevention

There are several criteria to use in deciding whether treatment should be terminated. Specifically, the counselor and client need to decide whether the symptoms have been reduced, the therapeutic goals have been achieved, and the beliefs underlying the problems have been effectively addressed (Dobson & Dobson, 2009). In the termination phase the frequency of the sessions is gradually reduced to one biweekly session and then to one monthly session. This gives clients the opportunity to see whether they can effectively use what they learned in therapy and reduces the impact of an abrupt closure. In the final sessions, the work will focus on reviewing what was learned, addressing the issue of a possible relapse, and practicing self-therapy sessions (J. S. Beck, 2011).

A well-conducted CT treatment should teach clients the knowledge and skills they need to try and prevent relapse or to deal with it if relapse does occur. The therapist should specifically address the possibility of a relapse and explain that there may be setbacks. Relapse prevention work should focus on identifying possible triggers and stressors, making a plan with specific strategies that clients could use to respond to symptoms and problems, as well as identifying possible obstacles that could prevent clients from following this plan. A few booster sessions in the year following termination are regularly scheduled to ensure that the gains made in therapy are maintained over longer periods of time (A. T. Beck et al., 1979; Freeman et al., 2004).

CT Interventions

As noted previously, CT uses a variety of therapeutic techniques and strategies, many of them borrowed from other therapeutic approaches. However, no matter their origin, CT uses these strategies in a cognitive framework, and the rationale behind their integration into the treatment plan is based on the underlying dysfunctional cognitions that should be targeted to achieve therapeutic goals. A few of the most common therapeutic techniques are described here.

Guided Discovery

Also called *Socratic questioning*, this technique is perhaps the hallmark of CT and at the same time one of the most difficult to master (DeRubeis et al., 2010). Guided discovery involves asking open-ended questions that help clients realize that their dysfunctional thoughts and beliefs are unrealistic as well as identify more realistic alternative thoughts. It also helps clients identify the worst, the best, and the most realistic interpretation of their life events, their coping skills and resources, and the advantages of changing their beliefs. Using open-ended questions such as "What evidence do you have that this thought about yourself is true?" and "What evidence do you have to the contrary?" will help clients realize that although some life experiences sustain dysfunctional thinking patterns, they are not generally valid; there is evidence against them, and more realistic ways of thinking are more appropriate (J. S. Beck, 2011). Although this might seem simple in theory, in practice there is a very thin line between guiding clients so that they discover the limitations of their own thoughts and beliefs and making them feel that the therapist has certain conclusions in mind that must be reached. The latter scenario will most likely discourage clients, and they will experience this strategy as a lecture about how they are supposed to think. It is important that questions be truly open ended, be guided by clients' responses, and not reflect a prior hypothesis formulated by the therapist (DeRubeis et al., 2010).

Thought Records

This is one the most commonly used techniques to identify and change negative automatic thoughts and is introduced in the early stages of therapy as a homework assignment between sessions. The thought record should be introduced after clients have been socialized to the CT model, acknowledge that their emotional and behavioral reactions to different events are due to their thoughts, and have some basic knowledge about how to address negative automatic thoughts. When these prerequisites have been met, the therapist will ask clients to keep track of negative events along with their emotional reactions and the thoughts that were going through their minds when the negative events were occurring. The thought record worksheet has some additional fields that ask clients to identify how they attempted to respond to their dysfunctional thoughts and describe the results. The thought record can help clients monitor and change automatic thoughts and also becomes a source of information for the therapist (J. S. Beck, 2011; DeRubeis et al., 2010; Freeman et al., 2004).

Cognitive Continuum

This technique can be used to challenge one of the cognitive biases that is frequently associated with psychological problems, namely, dichotomous/black-or-white thinking. When therapists observe that clients judge themselves or others in terms of either good or bad, success or failure, and so forth, they point this out and help clients develop a more balanced perspective. This is done by using a continuum, with one end being positive and the other end being negative, such as being a complete success or a complete failure. The therapist asks clients to point to a place on the continuum that represents their thinking. It is likely that clients with dichotomous thinking will place themselves on the negative end. Then, using sequential questions, the therapist helps clients search for examples (real or plausible) of other people who perform worse on this dimension. This example will become the new negative end, and the client's initial position on the continuum will be reappraised, usually higher on the scale. The therapist will help clients search for even worse examples through additional questions. The sequence repeats itself until a more balanced position on the scale is attained (J. S. Beck, 2011; Freeman et al., 2004).

Reattribution

Many clients tend to assume all of the responsibility for negative outcomes, whereas others tend to blame it all on others. To help clients develop a more realistic understanding of causes of and responsibility for negative events, the therapist might ask clients to discover other possible causes of the undesired outcome. Once a list of plausible causes has been developed, the counselor might ask clients to estimate the contribution that each of these causes had for the event. Percentage estimates can be used or a pie chart can be drawn to illustrate how it is unreasonable to assume full responsibility or to blame others for negative results or events (Dobson & Dobson, 2009; Freeman et al., 2004).

Downward Arrow Technique

This technique is used to identify the underlying beliefs that generate surface automatic thoughts related to distress and maladaptive behaviors. To implement this, the therapist asks a series of question that dig into the client's mind, trying to unveil how he or she makes sense of life events. The downward arrow exercise can start from an automatic thought related to a specific event. Instead of trying to test its validity, the therapist starts with the assumption that the thought is true and asks what implications this has for the client and what it says about him or her or about others or the world (J. S. Beck, 2011; DeRubeis et al., 2010). For example, if a client thinks that he or she has failed an exam, the automatic thought before the client views the results of the exam is "I will never be able to graduate if I fail this exam." The therapist then says, "Let us assume that this is true—that you do fail the exam and won't graduate. What does this mean to you?" The client might reply, "That it would be awful if I fail at something that is so important to me." The therapist continues in the same manner: "And what does it mean to you to fail?" The client might respond, "I'll become a nobody." The therapist asks one last question: "And what does it say about you if you become a nobody?" The client states some of his or her intermediate and core beliefs: "I have to achieve something in life. If not, I'm a failure, I'm worthless." Sometimes many more questions are needed to get to the core beliefs. However, the therapist will know they have been reached when the questions become repetitive and strong emotional reactions have been elicited (J. S. Beck, 2011). Learn more about this technique by referring to Sidebar 2.

Sidebar 2
Downward Arrow Technique

Think about an event in your life in which you experienced strong negative emotions. Identify the negative automatic thoughts that were associated with emotional reactions you had in that situation. Then start formulating questions following the description of the downward arrow technique and try to identify the beliefs and schemas that are underlying these thoughts. Assume that your thoughts are true and ask yourself what the thoughts and images in your mind mean to you. Write down the questions and responses so you can come back and reflect on them later.

Acting As If

This technique can be used to reinforce a new functional belief or schema that is not yet fully endorsed by the client. Applying this technique requires clearly defining how the client would act with the new belief and start adopting the new behavior. Acting from the perspective of a new belief might require changes in multiple aspects of the client's life, and thus the definition of the behavior should be detailed, not generic. The process might be simple if the dysfunctional belief that is being replaced with the new one is not very strong and more difficult if the less functional belief is strongly endorsed. Challenging the less functional belief using other techniques might be necessary before the client can implement the act-as-if strategy. Also, there could be positive as well as negative reactions from others as the client adopts new behaviors; the therapist should prepare the client for this in the event that there are negative responses and work on a plan for dealing with that. Changing behavior is a strong way of changing cognitions, and thus if the difficulties mentioned here can be overcome, this can be a very powerful therapeutic technique (J. S. Beck, 2011; Dobson & Dobson, 2009).

Role-Play Techniques

Role plays can be used in many creative ways to help clients identify and change automatic thoughts and beliefs. For example, if a dysfunctional schema has been identified and a more adaptive alternative has been formulated, the counselor and the client can engage in a role play in which each one of them is relating to an event through the perspective of one of the schemas. Roles can be reversed so that the client can experience both perspectives, which helps the client identify ways of responding to the old pattern of thinking and developing a new one (J. S. Beck, 2011; Dobson & Dobson, 2009).

Role-play techniques are particularly useful in work with children and adolescents. For example, with young children, the therapist might create an interaction between toys, mimicking the child's problems. Using this scenario, the therapist can ask the child to describe what a particular toy might think in this situation to assess the child's thoughts. Role plays can also be used to develop different skills in adolescents and adults, as described next.

Social Skills Building

It may be necessary to teach clients social skills such as communication or assertiveness. How to start a conversation, how to be a good listener, how to interpret nonverbal clues, and how to communicate assertively as opposed to aggressively are all useful skills for therapists to teach clients. In presenting these skills, it is very helpful for the therapist to serve as a model (Freeman et al., 2004) and to incorporate role playing so that clients can practice the skills. Teaching social skills and problem-solving techniques might be particularly necessary in work with youth, as youth might not have appropriate role models or the cognitive skills needed to use effective social and/or problem-solving skills (Albano, 2006).

Behavioral Experiments

Directly testing a dysfunctional cognition by confronting it with reality is probably one of the strongest methods of changing the cognition (Freeman et al., 2004). Some simple behavioral experiments can be done directly in session. For example, if a client thinks, "I am not able to concentrate; I can't even fill out a simple form," the therapist can ask him or her to fill out one or several forms to see whether this thought reflects reality. More complex behavioral experiments can be assigned as homework. It is important to clearly define the cognition that is being tested and to specify what would represent the proof that a belief is true or that it is not supported (J. S. Beck, 2011; Freeman et al., 2004). For example, "Others don't like to spend time with me" can be tested in an experiment in which the client asks some close friends to go out for coffee. If none of the friends agree to do so this week or in the next few weeks, then the belief might be true. However, if at least one friend responds affirmatively to the request, the belief will be regarded as unrealistic and a new alternative should be identified. The validity of almost any belief can be tested in similar ways through various experiences. Gain experience in designing behavioral experiments by referring to Sidebar 3.

Applications of CT

CT has been applied to a variety of problems and in various populations. It has been used to treat both mental health problems such as mood and anxiety disorders as well as psychosis and personality disorders and symptoms associated with medical conditions like chronic pain (David & Freeman, 2015). It has also been used with all age groups, including children and

Sidebar 3
Behavioral Experiments

Work with a partner and consider the following examples of clients with specific problems and beliefs. For each of them imagine a behavioral experiment in which you could test the validity of their beliefs. Try to make the behavioral experiments as detailed as possible. What would count as confirmation and what would count as disconfirmation of the belief? Can you also do the same for one of your real cases?

Case 1. A mother of two teenagers has developed depression and lost her job because of absenteeism. She holds the following belief: "I am a terrible mother and I don't deserve to be loved by my children."

Case 2. An adolescent has social anxiety and is too shy to go to a dance at her high school. She holds the following belief: "I am awkward and incapable of having a normal conversation."

adolescents. What follows is a brief overview of CT applications for some of the most common and/or prominent psychological problems as well as applications with youth.

CT for Mood Disorders

The cognitive model of depression can be used to conceptualize the symptoms of depression (A. T. Beck, 2008). The cognitive model asserts that depression is characterized by the cognitive triad, which involves a negative view of self, the world, and the future (A. T. Beck et al., 1979) expressed in clients' stream of thinking as negative automatic thoughts. The primary targets of CT for depression are the schemas that predispose individuals to depression and the negative automatic thoughts that maintain them (Freeman & Oster, 1998). Thus, the first step of CT is conceptualizing the problem according to the cognitive model while identifying relevant goals and appropriate strategies to reach them.

In the early phases, and usually with clients with severe depression, the intervention begins with a behavioral activation and planning component meant to restore clients' functioning (A. T. Beck et al., 1979). The behavioral component of the intervention is conceptualized as a series of experiments meant to test the validity of how clients view themselves. Thus, the behavioral strategies are viewed as indirect means of cognitive restructuring. As clients begin to engage in constructive activities, the focus of the cognitive treatment moves on to directly targeting the cognitive components of depression, which is done by addressing situation-specific negative thinking (automatic thoughts) as well as the underlying dysfunctional beliefs (schemas; A. T. Beck et al., 1979). Both verbal and behavioral strategies can be used to achieve these cognitive changes. As treatment progresses, clients are encouraged to take more control over their thinking patterns and identify, dispute, and change their automatic thoughts and core beliefs. Treatment ends with developing a strategy to prevent future relapses based on the skills and knowledge that clients have learned during therapy (A. T. Beck et al., 1979; J. S. Beck, 2011; Freeman & Oster, 1998).

With clients with bipolar disorder, CT therapists will focus first on developing a good therapeutic alliance, ensuring that the clients feel accepted. They use psychoeducation to help clients understand the role of stressors in activating mood swings. The goal of therapy is to teach clients skills to manage their symptoms and prevent the occurrence of manic and depressive episodes. Clients are taught to monitor their emotional state, to recognize prodromal symptoms, and to adopt adaptive strategies for each situation (e.g., reduce reward-approach behaviors when facing a prodromal manic episode and behaviorally engage in activities when getting close to a depressive episode). Emphasis is also placed on managing daily activities and sleep routines, which are relevant to manic outbursts. In addition, the therapeutic process will target dysfunctional beliefs that might be the basis for any of the mood symptoms. For example, absolutistic beliefs about achievement might result in dysfunctional behaviors that activate manic episodes while helplessness beliefs lead to depressed mood (Lam, Jones, & Hayward, 2010).

CT for Generalized Anxiety Disorder

Clients with generalized anxiety disorder hold exaggerated beliefs about the probability that different threats might occur. They also think that their anxiety undermines their own ability to cope with such threats by thinking that anxiety has helped them prepare for negative scenarios. Nevertheless, they consider themselves weak because they cannot control their anxiety (J. S. Beck, 2011; D. A. Clark & Beck, 2010). CT for generalized anxiety disorder aims to reduce the frequency, intensity, and duration of worry, which is considered the hallmark of this disorder. The treatment also addresses automatic and anxious intrusive thoughts and anxiety associated with this excessive and uncontrollable worry. The main strategies used to achieve these goals target the dysfunctional beliefs characterizing worry and the maladaptive control strategies that contribute to the chronic worry (D. A. Clark & Beck, 2010).

The treatment begins with psychoeducation on the cognitive model of worry and the distinction between productive and unproductive worry. Next the counselor and client begin working on threat appraisals that are reflected in primary worry content. Cognitive restructuring engages clients in gathering evidence that they are overestimating the probability of negative outcomes of the problems they worry about. Work in the therapist's office is extended with homework following the same goals.

In the next phase, the treatment focuses on teaching clients that worry is more controllable than they think and that their anxiety will be lower if they do not try to block or suppress the worry. To do this, the therapist uses worry induction techniques during the session, in which the client is asked to worry about the most catastrophic possible outcome of a certain event for about 10 minutes. Afterward, the therapist and client work on developing a plan to reduce the catastrophic consequences. Worry induction is continued with worry exposure at home, in which clients are required to engage in a 30-minute worry session, focusing again on the worst outcome of a single theme. Worries that emerge during the day outside of this interval are postponed to the next session. Also, clients are encouraged to fully engage in the worry process and not to adopt problem-solving strategies.

An important component of the treatment is to challenge clients' positive beliefs (e.g., worry helps problem solving) and negative beliefs (e.g., worry can lead to medical problems related to stress). The therapist also guides clients in changing unrealistic beliefs that support uncertainty intolerance. In the final phases, treatment focuses on improving problem-solving skills and increasing the focus on the present rather than on threat appraisal for future events. Relaxation training for generalized anxiety disorder is optional in CT (Borkovec, Alcaine, & Behar, 2004; D. A. Clark & Beck, 2010; Craske & Barlow, 2006).

CT for Panic Disorder

Clients with panic disorder tend to make catastrophic interpretations about bodily sensations. These interpretations are addressed in the cognitive model of panic disorder, which proposes the existence of two phases in the conceptualization of panic. The first phase, which includes the panic attack itself, is an immediate fear response in reaction to bodily and mental sensations, whereas the second phase refers to the apprehension about panic, which is avoidance. The apprehension about panic and avoidance of activities or stimuli that can trigger a panic attack maintain over the long term a state of heightened anxiety in relation to experiencing the symptoms, which is characteristic of panic disorders (D. A. Clark & Beck, 2010). In accordance with the CT model, the first phase of treatment focuses on reducing sensitivity to panic-relevant physical or mental sensations, disputing catastrophic misinterpretations and underlying dysfunctional schemas, and adopting more benign and realistic alternative explanations for the distressing symptoms. The protocol also targets a decrease in avoidant and control behaviors and an increase in tolerance of anxiety or discomfort (D. A. Clark & Beck, 2010).

The treatment protocol begins with psychoeducation about the cognitive model of panic. To access the dysfunctional appraisal of somatic reactions and to restructure catastrophic misinterpretations, the therapist performs symptom induction techniques (e.g., breathing or physical exercises). Using these exercises, the therapist demonstrates the impact of catastrophic thinking about normal physical reactions to panic symptoms. Alternative and functional beliefs about such reactions can be developed with clients. To reduce apprehension about having recurrent panic attacks, the therapist will engage clients in in vivo exposure exercises. Breathing retraining is usually offered only to individuals who clearly hyperventilate during a panic attack, and therapists should carefully monitor the use of this strategy to ensure that it is not used as a safety behavior (D. A. Clark & Beck, 2010).

CT for Social Anxiety Disorder

The cognitive theory of social anxiety disorder highlights three features of this disorder: (a) that the anxiety experienced in a social situation is accompanied by feelings of embarrassment and shame (A. T. Beck, Emery, & Greenberg, 1985; Hofmann & Barlow, 2002), (b) that intense anxiety associated with social situations is often associated with automatic inhibitory behaviors and attempts to conceal anxiety that disrupt social performance and thus result in a negative evaluation (A. T. Beck et al., 1985), and (c) that individuals consider how they might avoid the negative evaluation of others if they can conceal the anxiety they feel (D. A. Clark & Beck, 2010). This model is built on the cognitive theory of evaluative anxieties described by A. T. Beck and his collaborators (1985) and on models proposed by D. M. Clark and Wells (1995) and Rapee and Heimberg (1997).

Because individuals hold themselves to unrealistic standards of social performance and feel inferior when they perform, the main objective of CT for social anxiety disorder is to reduce anxiety, shame, and embarrassment while addressing cognitive distortions related to social threat and personal vulnerability, which will result in improvements in functioning in social interaction. Treatment progresses toward reducing evaluative situations (D. A. Clark & Beck, 2010). The strategies used during treatment are cognitive restructuring and exposure-based behavioral interventions that target the specific maladaptive thoughts and biases specific to this disorder. The first symptom addressed in treatment is anticipatory anxiety. The therapist challenges the unrealistic interpretation of perceived threat before engaging in a social interaction. Next a reduction in self-awareness and self-consciousness during social exposure can be achieved through role-play and video-recorded exercises in which clients can establish a connection between self-focused attention (e.g., focusing on their own reactions and behaviors) and anxiety, realizing that physical reactions and inhibitory behaviors might not be so obvious and disturbing to others as they might think. Next the therapist uses disputation and behavioral experiments, including exposure in vivo, to help clients challenge dysfunctional thinking patterns and beliefs that are activated during social interactions. In the final phases of the treatment, the client and therapist use cognitive techniques to reduce postevent rumination, which is maladaptive repetitive thinking that follows perceived negative performance in social situations (D. A. Clark & Beck, 2010).

CT for Pain Management

The CT model has been extended to understand and help clients who suffer from chronic pain. This approach focuses on the idea that there is a close connection between stress and pain and that certain beliefs that people hold might in fact exacerbate their experience of pain symptoms. The treatment protocol starts with psychoeducation about the ideas that chronic pain is a major stressor; that stress related to pain and other factors increase the level of pain; and that stress can be controlled by managing thinking patterns, such as negative automatic thoughts. CT also focuses on deeper dysfunctional beliefs that are responsible for the experience of distress as well as on core beliefs that are directly relevant to the pain experience, such as defining oneself as a vulnerable individual who is controlled by the pain. Cognitive change is achieved through classic techniques such as cognitive disputation and homework assignments to test the validity of the beliefs, but the main focus is on exercises that are related to pain-relevant cognitions (Thorn, 2004).

Applications With Children and Adolescents

CT applications with children and adolescents are not fundamentally different from applications with adults. However, several important characteristics of the therapeutic process need to be taken into consideration when one is working with this population. Therapy has to take into account the family, not only for the consent of the parents to see the child or adolescent but for other reasons as well. The family might represent the main source of psychological problems expressed and maintained by the young client. If this is the case, working in a family therapy format might be more appropriate to teach parenting skills and change disruptive interaction patterns. If the family is not the source of the problem, parental involvement will still be beneficial, as parents can reinforce the work that is done in sessions, such as assisting with homework assignments, encouraging change, and so forth. It is also possible that it might be impossible to perform some of the required changes without the parents and their explicit consent. Family involvement raises more complex issues regarding confidentiality, setting common goals (agreed on by everyone), and maintaining a good therapeutic alliance with everyone. It can be a delicate balance for the therapist in terms of what to share with parents about the therapeutic process when counseling adolescents who do not want their parents to know about their problems. However, parents have some right to know what is happening with their child.

It is also important to adjust the format of therapy to match the child's age and level of cognitive development. CT with children and adolescents takes a developmental social perspective in which problems are approached considering cognitive and emotional development in the context of the child's life, such as family, school, or friends (Reinecke, Dattilio, & Freeman, 2006). CT techniques will need to be adjusted according to the child's age, cognitive abilities, and verbal abilities, so instead of asking children to label their emotional states the therapist might instead use pictograph representations of emotions. Cognitive restructuring might be performed using games. Language should also be adjusted in accordance with the child's level of understanding (Freeman et al., 2004). Refer to Sidebar 4 for practice adapting CT for use with young clients.

Efficacy of CT

When reading about the efficacy of CT, you should remember that it can be difficult to differentiate between exclusive CT treatments and more generic CBT treatments. CT scholars sometimes call treatment protocols derived from the CT theory *CBT*. To make a clear-cut distinction between pure CT and other CBT approaches, you should consult treatment manuals and look for the theoretical foundation.

CT was developed as a treatment for depression (A. T. Beck et al., 1979), and it was the first psychological treatment with scientific support for its efficacy. A great deal of evidence has accumulated over the years, and now many randomized trials and meta-analyses show that CBT (most studies using the CT approach) is an efficacious intervention both for adults (Cuijpers, van Straten, Andersson, & van Oppen, 2008) and for children and adoles-

---

Sidebar 4

Adaptations for Young Clients

Review the CT interventions described in this chapter. Select two of them and discuss how you would adapt them for use with an adolescent whose boyfriend has just broken up with her. Share your ideas with a partner.

cents (Weersing & Brent, 2006). Meta-analytical data show that CT has been used effectively in treating clinical depression (Gloaguen, Cottraux, Cucherat, & Blackburn, 1998), with significantly better results than no-treatment controls, waitlist controls, antidepressants, and other psychotherapies. Moreover, it has been suggested that CT may prevent relapses better than pharmacotherapy (Gloaguen et al., 1998). Even in the case of severe depression, CT and pharmacotherapy are equally effective in treatment and relapse prevention (DeRubeis et al., 2005; Hollon et al., 2005).

There are also many randomized trials and meta-analyses pointing to the efficacy of CBT for various anxiety disorders. For instance, CBT was shown to be effective for obsessive-compulsive disorder with large effect sizes and effective for social anxiety disorder, panic disorder, and posttraumatic stress disorder with at least medium effect sizes (Hofmann, Asnaani, Vonk, Sawyer, & Fang, 2012). A more recent meta-analysis (Cuijpers, Cristea, Karyotaki, Reijnders, & Huibers, 2016) found that CBT yields high effect sizes for generalized anxiety disorder, panic disorder, and social anxiety disorder compared to waitlist, care as usual, or pill placebo. Furthermore, meta-analytical results show that CT is effective with large effect sizes in the treatment of anxiety disorders in combination with exposure (for specific and social phobia, obsessive-compulsive disorder, panic disorder, and posttraumatic stress disorder) and in the treatment of generalized anxiety disorder in combination with behavior therapy (Epp & Dobson, 2010). For social anxiety disorder, a recent meta-analysis (Mayo-Wilson et al., 2014) showed that individual CBT was more effective than placebos and more effective than other forms of psychotherapy (e.g., psychodynamic, interpersonal, mindfulness, and supportive therapies). For generalized anxiety disorder, CBT was recently found to be more effective than control conditions and more effective over the long term compared to applied relaxation, with similar effects whether the outcomes were self-reported or clinician based (Cuijpers et al., 2014).

Finally, some studies have focused on the utility of CT interventions for chronic pain and for the management of negative and positive symptoms of psychosis (Epp & Dobson, 2010; Hofmann et al., 2012). Also, some data suggest that adding CT treatment to medication for bipolar disorders might have some benefits, but in the long run relapse rates do not seem to change. There is some tentative evidence suggesting that symptoms associated with personality disorders might be reduced after CT treatment, but benefits are similar to other therapies and the quality of the studies seems to be low (Svartberg, Stiles, & Seltzer, 2004).

Verbatim Transcript: CT

The following verbatim transcript of a fourth session is presented in order to illustrate information about the principles and practice of CT as described in this chapter. I provide a brief overview of the case, the actual transcript, a short critique of the session, and an explanation as to why I think this theory effectively addressed the problem.

Overview

Andreas, age 22, was completing his final year in college and was majoring in computer science. He had worked hard in order to prepare himself for a career in information technology, getting good grades with the hope of landing a job in a top company after graduation. He was the only son of a wealthy family. His father was a well-known lawyer in their average-size hometown and his mother was a cardiologist. Andreas had always received lots of attention from his parents, and they ensured that he got a good education and had everything he wanted. Andreas described his parents as being very strict and critical, requiring that he work hard and receive good grades in order to increase his chances of doing something valuable with his life.

What triggered Andreas's depression was an event that took place at the beginning of the semester. At the end of summer holidays, a renowned multinational information technology company launched a contest inviting all students in their final year of computer science to submit a project on an emerging topic. The prize for this contest was a well-paid 6-month internship with the company, which for Andreas would have been the perfect start to a fabulous career. Twenty internships were awarded among more than 200 students who submitted projects, and Andreas was not among them. This made him feel terrible, especially because he had told his parents about this opportunity because he was confident he would be selected. When he received the news about not having been accepted, he initially did not tell his parents about it or about the fact that he was so depressed, lying to them about not receiving the results each time they asked about it.

As a result of being rejected for the award and lying to his parents, Andreas developed strong feelings of shame, guilt, and hopelessness, thinking that he would never be as he had been before. He saw himself as a failure both to himself and to his parents. He had tried to prove his worth by winning the internship, and now that opportunity was gone.

Andreas came to therapy after what he described as the worst period of his life in which he felt deeply depressed and experienced suicidal ideation. However, he did not intend to commit suicide and did not make any attempt, stating that he was very afraid of these thoughts. When he came to therapy he had not been to class for more than 3 weeks, and in the previous month he had only gone from time to time in his better moments. In the past 3 weeks, however, the depression had gotten so intense that he barely got out of house. He spent his time sleeping, playing video games, and thinking intensely about his situation and the fact that he would not be able to complete his graduation thesis.

In the initial session Andreas was introduced to the CBT model and behavioral activation, and in subsequent sessions he learned how to identify and dispute dysfunctional negative automatic thoughts. After the third session, Andreas started attending classes again and was able to study for winter exams, although he was very stressed about them. He also got up the courage to tell his parents that he had not received the award. He said that they were critical but did not dwell on it. In this fourth session the focus was on his deeper cognitions—the intermediate and core beliefs. I used Andreas's thought records from the previous week to initiate further exploration of his thoughts using the downward arrow technique to access deeper beliefs. At the end of the session we developed a behavioral experiment to test the functionality of these beliefs. What follows is the transcript of the fourth session.

Transcript of the Fourth Session

Therapist: Hi Andreas. It's good to see you. While you were completing the mood questionnaire I had a quick look over your daily thoughts record form from last week, and I think I have some more insights about you and your problems.

Client: Really? Can anything about me be insightful to others? [pause] Oh, I know, I shouldn't put myself down like that. So what are your insights?

Therapist: I will share them in a few minutes, but for now let's establish an agenda for today's session. You managed to do your homework, you seem to be sticking to your schedule and going to classes, and you are preparing for your exams. I think we are making some serious progress here! What do you think should be our next step? What would you like to work on today?

Client: Yes, I think I'm doing much better now. I'm so thankful to you for pulling me out of this.

Therapist: I helped you pull yourself up, but I didn't do it for you. Give yourself some credit! Now, what is it that you would like to work on today?

Client: I don't know . . . I mean, I don't know if it is possible or if it is something achievable.

Therapist: Come on, be brave, just tell me, and then together we will figure out if it is doable.

Client: There are two things that bother me . . . and it is not like they are deeply distressing me now, but I do think about them a lot, and I feel that this is where I am stuck.

Therapist: Okay, where are you stuck? You can tell me . . . I am not judging you. [smile]

Client: Yes, I know . . . [pause], so [sigh] . . . I was thinking that I will never trust myself the way I did before. I need that self-trust and self-confidence so that I can handle even the most challenging obstacles. Now, after all that has happened, after letting myself get so depressed about not getting the award, I don't think I can ever have that self-confidence.

Therapist: Okay, so let's put this on the table and we will get back to it. What is the second thing?

Client: The second thing is related to my parents. I understand that being critical is the way they are and this is what probably made them so successful, but I feel like I have disappointed them because I lost the internship. This last couple of months with being so depressed and not attending classes are the irrefutable proof that I have let them down. I don't think they will ever look at me the same after what's happened.

Therapist: Sounds like you are pretty upset about this.

Client: Yeah. Do you think I have disappointed them?

Therapist: Let's set aside what I think for now, because my opinion really doesn't matter. But it's that *you* think, and when you think they are disappointed, you feel depressed, right?

Client: Yes . . . [pause]

Therapist: Okay, let's put these two things on our agenda for today and see if we can work through them. What do you say? We might not finish, but we can always continue next time.

Client: I don't know, I don't know if we can tackle these . . .

Therapist: Well we can try and see what happens. What you are saying to me now seems important to you and it also relates to something I wanted to discuss today, which is what you think about yourself. I read in your daily records that you had negative thoughts about yourself when you last talked to your father. Let's start there.

Client: Okay . . . [pause]

Therapist: Can you recall the last phone call with your father? What did you discuss?

Client: Hmm . . . not much. He asked me how I was doing. He actually seemed kind and warm, and he advised me to get over it . . . not getting the award. But I am not sure if he was honest; perhaps he said that just to cheer me up for the exams.

Therapist: Okay . . . Or perhaps he really cares. What did you say to him when he asked how you were?

Client: That I am okay and I'm not bothered about the award anymore.

Therapist: But is that really true, that you aren't bothered by it?

Client: Well, I guess I am bothered . . . I mean, I got into therapy after that. Even if I don't care that much now, I did hide the truth from him and my mom about my depression over this.

Therapist: Tell me, what thoughts ran through your mind when you didn't tell your parents?

Client: What thoughts? That I am a liar and a coward and don't deserve to have parents who have done so much for me [somewhat increasing volume].

Therapist: And are there other thoughts?

Client: I thought about all the years that they took care of me, and now, when I had my chance to pay them back, I failed.

Therapist: Okay, I see . . . you think you didn't pay back your dues to your parents for taking care of you because you didn't get the internship award?

Client: Somehow, yes . . .

Therapist: Do you know others who have literally paid back their parents for raising them?

Client: No, of course not. Nobody pays them back.

Therapist: Okay, so does it make sense that you think you should?

Client: I am not saying I should pay them back literally. I just mean like honoring their memory, by taking care of them when they're old, by making them proud of me, stuff like this.

Therapist: But do you plan to do otherwise?

Client: No, of course not. I love my parents. With all their defects and all their criticism they are still good people and they take good care of me.

Therapist: I agree with all of what you're saying, except that I don't quite understand why you think you have failed them if you are not planning to do otherwise than what is regularly expected from a child to do for their parents like you mentioned . . . honoring them, taking care of them as they age, and so forth. It sounds like you think you owe your parents because?

Client: They took care of me, invested in me, and loved me, at least to some extent. I mean, they're not perfect because they can be critical.

Therapist: They might not be the perfect parents, if there are any perfect parents out there, but do you think that they love you?

Client: Yes.

Therapist: Good. Now, how do you think you should pay them back for their love and care?

Client: By doing what they are expecting of me . . .

Therapist: And what do you think they are expecting of you?

Client: To achieve something in life; to make them proud.

Therapist: Okay, we discussed in the last session that not getting this internship does not mean you have failed in life. You just failed to get the internship award. But have you really failed in life yet, when you are only 22 years old? And is it too late to try again?

Client: No, I guess that makes sense, but even failing once is proof that I am not what they expect me to be.

Therapist: We don't really have any proof of that at this point, but you seem to think so. Put that in relation to the idea of paying back their love. What does that mean?

Client: That I shouldn't fail, not even once, to deserve their love.

Therapist: Okay, what would you call someone who never fails?

Client: A perfect person.

Therapist: Yes, and do you think that you deserve the love of others only if you are perfect?

Client: Well, I don't know. Couldn't it be that I have this expectation only about my parents?

Therapist: It's possible . . . but let us think about this carefully. You told me in the last session that you thought that you had disappointed your math professor who had showed you some appreciation several times in the past by failing to solve a problem during seminar?

Client: Yes . . . it is the same thing. It feels the same.

Therapist: Okay . . . so this is what we call a deeper belief, a kind of an assumption you're making about your world. In your case, it sounds like "If I am not perfect, others will be disappointed and will not appreciate me, care about me, or love me."

Client: Yes . . . [longer pause]

Therapist: Okay . . . Let me explain something. In the cognitive model, assumptions are intermediate beliefs between the automatic thoughts that you experience daily and beliefs that are even deeper, called *schemas* or *core beliefs*. Schemas generate both assumptions and automatic thoughts.

Client: So, you are trying to tell me that I have some kind of schema deep in my mind that makes me think all these things?

Therapist: Yes, and the good news is that we are close to getting to that schema. Based on my knowledge and experience, your schema sounds something like this: "I am unlovable and I do not deserve others' love and appreciation." How does this sound to you?

Client: That sounds like me.

Therapist: Okay. Now, let me tell you something else. Because you have this core belief, you developed a rule that you should always appear perfect to others so that you can get appreciation and love. This rule has probably been guiding you and has been reflected mostly in your family relationships.

Client: Okay, I think you are right.

Therapist: So if that makes sense, I think we should put this belief to a test in order to see if you do not appear perfect, do significant others stop loving you?

Client: How do I test that?

Therapist: I think we should test it in real life by doing an experiment with someone you choose.

Client: Do you think I should try do this with my parents? What if they get upset with me?

Therapist: They might get upset, but does that mean they don't love you? Could it be that if they get upset it is *because* they love you and care about you? Think about it . . . is it really logical to think that they will reject you if you show them you are not perfect?

Client: Most likely.

Therapist: Pick a number, from 0 to 100%.

Client: Three quarters . . . 75%.

Therapist: Okay. Would you like to see if your prediction is right?

Client: I am scared about this.

Therapist: It's not mandatory that you do it now, but what will you gain by putting it off?

Client: Nothing, I guess. Okay . . . I'll do it.

Therapist: Great. So let's make this more specific and come up with a homework assignment. What could you tell them to test this belief?

Client: That I have developed depression because of losing the internship and now I am in therapy.

Therapist: Okay, that sounds good. But it will be more accurate to tell them that you developed depression when you lost the internship because you were worried about letting them down, about disappointing them?

Client: This way sounds much harder . . . but I'll try it.

Therapist: Perfect. Now for the next week I would also like you to keep tracking your thoughts and mood since it has proved to be so useful.

Client: Okay, I will do it.

Therapist: Good. I am sorry we did not manage to tackle the other problem as well. But I think we made some great progress today and you proved to be very courageous. Do you have any feedback to share?

Client: It was a very insightful session. Thank you. See you next week.

Therapist: You worked hard today. Thank you!

Session Critique

The session focused on identifying the client's dysfunctional intermediate and core beliefs using the downward arrow technique to move from automatic thoughts to deeper cognitions through direct questioning. Although there was some emphasis on changing faulty cognitions, more work needs to be done on this and more extensive homework should be assigned in future sessions. The therapeutic alliance was very good; the client seemed to feel accepted and more comfortable than in previous sessions, and the fact that I was encouraging and positive probably increased Andreas's involvement in the session. Getting Andreas involved in setting the agenda, deciding on homework, and challenging his own dysfunctional beliefs helped solidify the alliance. I think I did a good job explaining the cognitive conceptualization so that Andreas understood how his problems emerged. More attention could have been given to the introduction of a new/alternative schema, and the client could have been consulted more at this point.

Effectiveness of the Theory Relative to This Case

From the CT perspective, Andreas's depressive symptoms were generated by his core belief that he was unlovable, maintained by the assumptions and rules that he must appear perfect to others so that they could show him love and appreciation. CT is an effective treatment for depression, and historically it was developed to treat depression. Symptoms of depression are remitted by targeting cognitive factors from the conceptualization described previously. In this case, teaching Andreas how to identify and respond to negative automatic thoughts had an immediate and beneficial effect for his emotional state and helped him engage in his normal activities. Another CT strategy is to use behavioral experiments, one of the most effective methods of testing and changing dysfunctional beliefs and replacing them with more adaptive ones. Behavioral experiments can lead to long-lasting benefits for the client as well as significant others.

Numerous other CT interventions could be applied to a case such as this one. A direct approach such as CT works well with people of this age group, whose ability to generate effective problem-solving skills is often lacking. The encouragement and support that CT counselors model is also important in working with a client such as Andreas, who was initially skeptical about attending counseling.

Summary

CT is one of the main pillars of CBT and has wide applicability in treating almost the entire spectrum of mental disorders. According to the CT model, psychological problems are caused by dysfunctional schemas activated by negative life events, and specific mental disorders emerge from specific types of schemas. CT has developed specific cognitive models for different disorders, and treatment is tailored to target cognitions that are specific to the problem.

In CT the therapist and client work collaboratively as a team to identify and change dysfunctional schemas. CT counselors use a wide variety of cognitive and behavioral techniques that can be readily adapted to help clients develop more functional schemas. CT follows a rigorous scientific approach in which the theory and the efficacy of the treatment protocols are empirically tested and adjusted to fit the results. It is because of this commitment to science that CT has become one of the most influential therapeutic approaches under the CBT umbrella.

Suggested Resources and Websites

For more information about CT theory and practice, please refer to the following:

Fairburn, C. G. (2008). *Cognitive behavior therapy and eating disorders.* New York, NY: Guilford Press.

Freeman, A. (2013). *Cognitive therapy with couples and groups.* New York, NY: Springer.

Friedberg, R. D., & McClure, J. M. (2015). *Clinical practice of cognitive therapy with children and adolescents: The nuts and bolts.* New York, NY: Guilford Press.

Leahy, R. L. (2003). *Cognitive therapy techniques: A practitioner's guide.* New York, NY: Guilford Press.

Neenan, M., & Dryden, W. (2004). *Cognitive therapy: 100 key points and techniques.* New York, NY: Routledge.

- Academy of Cognitive Therapy
  www.academyofct.org
- Beck Institute for Cognitive Behavior Therapy
  https://www.beckinstitute.org/
- Center for Cognitive Therapy at the University of Pennsylvania
  www.med.upenn.edu/cct
- International Association for Cognitive Psychotherapy
  www.the-iacp.org

References

Aaron T. Beck. (n.d.). Retrieved from https://en.wikipedia.org/wiki/Aaron_T._Beck

Albano, A. M. (2006). Treatment of social anxiety disorder. In M. A. Reinecke, F. M. Dattilio, & A. Freeman (Eds.), *Cognitive therapy with children and adolescents* (2nd ed., pp. 128–161). New York, NY: Guilford Press.

Alford, B. A., & Beck, A. T. (1997). *The integrative power of cognitive therapy.* New York, NY: Guilford Press.

Beck, A. T. (1967). *Depression: Clinical, experimental, and theoretical aspects.* New York, NY: Harper & Row.

Beck, A. T. (1972). *Depression: Causes and treatment.* Philadelphia, PA: University of Pennsylvania Press.

Beck, A. T. (1976). *Cognitive therapy and the emotional disorders.* New York, NY: International Universities Press.

Beck, A. T. (2005). The current state of cognitive therapy: A 40-year retrospective. *Archives of General Psychiatry, 62,* 953–959.

Beck, A. T. (2008). The evolution of the cognitive model of depression and its neurobiological correlates. *American Journal of Psychiatry, 165,* 969–977.

Beck, A. T., & Alford, B. A. (2009). *Depression: Causes and treatment.* Philadelphia, PA: University of Pennsylvania Press.

Beck, A. T., Davis, D. D., & Freeman, A. (2004). *Cognitive therapy of personality disorders* (2nd ed.). New York, NY: Guilford Press.

Beck, A. T., & Dozois, D. J. (2011). Cognitive therapy: Current status and future directions. *Annual Review of Medicine, 62,* 397–409.

Beck, A. T., Emery, G., & Greenberg, R. L. (1985). *Anxiety disorders and phobias: A cognitive perspective.* New York, NY: Basic Books.

Beck, A. T., & Haigh, E. A. (2014). Advances in cognitive theory and therapy: The generic cognitive model. *Annual Review of Clinical Psychology, 10,* 1–24.

Beck, A. T., & Rector, N. A. (2000). Cognitive therapy of schizophrenia: A new therapy for the new millennium. *American Journal of Psychotherapy, 54*(3), 291–300.

Beck, A. T., & Rector, N. A. (2005). Cognitive approaches to schizophrenia: Theory and therapy. *Annual Review of Clinical Psychology, 1,* 577–606.

Beck, A. T., Rush, A. J., Shaw, B. F., & Emery, G. (1979). *Cognitive therapy of depression.* New York, NY: Guilford Press.

Beck, A. T., & Steer, R. A. (1993). *Manual for the Beck Anxiety Inventory.* San Antonio, TX: Psychological Corporation.

Beck, A. T., Steer, R. A., & Brown, G. K. (1996). *Beck Depression Inventory manual* (2nd ed.). San Antonio, TX: Psychological Corporation.

Beck, A. T., Ward, C. H., Mendelson, M., Mock, J., & Erbaugh, J. (1961). An inventory for measuring depression. *Archives of General Psychiatry, 4,* 561–571.

Beck, J. S. (2011). *Cognitive behavior therapy: Basics and beyond.* New York, NY: Guilford Press.

Borkovec, T. D., Alcaine, O. M., & Behar, E. (2004). Avoidance theory of worry and generalized anxiety disorder. In R. G. Heimberg, C. L. Turk, & D. S. Mennin (Eds.), *Generalized anxiety disorder: Advances in research and practice* (pp. 77–108). New York, NY: Guilford Press.

Butler, A. C., Chapman, J. E., Forman, E. M., & Beck, A. T. (2006). The empirical status of cognitive-behavioral therapy: A review of meta-analyses. *Clinical Psychology Review, 26*(1), 17–31.

Clark, D. A., & Beck, A. T. (2010). *Cognitive therapy of anxiety disorders: Science and practice.* New York, NY: Guilford Press.

Clark, D. M., & Wells, A. (1995). A cognitive model of social phobia. In R. G. Heimberg, M. R. Liebowitz, D. A. Hope, & F. R. Schneier (Eds.), *Social phobia: Diagnosis, assessment and treatment* (pp. 69–93). New York, NY: Guilford Press.

Craske, M. G., & Barlow, D. H. (2006). *Mastery of your anxiety and worry: Workbook* (2nd ed.). Oxford, UK: Oxford University Press.

Cuijpers, P., Cristea, I. A., Karyotaki, E., Reijnders, M., & Huibers, M. J. H. (2016). How effective are cognitive behavior therapies for major depression and anxiety disorders? A meta-analytic update of the evidence. *World Psychiatry, 15,* 245–258.

Cuijpers, P., Sijbrandij, M., Koole, S., Huibers, M., Berking, M., & Andersson, G. (2014). Psychological treatment of generalized anxiety disorder: A meta-analysis. *Clinical Psychology Review, 34,* 130–140.

Cuijpers, P., van Straten, A., Andersson, G., & van Oppen, P. (2008). Psychotherapy for depression in adults: A meta-analysis of comparative outcome studies. *Journal of Consulting and Clinical Psychology, 76,* 909–922.

David, D., & Freeman, A. (2015). Overview of cognitive behavior therapy of personality disorders. In A. Beck, D. Davis, & A. Freeman (Eds.), *Cognitive therapy of personality disorders* (3rd ed., pp. 3–18). New York, NY: Guilford Press.

Davison, G. C., Robins, C., & Johnson, M. K. (1983). Articulated thoughts during simulated situations: A paradigm for studying cognition in emotion and behaviour. *Cognitive Therapy and Research, 7,* 17–40.

DeRubeis, R. J., & Feeley, M. (1990). Determinants of change in cognitive therapy for depression. *Cognitive Therapy and Research, 14,* 469–482.

DeRubeis, R. J., Hollon, S. D., Amsterdam, J. D., Shelton, R. C., Young, P. R., Salomon, R. M., . . . Gallop, R. (2005). Cognitive therapy vs. medications in the treatment of moderate to severe depression. *Archives of General Psychiatry, 62,* 409–416.

DeRubeis, R. J., Webb, C. A., Tang, T. Z., & Beck, A. T. (2010). Cognitive therapy. In K. S. Dobson (Ed.), *Handbook of cognitive-behavioral therapies* (pp. 277–316). New York, NY: Guilford Press.

Dobson, D. J. G., & Dobson, K. S. (2009). *Evidence-based practice of cognitive-behavioral therapy.* New York, NY: Guilford Press.

Dozois, D. J., & Beck, A. T. (2008). Cognitive schemas, beliefs and assumptions. In K. S. Dobson & D. J. Dozois (Eds.), *Risk factors in depression* (pp. 121–143). San Diego, CA: Academic Press.

Dunkley, D. M., Blankstein, K. R., & Segal, Z. V. (2010). Cognitive therapy. In K. S. Dobson (Ed.), *Handbook of cognitive-behavioral therapies* (pp. 133–171). New York, NY: Guilford Press.

Ellis, A. (1962). *Reason and emotion in psychotherapy.* New York, NY: Institute for Rational Living.

Epp, A., & Dobson, K. S. (2010). The evidence base for cognitive-behavioral therapy. In K. S. Dobson (Ed.), *Handbook of cognitive-behavioral therapies* (pp. 39–73). New York, NY: Guilford Press.

First, M. B., Williams, J. B. W., Karg, R. S., & Spitzer, R. L. (2016). *Structured Clinical Interview for* DSM-5 *Disorders—Clinician Version (SCID-5-CV).* Arlington, VA: American Psychiatric Association.

Freeman, A., & Oster, C. (1998). Cognitive behavior therapy. In V. E. Caballo (Ed.), *International handbook of cognitive and behavioural treatments for psychological disorders* (2nd ed., pp. 108–138). Hoboken, NJ: Wiley.

Freeman, A., Pretzer, J., Fleming, B., & Simon, K. M. (2004). *Clinical applications of cognitive therapy* (2nd ed.). New York, NY: Springer.

Gloaguen, V., Cottraux, J., Cucherat, M., & Blackburn, I. M. (1998). A meta-analysis of the effects of cognitive therapy in depressed patients. *Journal of Affective Disorders, 49*(1), 59–72.

Hofmann, S. G., Asnaani, A., Vonk, I. J., Sawyer, A. T., & Fang, A. (2012). The efficacy of cognitive behavioral therapy: A review of meta-analyses. *Cognitive Therapy and Research, 36,* 427–440.

Hofmann, S. G., & Barlow, D. H. (2002). Social phobia (social anxiety disorder). In D. H. Barlow (Ed.), *Anxiety and its disorders: The nature and treatment of anxiety and panic* (2nd ed., pp. 454–476). New York, NY: Guilford Press.

Hollon, S. D., DeRubeis, R. J., Shelton, R. C., Amsterdam, J. D., Salomon, R. M., O'Reardon, J. P., . . . Gallop, R. (2005). Prevention of relapse following cognitive therapy vs medications in moderate to severe depression. *Archives of General Psychiatry, 62,* 417–422.

Hollon, S. D., & Kendall, P. C. (1980). Cognitive self-statements in depression: Development of an automatic thoughts questionnaire. *Cognitive Therapy and Research, 4*(4), 383–395.

Lam, D. H., Jones, S. H., & Hayward, P. (2010). *Cognitive therapy for bipolar disorder: A therapist's guide to concepts, methods and practice.* Chichester, UK: Wiley.

Marks, I., & Mathews, A. (1979). Brief standard self-rating scale for phobic patients. *Behaviour Research and Therapy, 17,* 263–267.

Mattick, R. P., & Clarke, J. C. (1998). Development and validation of measures of social phobia scrutiny fear and social interaction anxiety. *Behaviour Research and Therapy, 36,* 455–470.

Mayo-Wilson, E., Dias, S., Mavranezouli, I., Kew, K., Clark, D. M., Ades, A. E., & Pilling, S. (2014). Psychological and pharmacological interventions for social anxiety disorder in adults: A systematic review and network meta-analysis. *Lancet Psychiatry, 1*(5), 368–376.

Padesky, C. A. (2004). Aaron T. Beck: Mind, man and mentor. In R. L. Leahy (Ed.), *Contemporary cognitive therapy: Theory, research and practice* (pp. 3–24). New York, NY: Guilford Press.

Padesky, C. A., & Beck, A. T. (2003). Science and philosophy: Comparison of cognitive therapy and rational emotive behavior therapy. *Journal of Cognitive Psychotherapy, 17*(3), 211–224.

Rapee, R. M., & Heimberg, R. G. (1997). A cognitive-behavioral model of anxiety in social phobia. *Behaviour Research and Therapy, 35,* 741–756.

Reinecke, M. A., Dattilio, F. M., & Freeman, A. (2006). What makes for an effective treatment? In M. A. Reinecke, F. M. Dattilio, & A. Freeman (Eds.), *Cognitive therapy with children and adolescents* (2nd ed., pp. 1–18). New York, NY: Guilford Press.

Rogers, C. (2012). *On becoming a person: A therapist's view of psychotherapy.* New York, NY: Houghton Mifflin.

Rush, A. J., Beck, A. T., Kovacs, M., & Hollon, S. D. (1977). Comparative efficacy of cognitive therapy and pharmacotherapy in the treatment of depressed outpatients. *Cognitive Therapy and Research, 1*(1), 7–37.

Spielberger, C., Gorsuch, R., Lushene, R., Vagg, P., & Jacobs, G. (1983). *Manual for the State–Trait Anxiety Inventory.* Palo Alto, CA: Consulting Psychologists Press.

Svartberg, M., Stiles, T. C., & Seltzer, M. H. (2004). Randomized, controlled trial of the effectiveness of short-term dynamic psychotherapy and cognitive therapy for cluster C personality disorders. *American Journal of Psychiatry, 161,* 810–817.

Thorn, B. E. (2004). *Cognitive therapy for chronic pain: A step-by-step guide.* New York, NY: Guilford Press.

Weersing, V. R., & Brent, D. A. (2006). Cognitive behavioral therapy for depression in youth. *Child and Adolescent Psychiatric Clinics of North America, 15,* 939–957.

Wells, A. (2013). *Cognitive therapy of anxiety disorders: A practice manual and conceptual guide.* New York, NY: Wiley.

Wenzel, A. (2012). Modification of core beliefs in cognitive therapy. In I. R. de Oliveira (Ed.), *Standard and innovative strategies in cognitive behavior therapy* (pp. 17–34). Janeza Trdine, Croatia: INTECH Open.

Wills, F. (2009). *Beck's cognitive therapy: Distinctive features.* New York, NY: Routledge.

Rational Emotive Behavior Therapy

Michael Hickey and Kristene A. Doyle

Albert Ellis was a pioneer who revolutionized the field of psychotherapy when he became disenchanted with psychoanalysis and started putting his psychological and philosophical knowledge together in a different way, ultimately presenting his theory at the American Psychological Association meeting in 1955. He had a profound impact on the field of psychology, and his legacy lives on in that he trained and mentored thousands of counselors and therapists throughout the world who continue to practice and promulgate the theory.

The purpose of this chapter is to present pertinent information about Albert Ellis and his theory, with an emphasis on practical application of the theoretical concepts that have been so influential in the evolution of the field of cognitive behavior therapy. The therapeutic process, interventions, and efficacy of the theory are also addressed.

Albert Ellis: Key Theorist

Albert Ellis, considered the grandfather of cognitive behavior therapy, was born in Pittsburgh, Pennsylvania, in 1913 but lived most of his life in New York City. In his lectures and the books he authored, Ellis often referred to his mother as self-absorbed and his father as emotionally distant (Ellis, 2004), and when he was hospitalized eight times between the ages of 5 and 7 for various illnesses, visits from his parents were reportedly infrequent. Public speaking and social anxiety (particularly with women) afflicted Ellis during his adolescence, but because he was very interested in sexual and romantic relationships, he took it upon himself at age 19 to overcome this anxiety by forcing himself to initiate conversations with 100 women at the Bronx Botanical Gardens in the hopes of securing a date. Although he did not achieve success with that goal, this self-imposed exercise enabled him to overcome his fear of rejection (Ellis, 1998). Ellis was married briefly to two different women, had a long-term relationship with another, and married again when he was 90 years old.

Ellis received a bachelor of arts degree in business from City College of New York. He went on to receive a doctorate in clinical psychology from Teachers College of Columbia University in 1947. The theoretical orientation largely emphasized and taught during his graduate work was psychoanalysis. Ellis was influenced by the writings of Karen Horney, Alfred Adler, Erich Fromm, and Harry Stack Sullivan. He also referenced Dr. Robert Woodworth's principle of stimulus–organism–response as a key contributing factor in his system and acknowledged Alfred Korzybski and general semantics as responsible for creating his interest in philosophy. In 1953 Ellis broke away from analysis, as he did not see his patients making progress as efficiently as was possible. In 1955 he developed what was then called *rational therapy* (later to be called *rational emotive therapy* and then *rational emotive behavior therapy* [REBT]; Ellis & Dryden, 2007). Unlike previous forms of psychotherapy (e.g., Freudian psychoanalysis), REBT is a system of psychotherapy that combines both reason and emotion (Ellis, 1962b).

Many in the therapy/counseling field initially opposed Ellis and his work. However, as cognitive behavior therapy became more recognized because of the research supporting its efficacy, Ellis's reputation continued to grow. He held numerous positions in professional organizations and societies and in 1982 was ranked the second most influential psychologist in history. He authored or coauthored more than 1,200 articles and more than 80 books on sex therapy, marital and family therapy, and psychotherapy (Vernon, 2016). In 1959 Ellis founded a nonprofit organization, the Institute for Rational Living, which became chartered by the New York State Board of Regents in 1968 (and is now called the Albert Ellis Institute). The Albert Ellis Institute's headquarters is in New York and, because of the profound influence of REBT, there are 26 affiliated training centers in the United States and around the world. Ellis's mission and vision to train as many mental health providers in REBT is alive and strong.

Theoretical Overview of REBT

As stated previously, Albert Ellis was trained as a psychoanalyst and had a background in the Jungian, Horney, and Freudian schools of psychoanalysis. While practicing psychoanalysis on his patients, Ellis found that although they experienced relief from many of their symptoms, he was not satisfied with the overall results. Patients would gain insight into their problems and would see the connection between their present behavior and their past behavior, but they would not ultimately change their present behavior. Although they were able to acknowledge their disturbances through this process, they continued to maintain them (Ellis, 1962a).

Ellis was greatly influenced by philosophy, the Stoics in particular, who taught people how to behave differently. In line with Stoic philosophy, Ellis posited that it is not experiences from childhood that make an individual disturbed; rather, it is the attitude and the philosophy of life one takes at an early age. This is consistent with the philosophy of Epictetus, who stated, "Men are disturbed not by things, but by the views which they take of them" (Dryden, 2002, p. 349).

Based on the aforementioned philosophical influence, Ellis developed the ABC personality system. In this system, A stands for *activating event,* B stands for *beliefs,* and C stands for *consequences.* The activating event is something that happens to a person (e.g., situations, thoughts, emotions). Almost immediately following A, an emotional reaction to that occurs (C); although individuals erroneously believe that A causes C, it is actually what one *tells* oneself about A (B) that causes C. Emotional and behavioral disturbances are a result of *irrational beliefs,* which are defined as rigid, absolutistic, inconsistent with reality, and illogical and block goal attainment. Furthermore, they result in self-defeating or maladaptive behaviors. In theory, irrational beliefs create unhealthy negative emotions (e.g., depression, anxiety, unhealthy anger, shame, hurt, guilt, jealousy, unhealthy envy). The goal of REBT is to challenge and question irrational beliefs and replace them with *rational beliefs,* which are defined as flexible, reasonable, self-enhancing, consistent with reality, and logical and facilitate goal attainment. In addition, rational beliefs are theorized to result in healthy but still negative emotions (e.g., sadness, concern, healthy anger or annoyance, disappointment, regret; David, Lynn, & Ellis, 2009). A detailed explanation of the categories of irrational beliefs is given later in this chapter.

To better understand the aforementioned concepts, consider the following scenario. Suppose you are driving on a highway with a speed limit of 60 mph. You are driving behind a car that appears to be going around 35 mph. You get angry because you think to yourself, "This stupid driver *should* be driving the speed limit." You then realize that you are behind a funeral procession. Immediately the anger subsides because you change your demand based on the new information (i.e., a funeral procession), which results in a different emotional reaction. This illustrates the ABC system Ellis developed, in which he concluded, "It is not the external environment which influences you, it is what you tell yourself—your philosophy of life about that environment" (Ellis, 1962a). Also, the relationship between the past and the present is not a focus in REBT as it is in other forms of therapy. Rather, the focus is on what individuals are telling themselves *in the present* about the past events. As a result of this insight, Ellis modified his psychoanalytic techniques and methods of therapy on an empirical and theoretical basis.

A unique feature of Ellis's theory in the 1950s and 1960s was the recognition of the biological tendency toward emotional disturbance and human fallibility (Ellis, 1962b). Ellis argued that individuals must be trained to overcome their biological limitations. In order to acquire a healthier philosophy, hard work and commitment are required. Ellis proposed that counseling can help individuals accept their biological handicaps and human fallibility, thereby reducing emotional disturbance. He posited that the two main aspects of human disturbance are being dependent on others and lacking frustration tolerance.

Some of the major principles of REBT include the following (DiGiuseppe, Doyle, Dryden, & Backx, 2014; Ellis & Harper, 1997):

1. REBT stresses the B–C connection. From the beginning of therapy clients are taught the connection between their emotional and behavioral upset (C) and their irrational beliefs. Emotional and behavioral responsibility is emphasized at the outset of therapy. Understanding the B–C connection is a prerequisite to challenging irrational thinking.
2. REBT emphasizes the concepts of unconditional self, other, and life acceptance. Specifically, an individual's worth cannot be determined by external factors such as others' love and approval or his or her own achievements. Humans and life are too complex to be given a global rating of worth. The concept of unconditional acceptance of self and other promotes tolerance of differences in gender, sexual orientation, ethnicity, religion, disability, and so forth. The assumption is that all individuals have equal worth as human beings. Learn more about self-acceptance by referring to Sidebar 1.

Sidebar 1
Self-Acceptance

You can use this pie chart exercise to help your clients see that they possess positive and negative traits, behaviors, interpersonal roles/relationships, and so forth. Have them fill in the pie chart with what they view as both the positive (+) and negative (–) aspects of themselves. The goal is to show clients that they cannot logically rate themselves on any one given piece of the pie, thus fostering the concept of self-acceptance. Now work with a partner and develop other ways to convey this concept to clients.

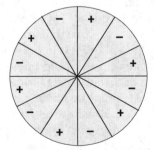

3. According to REBT, insight is not enough to overcome emotional disturbance. One has to *question* the beliefs that are creating the disturbance rather than uncritically accepting them as true. This can be done both through verbal challenging and behavioral experiments, such as exposure exercises.
4. REBT emphasizes how present emotional disturbance is *perpetuated* rather than how it was *acquired*. Although the past is important, it is not typically a focus in REBT.
5. In REBT the counselor–client relationship is one of collaboration rather than one that emphasizes analysis of transference.
6. REBT counselors and therapists educate clients about the origin of their disturbance and how to change it. Psychoeducation is a key component of the theory.
7. According to REBT, change requires establishing realistic goals, which are attained through hard work and practice. Homework assignments are a fundamental aspect of REBT.
8. As REBT emphasizes efficiency in its therapeutic methods and strategies, a crucial objective is to help clients learn how to become their own counselors.

As noted, the concepts of unconditional acceptance of self, other, and life promote tolerance and understanding of differences among diverse populations. Consequently, REBT is a very culturally sensitive theory. Furthermore, REBT is very helpful for clients whose own values conflict with those that are endorsed by their cultural and/or religious upbringing. The concept of acceptance (whether of self, other, or life) does not necessarily translate to liking or agreeing with conflicting values but rather refers to acknowledging and tolerating differences in sexual orientation, religion, gender identification, and so forth. Through unconditional acceptance of self, other, and life, people not only resolve their own emotional disturbance but also decrease the denigration and discrimination of others due to differences.

The ABC Model

Ellis developed the ABC model to illustrate the process of change (DiGiuseppe et al., 2014; Dryden & Branch, 2008). This model is followed by all REBT practitioners, although some modifications are needed for younger clients whose ability to express themselves verbally or emotionally may be limited. However, through games, stories, and other expressive arts techniques, school-age clients are able to learn basic rational concepts (Bernard, 2009; Vernon, 2009).

After the goals for counseling have been identified, the counselor begins to implement the ABC model. Identifying a specific, concrete activating event (A) is important in the therapeutic process of REBT for two reasons. First, most people think that the activating event is what *makes* them feel as they do, and therefore they want to talk in detail about this event, which could be something that happened in the past, that is currently occurring, or that they think might happen. Second, identifying a specific event helps elicit specific beliefs that may be rational or irrational, as described previously. Demands against self, others, or the world constitute irrational beliefs, whereas rational beliefs are preferences rather than demands and result in healthy but still negative emotions and adaptive behaviors (DiGiuseppe et al., 2014; Dryden & Branch, 2008; Ellis, 2001).

Occasionally clients may talk about an activating event and there are no unhealthy negative emotions because the beliefs are rational. If this is the case, the counselor can reinforce the rational way of thinking as well as contrast this to what beliefs would be present if clients were thinking irrationally. This form of psychoeducation is effective in teaching clients the difference between the two types of beliefs. More often than not, however, clients are seeking counseling because they have dysfunctional negative emotions and/or maladaptive behaviors, which would also signal the presence of irrational beliefs.

As the counselor attempts to elicit a specific event, the client may identify several different events that may or may not be related. Therefore, it is important for the counselor to listen carefully and help the client identify the most disturbing or the most pressing A. The REBT counselor discourages the client from providing overly detailed information about A; however, this may depend somewhat on the nature of the problem. For example, if a client was just fired from a job the day before, he or she may require more attention to details about A.

The next step in the ABC model is to ask clients to identify the emotional and behavioral consequences (C)—how they felt and behaved in relation to the activating event. It is important for you to note that assessing emotions is a critical step in this model, as a common misconception is that this theory does not address emotions or that REBT counselors aim to eliminate clients' emotions. On the contrary, helping clients develop healthier emotions and more adaptive behaviors is a major goal.

Clients often have difficulty identifying how they feel, and it is not uncommon for clients to provide a thought rather than a feeling in response to the question "How did you feel when that happened?" If the client fails to identify a feeling, the counselor would then say, "That's what you think . . . but how did you feel?" Some clients, especially children and adolescents, may benefit from affective education. This can also be helpful if there is a language barrier and/or cultural differences in emotions between the client and counselor, in which case the counselor might want to use feeling word lists and mood meters. Younger clients may be better able to express feelings through drawing, painting, music, or acting them out (Vernon, 2002, 2009).

In addition to asking about feelings, the REBT counselor asks clients to specify how they behaved in relation to the feeling and activating event. This is important because REBT is a comprehensive theory and the behavioral component is very significant for overall change. In addition, it is important in assessment, which includes an accurate identification of emotions. For instance, if a client says that she was angry, the counselor would expect that the behavioral reaction would be consistent with the feeling. But if the client who is angry says that she isolated herself and cried for 2 days, the client may be experiencing more depression than anger.

Once the counselor has identified a specific A and the subsequent emotional and behavioral consequences (C), the next step is to elicit clients' beliefs (B) about A. As noted previously, beliefs are either rational or irrational, although most clients who seek counseling have irrational beliefs but often have difficulty recognizing that they are irrational. There are four types of irrational beliefs: demandingness; awfulizing; frustration intolerance; and condemnation of self, other, and life (DiGiuseppe et al., 2014). Demandingness is the expectation that people, events, and life *should* be exactly the way a person wants them to be. Awfulizing is end-of-the-world thinking and exaggeration of the negative consequences of something. When reactions to traumatic events (e.g., death of a loved one) occur, counselors are advised not to immediately challenge the awfulness of the event to avoid a rupture in the therapeutic alliance. Frustration intolerance refers to the belief that things in life should come easily and/or the belief that one cannot tolerate or stand discomfort. Frustration intolerance is also referred to as "I-can't-stand-it-itis" (Ellis & MacLaren, 2005). The irrational belief of condemnation refers to the global rating of oneself, others, or life based on any given behavior, performance, external facts, and so forth.

There are several ways to help clients identify irrational beliefs. First, counselors can listen for words that typically reference demandingness statements (e.g., *shoulds, musts, needs,* and *oughts;* Ellis, 1997, 2001). Second, dysfunctional negative emotions and/or self-defeating behaviors usually signal the presence of irrational beliefs. For example, unhealthy anger is correlated with a demand and/or frustration intolerance, and guilt or depression is related to some form of self-condemnation. Anxiety often signals some type of "what if" questioning with catastrophic answers.

Once the irrational beliefs are identified and the B–C (beliefs and emotional/behavioral consequence) connection is reinforced, the *disputation* (D) process begins. The counselor now helps the client examine and question one irrational belief at a time. This is an active process, with the goal being to generate alternative rational beliefs to produce healthier emotions and more adaptive behaviors in line with the client's stated goals. Not only is it important to dispute or challenge irrational beliefs and replace them with rational alternatives, but it is critical to strengthen the conviction of the new rational beliefs. This is done through repeated vigorous rehearsal of the rational alternative. To help convey the importance of rehearsal, it can be helpful to use analogies. For example, we often ask clients how someone would increase muscle strength and whether this could be achieved by lifting a weight only once a week. Clients generally understand the significance of repetition. Much like strengthening their muscles, clients see the necessity of hard work in strengthening their emotional muscles.

There are several types of disputes counselors can use to effect cognitive, emotive, and behavior change. The *empirical* dispute involves gathering data to refute the irrational belief and/or support the rational alternative (e.g., "Where is the evidence that you are a complete failure as a person because you got an F on an exam?"). The *logical* dispute uses reason to examine and question the belief system (e.g., "How does it logically follow that because you want the job you therefore *must* get it?"). The *functional* or *pragmatic* dispute helps clients examine whether the specific irrational belief is helping them achieve their goals or is preventing goal attainment (e.g., "How does telling yourself that 'all people *must* respect you' help you to achieve your goal of getting along with difficult coworkers?" "How does demanding that all people respect you interfere with your stated goal?"). The *philosophical* dispute helps clients cope with their worst case scenario (e.g., "Suppose you never get accepted into graduate school. Could you still find some happiness and satisfaction in your life?"). The *best friend* dispute is often effective when working with clients who engage in self-condemnation (e.g., "If your best friend came to you and told you that she was a worthless human being because her partner left her for another woman, would you agree with her that she is worthless? If not, how can you define yourself as worthless but not your best friend, given the same circumstance?").

Younger children may have difficulty with the disputing process, in which case it may be better accomplished in a more didactic manner in which the counselor explains the difference between rational and irrational beliefs and uses games, stories, experiential activities, and other psychoeducational methods to teach the concepts (Vernon, 2002, 2016). For specific strategies and activities for working with children and adolescents, please see Vernon (2002, 2009).

After disputation, the next step in the model is *achieving a new effect* (E), which involves strengthening the conviction of the rational beliefs by continuously rehearsing them. The counselor might say something like "So instead of thinking that you are a complete failure as a parent because your teenage daughter got arrested for driving under the influence, what could you tell yourself instead?" After the client generates new rational beliefs, the client and counselor collaborate on homework assignments, which are integral to facilitating change and strengthening conviction in the new belief system. When working with children and adolescents (and many adults!), we recommend avoiding the term *homework*, as this is often aversive. *Practice, experiments, field work,* and *exercises* can be used to replace the term *homework*.

The Therapeutic Process in REBT

As Dryden (2002, 2012) noted, REBT counselors and therapists may practice REBT in different ways, but they adhere to the same theoretical principles. This is very important to note, because although Ellis's public persona was at times viewed as abrasive, the real Albert Ellis was much more empathic, supportive, and encouraging of his clients, supervisees, and professional training participants.

In the following paragraphs we describe how an REBT counselor would engage the client in the counseling process. The establishment of goals, the development of rapport, the process of change, and the termination process are described.

Goals of Counseling and Therapy

As REBT is an active-directive therapy, goal setting is an integral part of the therapeutic process and usually begins in the first session. When REBT counselors assess clients' goals, many of them look for practical solutions. As a result, one of the first jobs for the counselor is to teach the concepts of emotional and behavioral responsibility. In other words, regardless of what is happening in clients' lives, ultimately they are responsible for their emotional and behavioral reactions. This is why understanding and buying into the B–C connection is essential to the therapeutic process, and counseling cannot progress effectively until this is established. For many clients who have difficulty grasping the relationship between thoughts, feelings, and behaviors, utilizing stories and metaphors to explain the B–C connection can help facilitate comprehension of this concept. For example, ask the client to imagine twin sisters around the age of 9 who are going to the ocean for the first time. They are both wading in the water and a wave comes over them. One of the girls starts laughing hysterically and says, "This is so much fun! I can't wait for the next wave!" Her sister is crying hysterically and runs out of the water toward her parents, screaming, "Noooooo! I hate this! That was really scary!" After telling this story, ask the client if what happens to people makes them feel a certain way, how can he or she explain the differences in the girls' emotional responses to the *same* experience? Stories such as this one have proven to be helpful in solidifying the concept of the B–C connection. In working with adults, it is also good to use metaphors or stories, but older clients generally see the connection more readily when the counselor asks something like "Do you think all parents in the world would feel very angry as you do when their teenagers are spending most of their free time on their phones instead of with the family? If not, what do you think they might be feeling or thinking?" Assuming that the client says something to the effect that other parents might just feel irritated or think that it is just typical teenage behavior, the counselor would say, "Can you see then that it is not the *event* that makes you upset, but rather it is what you *think* about the event that causes you to feel a certain way?" If the client does not make the connection, the counselor can explain it more didactically. Complete the assignment in Sidebar 2 to better understand the B–C connection.

Sidebar 2

The B–C Connection

Remember that before you challenge irrational beliefs, it is important to make sure the client understands and buys into the B–C connection! Generate several of your own examples to teach clients the B–C connection and share with a partner.

Goal setting is also done in part through the process of psychoeducation. As the counselor orients them to the ABC theory of REBT, clients begin to learn how their emotional and behavioral disturbance is caused and maintained by the beliefs and perceptions that they hold about self, others, and life events. This also involves the process of emotional education—helping clients see the link between unhealthy negative emotions and maladaptive, goal-interfering behavior in contrast to the link between healthy negative emotions and adaptive, goal-oriented behavior (DiGiuseppe et al., 2014).

Once clients have a satisfactory understanding of the basics of REBT, they can develop specific short- and long-term goals. The counselor plays a role in facilitating this process by having them generate specific, measurable goals. For example, the counselor may ask a client to picture his or her life a few months from now and ask, "What would you like to be different? How would you like to be *feeling* differently, and what would you be *doing* differently?" This form of questioning not only helps the client generate concrete, measurable goals but also often serves as a form of motivation for change. The counselor may then ask the client to make a list of the emotions, behaviors, and thoughts he or she would like to increase as well as decrease. Learn more about this process in Sidebar 3.

Once the goals are established, the first question posed to the client in an REBT session is often "What problem would you like to work on today?" This question sets the stage for a working relationship between the counselor and client that is oriented toward solving emotional and behavioral problems, which results in getting better, not just venting and feeling better.

Sidebar 3
Identifying Goals of Therapy

You can help clients establish clear, measurable goals by having them make a list of what they would like to be different 3 months from now. Clients will often confuse behaviors, emotions, and thoughts. Determine whether the responses here are accurately categorized or operationally defined. If they are not, correct them. (See p. 141 for the answer key.)

1. Behaviors you would like to increase:
   I want to exercise more.
2. Behaviors you would like to decrease:
   Overeating.
3. Emotions you would like to increase:
   Feeling calm.
4. Emotions you would like to decrease:
   Feeling like a failure.
5. Thoughts you would like to increase:
   I'm a good person.
6. Thoughts you would like to decrease:
   I feel stupid.

As REBT is an evidence-based practice, goal attainment and progress monitoring is done throughout the course of therapy. This helps the counselor and client stay on track, as therapeutic goals may also change over time.

The Therapeutic Alliance

REBT has received criticism from some individuals who equate the theory with its founder, Albert Ellis, regarding a lack of emphasis on the therapeutic alliance. On the contrary, Dryden (2002) stressed that the literature has underplayed the importance of the relationship and that it actually is very important. Also, present-day REBT practitioners are acutely aware of the importance of establishing and maintaining a strong working therapeutic alliance. Careful monitoring of any ruptures in the alliance is addressed throughout the course of therapy. That having been said, both Dryden (2002) and O'Kelly (2010) pointed out that unlike in other forms of therapy, such as client-centered therapy, a strong therapeutic alliance is not sufficient to bring about client change.

Several factors contribute to the development of the therapeutic alliance in REBT. One key component is that the counselor and client work *collaboratively* to achieve the client's goals. A unique aspect of REBT that distinguishes it from many other forms of counseling and psychotherapy is that the client often leaves the first session with some type of skill or coping strategy that can be implemented immediately. Rather than spending multiple sessions obtaining background and diagnostic information about a client, REBT counselors can establish goals, teach the model, and also help the client with a specific emotional or behavioral problem in the first session (Yankura & Dryden, 1997). Clients often appreciate this approach and frequently experience a sense of hope as they immediately begin to acquire ways to address their disturbance. As a result, a trusting bond often forms between client and counselor, thus setting the stage for a collaborative working alliance.

The therapeutic alliance is often further strengthened throughout the course of treatment in REBT. As the counselor frequently utilizes a Socratic style (rather than lecturing), the client sees that the counselor is working toward the client's agenda and not the counselor's agenda. As the counselor continues to connect the client's irrational beliefs to his or her emotional and/or behavioral disturbance, the client sees how his or her irrational beliefs interfere with goal attainment. This helps the client understand the rationale behind the counselor's interventions (e.g., challenging/questioning irrational beliefs) and builds momentum for the client to actively engage in the therapy (DiGiuseppe et al., 2014).

Other ways of developing and maintaining a working relationship include being sensitive to the client's readiness to change, using encouraging and supportive language, giving positive feedback (O'Kelly, 2010), using humor appropriately (Dryden, 2002), and demonstrating unconditional positive regard for the client (Vernon, 2016).

The Process of Change

As emphasized in previous sections of this chapter, REBT is a form of psychotherapy that helps people not just *feel* better but actually *get* better (i.e., changing cognitive reactions in order to change emotional and behavioral reactions). The process of change occurs through ongoing practice and rehearsal identifying and challenging/questioning irrational beliefs that lead to unhealthy negative emotions and maladaptive behaviors. In the early stages of REBT, clients often state, "I understand the error in my thinking at an intellectual level, but I still have difficulty on the emotional level when I am confronted with certain triggers." This is typically the result of a client being able to identify a rational alternative but not really believe it. Real change in REBT comes when clients can actually make a philosophical shift in their ways of thinking by truly believing the rational alternative.

For example, a client who believes that she is worthless because she does not have a significant other is only going to overcome her depression when she actually *believes* that her worth as a human is not based solely on being in a relationship. When she comes to believe this, the client will have made a philosophical shift in her core belief system. This shift is not something that usually comes easily. It requires a lot of practice and hard work on the part of the client both during and in between sessions. Counselors can help their clients achieve this through a variety of cognitive, emotive, and behavioral interventions, many of which are detailed later in this chapter. These interventions are subsequently illustrated in the verbatim case study at the end of this chapter and in the case of Marcos in Chapter 9.

The Termination Process

Unlike in other forms of therapy, in which the counselor may dictate the termination process, ending therapy in REBT is typically a collaborative process between the counselor and the client. As REBT is highly goal oriented, the ideal termination occurs when the client has successfully achieved his or her emotional and behavioral goals, mastered the skills and strategies learned over the course of therapy, and can successfully implement these strategies on his or her own when encountering difficult activating events. Essentially, through hard work and practice the client learns how to become his or her own REBT counselor (DiGiuseppe et al., 2014).

Because there is ongoing monitoring of the client's progress and goal attainment throughout the course of therapy, the termination process is typically smooth and occurs as a natural progression of the therapy. The client and counselor may choose to fade out counseling or therapy (e.g., reduce sessions from weekly to biweekly to monthly) to assess how the client maintains the therapeutic gains with reduced sessions.

When both the client and counselor agree that termination of therapy is appropriate based on the factors discussed previously, the counselor reviews the client's progress and the skills that he or she has learned. To obtain an idea of the client's ability to put these skills to use, the counselor may pose a hypothetical problem that is relevant to the client's reason for referral. The counselor will then ask the client to identify potential unhealthy emotions and the irrational beliefs that would likely contribute to these emotions. The client is next asked to challenge/question these irrational beliefs and formulate alternative rational beliefs that would lead to healthier emotional and behavioral responses (Ellis & Dryden, 2007). This allows the counselor to see how well the client has mastered the REBT process and also serves as a form of relapse prevention.

Sometimes there is disagreement between the counselor and client regarding the timing of and/or reasons for termination of therapy. If the client wants to discontinue therapy but has not reached his or her goals, it is important for the counselor to try to obtain the client's reasons for termination, help the client generate pros and cons of this decision, and also express reasons why termination may not be clinically recommended. REBT counselors will look for any irrational beliefs contributing to reasons for termination (e.g., frustration intolerance: "It's *too* uncomfortable to do this work!"). Nevertheless, it is not the REBT counselor's role to forcefully convince or strong-arm the client into continuing therapy, regardless of the reason for termination. Of course there are exceptions to this rule, such as if the counselor believes the client is in imminent danger to himself or herself or others. In general, if the client is no longer motivated to continue in counseling, it is unlikely that he or she will benefit significantly from further sessions, in which case the counselor should make sure that the client is given appropriate referrals should he or she choose to resume therapy elsewhere.

REBT Interventions

REBT focuses on cognitive, emotive, and behavioral interventions to effect change. We provide examples for each category to illustrate.

Cognitive Interventions

- *Inference chaining.* Inference chaining is an effective way of assessing a client's irrational belief(s). The process is to temporarily assume that the client's automatic thoughts or inferences are true and to chain the thoughts with conjunctive phrases (e.g., "And that would mean?" "And if that happened, what then?"; DiGiuseppe et al., 2014). For example, if a client reports feeling depressed, the counselor asks the client what she was thinking in a specific situation in which she felt that emotion. The client starts by saying that she had the thought "I have no friends." The counselor responds by saying, "Let's suppose for the moment you don't have friends. What would that mean to you?" The client responds, "I have no one to hang out with." The counselor then follows with "And if you have no one to hang out with, then what?" The client responds, "That would mean I'm a loser." "I'm a loser" is an irrational belief (global evaluation of worth) that would be the target of therapy, rather than the inferences "I have no friends" and "I have no one to hang out with." In REBT counselors tend not to challenge inferences because they could be true, and doing so does not help the client cope with what is sometimes a bad reality. Practice inference chaining by referring to Sidebar 4.

When working with children and adolescents, however, it is sometimes effective to first challenge inferences (rather than go directly to any irrational beliefs). When young clients are in the concrete stage of development, they naturally awfulize and overgeneralize and therefore are easily overwhelmed. Vernon (2009) argued that challenging inferences can help young clients see a problem more realistically. For example, if a teenager says that his girlfriend must not love him because she did not call him the night before as promised, it is helpful for the counselor to confront this by saying, "So where's the evidence that she doesn't love you just because she didn't call you? Could there be any other explanation?" Once he acknowledges that this could be possible, the counselor could then say, "Suppose your assumption is correct. What would this say about you? And if it were true, do you think you could eventually stand it?" By helping him develop other possible perspectives first, the counselor can gradually move into the more elegant philosophical dispute, depending on the age of the child.

- *Disputation.* This is one of the most recommended interventions for changing a client's belief(s). This intervention is both used in sessions as well as assigned for homework. It is very important that clients learn how to challenge their unhelpful thinking in an active manner. As discussed previously, there are several commonly used disputes: functional, empirical, logical, and philosophical (Ellis & Dryden, 2007).
- *REBT worksheets.* These serve as a great way to determine whether clients understand the ABC process as well as to determine clients' ability to challenge and replace their irrational beliefs. It is very helpful to utilize these worksheets in session (especially with clients who are tangential, easily distracted, or overly detailed in nature) as well as for homework. Please refer to the Appendix for a copy of this worksheet (Albert Ellis Institute, 2017).

Sidebar 4

Inference Chaining

In dyads or alone, practice inference chaining with each of the following automatic thoughts:

"I'm going to fail this test"
"My teacher doesn't like me"
"My partner is going to break up with me"
"I'll never get this great job that I applied for."

- *Rational beliefs rehearsal.* Having clients rehearse the new, healthy, rational beliefs can be as important as disputing the irrational beliefs, and having them practice a different way of thinking both in and out of session is integral to effecting change. Specifically, clients are often asked to audio record the healthier rational belief and listen to it on a daily basis. It is helpful to have younger clients write the new rational belief and/or coping statement on an index card and review it in between sessions (Ellis & MacLaren, 2005).
- *Bibliotherapy.* Assigning books to read, movies to watch, or audio files to listen to serves as an effective intervention for clients of all ages to reinforce the concepts being addressed in counseling. It is important to discuss with the client how he or she learns best in order to determine whether this will be an effective intervention (Ellis & MacLaren, 2005).
- *Stop and monitor.* Many clients will not be aware of what they are thinking throughout the day when they are experiencing different emotions. A very effective strategy to help clients think about their thinking is to have them stop and monitor their thoughts. Clients are asked to set an alarm on their phone or put a sticky note on their computer so that every time they see or hear the cue, they remember to stop and check what they are thinking. This exercise helps clients understand that they have many cognitions throughout the day, ranging from neutral to positive, negative, irrational, or rational (Ellis & MacLaren, 2005).
- *Proselytizing.* This intervention is very popular with children and adolescents. Ask clients to spend the week identifying their parents' and siblings' irrational thinking and pointing it out to them. This is sometimes easier for some clients who are not ready to take a look at their own irrational beliefs (Ellis & MacLaren, 2005).
- *Referenting.* Referenting is a type of cost–benefit analysis that helps clients identify the positive and negative short-term and long-term consequences of a particular way of thinking, feeling, or behaving. For example, a counselor working with an individual struggling with whether to come out to his or her parents could generate the short-term versus long-term pros and cons of this disclosure.
- *Changing semantics.* Clients often say "I can't" or "I need this" or "I can't help it, that's just the way I feel." Counselors can help clients change their semantics by asking, "Do you really mean you *can't* or just that you are *choosing* not to?" "Do you really *need* it or do you just *want* it?" In addition, REBT counselors are diligent in operationally defining abstract terms their clients use (*it, that, you know what I mean,* etc.).

Emotive Interventions

- *Rational emotive imagery.* This intervention should be done *after* clients understand the B–C connection. The counselor asks clients to make themselves feel extremely angry, anxious, guilty, depressed, or so on.

Once they do so, they are asked to change the unhealthy negative emotion to a healthy negative emotion and tell the counselor how this was accomplished. The proper response is that this was done by changing the irrational beliefs to rational beliefs (Ellis, 2000).

- *Forceful coping statements.* Have clients repeat aloud, with force and emotion, their coping statements, such as "I *don't* like it but I *can* stand it!!"
- *Forceful recorded disputing.* Much like forceful coping statements, ask clients to record themselves disputing their irrational beliefs with force. The idea is that using force in their disputes will assist in the shift from irrational thinking to rational thinking. Repetitive listening to the recording will further strengthen this shift.
- *Role playing.* In session, the counselor and client identify an activating event that triggered an unhealthy negative emotion for the client in the recent past. The client plays himself or herself, and the counselor plays the role of the individual who triggered the problem. After the role play, the counselor processes the client's thoughts and feelings during the exercise and identifies anything he or she would prefer to do differently in the future. During this conversation, emphasis is placed on identifying and challenging any irrational beliefs leading to emotional and behavioral disturbance (Ellis & MacLaren, 2005).
- *Reverse role playing.* After the counselor has challenged the client's irrational beliefs, it is often helpful to switch roles with the client. The counselor takes on the client's irrational thinking, and the client is asked to be the counselor and challenge the beliefs. This strategy determines whether the client actually believes the healthier way of thinking as well as reinforces the client's new belief system.
- *Watching movies and television programs.* Many clients, including children and adolescents, do not have a strong emotional vocabulary or good problem-solving skills. Carefully selected movies and TV programs that convey good problem-solving skills and emotional expression can be very helpful when used and discussed in session.
- *Happiness assignments.* Although REBT tends to focus on changing unhealthy negative emotions to healthier negative emotions, counselors do help clients work on achieving happiness. Homework assignments include having clients engage in activities that contribute to happiness and having clients be mindful of things that contribute to their happiness.
- *Humor.* REBT emphasizes the use of humor in treatment. Counselors help clients learn how to laugh at their irrational thinking as a means to change. It is crucial that counselors emphasize that the humor is directed toward the client's thinking and not the client.

Behavioral Interventions

- *Staying in difficult situations.* Many clients opt to escape situations that they find uncomfortable or in which they overestimate the actual threat. This reaction is problematic because it reinforces to the client that he or she *cannot* tolerate uncomfortable situations and reinforces the misperceived threat. Having clients stay in difficult and uncomfortable situations affords the opportunity for them to see that although uncomfortable, they are not intolerable or as harmful as clients initially believed (Ellis, 1997).

- *Acting on rational beliefs.* For some clients, waiting to see cognitive change can take a while. We will often have clients act *as if* they believed the rational belief in order to produce change. In other words, act how you want to feel (Ellis & MacLaren, 2005).
- *Stimulus control.* For clients working on changing a behavior, we advocate stimulus control at the beginning of such change. Examples include having clients who have problems with alcohol get rid of all of the alcohol in their home and avoid going to bars or having clients with eating disorders throw away certain foods that are likely to trigger a binge.
- *Risk taking and shame attacks.* Albert Ellis was well known for the use of shame attacks with clients who were prone to feeling shame. One effective way to overcome the problem of shame is to have clients engage in exercises that they avoid because they would experience shame and rehearse a coping statement (e.g., standing in an elevator facing the wall instead of the door, calling out the subway or bus stops, walking a banana on a leash in a populated area). Obviously clients should do nothing illegal or dangerous but rather something they find to be embarrassing or shameful. They learn that they can tolerate others' disapproval (if anyone even pays attention to them) and that they can tolerate feeling embarrassed and uncomfortable.
- *Relaxation training.* Many clients with severe physiological arousal require relaxation training *prior* to cognitive work. Clients with anger and anxiety in particular will benefit from this approach.
- *Skills training.* Although REBT emphasizes the emotional solution before the practical solution (in other words, disputing irrational beliefs in order to achieve healthier negative emotions before doing skills training), it should be noted that skills training is often a part of REBT counseling. Social skills training, assertiveness training, and behavior management training can be very helpful interventions for clients with skills deficits.

Applications of REBT

REBT can be applied to a wide range of psychological, emotional, and behavioral problems: internalizing disorders such as mood disorders, anxiety disorders, obsessive-compulsive and related disorders, trauma and stressor-related disorders; and externalizing disorders such as anger, disruptive or impulsive behavior, conduct disorders, and attention-deficit/hyperactivity disorder. Other problems treated with REBT include addictions, eating disorders, relationship issues, grief and loss, sexual identity concerns, psychosis, and personality disorders (Ellis & Bernard, 2006; Ellis & Dryden, 2007;

Vernon, 2016). REBT can be applied individually, in small groups, in class-rooms as a preventive emotional education curriculum for children and adolescents, and in consultation with parents or teachers. Several specific applications are described here.

REBT Applications With Eating Disorders

When treating eating disorders, a common misunderstanding is that the issues presented in therapy are related to food. Although it is true that the problem manifests itself in eating disturbances, the issue is not the food per se but rather one's self-worth defined by one's ability to control caloric intake and/or control one's weight and shape. Consequently, REBT is uti-lized to target and address the typically held irrational beliefs of global eval-uations of self-worth and frustration intolerance. It should be noted that a strong therapeutic alliance is a necessary prerequisite for carrying out any intervention strategies when treating this population, as trust is such a struggle for these clients. Many clients with eating disorders will engage in exercises and homework assignments because they trust the counselor, despite how fearful they are of doing so.

Working with this population requires being patient and slowing down one's tempo so as not to lose the client during the therapeutic process. Prior to any cognitive interventions being done, behavioral interventions (e.g., in-session weighing, real-time self-monitoring of eating, and planned meals and snacks) are often used (Fairburn, 2008). These behavioral strat-egies, which are done at the outset of therapy, address many of the main-taining mechanisms seen in eating disorders. Once this is done, moving onto cognitive interventions is typically the next step. Teaching the REBT concept of *unconditional self-acceptance* is crucial with this population to help clients acknowledge that they are human and therefore have flaws (not that they have to like them) and that they should avoid global ratings of their worth based on such flaws. Expanding clients' concept of self-worth beyond their ability to control their shape, weight, or caloric intake is necessary in treatment. In addition, helping clients learn to tolerate uncomfortable emotions or activating events is a priority (Doyle, 2000) because thinking that they cannot tolerate discomfort is what often triggers event- and/or mood-related changes in eating. A good homework assignment to increase frustration tolerance for clients who binge and purge is to have them sit in discomfort after they purge for 30 seconds (or 1 minute, 2 minutes, etc.). While they are sitting with the discomfort, they are to rehearse a rational coping statement such as "I don't like this discomfort, but I certainly can stand it, and it is in my best long-term interest to do so." After the allot-ted time period, they can go and purge. The next time they binge they are asked to sit for a bit longer while they rehearse their coping statement before they purge. They do this repeatedly, which serves two functions: (a) It shows clients that they *can* tolerate discomfort, and (b) it increases their overall level of tolerance for discomfort. Other homework assignments for this population include interviewing individuals who appear happy and self-accepting but are *not* thin by cultural standards; having clients who catastrophize about gaining weight if they eat something off their bad-food list take risks to incorporate such foods into their diet; and having clients prepare a closing argument on why they can accept themselves regardless of shape, weight, and control to present to a jury as if they were a prosecutor in court (Doyle, 2000).

REBT Applications With Couples

In addition to being used with individuals to treat a variety of problems, REBT is often used with couples. As A–C (activating event, emotional/behavioral consequences) connections are frequently made by individuals in couples counseling, counselors using REBT focus heavily on helping each individual take responsibility for his or her own emotions and behaviors. This addresses the problematic philosophy of blame and punishment that is often a barrier to progress (Broder, 1994). Furthermore, in couples counseling, the REBT counselor works to elicit each partner's goals and helps them identify mutually agreed-on goals. Establishing goals for both the individual as well as the relationship is an integral component of REBT couples counseling.

Similar to the emphasis on effective goal establishment, other aspects of the theory and philosophy of REBT prove to be quite useful in work with couples. McMahon and Siu Woo (2012) highlighted a core difference between REBT and other forms of cognitive therapy (CT) when it comes to the theoretical approach of working with couples. REBT emphasizes unconditional acceptance of oneself and others rather than on focusing on the validity of one's inferences. For example, if one partner complains that the other never does her share of the chores, emphasis would be placed on condemning the behavior and not the individual or her worth. Other forms of CT may immediately jump to challenging the inference that the person "never" does her share of the chores. Although this may be an exaggeration, it may also be the truth or close to it. Therefore, challenging the inference will likely have little impact on the partner's unhealthy negative emotion. In contrast, the elegant solution of accepting the partner as a fallible human being, as is emphasized in REBT, will likely change the unhealthy anger to healthy anger/frustration, which can assist the couple in moving toward their relationship goals.

Although REBT is effective in addressing numerous problems that arise in relationships, it is particularly useful when working with infidelity (Abrams, 2012). If it is the shared goal of both partners to work through the betrayal and stay together, REBT emphasizes the importance of changing the unhealthy negative emotions of each partner. The experience of unhealthy negative emotions such as anger, hurt, shame, and guilt will likely serve as an obstacle to the goal of eventually returning to a healthy relationship. For example, Abrams (2012) emphasized the significance of helping the offended partner challenge irrational beliefs that lead to anger, hurt, and vengefulness, as these emotions are not consistent with the goal of restoring the relationship. In addition, helping the unfaithful partner identify irrational beliefs that led to the infidelity in the first place is essential in preventing recurrence and also in helping the offended partner regain trust. When the emotional disturbance and irrational beliefs of each of the partners is effectively addressed, the stage is set to work on other problematic areas of the relationship that can benefit from improvement, such as communication skills or intimacy.

In summary, core methods and concepts in REBT are applied very effectively in work with couples. Establishing agreement on goals, addressing unhealthy emotional disturbance before engaging in practical problem solving, and emphasizing unconditional acceptance of self and other are all key components in helping couples with a wide range of presenting problems meet their goals in therapy.

REBT Applications With Children and Adolescents

REBT can be readily modified for use with children and adolescents and has been used successfully with this population to address a variety of internalizing and externalizing disorders as well as typical developmental issues (Vernon, 2002, 2009, 2016). REBT is especially applicable for this age group for several reasons. It is generally a briefer form of therapy, which is ideal for children, as their sense of time is more immediate. It also empowers children by teaching them methods of coping with situations out of their control. For example, children usually do not decide whether their parents will get divorced, but they can control their emotional and behavioral reactions to events of this nature. In addition, this theory teaches emotional and behavioral self-control, which is very important for young people, whose abilities to generate alternatives and solve problems is often limited (Vernon, 2009).

Bernard, Ellis, and Terjesen (2006) recommended that disputation be aligned with the child's developmental level. For example, it can be difficult for children younger than age 11 who have not yet developed abstract reasoning skills to understand the concept of disputation. Instead, REBT counselors can use affective education methods and teach them what to think when they encounter specific activating events, or they can use games, stories, experiments, and other creative strategies to help children learn disputation (Doyle & Terjesen, 2006; Vernon, 2002, 2009). In general, at around 11 years of age, when children have developed more abstract reasoning abilities, counselors can begin to challenge distorted cognitions and irrational beliefs.

Other considerations when working with children and adolescents include taking some of the responsibility for the problem off of the child or adolescent at the outset of therapy. This is because young clients are often labeled a *problem child* by parents and/or school personnel. By removing some of the responsibility from the child, the counselor is demonstrating that he or she is on the child's side, which typically helps build the therapeutic alliance. Because many children and adolescents are in counseling against their will, it is important for the counselor to gain leverage by showing how the child or adolescent may benefit from participating (e.g., getting their parents to stop nagging, having an additional hour of computer time on the weekend, having a friend sleep over; DiGiuseppe & Bernard, 2006). In addition, the use of relevant technology (e.g., YouTube, websites, mobile phone apps) can help to keep the child or adolescent engaged while teaching pertinent concepts.

Furthermore, there are some very specific considerations when working with adolescent clients to build a sound therapeutic relationship. The counselor should be prepared for long periods of uninterrupted listening as well as avoidance of silence in session. This is often in contrast with how REBT addresses adults in that discussion of activating events is kept to a minimum and silence is encouraged during the disputation process. Although adolescents' perspectives of reality are often quite distorted, REBT practitioners will not challenge their reality. Provided that it is appropriate and relevant to the content of the session, REBT practitioners will discuss their own opinions and attitudes if asked by the teenager.

Consultation With Parents and Teachers

When REBT is used with children and adolescents, the work often extends beyond the identified client to parents and school personnel. It is important to address any irrational beliefs and emotional disturbance that can interfere with effective parenting and effective teaching (DiGiuseppe & Kelter, 2006). For example, parents who are awfulizing about their child's learning disorder will typically experience anxiety and in turn may model maladaptive coping. A teacher may have the irrational belief "I can't stand it when this child doesn't pay attention." As a result, she may experience anger and may be less effective in managing her classroom. We recognize that when working with this population, it is crucial to utilize a multisystem approach, which is encouraged at the outset of therapy.

Classroom and Small-Group Applications

Ellis was a firm believer in emotional education, and he felt strongly that if all students could be introduced to rational concepts throughout their school experience, they would live much happier lives. As Ellis himself stated, "I have always believed in the potential of REBT to be used in schools as a form of mental health promotion and with young people experiencing developmental problems" (Ellis & Bernard, 2006, p. ix). Although not all problems can be prevented with this approach, students will have more skills to deal with issues as they arise; REBT helps them develop emotional muscle.

Several curriculums have been developed for this purpose by Vernon (2006a, 2006b), Bernard (2001), and Knaus (1974). Structured lessons that can be facilitated in the classroom by teachers or school counselors and psychologists address topics such as feelings and behaviors; sensible and insensible (rational and irrational) beliefs; changing thoughts, feelings, and behaviors; learning frustration tolerance; developing acceptance of self and other; and problem-solving skills. Concepts are presented in developmentally appropriate ways through role playing, games and other experiential activities, music, stories, art activities, and expressive writing.

These topics can also be introduced in a small-group format (Vernon, 2007). For example, a group of four to eight children may benefit from learning how to reduce anger and frustration or how to get along more effectively with others by learning other-acceptance and assertive communication skills. Adolescents can benefit from a more open-ended group in which members bring problems they would like to discuss in the group and, after having been introduced to REBT concepts, other group members help the identified member think more rationally about his or her issue. The advantages of using small groups are numerous, and you are encouraged to use this format not only with children and adolescents but also with adults in hospital, mental health, rehabilitation, or other settings to deal with problems such as addiction, eating disorders, obsessive-compulsive disorder, grief and loss, or relationship issues. The benefits of group work include more creative homework assignments, better accountability, and a wider range of disputation (compared to individual counseling). Furthermore, as group members help other group members change their irrational beliefs, they learn to talk themselves out of their own irrational thinking (Ellis & Dryden, 2007).

Efficacy of REBT

Prior to 1970 most of the research on REBT consisted of case studies or research utilizing a quasi-experimental design. Until relatively recently, REBT has not been tested in scientifically rigorous, controlled experimental designs (David, Szentagotai, Kallay, & Macavei, 2005). This gap in the REBT efficacy literature is currently being addressed.

In a randomized clinical trial, David, Szentagotai, Lupu, and Cosman (2008) compared REBT, CT, and selective serotonin reuptake inhibitors (fluoxetine) to determine the relative efficacy of these three forms of treatment for individuals diagnosed with major depressive disorder. They found that all three treatment modalities resulted in a significant reduction in depressive symptomology as measured by the Beck Depression Inventory and the Hamilton Rating Scale for Depression. After 6 months, participants were reassessed, and the REBT and CT groups maintained treatment effects more than the psychopharmacology (fluoxetine) group, with the REBT group showing significantly fewer depressive symptoms than the psychopharmacology group. This is consistent with previous research indicating that various forms of cognitive behavior therapies, including REBT, are as effective as medications (if not more so) for the treatment of depression (DeRubeis et al., 2005).

In addition to having noteworthy clinical implications, David and colleagues' (2008) findings are also quite relevant with regard to the health care system's growing pressure on providers to utilize short-term evidence-based practice. Sava, Yates, Lupu, Szentagotai, and David (2009) used the results of David and colleagues' (2008) study to examine the cost effectiveness and cost utility of the three treatment modalities (i.e., CT, REBT, and fluoxetine). Both CT and REBT were found to be notably less expensive than fluoxetine (Prozac), which is a common antidepressant medication used to treat major depressive disorder. Statistical analysis revealed that the same effect obtained at a cost of $100 for fluoxetine could be obtained by spending about $70 for cognitive behavior therapy (CT or REBT). Although CT was found to be slightly less expensive in comparison to REBT relative to fluoxetine, it should be noted that REBT yielded the best maintenance in symptom reduction at 6-month follow-up (David et al., 2008). Therefore, one may argue that REBT may be the most cost effective of the three treatment modalities when one takes into consideration maintenance of treatment effects.

The REBT research literature also includes a significant number of studies examining treatment outcomes in children and adolescents. In a meta-analysis of REBT with children and adolescents conducted by Gonzalez and colleagues (2004), the average child or adolescent scored 69% better than untreated control groups on various outcome measures. In these studies, it was determined that REBT had the most prominent impact on the reduction of disruptive behaviors. It was also suggested that REBT may be useful in both intervention and prevention, as REBT was almost equally as effective for children and adolescents with and without an identified problem. Overall, this study supports the efficacy of using REBT in treating children and adolescents, especially those with externalizing problems.

Criticisms of the theory include the claim that REBT lacks vigorous scientific research in comparison to other cognitive behavior therapies, as noted at the outset of this section. After 1970 better controlled outcome studies were conducted. However, most of them were transdiagnostic rather than examinations of specific category-based disorders and/or investigated effectiveness rather than efficacy. David and colleagues (2005) suggested that these studies be reexamined given the trend in the field to encourage transdiagnostic and effectiveness-based research.

Verbatim Transcript: REBT

The following verbatim transcript of a fourth session is presented in order to illustrate information about the principles and practice of REBT as described in this chapter. We provide a brief overview of the case, the actual transcript, a short critique of the session, and an explanation as to why we think this theory effectively addressed the problem.

Overview

Allison was a 13-year-old African American female referred by her homeroom teacher in response to recent events of being bullied, specifically regarding her physical appearance. Allison presented with depressive symptomology that was triggered by self-downing as well as anger toward classmates who were reportedly making fun of her on a regular basis. At school, she began isolating herself from her peers at lunchtime, and her absences had increased over the past month, prompting the teacher to reach out to the therapist, who had worked with other students from this school. The first three sessions focused on building rapport with Allison by establishing agreement on the goals and tasks of therapy (e.g., explaining the connection between thoughts and emotions, emphasizing the importance of emotional and behavioral responsibility, validating her difficulties, and explaining the importance of practice in between sessions). Allison shared that she wanted to work on her problems. What follows is the transcript of the fourth session, in which Kristene was the therapist.

Transcript of the Fourth Session

> *Therapist:* Hey Allison! How did you do on your homework we came up with last week? If you remember, you agreed to monitor and log your self-downing thoughts like "I'm a loser" throughout the week when you were feeling depressed. How did you do with this?
>
> *Client:* I guess I did better than last week. Here is my log [takes out log and shows therapist].
>
> *Therapist:* You did great this week Allison! Let's see what we have. So from looking at this, it seems like your negative thoughts of "I'm a loser" tend to come up during lunchtime and after school, which makes sense since these are the times the other girls are together and talking about you. When you noticed you were thinking "I'm such a loser," how did you feel?
>
> *Client:* I felt down.
>
> *Therapist:* What does down mean for you? Down could be sad, angry, depressed.
>
> *Client:* When I was down I was trying my best not to cry, so I guess I was feeling a little depressed. But I was also angry at them for making me feel this way.
>
> *Therapist:* Okay, so you were feeling both depressed and angry. If you recall from two sessions ago, we talked about how no matter what happens to us, nobody has the power to make us feel anything. We *feel* and *behave* based on how we *think* about what is happening. Do you remember that?
>
> *Client:* Yes I remember; it's still a little hard for me to not blame them.
>
> *Therapist:* I get it, that makes sense, but it's super important you realize that the one thing you have control over is your reactions. So we may not be able to control what the girls do and say about you, but we can control how you respond emotionally and behaviorally. Any questions so far?
>
> *Client:* No, I remember a couple of weeks ago when you asked me to think this way I actually did feel a little better. This week was especially hard though.

Therapist: So you mentioned feeling both a little depressed, as well as angry at the other girls. To be most helpful, let's pick one of those feelings to focus on first. We'll get to both eventually, but it makes most sense to look at them one at a time. Do you want to look at the depression or the anger first?

Client: I think because I was so upset, actually, depressed, I, that, is more important. I don't think I would be so angry if I wasn't feeling so down.

Therapist: Okay, that sounds good. So let's take a look at what was happening during one of these times this week you felt depressed. Can you look back at your log and pick one time that you recall feeling depressed? Do you remember what happened?

Client: Okay [looking at log from homework assignment], on Friday at lunchtime I got so upset I started to cry and tried to hold back my tears.

Therapist: Do you remember what happened right before you started to cry?

Client: Friday was pizza day and I was eating by myself and I noticed a few of the girls from my class that we have spoken about before walked by me and stared. I heard one of them say under her breath "Should she really be eating that?" and then they started to laugh.

Therapist: I'm sorry about this Allison—that must have been really difficult to hear. So it was at this point when you started to feel depressed?

Client: Yes.

Therapist: Okay, going back to that Friday when you heard the girl say that to you and started to feel depressed and cried, can you think back to that moment and recall what was going through your mind?

Client: [Looks at log] I wrote in my log "I have no friends. Nobody likes me."

Therapist: Okay so when you heard the comment from the girl and saw them laugh, you thought—I have no friends, and nobody likes me.

Client: Yes.

Therapist: Let's just say for now, we can't control what the girls are doing and saying. Is there a different feeling than depressed that would be better for you when the girls are making fun of you? Remember you had told me in our first session that one of the things you would like is to have more friends. You also told me that when you are depressed you isolate yourself from your classmates.

Client: Less depressed.

Therapist: Do you remember when we started working together we spoke about different emotions? Do you remember when I talked to you about the difference between sad and depressed?

Client: Yes.

Therapist: Can you tell me what you remember?

Client: I remember that when I feel sad I don't cry and I'm not isolating myself so much. And when I get depressed I have a hard time not crying and don't want to be around other people. I also don't want people to see me crying so I try harder to hide it by staying away from the other girls.

Therapist: Great. So do you think it would be helpful if we work on going from being depressed to being sad when the girls are making fun of you?

Client: That sounds good.

Therapist: Okay, so this is really important Allison. I'm going to explain something to you and I want to hear what you think. Some people your age may think, "I have no friends and nobody likes me," and might feel frustrated, disappointed, or sad. But you had those same thoughts and felt depressed. So I'm wondering if I could ask you a little more about what you were thinking?

Client: Sure. Do you think this could help me?

Therapist: Yes, I am confident this will help.

Client: Okay.

Therapist: Let's suppose—just let's assume for now you don't have any friends and nobody likes you. I don't know if this is true or not, but for *now*, let's just suppose it is true. I'm wondering if you are thinking something about *you* that you don't have friends and nobody likes you?

Client: Yeah, how could it not say something about me if nobody likes me. I feel like such a loser.

Therapist: Okay, do you see by having the *thought* "I am such a loser" that would make you feel depressed? I know I would feel depressed if I was thinking I'm a loser.

Client: Yeah, that makes sense. But I don't know how to stop thinking that. It's so hard when you hear such mean things.

Therapist: I get it Allison, I know it's hard. But you've already started to help yourself by doing the homework and seeing that there are certain times when you feel depressed and during those times you have certain thoughts.

Client: I'm starting to see how my thoughts are making me feel bad. How do I change this?

Therapist: That's a really good question. So just to make sure we're on the same page: We agree it would be better for you to feel sad, rather than depressed, correct?

Client: Yes.

Therapist: And you see how thinking "I am such a loser" leads you to feel depressed which then interferes with you making friends, which I know is really important to you.

Client: Yeah.

Therapist: So perhaps we can take a look at this thought "I am such a loser" and ask a few questions?

Client: Okay.

Therapist: I know you mentioned in our first session that you have a younger sister that you are really close to. If she was having some trouble with her classmates and they were making fun of her, do you think she would be a loser?

Client: No way.

Therapist: Reaaaally, huh . . . that's interesting. How come she wouldn't be a loser but you think you are? It's the same situation . . .

Client: She's the last thing from a loser—she's sweet, funny, she listens to me when I have problems, and she does her chores.

Therapist: So . . . I know from your mother and your counselor at school that you are very helpful in class, you also help your parents by doing your chores, and you get good grades. So you and your sister both have some really good qualities. So I'm wondering when those girls at school make fun of you, does that erase all of your positive qualities?

Client: I guess not.

Therapist: So while it may be true at the moment that you have less friends than the other girls at school, does that make you a total loser as a person?

Client: [Pauses] . . .

Therapist: Remember what we talked about in terms of your sister. She has many good qualities, but I'm guessing because she's human, she also has some negatives. And she is not a loser according to you.

Client: You're right. She is a good person but can also be a pain in my butt sometimes.

Therapist: Okay, now that we've established there is no evidence that you are a loser because of what other people say about you, next question: How is telling yourself that "I am such a loser" when you're being teased helping you to achieve your goal of feeling sad but still be and make other friends?

Client: It's not at all.

Therapist: How is telling yourself that "I am such a loser" preventing you from making new friends?

Client: It makes me feel depressed, and then I cry, and then I stay as far away from the other girls as possible.

Therapist: Good—well, not good, but that was good that you see how this thought is not helping you at all.

Client: Great . . . so now what?

Therapist: So now we have to change how you think when you notice the girls saying mean things so you don't feel depressed and isolate yourself.

Client: What should I think instead?

Therapist: I don't know. What do you think might be more helpful than "I'm such a loser"?

Client: Maybe I could tell myself what I would tell my sister?

Therapist: Which is . . .?

Client: I don't like when the girls say mean things about me, but it doesn't mean I'm a loser.

Therapist: That's a great start. So what does it mean about you when they say mean things about you?

Client: Nothing!

Therapist: Cool. That's awesome Allison. How do you feel now when you say, "I don't like it when they say mean things about me but it doesn't mean anything about me when they do?"

Client: I guess it's like we talked about before—I definitely still feel sad because it's hard to hear those things, but definitely feel better than depressed. I don't feel like crying when I think this way.

Therapist: And do you feel like staying away from the other kids when you feel sad?

Client: Not as much.

Therapist: Good! So since we're getting close to time being up, maybe we can come up with something for you to practice this week based on what we talked about today. Do you have any ideas?

Client: I could try to sit with people from my class instead of sitting in the corner alone.

Therapist: That's great. And what if you have the thought "I am such a loser" this week? What can you do if this happens?

Client: I'll remind myself that no matter what they may say, it doesn't make it true.

Therapist: Can you rehearse a specific thought to help replace "I am such a loser"?

Client: What about "Less friends does not make me a *loser.*"

Therapist: That's really good. So can you think of anything that might interfere with doing this homework this week?

Client: I might forget.

Therapist: So how could we make sure you remember? Do you want to write it down in your therapy book? Or set your smartphone to go off right before lunch to remind you to sit with other kids and practice your new thought? How does that sound?

Client: I like the phone idea.

Therapist: Great. So you did a really nice job today Allison. I'll see you next week and look forward to seeing how you do.

Session Critique

This session demonstrates a collaborative approach to working with adolescents. The therapeutic style was a balance between Socratic and didactic, which is optimal for this particular age group. The presenting problem was quite challenging as well as very typical for a young adolescent. By validating the client's problem and subsequent emotional and behavioral difficulties, I (Kristene) increased the bond and trust with Allison. A considerable amount of time was dedicated to establishing a realistic goal for the session, with integration and repetition of information obtained from previous sessions. Looking back, I could have allocated more time at the end of the session to having the client summarize the main points from the session to ensure that she understood the process and content.

Effectiveness of the Theory Relative to This Case

One of the key tenets of REBT is that of unconditional self-acceptance. Helping this adolescent to separate her worth and value as a person from what others think, do, or say about her is the most elegant solution and will help her to cope with future adverse events. Rather than challenging clients' automatic thoughts (e.g., "I have no friends," "Nobody likes me"), REBT challenges the evaluations clients make about their automatic thoughts and inferences. This approach is extremely effective for Allison's problem, because in many cases clients' inferences (e.g., "I have no friends") are true. REBT's elegant solution helps clients cope with their worst case scenarios, thereby enabling them to better manage future difficulties. Helping Allison effectively change her unhealthy negative emotion of depression to a healthy negative emotion of sadness brought her closer to achieving her goal of making friends.

Summary

Originally trained as a psychoanalyst, Dr. Albert Ellis believed that there was a more efficient means of effecting psychological change. Ellis was greatly influenced by Stoic philosophy and developed REBT in 1955 as the original, pioneering form of cognitive behavior therapy. Ellis posited that it is not experiences from childhood that make an individual disturbed; rather, it is the attitude and the philosophy of life one takes at an early age. Emotional and behavioral disturbance is a result of *irrational beliefs:* demandingness, frustration intolerance, awfulizing/catastrophizing, and global evaluations of human worth. Irrational beliefs are theorized to create unhealthy negative emotions (e.g., depression, anxiety, unhealthy anger, shame, hurt, guilt, jealousy, unhealthy envy). The goal of REBT is to challenge and question irrational beliefs and replace them with *rational beliefs*, which are more flexible preferences, desires, and wishes. Rational beliefs are theorized to result in healthy but still negative emotions (e.g., sadness, concern, healthy anger or annoyance, disappointment, regret). As an active-directive therapy, REBT utilizes various cognitive, emotive, and behavioral interventions to help clients achieve their goals. Inference chaining, disputation, role playing, reverse role playing, staying in difficult situations, and shame attacks are some of the many strategies counselors use with their clients both in and out of session.

REBT can be applied to a wide range of psychological, emotional, and behavioral problems. It is designed for individuals at the action stage of change but can be modified to treat clients who are at the precontemplative or contemplative stage of change (e.g., children, adolescents, and mandated clients). The concept of acceptance, as it applies to oneself, others, and life, promotes understanding and tolerance of differences (in gender, ethnicity, sexual orientation and identity, religion, and so forth) among individuals. The elimination of global ratings of worth (self, other, and life) fosters prosocial attitudes and behaviors.

Suggested Resources and Websites

For more information on REBT theory and practice, please refer to the following resources and websites:

DiGiuseppe, R. A., Doyle, K. A., Dryden, W., & Backx, W. (2014). *A practitioner's guide to rational emotive behavior therapy* (3rd ed.). New York, NY: Oxford University Press.

Dryden, W. (2012). *Dealing with emotional problems using rational-emotive cognitive behavior therapy: A practitioner's guide.* New York, NY: Routledge.

Ellis, A. (1962). *Theory and practice of RET* [CD-Rom]. Available at www.albertellis.org

- REBT worksheet (see the Appendix)
- Albert Ellis Institute
  www.albertellis.org
- Albert Ellis Institute, On Demand Pages
  https://vimeo.com/user38239091/vod_pages

References

Abrams, M. (2012). Helping couples deal with intimacy and sexuality. In A. Vernon (Ed.), *Cognitive and rational-emotive behavior therapy with couples: Theory and practice* (pp. 97–115). New York, NY: Springer.

Albert Ellis Institute. (2017). *REBT worksheet.* New York, NY: Author.

Bernard, M. E. (2001). *Program Achieve: A curriculum of lessons for teaching students how to achieve and develop social-emotional behavioral well-being* (Vols. 1–6). Laguna Beach, CA: You Can Do It! Education.

Bernard, M. E. (2009). Dispute irrational beliefs and teach rational beliefs: An interview with Albert Ellis. *Journal of Rational-Emotive & Cognitive-Behavior Therapy, 27,* 66–76.

Bernard, M. E., Ellis, A., & Terjesen, M. (2006). Rational-emotive behavioral approaches to childhood disorders: History, theory, practice, and research. In A. Ellis & M. E. Bernard (Eds.), *Rational-emotive behavioral approaches to childhood disorders: History, theory, practice, and research* (pp. 3–84). New York, NY: Springer.

Broder, M. S. (1994). *The art of staying together.* New York, NY: Avon Books.

David, D., Lynn, S. J., & Ellis, A. (2009). *Rational and irrational beliefs: Research, theory, and clinical practice.* New York, NY: Oxford University Press.

David, D., Szentagotai, A., Kallay, E., & Macavei, B. (2005). A synopsis of rational emotive behaviour therapy (REBT): Fundamental and applied research. *Journal of Rational-Emotive & Cognitive-Behavior Therapy, 3,* 175–221.

David, D., Szentagotai, A., Lupu, V., & Cosman, D. (2008). Rational emotive behavior therapy, cognitive therapy, and medication in the treatment of major depressive disorder: A randomized clinical trial, posttreatment outcomes, and six-month follow-up. *Journal of Clinical Psychology, 64,* 728–746.

DeRubeis, R. J., Hollon, S. D., Amsterdam, J. D., Shelton, R. C., Young, P. R., Salomon, R. M., . . . Gallop, R. (2005). Cognitive therapy vs. medications in the treatment of moderate to severe depression. *Archives of General Psychiatry, 62,* 409–416.

DiGiuseppe, R., & Bernard, M. E. (2006). REBT assessment and treatment with children. In A. Ellis & M. E. Bernard (Eds.), *Rational-emotive behavioral approaches to childhood disorders: History, theory, practice, and research* (pp. 85–114). New York, NY: Springer.

DiGiuseppe, R. A., Doyle, K. A., Dryden, W., & Backx, W. (2014). A *practitioner's guide to rational emotive behavior therapy* (3rd ed.). New York, NY: Oxford University Press.

DiGiuseppe, R., & Kelter, J. (2006). Treating aggressive children: A rational-emotive behavior systems approach. In A. Ellis & M. E. Bernard (Eds.), *Rational-emotive behavioral approaches to childhood disorders: History, theory, practice, and research* (pp. 257–280). New York, NY: Springer.

Doyle, K. A. (2000). Cognitive and behavioral techniques for disputing core irrational beliefs in clients with eating disorders. In M. E. Bernard & J. L. Wolfe (Eds.), *The REBT resource book for practitioners* (2nd ed., I-36–I-39). New York, NY: Albert Ellis Institute.

Doyle, K. A., & Terjesen, M. D. (2006). Rational-emotive behavior therapy and attention deficit hyperactivity disorder. In A. Ellis & M. E. Bernard (Eds.), *Rational-emotive behavioral approaches to childhood disorders: History, theory, practice, and research* (pp. 281–309). New York, NY: Springer.

Dryden, W. (2002). Rational emotive behaviour therapy. In W. Dryden (Ed.), *Handbook of individual therapy* (4th ed., pp. 347–372). London, UK: Sage.

Dryden, W. (2012). *Dealing with emotional problems using rational-emotive cognitive behavior therapy: A practitioner's guide.* New York, NY: Routledge.

Dryden, W., & Branch, R. (2008). *The fundamentals of rational emotive behavior therapy* (2nd ed.). West Sussex, UK: Wiley.

Ellis, A. (1962a). *On theory and practice of RET.* New York, NY: Albert Ellis Institute.

Ellis, A. (1962b). *Reason and emotion in psychotherapy.* New York, NY: Institute for Rational Living.

Ellis, A. (1997). *How to control your anger before it controls you.* New York, NY: Kensington.

Ellis, A. (1998). *How to control your anxiety before it controls you.* Secaucus, NJ: Carol.

Ellis, A. (2000). Rational emotive imagery. In M. E. Bernard & J. L. Wolfe (Eds.), *The REBT resource book for practitioners* (2nd ed., II-8–II-10). New York, NY: Albert Ellis Institute.

Ellis, A. (2001). *Feeling better, getting better, and staying better.* Atascadero, CA: Impact.

Ellis, A. (2004). *Rational emotive behavior therapy: It works for me—it can work for you.* New York, NY: Prometheus Books.

Ellis, A., & Bernard, M. E. (2006). *Rational emotive behavioral approaches to childhood disorders: Theory, practice, and research.* New York, NY: Springer.

Ellis, A., & Dryden, W. (2007). *The practice of rational emotive behavior therapy* (2nd ed.). New York, NY: Springer.

Ellis, A., & Harper, R. A. (1997). *A guide to rational living.* Chatsworth, CA: Melvin Powers Wilshire.

Ellis, A., & MacLaren, C. (2005). *Rational emotive behavior therapy: A therapist's guide.* Atascadero, CA: Impact.

Fairburn, C. G. (2008). *Cognitive behavior therapy and eating disorders.* New York, NY: Guilford Press.

Gonzalez, J. E., Nelson, R., Gutkin, T. B., Saunders, A., Galloway, A., & Shwery, C. S. (2004). Rational emotive therapy with children and adolescents: A meta-analysis. *Journal of Emotional and Behavioral Disorders, 12,* 222–235.

Knaus, W. J. (1974). *Rational-emotive education: A manual for elementary school teachers.* New York, NY: Institute for Rational Living.

McMahon, J., & Siu Woo, C. (2012). Introduction to counseling couples. In A. Vernon (Ed.), *Cognitive and rational-emotive behavior therapy with couples: Theory and practice* (pp. 1–16). New York, NY: Springer.

O'Kelly, M. (2010). *CBT in action: A practitioner's toolkit.* Melbourne, Australia: CBT Australia.

Sava, F., Yates, B. T., Lupu, V., Szentagotai, A., & David, D. (2009). Cost-effectiveness and cost-utility of cognitive therapy, rational emotive behavior therapy, and fluoxetine (Prozac) in treating depression: A randomized clinical trial. *Journal of Clinical Psychology, 65,* 36–52.

Vernon, A. (2002). *What works when with children and adolescents: A handbook of individual counseling techniques.* Champaign, IL: Research Press.

Vernon, A. (2006a). *Thinking, feeling, behaving: An emotional education curriculum for children* (Grades 1–6). Champaign, IL: Research Press.

Vernon, A. (2006b). *Thinking, feeling, behaving: An emotional education curriculum for adolescents* (Grades 7–12). Champaign, IL: Research Press.

Vernon, A. (2007). Application of rational emotive behavior therapy to groups within classrooms and educational settings. In R. Christner, J. Stewart, & A. Freeman (Eds.), *Cognitive behavior group therapy with children and adolescents: Specific settings and presenting problems* (pp. 107–127). New York, NY: Routledge.

Vernon, A. (2009). *More what works when with children and adolescents: A handbook of individual counseling techniques.* Champaign, IL: Research Press.

Vernon, A. (2016). Rational emotive behavior therapy. In D. Capuzzi & M. Stauffer (Eds.), *Counseling and psychotherapy: Theories and interventions* (6th ed., pp. 283–310). Alexandria, VA: American Counseling Association.

Yankura, J., & Dryden, W. (1997). *Special applications of REBT: A therapist's casebook.* New York, NY: Springer.

Answer Key for Sidebar 3

1. This is an example of a vague goal. Have the client operationally define the number of times per week or the number of hours per week that he or she would like to exercise.
2. This is a vague goal. What does overeating mean for this client? What would a reduction in this behavior look like specifically (e.g., one dessert per day/week/month)?
3. Calm is not an emotion. It is more of a physiological response to a healthy emotion. Many clients will indicate wanting to feel calm as an emotional goal. Be careful to clarify the difference between sensations and emotions.
4. Feeling like a failure is not an emotion. Clients will couch a thought as a feeling. Counselors can rephrase their question to something like "When you *think* you are a failure, how do you *feel?*" This will also reinforce the B–C connection.
5. Be careful not to reinforce the concept of global ratings. Restate the goal as something like "I'm a fallible human being, with strengths and flaws."
6. Feeling stupid is not an emotion. Clients will couch a thought as a feeling. Counselors can rephrase their question to something like "When you *think* you are stupid, how do you *feel?*" (Typically the accompanying emotion is depression or shame.)

APPENDIX
REBT Worksheet

Have your client complete this worksheet during the session as well as in between counseling sessions. This worksheet provides practice in identifying, disputing, and replacing irrational beliefs with healthier alternatives for both the new REBT counselor as well as the client.

A Activating Event(s)	B Beliefs	C Consequences	D Disputes/ Interventions	E Effective Emotional Responses

Homework:

Notes:

Chapter 5

Multimodal Therapy

Gary B. Kelley

Multimodal therapy (MMT) is a comprehensive psychotherapy that was developed by Dr. Arnold Lazarus, the first psychologist to apply desensitization in treating phobias in a group therapy modality. Currently, MMT is assumed in the framework of cognitive behavior therapy and is supported by the same research and empirical studies. However, this approach to clinical treatment still remains distinct and continues to be clinically relevant.

The purpose of this chapter is to describe the features that distinguish MMT from other forms of cognitive behavior therapy, with specific information on the fundamentals of the theory as well as the process of therapy. Practical interventions and applications are also addressed.

Arnold A. Lazarus: Key Theorist

Arnold A. Lazarus, born in South Africa in 1932, has been known as "the man who ushered in the era of effective therapy" (C. N. Lazarus, 2013, p. 1). Initially influenced by Joseph Wolpe, the noted behaviorist, Lazarus recognized that behavior change was often clinically more significant than insight or beliefs alone and that performance-based psychotherapy methods resulted in more durable change. In fact, he observed that when people behave differently they often report feeling and thinking differently. In an effort to move behavioral interventions into clinical practice, he coined the term *behavior therapy* and introduced it into the literature in 1958 (A. A. Lazarus, 1958).

It is interesting that despite adhering to many behaviorist principles, Lazarus was never a fervent behaviorist. In fact, he was not overwhelmed the first time he observed a demonstration of behavioral treatment. However, as the story goes, a friend was seriously considering a lobotomy for recalcitrant agoraphobia that psychodynamic therapy had failed to treat successfully. Lazarus recommended that the friend receive systematic desensitization with Dr. Wolpe. That treatment was so successful that Lazarus was convinced that there was considerable value in a behavioral approach.

Lazarus received his doctorate in clinical psychology in 1960 from the University of Witwatersrand in South Africa. Dr. Wolpe was the chair of his thesis committee. Having been impressed by conditioning therapy, Lazarus's thesis topic was a comparison of systematic desensitization and insight-oriented methods with phobic subjects. After completing his doctorate, Lazarus was invited in 1963 by Albert Bandura to become a visiting assistant professor at Stanford. At Stanford he became familiar with operant conditioning, which was a step forward from his traditional classical conditioning orientation, and incorporated it into his classical conditioning thinking. He published a paper on the use of these methods in the treatment of school phobia (A. A. Lazarus, Davidson, & Polefka, 1965). He left Stanford in 1967 to assume a position at the Temple University medical school, where he became a full professor and joined his mentor, Joseph Wolpe. Lazarus and Wolpe collaborated on a noteworthy book, *Behavior Therapy Techniques* (Wolpe & Lazarus, 1966), which contained the major methods characteristic of behavior therapy at that time. It is important to note that Lazarus had already begun to incorporate a variety of nonbehavioral, non-Wolpian techniques into his thinking, viewing strict behavior therapy as being too constricting. Even before publishing the book with Wolpe, Lazarus had already begun to see the value in a more robust approach to treatment, feeling that Wolpe overemphasized behavioral techniques and behaviorism at the expense of a variety of useful techniques. He wrote an article on the multidimensional approach to treating alcoholics (A. A. Lazarus, 1965) and elaborated on his views in his highly regarded 1971 publication *Behavior Therapy and Beyond*. Soon thereafter a great divide grew between Wolpe and Lazarus, as Wolpe viewed Lazarus's position as a betrayal. This severe disaffection was never resolved. Lazarus subsequently left Temple and went to Yale University as director of clinical training in 1970, and in 1972 he took a position at Rutgers University as a distinguished professor where he taught until 1997. He founded the Center for Multimodal Psychological Services in Princeton, New Jersey (A. A. Lazarus, 2000).

His first book on MMT, *Multimodal Behavior Therapy* (A. A. Lazarus, 1976a), outlined his clinical approach to treatment. This was followed by *The Practice of Multimodal Therapy*, published in 1981. In total, Dr. Lazarus authored or edited 18 books and more than 250 publications. He was considered a brilliant clinician who was pragmatic in his thinking and gifted in his approach to treatment. In 1982 he was identified as one of the five most influential psychotherapists by practicing clinicians in a survey published by the American Psychological Association (Smith, 1982). Thus, it is not surprising that when a 1978 follow-up was made to the film *Three Approaches to Psychotherapy*, which initially featured Carl Rogers, Fritz Perls, and Albert Ellis, Arnold Lazarus was chosen as one of the three psychotherapists featured. He died in 2013, but his legacy lives on.

Theoretical Overview of MMT

MMT is an outgrowth of behavior therapy. Lazarus introduced the term *behavior therapy* in an effort to legitimize behavioral interventions as important aspects of clinical practice. However, despite his appreciation for behavioral approaches, he had some reservations. For example, in a 3-year follow-up of clinical populations that were effectively treated via behavior therapy, Lazarus discovered an unacceptably high rate of relapse (A. A. Lazarus, 1971, 1976a, 1989). Although some impressive improvements were made with seriously impaired clients, individuals with addictions and extended interpersonal problems did not fare so well. He also found behavior therapy less effective when cognitive restructuring required more than mere corrections of misconceptions or restructuring of a negative personal narrative, such as when individuals had intrusive images involving self-defeating future projections or protracted emotional reactions. Although the behavioral approach successfully addressed many complex problems, 67% of clients relapsed within a 2-year period (A. A. Lazarus, 1989), which prompted Lazarus to expand his focus in an attempt to develop a more effective, multidimensional approach. It is important to note, however, that MMT did not abandon its behavioral underpinnings. Quite the opposite is true. Classical conditioning, operant conditioning, social learning theory (including modeling), and cognitive theory are all at the foundation of MMT.

Of note is that MMT is client specific. That is to say, it can easily be applied to a wide range of client populations without bias. The goal of MMT is to create an individualized treatment plan consisting of what will work best for a particular client. In other words, the multimodal therapist is less concerned with theoretical orientation and more focused on what works for whom and under which particular circumstances. This is in contrast to most unimodal therapies, which force clients into their theory; for instance, clients who go to a Rogerian counselor get Rogerian counseling, and clients who go to a rational emotive behavior therapy counselor get rational emotive behavior therapy counseling. In MMT two clients with a depressive disorder could very easily receive two very different treatments depending on how their depression presents, with clear awareness of each client's specific BASIC ID and Structural Profile.

The Seven Constructs and BASIC ID Modalities

Personality is shaped and maintained by the following seven constructs: associations and relations among events, modeling and imitation, nonconscious processes, defensive reactions, private events, metacommunications, and thresholds. Each of these is subsequently described.

People make connections and associations in life that result in experiences and learnings that have varying impacts on them and how they make their way in the world (A. A. Lazarus, 1997). Thus, conditioned responses, of both a classical and operant conditioning nature, as well as concepts such as stimulus generalization, reinforcement, negative experiences, and other learning theory principles can initiate and maintain a variety of human behaviors. Likewise, observation, identification, and imitation are the source of a great many aspects of human learning, for better or for worse. Human self-awareness varies, but it is not assumed that this lack of awareness (or nonconscious awareness) limits the influence of these nonconscious mental functions. Defensive reactions are observed in individuals all of the time as a means of avoiding something about themselves or actions that need to be taken. Private events consisting of beliefs, thoughts, internalized self-knowledge, values learned in life, or attitudes about things that one has internalized across one's lifetime impact people. In terms of shaping one's personality, these private events need not be negative but rather are merely seen as life occurrences that one has assimilated that serve as internal filters for how one interacts with the world. This in turn heavily influences one's behaviors and interpersonal relationships. Metacommunications reveal one's ability to be reflective and communicate regarding one's own communications. This ability to be reflective is quite significant at important junctures in life, particularly when change in decision making or behavior is required for effective outcomes. Finally, although many things in life appear to surround the normal or average, it is readily seen that people have different tolerances and capacities for many important human experiences, such as regulating emotions or tolerating stress, pain, or frustration, all of which contribute to individual differences and interpersonal strife. As these thresholds are exceeded, it frequently is a signal that therapeutic attention may well be necessary (A. A. Lazarus, 2003).

Problems develop in one of these seven constructs and/or an interaction between or among them. Treatment addresses and alters the origin and evolution of the particular difficulties. In many ways MMT is both a novel approach to treatment and a treatment in and of itself. A basic assumption explicit in MMT is that people move, feel, sense, imagine, think, and relate interpersonally. Accordingly, from this perspective, thorough treatment must include an assessment of each of seven modalities of human functioning for possible difficulties: behavior (B), affect (A), sensation (S), imagery (I), cognition (C), interpersonal relationships (I), drugs and basic biological processes (D). The acronym for this assessment is the BASIC ID. In addition, if treatment is to be effective and lasting, the seven constructs previously described must be referenced because this is where errant functioning arises. A closer look at these modalities follows:

B *Behavior* includes everything a person does, including habits, verbalizations, and actions. What actions or habits is the person engaging in that interferes with his or her overall contentment? What is the person doing (or not doing) that contributes to his or her current level of distress, both excesses and deficits? When dealing with behaviors it is important to count or quantify. Obtaining a gauge as to the frequency, duration, and intensity of unwanted, disturbing behaviors is always important.

A *Affect* refers to the person's emotions and feelings. What reactions are most notable? What is the frequency, intensity, and duration of these emotions? What are the apparent precursors to their appearance, and how do they connect with the other modalities?

S *Sensation* includes information that comes into the person's senses as well as his or her bodily sensations. What are the person's most prominent sensations or sensory complaints? What are the positive sensations that the person experiences as well as the negative sensations? Included in this area are sexual as well as sensual functions.

I *Imagery* refers to the pictures in the person's mind as well as fantasies, daydreams, self-image, visual memories, and future projections. Are the person's fantasies or daydreams realistic? Does the individual experience flashbacks to earlier negative experiences? Are the fantasies, daydreams, and images of himself or herself under the person's control, or are they intrusive or serendipitous? Do these images relate to other modalities, such as cognitions or affective reactions?

C *Cognition* refers to thoughts, attitudes, beliefs, assumptions, presuppositions, insights, internal dialogue, opinions, and judgments. Are there self-limiting aspects to the person's cognitions, such as irrational or delusional thoughts or beliefs? Is the person struggling with overly strict internal imperatives, such as *should, must,* or *ought?*

I *Interpersonal relationships* refers to how the person relates to people in general as well as in specific relationships, including love relationships, family-of-origin and current family relationships, work relationships, friendships, and relationships with authority figures. This also includes how the person views relationships, what kind of relationships the person wants with others, how much the person values relationships, and what the person derives from relationships (for better or worse). What kind of relationships does the person form (mutual, trusting, reciprocal, one sided, dependent, distant, etc.)?

D *Drugs and basic biological processes* refers to the person's physical health and functioning. It includes his or her genetic history as well as acquired history. It is worth noting that the drugs and basic biological processes modality is an overriding modality. It goes without saying that providing a thorough physical assessment, reviewing medications or the need for medications, and determining the presence and/or effects of substance use/abuse are paramount to providing comprehensive treatment. Also, issues of sleep, diet, nutrition, exercise, rapid or unexplained weight gain or loss, the use of supplements, and the person's general overall sense of physical well-being need to be explored.

The BASIC ID Assessment Process

To better understand the BASIC ID, refer to Sidebar 1. The assessment process is straightforward. The BASIC ID assessment proceeds along the following lines: First explain the modalities to the client, one at a time. Then, after a thorough discussion of each modality, simply ask what problems or concerns the client is experiencing in each modality. It is also helpful to ask what the client would like to experience more or less or to start or stop experiencing. For example, ask what he or she would like to do more often or less often, feel more or feel less, sense more or sense less, and so forth. Or ask the client what he or she would like to start or stop doing, feeling, sensing, thinking, imagining, and so forth. In essence, the question is "What do you want?"

Important information is also gleaned from the Multimodal Life History Inventory. This is a 15-page personal inventory developed by Lazarus and his son Clifford, also a clinical psychologist, to assess each of the client's seven modalities of functioning (A. A. Lazarus & Lazarus, 1991). In general, it is gender and culture neutral. Sections include general information, personal and social history, descriptions of the presenting problems, expectations regarding treatment together with a modality analysis of current problems via questions, fill-in-the-blank statements, rating scales, and checklists for the seven modalities. Childhood memories and significant life experiences are also queried. It is always important to assess how the modalities play out in the client's interpersonal context. A version for teenagers is available for use with older middle school clients and clients of high school age (Adams & Weitz, 1981).

When the client's interpersonal stance is unclear or unable to be gleaned from interview dialogue or the Multimodal Life History Inventory, the MMT counselor will use the deserted island fantasy technique (A. A. Lazarus, 1981, 1989). This is a projective technique developed to gain clinical insight into and understanding of the client's interpersonal dynamics and ability to form relationships. Briefly stated, the counselor enlists the client's cooperation and encourages him or her to engage in the spirit of the fantasy. The counselor then presents the following scenario: A magician is going to enter the room and transport the client to a deserted island for 6 months where all physical needs are completely taken care of. The

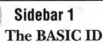

Sidebar 1

The BASIC ID

Reflect on a client with whom you have recently worked. Make a list of the issues that have been identified as targeted treatment problems. What modalities in the BASIC ID do these problems coincide with? As you reflect on this client, consider what other modalities not already addressed may need to be assessed. Discuss with a partner.

client does not have any choice about going, and time will stop for everyone else in the world. When the 6 months are over and the client returns, everything will be as it was prior to leaving. The first decision the client needs to make is whether to be on the deserted island alone or to have a pleasant companion of the same or opposite sex with him or her on the island. Although some may choose solitude, most prefer companionship. If the client chooses companionship, for the entire 6 months the client and companion are completely reliant on each other for entertainment and interactional needs because there are no distractions: no television, radio, books, iPads, or phones. Once the companionship/solitude choice has been made, the client instantly appears on the island. Once there, he or she begins to visually explore the island and is encouraged to create images and mental pictures in order to become immersed in the story. The idea is to develop a sense of what happens, to let it flow freely and to describe what happens on that deserted island.

Possible outcomes are endless. For example, how does the client conceptualize the companion, and how does their relationship develop? In the fantasy, is the companion a lover, a friend, or a relative? Whose needs are primary, and what needs are revealed? Is there harmony or conflict? If there is conflict, does it get resolved, and if so, how? Does the relationship resemble real-life relationships in the client's life? Does normal reciprocity emerge, or is the relationship one sided? Does the client strive for dominance and power, or does equality prevail? Does the companion become a trusted confidant? As the client describes the fantasy, clinical information relevant to his or her interpersonal attitudes, inclinations, and learnings becomes apparent, and this information can be therapeutically useful.

Other Features of MMT

In addition to the BASIC ID, other unique features of MMT include tracking the sequence of modalities involved in psychological problems (also known as tracking the firing order), bridging, the Second Order BASIC ID, and the Structural Profile. Tracking is helpful when progress on a particular issue begins to stall and is accomplished by asking the client to relate how he or she has been experiencing that particular problematic situation and then asking the client to notice which of the seven modalities comes to mind. If the client is vague or unsure, the counselor can assign homework between sessions, asking the client to observe his or her experience relative to the problem and record the findings. Once the client has clearly identified the initial modality, the counselor asks what else he or she noticed or experienced. This procedure is followed until three or four modalities related to the problem area are identified in their order of occurrence. This can prove to be extremely beneficial in developing interventions that are consistent with the nature in which the client experiences the particular problem. For example, treating a depressed person who is lethargic and cannot get out of bed and thinks "I am inadequate" would require a different approach than treating a depressed person who is feeling worthless, which leads to interpersonal isolation and avoidance. With the first client the counselor might start the interventions with behavioral activation and contracting, whereas with the second the counselor might begin by processing the feelings of worthlessness.

Bridging involves easing a client through the various modalities. For example, when a client begins to discuss an issue or problem, the counselor will hone in on and follow the modality preferred by the client. So if the client begins by discussing feelings about his or her situation, the counselor will explore those feelings. After a period of time, the counselor might take the discussion down another avenue and inquire about what else might have come into the client's awareness in terms of other modalities. Or perhaps the counselor might ask about a specific modality that the counselor thinks might yield more productive information. Sometimes, in addition to gaining a more robust understanding of the problem, bridging to another modality can help in deescalating an otherwise overly intense situation for the client. Switching from disturbing imagery to the behavior modality ("You are sitting in the chair, breathing in and out," etc.) can be useful. Concrete here-and-now sensations sometimes can be less threatening than emotions or images.

There are occasions when greater specificity is needed in order to clarify a particular problem, in which case a Second Order BASIC ID is helpful. In this process, the client focuses on one specific issue and applies the seven-modality analysis to it. For example, suppose that during the initial BASIC ID one of the identified problems for an elderly woman is social isolation. The counselor would work with the client to identify how she behaves, feels, senses, imagines, thinks, relates interpersonally, and responds physically to the lack of social contact. According to A. A. Lazarus (2003), "This recursive application of the BASIC I.D. to itself adds depth and detail to the macroscopic overview afforded by the initial Modality Profile" (p. 249).

The Structural Profile depicts tendencies and characteristics with regard to each modality. This profile may be constructed by completing the Structural Profile Inventory, which consists of 35 items that yield a quantitative BASIC ID that graphs a person's functional tendencies along the seven modalities (A. A. Lazarus, 1997). Recognizing the uniqueness of each individual and the need for a rapid assessment of a person's modality profile, A. A. Lazarus (2008) created an abbreviated Structural Profile Inventory that requires clients to rate themselves on each modality from 0 (*lowest*) to 6 (*highest*), asking themselves the following questions:

> *Behavior* How active are you? How much of a doer are you? Do you like to keep busy?
>
> *Affect* How emotional are you? How deeply do you feel things? Are you inclined to impassioned or soul-stirring reactions?
>
> *Sensation* How much do you focus on the pleasures and pains derived from your senses? How tuned in are you to your bodily sensations—to sex, food, music, art?

Imagery Do you have a vivid imagination? Do you engage in fantasy and daydreaming?

Cognition How much of a thinker are you? Do you like to analyze things, make plans, reason things through?

Interpersonal How much of a social being are you? How important are other people to you? Do you gravitate to people? Do you desire intimacy with others?

Drugs/biology Are you healthy and health conscious? Do you take good care of your physical body and health? Do you avoid overeating, smoking, or ingesting unnecessary drugs or alcohol? (A. A. Lazarus, 2008, p. 378)

This information can be very valuable in several instances. For example, it may be particularly helpful for clients to gain personal insights by comparing their subjective self-assessment with the seven modalities to the Structural Profile Inventory findings. It is also quite useful in couples counseling. Couples can rate themselves as well as their partners across the seven modalities to identify functional and experiential similarities and dissimilarities that may need to be accounted for in the relationship. Also, when feedback regarding their partner's profile is provided, beliefs and expectations about each partner can be adjusted. Finally, data suggest that counselors tend to gravitate toward specific therapeutic approaches and utilize interventions consistent with their own Structural Profile rather than those of their clients. There are also data to support the commonsense notion that the more similar the Structural Profile between the therapist and the client, the more effective the client considers the therapy (Herman, 1991, 1997). Learn more about your own Structural Profile by referring to Sidebar 2.

Another feature of MMT is technical eclecticism. In an MMT framework, techniques are separated from the theories from which they were developed. In fact, it is believed that techniques may well be effective for reasons not at all connected to their theoretical origins. What matters is not where techniques originated but whether the techniques work. This is *not* theoretical integration. Oftentimes attempts to integrate theories result in confusion rather than clarity. Thus, MMT maintains its theoretical under-

Sidebar 2

Personal Structural Profile

Review the seven modalities that make up the Structural Profile. Using the abbreviated inventory on pages 150–151, rate yourself on each modality by asking yourself the questions to determine your top three modalities. Share your results with a partner, discussing what you learned about yourself by completing this inventory and what implications this has relative to your approach to counseling.

pinnings while at the same time utilizing techniques from many theories of counseling and personality.

In summary, MMT is unique in its specific yet comprehensive assessment across seven modalities of human functioning, use of intentional bridging techniques, tracking of modality firing orders, use of modality profiles, use of Second Order BASIC ID assessments, and technical eclecticism. All modalities of functioning are viewed as important and have a critical interrelationship with one another. Successful treatment requires that all modalities of functioning be assessed and that those areas of significant difficulty be addressed.

The Therapeutic Process in MMT

The overreaching goal of MMT is to create a specific treatment plan unique for each client based on the psychological/behavioral issues presented in counseling. Again, it is what works best for whom, under what circumstances, and in what context. The MMT position embodies the following four principles: (a) Human beings act and interact across the seven modalities of the BASIC ID; (b) these modalities are connected by complex chains of behavior and other psychophysiological events, and they exist in a state of reciprocal transaction; (c) accurate assessment/diagnosis is served by the systematic assessment of each modality and its interactions with all others; and (d) comprehensive counseling calls for specific corrections of significant problems across the BASIC ID (A. A. Lazarus, 1997).

From an MMT framework, effective counseling or therapy depends on engaging in creative problem solving, having a constructive focus, and being brief but comprehensive. The following issues must be addressed sufficiently for treatment to be successful: conflicting or ambivalent feelings or reactions, maladaptive behaviors, misinformation (especially dysfunctional beliefs), missing information (e.g., skill deficits, naïveté), interpersonal pressures and demands, biological dysfunctions, external stressors outside the immediate interpersonal network (e.g., poor living conditions, unsafe environments), and traumatic experiences (e.g., abuse or neglect; A. A. Lazarus, 1997).

The Role of the Counselor

The role of the counselor is both educational and therapeutic. Assisting the client in recognizing cueing and maintaining variables and events that are connected to the client's problems—as well as helping the client learn skills, correct errors and misconceptions, and become functionally competent—are major concerns of the counselor functioning in a multimodal framework. Homework and practice are essential in this approach, and Lazarus favored bibliotherapy as an effective means of helping clients educate themselves. When he was unable to find specific resources that would be beneficial to a client, he would create them. For example, clients who were stuck in basic life mistakes that required changes in thinking and/or behavior benefitted from the book he wrote to address this problem, *I Can if I Want To* (A. A. Lazarus & Fay, 2000). For clients who had faulty beliefs or ideas he wrote *Don't Believe It for a Minute!* (A. A. Lazarus, Lazarus, & Fay, 1993), and for couples he wrote *Marital Myths Revisited* (A. A. Lazarus, 2001).

In the MMT framework, 90% of treatment revolves around building the BASIC ID profile, and working with the client to develop this profile is in and of itself an educational endeavor for both client and counselor. The idea is that more learning leads to more personal resources, which leads to better coping, which leads to a reduced likelihood of relapse.

The Therapeutic Alliance

Along these lines, less emphasis is placed in the multimodal framework on investing extraordinary effort in rapport building. Rather, the focus is on establishing a relationship based on respect. Certainly the encouragement and support necessary to help clients achieve their therapeutic goals and establish trust sufficient to feel comfortable with self-disclosure are required. Although multimodal counselors consider the counselor–client relationship very important, it is not the total picture. It is also necessary to address dysfunctional behaviors and cognitive distortions as well as the other modalities in the BASIC ID framework. Effective therapy requires the development of coping skills and problem-solving and decision-making skills, among other things (A. A. Lazarus, 2003), and no matter how good the relationship is, it is more important for the multimodal counselor to have solid knowledge of treatment techniques. In this regard, a multimodal counselor would prefer to be viewed as a skillful practitioner who is capable of assisting counselees resolve bothersome life problems.

Stages of Therapy

In terms of the steps and stages of therapy, in MMT there is no typical session. The counselor does not wait to intervene if it is clear that the client has immediate needs that require intervention (A. A. Lazarus, 2008). That being said, the counseling process begins with an initial interview, which is consistent with most clinical approaches. During this initial interview, precipitating events and major complaints are elicited. Significant antecedent factors and maintaining variables related to the client's current distress are evaluated. Attention is paid to all problematic issues revealed in the BASIC ID, and it is helpful to ascertain differences between presymptomatic and postsymptomatic environments. The "Why now?" question is asked to determine the motivation for seeking counseling at this point. It is also important to determine what the client wants to achieve from counseling, what strengths and positive attributes he or she possesses that can be used as resources, and whether there is realistic evidence for the client to believe that he or she can overcome the problems.

The counselor takes notes to document how the client presents himself or herself both physically and psychologically, noting any signs of severe mental illness, suicidal thinking, major depression, bipolar disorder, or severe anxiety. The counselor or therapist also determines whether a formal mental status examination needs to be performed and whether there is a good fit between the counselor and the client or the client would be better served with another professional. The counselor will also want to decide whether any information presented suggests a particular therapeutic stance or approach. For example, if the client appears to be very analytical, psychoeducational approaches in which information is shared may be more successful than the use of imagery or emotive techniques, at least initially.

The goal of the initial interview is to identify problems and issues and also to gain information that will help the counselor decide how to proceed. At the end of the first session the Multimodal Life History Inventory is given to the client to complete before the next session. If one is working with children and adolescents, the teenage version of the Life History Inventory interview form, which follows the Keat HELPING model, can be used (Keat, 1990, pp. 23–26). Keat also developed a Multimodal Child Interview Schedule, which can be used by the counselor for assessment purposes (pp. 133–136). Once the assessment is done and the Multimodal Life History Inventory is completed and reviewed, the treatment stage begins. Treating problems across the BASIC ID is essential for effective treatment. Thus, the sequence is as follows.

Treatment Sequence

The first step in the treatment sequence is to determine whether problems exist in each of the seven modalities: behavior, affect, sensation, imagery, cognition, interpersonal relationships, drugs and basic biological processes. During this process, the multimodal therapist keeps in mind salient issues such as conflicting emotions, problematic behaviors, dysfunctional beliefs, skill deficits, interpersonal conflicts, stressors, traumatic experiences, and biological dysfunction. This can help determine the presence of important problems that need to be addressed for treatment to be successful.

Second, the counselor and client need to choose three or four salient problems or issues that appear to be most important and that the client agrees to work on. Third, if it is necessary or appropriate, the client may need to be referred for medical or psychiatric treatment. Finally, the counselor must select interventions that are empirically validated whenever possible (A. A. Lazarus, 1997).

Keep in mind that the underlying assumption in the multimodal framework is that treatment must be comprehensive in order to prevent relapse. Furthermore, treatment is not complete until all of the essential problems and concerns revealed by the BASIC ID assessment have been addressed in some fashion. Whenever possible, specific techniques and solutions should be selected and implemented for each specific problem. When this has been completed, techniques such as future rehearsal, along with role playing, can be used to further avoid relapse.

Consider the example of a Juan, a 35-year-old Hispanic male who voluntarily initiates counseling. In the first session he shares that he has been abusing alcohol for the past 6 months, which has created significant problems between him and his spouse. In addition, he recently lost his job when the company he worked for outsourced his job function. He did not see this coming, so in addition to feeling extremely angry he also feels betrayed by the company. Although he has sent out more than 50 job applications, he has not had an interview. As a result, he is behind on his mortgage payments, has depleted most of his savings, and is incurring significant debt because he cannot pay his bills. His wife, who stayed home for years to raise their children, was recently able to find part-time work in a supermarket working for minimum wage. Juan thinks he has let her down and feels ashamed and hopeless.

From this brief description we can identify a variety of problems across the BASIC ID. Behaviorally speaking his alcohol abuse must be addressed. Developing a substitute activity such as exercise to reduce the level of stress and agitation that leads to drinking could be helpful. In addition, joining Alcoholics Anonymous could provide support to help him reduce his alcohol dependence. Affectively speaking, Juan has revealed feelings of anger, anxiety, shame, and betrayal. Creating activities that may increase his sense of self-efficacy, such as doing projects around the house, coaching a sports team, or volunteering in a community agency, may help Juan develop more positive feelings about himself. Certainly anger management, whether individually or in a group setting, would be important. Cognitive restructuring should be helpful for dealing with his shame and his image of himself as a failure. For example, the counselor might ask Juan how helpful it is to continue to focus on his shame, helping him see that he did not lose his job because he was incompetent—he lost it because of organizational restructuring. It might be beneficial for him to deal with his sense of betrayal by writing a letter to his former employer (but not sending it), then tearing it up and burying it as a symbolic way of letting go of the past so he can focus on the present. Anxiety could be reduced through relaxation training and through cognitive restructuring, helping Juan learn how to challenge catastrophic thinking and awfulizing in order to reduce emotional disturbance, which will in turn enable him to be better able to problem-solve.

Interpersonally speaking, the marital problems should also be addressed through conjoint as well as individual sessions. Bibliotherapy, movies, or audio recordings can be very enlightening. After reading, watching, or listening to media addressing aspects of the relationship they are struggling with, Juan and his wife can discuss what they learned and how they can apply the concepts to their relationship. If they have difficulty communicating without arguing, they can express their opinions in writing and share them with their partner. Given the extent of his concern, anxiety, and frustration over his inability to obtain work and keep up with his household expenses, it might be worthwhile for Juan to consider the possibility of consumer credit counseling and/or a referral to a career counselor to help him identify his skill sets and jobs that might be a good fit. As each of these modalities and the associated problems are explored, it is very likely that more data and information will surface, and with that new information additional treatment techniques will need to be developed to address these issues. It is important to note that all of the modalities interconnect with one another, which impacts how they present and assert themselves in a person's moment-to-moment functioning. For example, Juan's problem drinking behavior adversely affects the marital relationship. The anger, shame, hopelessness, and anxiety contribute to the problematic alcohol abuse and negatively impact his ability to constructively address his problems.

Systematically dealing with each of the BASIC ID modalities that are problematic may involve multiple interventions that overlap and ultimately result in a comprehensive treatment approach. A Second Order BASIC ID assessment would be beneficial for more thoroughly addressing Juan's problems. Gain practice with the Second Order BASIC ID in Sidebar 3.

Multimodal Interventions

In selecting and developing techniques in MMT, the most reasonable approach is to apply the technique that is most likely to address each problem identified in each of the BASIC ID modalities. As has been noted, the multimodal framework espouses technical eclecticism, so in essence the treatment intervention that will pay the greatest dividends in terms of successful attainment of client goals is the technique of choice. Unique to MMT is the fact that it uses a wide variety of techniques, and the MMT counselor is free to draw from any theory-specific intervention. The following is a brief list of frequently used techniques:

Behavior: behavior rehearsal, modeling, non-reinforcement, positive reinforcement, recording and self-monitoring, stimulus control, systematic desensitization, contingency contracting, paradoxical intention, systematic exposure, the empty chair technique, acting as if, role play/reverse role play

Affect: anxiety and anger management training, pleasant activity scheduling, journaling, bibliotherapy, relaxation training, expressive writing as a means of clarifying and releasing feelings, imagery

Sensation: focusing, biofeedback, hypnosis, meditation, mindfulness training, relaxation training, yoga, massage therapy, anxiety management training

Imagery: future-rehearsal imagery (preparing for future possible outcomes or eventualities), associated imagery (becoming immediately

Sidebar 3
The Second Order BASIC ID

Referring to the case study of Juan, select one or two problems from the initial BASIC ID assessment and do a Second Order BASIC ID. Share with a partner, discussing any questions you might have about this process.

aware of what imagery occurs with the onset of an unwanted feeling), aversive imagery, goal rehearsal or coping imagery, positive imagery, the step-up technique (picturing the worst possible future outcome to a situation and imagining oneself surviving and coping), mastery imagery, guided imagery, time projection (imagining how the future will look if certain actions occur or decisions are made), hypnosis

Cognition: problem solving, self-instruction training, positive self-talk, rational disputation, reframing, cognitive restructuring, thought records, bibliotherapy, skill training, homework assignments

Interpersonal relationships: friendship training, contingency contracting, communication training, social skills and assertiveness training, role reversal, intimacy training, bibliotherapy, stepping into their shoes (taking the perspective of the other person), conflict resolution strategies

Drugs and basic biological processes/health: healthy eating practices, exercise, recreation, good lifestyle habits, medical evaluation, habit control (tobacco/nicotine discontinuation, weight control), sleep habits and schedules, substance use control/discontinuation

Specific Examples of Interventions

As noted, multiple interventions can be used with MMT. Although MMT focuses on a systematic, comprehensive approach to counseling, it is driven by the selection of techniques that are appropriate for a particular client and, whenever possible, empirically validated. Very few techniques would be considered unique to MMT. To illustrate the multimodal approach and interventions, I present three short case examples. The first is a 10-year-old African American girl who is being bullied at school. The second is a 15-year-old Caucasian male who is referred for anger issues. The third is an adult female who is currently experiencing emotional distress in relation to the dissolution of her marriage. For demonstration purposes, only one problem is listed for each modality, but in reality there are typically several problems in many of the various modalities.

The Case of Mary

Mary is a 10-year-old girl who is somewhat socially awkward and quiet. She is slightly larger than average in terms of size, although not height. Mary is an average student with a slight speech articulation problem, one of those students who typically goes unnoticed and in general flies under the radar. Usually she eats lunch alone and plays by herself at recess. Having recently moved to this community, Mary finds her school to be very different from her former school because her current school is located in an affluent community where most are employed in professional or managerial careers. Most students wear designer clothing and have the latest electronic devices. Such is not the case with Mary, whose father works in a factory and whose mother works as a waitress in a neighboring community. Because they have to work hard to make ends meet, designer clothing and electronic gadgets are not part of Mary's everyday life. Since arriving at the school she has been feeling like an outsider and other students have treated her as such, letting her know that there is no place for her in their social groups. Two girls in particular have been threatening and unkind to her, regularly making nasty comments about her clothes, her weight, and her speech. As result, Mary does not want to go to school, complaining of headaches, stomachaches, and general unhappiness. She has become very withdrawn at home and shows no interest in doing schoolwork. On several occasions her mother has found her crying in her bedroom after school, but Mary has been reluctant to talk about her feelings. Eventually she tells her mother about the girls at school and that she feels ugly, stupid, and like a loser. She says that she thinks other kids are better than she is and that she will never fit in at school. She wants to have friends and feel like she belongs so that she can be happy again.

Table 5.1 shows an adaptation of the BASIC ID assessment and intervention process for children. This HELPING model is described in more detail later in this chapter.

The Case of Jalen

Jalen is a 15-year-old Caucasian male who has been referred for counseling in relation to behavioral difficulties in the classroom. Although nonviolent, he frequently uses inappropriate language, talks back to teachers, and challenges administrators and at times can be threatening to others. In general, his fellow students are afraid of him, as he tends to be angry and unpredictable. When the counselor meets with his parents, his father in particular presents himself in a similar fashion. Thus, there may well be some role modeling influencing Jalen's behavior. Also, the possibility of abuse at home is suspected but not yet proven. This is Jalen's first counseling experience, and although he does not think he needs counseling, he is relatively cooperative. Nevertheless, the counselor's first goal is to strengthen the therapeutic alliance in order to develop trust. For this reason, a more Rogerian client-centered approach is used initially to help Jalen feel more comfortable in the counseling setting. Following the initial rapport building and acceptance, the BASIC ID for Jalen is developed, as demonstrated in Table 5.2.

The Case of Ruth

Ruth is a 39-year-old Caucasian female who has recently divorced. She was caught off guard when her husband approached her about ending the marriage because she thought the relationship was satisfying and she was unaware of her husband's unhappiness. They had been together since they were 19 years old, and this is the first time she has lived independently since she left her parents' home to get married. She is depressed, anxious, and overwhelmed and is having difficulty motivating herself to do anything. Her husband had always taken care of all financial matters as the primary wage earner, and she only recently began working part time after their only child left for college. At the current time she feels confused and ill prepared to deal with the task ahead of her. Ruth's BASIC ID is shown in Table 5.3.

Table 5.1
Mary's BASIC ID

Modality	Problem	Interventions
Health	Slightly overweight	1. Initiate activities such as dance classes or school/community recreational activities 2. Consult with parents about healthy eating practices
Emotions/feelings	Sad/depressed	1. Normalize feelings 2. Develop a feeling vocabulary 3. Schedule fun activities 4. Journaling
Learning/school/sensations	Somatic complaints: headaches, stomachaches	1. Positive guided imagery 2. Relaxation training 3. Refer to physician
People/personal relationships	Withdrawn, has no friends	1. Bibliotherapy: *Speak Up and Get Along: Learn the Mighty Might, Thought Chop, and More Tools to Make Friends, Stop Teasing, and Feel Good About Yourself* (Cooper, 2005) 2. Arrange for speech and language therapy in a group setting 3. Social skills training 4. Friendship group
Imagination/interest	Sees herself as ugly/poor self-image	1. Bibliotherapy: *Vulture* (Simon, 1977) 2. Exploring self-esteem game (creative therapy)
Need to know/think/believe	Thinks she's a loser	1. Cognitive disputation and reframing 2. Positive self-talk
Guidance of acts, behaviors, and consequences	Being teased and left out	1. Emotional validations 2. Role play assertiveness 3. Problem solving 4. Tease tolerance training 5. Bibliotherapy: *Simon's Hook* (Burnett, 2000)

Diversity Implications

In using any of the aforementioned interventions, it is imperative to be sensitive to cultural issues and applications, using approaches that respect diversity and facilitate effective counseling outcomes. Whereas many traditional counseling theories may not take into account the sociocultural and systemic factors of diverse clients (Constantine, 2001), MMT is unique in that it does not adhere to a strict set of theoretical principles or specific techniques, so assessment and intervention can readily be tailored to what best fits the specific client population. For example, many diverse populations flourish in the arts and do extremely well with expressive arts approaches (Vernon & Clemente, 2005),

Table 5.2
Jalen's BASIC ID

Modality	Problem	Plan

Behavior
  Actions, reactions,
    avoidance
	Talking back to the teacher in class, defensive	1. 3 Cs
		    Catch a thought
		    Check a thought
		    Change a thought

Affect/emotions	Anger over perceived criticism	1. Teach anger management skills 2. Bibliotherapy: *How to Control Your Anger Before It Controls You* (Potter-Effron, 1998)

Sensation
  See, hear, taste, smell,
    touch, pain, tension
	Tense, hand balled up in a fist	1. Progressive relaxation training

Imagery
  Thinking in images, self-
    image, dreams, fantasies
	Sees himself as the only student willing to stand up to authority	1. Coping imagery
		2. Cognitive reframing and rehearsal: "It is not that you stand up but *how* you stand up that matters"

Cognition
  Thought, attitudes, beliefs,
    values, assumptions
	Believes he has a right to be angry because he feels attacked by teachers	1. Rational disputation of the cognitive distortion of emotional reasoning (if I feel it is true, then it is true)

Interpersonal relationships	Other students are often distant because of his attitude; poor relationships with peers	1. Identification of strengths and skills 2. Involvement in school activities 3. Group counseling 4. Teaching assertive communication versus aggressive communication and behaviors
Drugs/biology	Indirectly suggested that he smokes marijuana	1. Provide drug use information

so MMT counselors would be free to use techniques such as drawing, painting, or music to address their clients' needs. Likewise, some populations do better with a time-limited approach, whereas others may respond poorly under the same circumstances. For some, concrete solutions are more helpful than elaborate intellectualized techniques. In some cultures the counselor as an expert is viable, whereas in others taking a more subtle, reduced status position may be received more openly (Ratts, McCullough, & Rubel, 2016). Collaborative problem solving may be important in some cultures, whereas other populations might prefer a more directive, authoritative style (Sue & Sue, 2013). Failure to give the correct interpretation and sensitivity to nonverbal behaviors may be taken as an insult in some cultures, and it is important to recognize that because English is a second language for some clients, avoiding idioms that require abstract interpretations or slang is essential. In essence, counselors need to be self-aware and knowledgeable about diversity, taking into account clients'

Table 5.3
Ruth's BASIC ID

Modality	Problem	Plan
Behavior Actions, reactions, avoidance	Unmotivated, just sits alone around the house	1. Set behavioral activation goals 2. Start an exercise program (e.g., go for walks for increasing amounts of time) 3. Do one household chore every day 4. Set social dates with friends
Affect/emotions	Depressed, anxious, worthless	1. Explore feelings of depression, anxiety, and worthlessness 2. Dialectical behavior therapy/radical acceptance 3. Depression toolbox (Vernon, 2009) 4. Journaling 5. Bibliotherapy: *The Journey From Abandonment to Healing* (Anderson, 2000)
Sensation See, hear, taste, smell, touch, pain, tension	Nervous and anxious about assuming new responsibilities	1. Mindfulness meditation 2. Create a budget 3. Seek financial counseling 4. Contact creditors to negotiate payments
Imagery Thinking in images, self-image, dreams, fantasies	Pictures being old and alone; sees herself as incapable of assuming new responsibilities	1. Positive future projection 2. Review and challenge cognitive distortions of magnification and fortune telling
Cognition Thought, attitudes, beliefs, values, assumptions	Belief that she did not do enough to save the marriage	1. Rational emotive behavior therapy disputation 2. Reverse role play—making arguments for the positive things she contributed to the marriage 3. Reframe beliefs
Interpersonal relationships	Withdrawn and avoiding friends and extended family	1. Provide abandonment/grief counseling 2. Divorce recovery group
Drugs/biology	Losing weight due to poor appetite and difficulty sleeping	1. Contact/make appointment with health care provider for a consultation 2. Create a weekly meal plan 3. Cognitive behavior therapy for insomnia (Perlis et al., 2005)

communication styles, their life experiences, their values, and their beliefs. Sue and Sue (2016) recommended that culturally sensitive counselors become familiar with a variety of theoretical orientations and be open to interventions that are more nontraditional, such as the arts. Based on these recommendations, MMT meets the criteria for a culturally sensitive approach.

Applications of MMT

Like most treatment approaches, MMT will be effective with most problems. However, as problems present that are more complicated or severe, the theory and approach to treatment becomes much more significant. As noted previously, MMT is a comprehensive approach that works well with a variety of problems and populations. It has been adapted and used with children (Keat, 1985, 1990) and patients in psychiatric hospitals (Burnell & Young, 1982). It has been used to treat problems such as depression (A. A. Lazarus, 1976a), anxiety (Rudolph, 1985), sexual dysfunction (A. A. Lazarus, 1976b), enuresis (Keat, 1985), eating disorders (Kwee & Duivenvoorden, 1985), and bipolar disorder (Blasucci, 1985). It has been used with hypnosis (A. A. Lazarus, 2010) and has been combined with individual therapy (Burnell & Young, 1982) and with group therapy (Mitchell, 1982). Despite the sparsity of recent research, practitioners should not be dissuaded from utilizing this versatile and effective approach to counseling. To do so would be to diminish an approach that can be used successfully in the counseling process across populations and with a variety of psychological problems and issues.

Probably the most elaborate adaptation of MMT was done by Donald Keat II, a child psychologist who specialized in counseling children using MMT. Keat transformed the acronym BASIC ID to the acronym HELPING (Keat, 1990), which he believed was more specifically applicable. The HELPING model is described in Table 5.4 along with the corresponding BASIC ID modalities.

Although the overall categories are similar, sensation (S) was left out of the HELPING model. Keat felt that school was an essential component of the child's life. Lazarus criticized this because he felt that school was an external variable and, although valuable to explore, violated the comprehensive integrity of the BASIC ID, which he considered to be the pillars of personality (A. A. Lazarus, 1985). Lazarus nonetheless admired Keat's giftedness in conceptualizing and working with children, and Keat subsequently included sensations in his assessment model under the learning modality (L).

The multimodal process of assessing each modality, performing Second Order BASIC ID assessments, and developing comprehensive treatments for

Table 5.4
HELPING Model/BASIC ID Model Comparison

HELPING Modalities	BASIC ID Modalities
Health	Drugs and basic biological processes
Emotions/feelings	Affect
Learning/school (sensation)	Sensation
People/personal relationships	Interpersonal relationship
Imagination/interests/image of self	Imagery (self-image)
Need to know/think	Cognition
Guidance of acts, behaviors, consequences	Behavior

each problem is exactly the same with the HELPING model as with the BASIC ID. The only difference is the school component in the HELPING model and the types of interventions used to address problems in each modality, as it is essential to use developmentally appropriate strategies with younger clients.

As illustrated in the three case studies described previously, MMT can be applied to virtually any problem. It is particularly useful in a school setting, where the BASIC ID or HELPING model can be used very effectively in consultation with teachers and parents. A distinctive advantage is that often multiple professionals, as well as parents, implement various interventions, so the BASIC ID is not only a way to track interventions but an excellent method of holding the client accountable. The following case study provides an example of the assessment and intervention process.

The Case of Amanda

Amanda, an 8-year-old only child, was referred to the school counselor by her mother. The initial presenting problem was that Amanda's parents had recently divorced and she appeared to be having difficulty adjusting to living in two homes. Normally a very good student, she now frequently came to school without her homework completed, her level of concentration had declined, and her school performance in general was not as good as it had been prior to the divorce. One of her teachers noted that she appeared tired in class. She still interacted with her peers and seemed to enjoy doing her usual activities with them, but she mentioned to one of her teachers that she missed being able to walk home with her best friend every day because now she had to spend half of the week with her father, who lived on the other side of town.

In initiating the assessment process, the counselor first met with the team of three teachers. She gave each of them a copy of the HELPING model, and together they went through each of the modalities, discussing what they knew to be problematic or notable in each of the categories. If there was no information for specific modalities, additional methods of assessment were identified. The counselor also met with the school nurse because Amanda had been frequenting her office, then met with Amanda's mother in person and her father by phone. With each of these parties she asked targeted questions in each of the HELPING modalities. Following is an example of how this process worked.

In the meeting with the teachers and the nurse, they identified the following during the assessment process:

H = Health
    H1. Appears tired; need to assess how much sleep she is getting in both homes
    H2. Frequent visits to the school nurse for nonspecific complaints
E = Emotions
    E1. Appears to be somewhat anxious about the divorce and this transition; need to assess this further to determine how she is coping with this situation and exactly how she feels

L = Learning/school
  L1. Incomplete homework
  L2. Declining grades
  L3. Decreased concentration
P = Personal relationships
  P1. Peer interactions are good
  P2. Relationship with parents? Needs further assessment
 I = Image of self/imagery
  I1. May see herself as caught between her two parents
N = Cognitions/need to know
  N1. How to express her feelings about the divorce and transition
  N2. Coping skills for moving back and forth
  N3. How to complete homework
G = Guidance of actions, behaviors
  G1. Arriving at school without homework completed
  G2. Concentration is more difficult
  G3. Difficulty adjusting to living in two homes
  G4. Declining grades

Note that some of the problems overlap—for example, problems with concentration can be categorized as behavior but also as school performance. It is more important to be thorough in the assessment as opposed to worrying about what should be in which modality.

After the initial assessment with the teachers and school nurse, who contributed the aforementioned information, the counselor met with the mother (and talked with the father), asking pertinent questions in each modality, specifically inquiring about how much sleep Amanda was getting and whether she complained of headaches and stomachaches at home as she did at school. She suggested that the parents monitor her sleep in each home and get a medical evaluation to address these health-related complaints at school. The counselor asked both parents how they felt Amanda was dealing with the transition: Had she expressed her feelings? Had they seen more tears, tantrums, or other signs of anxiety or sadness/depression? In general, how did they see her at home, and how did her present behavior compare to how she had been before the divorce? Both parents were very forthcoming, sharing that initially when they separated Amanda had appeared sad and was quite tearful, but now that had subsided. They both claimed that they were trying to maintain a routine and that they did structure in time for her to do homework, but because she had always been a good student, they had not been checking it, which the counselor suggested they start doing. Although both parents seemed concerned about her declining grades and lack of concentration, they did not think she was terribly sad about their divorce or anxious about living in two homes. They both shared that Amanda was very loving toward them both and that they got along quite well, so there was no arguing or tension.

After gathering this information, the counselor added what she had learned from the parents to the HELPING assessment and decided on a plan of action to collect further data. She thought that it was imperative to do an assessment of how Amanda was feeling about the divorce and living arrangements, and she did this by selecting a book about parental divorce. After she and Amanda read it, they discussed how the feelings of the characters in the story were like or unlike Amanda's feelings. The counselor also had Amanda draw a picture of what it was like to transition between two homes and make a collage about how she felt about her parents' divorce. In addition, she developed some unfinished sentences that directly asked for feelings about Amanda's living situation. Consequently, she learned that Amanda was indeed very sad and somewhat anxious about living in two homes.

The next step after this assessment was to meet with the parents, teachers, and nurse in order to share any new data and develop specific interventions to address the problems identified in each modality. Everyone agreed that the most important modality to address was emotions because that probably impacted Amanda's inability to sleep, her lack of concentration, and consequently her declining grades. The counselor suggested putting Amanda in a small group with other children her age whose parents had also divorced. She also planned to meet with Amanda individually, inviting her to write and illustrate a book expressing how she felt about her parents' divorce. The counselor thought she would use bibliotherapy and have Amanda keep a feelings journal, drawing pictures or writing about her feelings each day. They would also play several feelings games. The counselor suggested that the parents talk to their daughter more openly about how she was dealing with things and reassure her that they both loved her and cared about her feelings. In addition, the teachers said that they would e-mail or text both parents about homework assignments so that they could monitor this more carefully.

After several weeks, Amanda's journal began to reflect less sadness and more acceptance of her situation. The divorce group was very instrumental in helping her see that she was not alone and that others were dealing with similar issues. Over time, Amanda's grades started to improve, and her teachers as well as her parents felt like she was getting back on track.

As this case illustrates, the HELPING model is a very comprehensive assessment model that elicits information from multiple sources. Furthermore, interventions are often implemented by teachers, parents, as well as the counselor, depending on the main issues that are targeted. In this example, because emotions were targeted first, the counselor was the best person to implement the interventions, but this could vary depending on the problems and who is best suited to implementing appropriate strategies to address them. Gain more experience with the BASIC ID and the HELPING models by referring to Sidebar 4.

Efficacy of MMT

MMT is pragmatic in its application, comprehensive in its assessment and interventions, brief in nature, and based on a foundation of cognitive–

> **Sidebar 4**
> ### Assessing Modalities
> Having been exposed to Lazarus's BASIC ID and Keat's HELPING model, and having created your own Structural Profile, identify the modalities you typically use when working with clients. Further reflect on how you might broaden your approach in terms of utilizing other modalities in order to meet the needs of clients with a variety of presenting problems. Discuss in a small group.

behavioral research. It has been applied to many different problems and populations and focuses on empirically validated treatment strategies. However, there is little in terms of research specifically on MMT. This is partly because it is easier to research a single modality than multiple modalities. In addition, because the treatment is so individualized there is no standardized form of treatment other than the basic approach. As has been noted, two people with the same diagnosis (e.g., depression), because of their unique personalities, life experiences, histories, genetics, and so forth, are unlikely to receive the same treatment interventions.

Dr. Lazarus was the driving force behind MMT. There was a flourish of publications when the approach first entered the psychotherapy field from the mid-1970s to the late 1990s. Since that time there have been very few new professional publications on and very little new research utilizing this approach. The sparse research includes one study done with children with learning disabilities that supported the use of a multimodal framework (Williams, 1988). Another study completed with hospitalized patients diagnosed with either obsessive-compulsive disorder or phobias who had experienced prior treatment failure revealed that the multimodal approach provided substantial improvement that was maintained at a 9-month follow-up (Kwee, 1984). When recovery-focused MMT was combined with standard care, significant improvements in symptoms and functioning were obtained in an inpatient treatment-resistant psychotic population compared with a control group (Patte, Simpson, & Laidlaw, 2003). Some informative research has been completed using the Structured Profile Inventory. It was found that when clients and counselors are widely discrepant on the Structural Profile Inventory, treatment outcomes are negatively affected (Herman, 1991).

There is also the issue of whether there is a need to assess more than the three prominent aspects of counseling addressed by most practitioners, particularly those of the cognitive–behavioral orientation. Specifically, is dealing with thoughts, feelings, and behaviors not sufficient? Don't practitioners typically include the other four modalities as a rule in their practice? Although there may be some validity to this position, separating out interpersonal relations from behavior, sensations from affect, and imagery from cognitions as well as focusing on a robust modality of basic biological functioning and the relationship between these modalities ensures greater focus in both assessing and understanding a client's condition and treatment.

Burnell (Burnell & Young, 1982) wrote an incisive appraisal of the MMT approach. In this thorough assessment, she provided strong, logical support in favor of the multimodal approach. She addressed the criticisms levied at MMT by Aaron Beck, who questioned whether MMT is a therapy or merely an approach, referring to the three components of the MMT framework (Beck, 1977). These components are the comprehensiveness/completeness assumption, the separate but equal assumption, and the idea that MMT is a theoretical position. Concerns over technical eclecticism and the notion that this framework is too mechanistic, which renders the counselor merely a technician, diminish the integrative role that the counselor performs. It should be pointed out that the BASIC ID assessment is not a static event but rather an emerging process that occurs throughout the counseling process as new data arrive and context changes. It must also be noted that a ripple effect occurs in counseling whereby movement in one modality can, and frequently does, affect other modalities of functioning. The multimodal framework provides a roadmap for counselors to follow that facilitates completeness. It also allows for the rational sequencing of interventions, with priority given to the most urgent needs while interventions that, although important, do not necessitate immediate implementation are delayed. The idea that theory drives the therapy, as is the case with cognitive–behavioral treatment, would appear to be equally as accurate or more accurate in the multimodal framework. The technical eclecticism position (again as opposed to theoretical integration) allows the counselor to be specific and precise in exactly what interventions to use under what conditions, which can then be assessed for their effectiveness in terms of behavior change. This is as opposed to staying within a particular theoretical framework that, when treatment is ineffective, resorts to the same treatment framework and intervention.

Verbatim Transcript: MMT

The following verbatim transcript of a fourth session is presented in order to illustrate the information about the principles and practices of MMT as described in this chapter. I provide a brief overview of the case, the actual transcript, a short critique of the session, and an explanation as to why I think this theory effectively addressed the problem.

Overview

Jason was a third-generation 17-year-old Asian American male. His father was an American Vietnam War veteran and his mother a Vietnamese refugee. Jason was referred for counseling by his parents because of anxiety and had been seen on three prior occasions. In the first session an initial diagnostic interview was completed; it was determined that he was a suitable candidate for counseling and had no serious dysfunction. Jason was polite and respectful, but he avoided eye contact, and it was clear that anxiety played a significant role in his interactions. As a result, a very nonthreatening relaxation exercise consisting of tightening and relaxing various large muscle groups was conducted. This exercise appeared beneficial, and Jason's tension was noticeably reduced after the exercise was completed.

During the second session a BASIC ID profile was configured, and Jason was asked to complete the Multimodal Life History Questionnaire for Teenagers before the third session. During the third session the questionnaire was reviewed with Jason. Results of the BASIC ID profile revealed the following: behaviors of staying around the house and avoiding eye contact, feelings of loneliness and anxiety, sensations of butterflies in his stomach and tension in his body, images of rejection and fear of the future, cognitive distortions of all-or-nothing thinking and emotional reasoning, relationships characterized by avoiding peers, and excessive amounts of sedentary activity. Jason acknowledged being quite anxious in the following performance-based situations: taking tests and quizzes, giving a presentation in front of the class, and performing on stage with the school orchestra. He also shared that he was quite shy around girls and was worried about graduating from high school and moving away from home to attend college. His anxiety about college was along the lines of anxious future projections, even though he was an excellent student who was well prepared to compete successfully at even the most challenging universities. Thus, worry/generalized anxiety was also a major component.

After reviewing the BASIC ID during the third session, Jason agreed to work on his anxiety utilizing a relatively safe and nonthreatening intervention. He chose to begin a program of aerobic exercise at the fitness center where his family had a membership. Having experienced the benefits of the relaxation exercise, this seemed like a reasonable starting place. He agreed to exercise twice between sessions. What follows is the transcript of the fourth session, with me as the counselor.

Transcript of the Fourth Session

Therapist: So Jason, how did things go this week? We had decided that you would begin exercising between sessions.

Client: Not so well!

Therapist: Not so well? Tell me about that.

Client: Well, I had planned to go to the fitness center on Tuesday and Thursday of last week. However, when I started to get ready to go, I guess I found other things to do.

Therapist: Found other things to do? Please tell me more about that.

Client: Well, you know, like playing on the Xbox, that sort of thing.

Therapist: Playing on the Xbox. Anything else?

Client: Not really! The Xbox is in my bedroom so it's really easy to get on it. I have a lot of games on it that are really cool.

Therapist: I'm wondering if you also have difficulty getting started on other things, like chores or family activities?

Client: I don't know. I guess you'd have to ask my parents.

Therapist: Well, that would be a good idea, but your parents are not here right now, so why don't you tell me how you see it as best you can.

Client: Maybe; I do, but I don't think any more than other kids my age.

Therapist: So what happened was that you started getting ready to go to the fitness center and instead you played on your Xbox. Is that right?

Client: Yeah that's pretty much it.

Therapist: Sometimes there is more going on than what we are aware of at the moment when we fail to accomplish things that we set out to do. For example, when you were starting to get ready to go to the fitness center, what were you thinking? What sorts of things came to mind? What were you aware of?

Client: To be honest, I was really thinking about being at the fitness center with all those people. You know how fitness centers are, they are always crowded and people always seem to know other people. I guess I just got nervous thinking all those people will be staring at me.

Therapist: The thought of people looking at you while you were exercising made you nervous. Tell me more about that!

Client: I'm not a big exercise person, so I'm sure that the other people there will know how to use the machines and be able to do the exercises much better than me.

Therapist: In essence you were thinking that other people would be judging you and that if you didn't do things exactly right that it would mean that you are somehow inferior or defective? Is that right?

Client: Partly! There are not very many people who are Vietnamese in this area, and I always kind of feel out of place. Maybe it's just me, but it seems that people stare at me an awful lot.

Therapist: Always kind of feel out of place? Help me out. Tell me what that's like for you.

Client: It's not like I think that I'm really weird or anything like that. It's more like everyone else is wearing a red jacket and I'm the only one wearing a green one. Like I'm different, like I stand out. I just don't feel comfortable.

Therapist: So let me just take a moment here to catch up with what you are telling me. You started to get ready to go to the fitness center but then you began to think about what might happen if you in fact went there. You began thinking that other people might be looking at you and judging you, and you felt uncomfortable. It sounds like some of that comes from not being familiar with the equipment, but some of it has to do with feeling like you don't fit in with other people because of your Asian heritage. You feel uncomfortable, like you stand out. And because of that you avoided going to the fitness center and instead played with your Xbox. Did I get that right?

Client: That's pretty much it. But when I hear it out loud that way it sounds strange. I mean I've really never stopped to think about things that way.

Therapist: As I was going over what you are telling me, were there any pictures or images that came to mind?

Client: I did see, in my head, being at the fitness center and people staring at me. It was kind of creepy to be thinking that. I mean, it's not like I haven't had those kinds of pictures in my head before, but I never talked about them with anybody or even spent much time thinking about them myself.

Therapist: Are there other pictures or images that you are aware of?

Client: Not that I can think of right now.

Therapist: It seems that going to the fitness center initially may have seemed like a low-stress activity to help you reduce your anxiety, but as it turns out, going there created more anxiety for you.

Client: Yeah, it does seem that way now.

Therapist: But now that we've started down this path of going to the fitness center, how would you feel about continuing to use this opportunity at the fitness center to address your anxiety in a little different way?

Client: Can you tell me what you're thinking first before I give you my answer?

Therapist: Of course! If you are uncomfortable with what I'm suggesting, we can do something else. What I was thinking was that perhaps we could use the fitness center to help you get more comfortable in places where people might look at you. I was thinking that perhaps you could drive to the fitness center and just walk into the building and check it out without intending to exercise. This would give you an opportunity to become more comfortable there and to notice how people are acting. Specifically, you might spend a few moments looking around the room and noticing that most people are totally focused on their own activities when they're exercising. While I am sure some of the people there may notice you and look in your direction, you may also find that most of the people are focusing on their own goals and activities. What do you think about that?

Client: I think I could do that!

Therapist: Have you ever heard of the 5 Ps?

Client: No!

Therapist: It stands for "Prior planning prevents poor performance." So let's make a plan so that things will turn out better this time. To start with, when you are getting ready to go to the fitness center, what would be helpful for you to be thinking?

Client: I start to get real uncomfortable!

Therapist: Right, you get uncomfortable and just before that, what are you thinking?

Client: I'm thinking that people will be looking at me.

Therapist: People will be looking at you! So?

Client: When people look at me I think they are judging me, and that's what makes me feel uncomfortable.

Therapist: And how do you know that they are judging you or even thinking about you at all?

Client: I don't know for sure; I just feel they are.

Therapist: Sometimes we think we know what other people are thinking, but in reality, we really don't. In fact, most of the time we have no idea what other people are actually thinking. Some people refer to this as *mind reading*. We act and think as if we can read other people's minds. And this gets worse when the mind reading creates uncomfortable feelings because when we feel something is true, we act as if it is true in reality. This is sometimes referred to as *emotional reasoning*. If we feel something, it must be true! We treat feelings and thoughts as facts when all they are is just feelings and thoughts. I'm wondering if this is making sense to you.

Client: I get it. No one really knows what someone else is thinking unless they tell us. Feelings are just feelings.

Therapist: That's right! Our thoughts can give rise to feelings. If the thoughts are not accurate it's likely that the feelings will be off track. So when you are planning on going to the fitness center it will be helpful if you can think in a way that will not result in you feeling uncomfortable, but rather, at the very least, neutral or more relaxed. How might you be thinking as you prepare to go to the fitness center?

Client: I could be thinking that I don't know anyone there and I really can't know what they are thinking or not thinking.

Therapist: That's good! And if you think that way, how would you feel?

Client: I'll probably feel okay.

Therapist: And what kind of images do you think you'll have in your mind if you think and feel that way?

Client: As I think about it now, I can see people just exercising and not paying any attention to me.

Therapist: And how about that feeling like you stand out, you know, that red and green jacket thing we talked about earlier?

Client: I don't know about that right now. It doesn't seem to be real important, but I don't know.

Therapist: Fair enough! So back to the 5Ps. Our plan right now is for you to go to the fitness center to just look around rather than to exercise in order to become familiar with the facility. The idea here is to engage in an exposure exercise to desensitize you to the environment there. Before you go you are going to have an open mind about the people there. You can have a neutral picture of how the people are acting there in your mind. In doing so, you can maintain a more neutral emotional spot. While there, just notice what the people are doing. Does that sound like something you are willing to do?

Client: Yes I can do that.

Therapist: And will you do that?

Client: Yes I will do that.

Therapist: Great! And we can evaluate how things went for you during our next session.

Session Critique

This session demonstrates the utilization of a variety of the seven modalities in the understanding of the problem and in the development of an intervention. Tracking modalities, bridging, pacing, and leading, along with intervention development based on the modality firing order implicit to the problem, were used. The session was focused as well as educational, which can be especially effective with adolescents.

Many different directions could have been taken in this session. The issue of Jason's discomfort due to his ethnicity could easily have become the target problem. However, I decided that addressing his overall interpersonal sensitivity would provide additional data as to whether the ethnicity issue would need further attention. When questioned, he responded that he was not sure where he was at with it. Overall, the session was fairly consistent with the multimodal approach to problem identification and intervention development utilizing multimodal features.

Effectiveness of the Theory Relative to This Case

MMT posits that there is more to human functioning than a single modality. To be effective in counseling it is necessary to assess and address various modalities of functioning. In Jason's case, it was clear that he had faulty beliefs, distorted cognitions, upsetting emotions, negative images, and unpleasant sensations that all interfered with his ability to interact effectively in interpersonal settings. The multimodal counselor maintains that correcting the difficulties in the various modalities in more or less the same order in which they occurred in the problem offers the most effective means of providing successful treatment.

Summary

In conclusion, MMT can be used very effectively with clients of all ages and for a multitude of problems. Counselors and therapists can draw from a wide variety of interventions that are developmentally and culturally appropriate and also those that most directly relate to the client's learning style. The versatility of this theory is a salient feature of this approach.

MMT was developed as a brief, empirically based, comprehensive approach to providing counseling and treatment. It is based in behavior and learning theory but is flexible in terms of the inclusion of interventions. It follows the axiom of what will work best for a particular counselee and under what conditions. It provides a basic structure for understanding personality, referred to as the *BASIC ID*, and represents the seven modalities or components of human personality and experience: behavior, affect, sensation, imagery, cognition, interpersonal relationships, and drugs and basic biological processes. It espouses technical eclecticism and uses unique features such as the Second Order BASIC ID (tracking firing order) when necessary for specific problems requiring more thorough individual assessment. In a Second Order BASIC ID assessment, all of the modalities are explored for depth and greater understanding of the particular problem so that effective intervention can be accomplished. Also unique to this treatment approach is the process of bridging, which allows the client to smoothly shift from one modality to another and results in a more robust understanding of the problem. Diagnostic materials have been developed to assist with treatment, including the Multimodal Life History Inventory as well as the Structural Profile Inventory.

This multimodal orientation has been applied to a variety of populations and problems. Despite the limited current research, it remains a viable, dynamic, effective form of treatment. If counseling is about change, then MMT is the blueprint for that change to occur. Learn more about this process of change by reading the case of Marcos in Chapter 9.

Suggested Resources and Websites

For more information on MMT theory and practice, please refer to the following resources and websites. These websites provide abbreviated, condensed overviews of MMT. However, they do not contain the in-depth information provided by the books and journals in the reference list.

- Education Resources Information Center
  http://eric.ed.gov; search "multimodal therapy"
- "Multimodal Therapy: A Primer"
  www.zurinstitute.com/multimodaltherapy.html
- Multimodal Therapy: Basic I.D.
  www.get.gg/mmt.htm
- Zur Institute Site Search Results
  www.zurinstitute.com/search.html?q=multimodal%20therapy

References

Adams, E. M., & Weitz, S. (1981). *Multimodal questionnaire for teenagers.* Kingston, NJ: Multimodal Therapy Institute.

Anderson, S. (2000). *The journey from abandonment to healing.* New York, NY: Penguin.

Beck, A. (1977). Review of *Multimodal Behavior Therapy* by A.A. Lazarus & Contributors. *Behavior Therapy, 8,* 292–294.

Blasucci, A. P. (1985). The case of Joan: The "bipolar" agoraphobic. In A. A. Lazarus (Ed.), *Casebook of multimodal therapy* (pp. 168–175). New York, NY: Guilford Press.

Burnell, L. F., & Young, W. T. (1982). Individual psychotherapy. In L. F. Burnell & W. T. Young (Eds.), *Multimodal handbook for a mental hospital* (pp. 89–105). New York, NY: Springer.

Burnett, K. G. (2000). *Simon's hook.* Roseville, CA: Grandma Rose.

Constantine, M. (2001). Multicultural training, theoretical orientation, empathy, and multicultural case conceptualization ability in counselors. *Journal of Mental Health Counseling, 23,* 357–372.

Cooper, S. (2005). *Speak up and get along: Learn the mighty might, thought chop, and more tools to make friends, stop teasing, and feel good about yourself.* Minneapolis, MN: Free Spirit.

Herman, S. M. (1991). Client-therapist similarity on the Multimodal Structural Profile is predictive of psychotherapy outcome. *Psychotherapy Bulletin, 26,* 26–27.

Herman, S. M. (1997). Therapist-client similarity on the Multimodal Structural Profile Inventory is a predictor of early session impact. *Journal of Psychotherapy Practice and Research, 6,* 139–144.

Keat, D. B. (1985). Multimodal therapy with children: Ernie the enuretic. In A. A. Lazarus (Ed.), *Handbook of multimodal therapy* (pp. 70–80). New York, NY: Guilford Press.

Keat, D. B. (1990). *Child multimodal therapy.* Norwood, NJ: Ablex.

Kwee, M. G. T. (1984). *Klinishe multimodale gedragtstherapie* [Clinical multimodal behavior therapy]. Lisse, The Netherlands: Swets & Zeitlinger.

Kwee, M. G., & Duivenvoorden, H. J. (1985). Multimodal residential therapy in two cases of anorexia nervosa (adult body weight phobia). In A. A. Lazarus (Ed.), *Casebook of multimodal therapy* (pp. 116–138). New York, NY: Guilford Press.

Lazarus, A. A. (1958). New methods in psychotherapy: A case study. *African Medical Journal, 32,* 660–664.

Lazarus, A. A. (1965). Towards the understanding and effective treatment of alcoholism. *South African Medical Journal, 39,* 736–741.

Lazarus, A. A. (1971). *Behavior therapy and beyond.* New York, NY: McGraw-Hill.

Lazarus, A. A. (1976a). *Multimodal behavior therapy.* New York, NY: Springer.

Lazarus, A. A. (1976b). Sex therapy in the BASIC ID. In A. A. Lazarus (Ed.), *Multimodal behavior therapy* (pp. 205–212). New York, NY: Springer.

Lazarus, A. A. (1981). *The practice of multimodal therapy.* New York, NY: McGraw-Hill.

Lazarus, A. A. (1985). Introductory comments to Multimodal Therapy With Children: Ernie the Enuretic; D.B. Keat. In A. A. Lazarus (Ed.), *Casebook of multimodal therapy* (p. 70). New York, NY: Guilford Press.

Lazarus, A. A. (1989). *The practice of multimodal therapy: Systematic, comprehensive, and effective psychotherapy.* Baltimore, MD: Johns Hopkins University Press.

Lazarus, A. A. (1997). *Brief but comprehensive psychotherapy: The multimodal way.* New York, NY: Springer.

Lazarus, A. A. (2000). Multimodal therapy. In F. Dumont & R. J. Corsini (Eds.), *Six therapists and one client* (2nd ed., pp. 145–147). New York, NY: Springer.

Lazarus, A. A. (2001). *Marital myths revisited.* San Luis Obispo, CA: Impact.

Lazarus, A. A. (2003). Multimodal therapy: Technical eclecticism with minimal integration. In J. C. Norcross & M. R. Goldfried (Eds.), *Handbook of psychotherapy integration* (pp. 231–263). New York, NY: Oxford University Press.

Lazarus, A. A. (2008). Multimodal therapy. In R. J Corsini & D. Wedding (Eds.), *Current psychotherapies* (8th ed., pp. 368–401). Belmont, CA: Thompson Brooks/Cole.

Lazarus, A. A. (2010). A multimodal framework in clinical hypnosis. In S. J. Lynn, J. W. Rhue, & I. Kirsch (Eds.), *Handbook of clinical hypnosis* (2nd ed., pp. 239–264). Washington, DC: American Psychological Association.

Lazarus, A. A., Davidson, G. C., & Polefka, D. A. (1965). Classical and operant factors in the treatment of school phobia. *Journal of Abnormal Psychology, 70*, 225–229.

Lazarus, A. A., & Fay, A. (2000). *I can if I want to.* New York, NY: Morrow.

Lazarus, A. A., & Lazarus, C. N. (1991). *The Multimodal Life History Inventory.* Champaign, IL: Research Press.

Lazarus, A. A., Lazarus, C. N., & Fay, A. (1993). *Don't believe it for a minute! 40 toxic ideas that are driving you crazy.* San Luis Obispo, CA: Impact.

Lazarus, C. N. (2013, October). *The man who ushered in the era of effective psychotherapy.* Retrieved from https://www.psychologytoday.com/blog/think-well/201310/the-man-who-ushered-in-the-era-effective-psychotherapy

Mitchell, B. A. (1982). Group psychotherapy. In L. F. Burnell & W. T. Young (Eds.), *Multimodal handbook for a mental hospital* (pp. 106–123). New York, NY: Springer.

Patte, R., Simpson, A., & Laidlaw, T. (2003). Can recovery-focused multimodal psychotherapy facilitate symptom and function improvement in people with treatment-resistant psychotic illness? A comparison study. *Australian and New Zealand Journal of Psychiatry, 37*, 720–727.

Perlis, M. L., Jungquist, C. R., Smith, M. T., & Posner, D. A. (2005). *Cognitive behavioral treatment of insomnia: A session-by-session guide.* New York, NY: Springer/Verlag.

Potter-Effron, R. (1998). *How to control your anger before it controls you.* Center City, MN: Hazelden.

Ratts, M. J., McCullough, J. R., & Rubel, D. J. (2016). Diversity and social justice issues in counseling and psychotherapy. In D. Capuzzi & M. Stauffer (Eds.), *Counseling and psychotherapy: Theories and interventions* (6th ed., pp. 35–65). Alexandria, VA: American Counseling Association.

Rudolph, J. A. (1985). Multimodal treatment of agoraphobia: A problem-focused approach. In A. A. Lazarus (Ed.), *Casebook of multimodal therapy* (pp. 35–49). New York, NY: Guilford Press.

Simon, S. B. (1977). *Vulture: A modern allegory on the art of putting oneself down.* Boston, MA: Argus Communications.

Smith, D. (1982). Trends in counseling and psychotherapy. *Journal of the American Psychological Association, 37,* 802–809.

Sue, D. W., & Sue, D. (2016). *Counseling the culturally diverse: Theory and practice* (7th ed.). New York, NY: Wiley.

Vernon, A. (2009). *More what works when with children and adolescents: A handbook of individual counseling techniques.* Champaign, IL: Research Press.

Vernon, A., & Clemente, R. (2005). *Assessment and intervention with children and adolescents: Developmental and multicultural approaches.* Alexandria, VA: American Counseling Association.

Williams, T. A. (1988). *A multimodal approach to assessment and intervention with children with learning disabilities* (Unpublished doctoral dissertation). University of Glasgow, Glasgow, Scotland.

Wolpe, J., & Lazarus, A. A. (1966). *Behavior therapy techniques.* New York, NY: Paragon.

Chapter 6

Acceptance and Commitment Therapy

Ioana R. Podina and Daniel David
Case study contributed by
Cristina Mogoaşe

Acceptance and commitment therapy (ACT) is part of the third-wave movement in cognitive behavior therapies (CBTs) and has become increasingly popular in recent years. Unlike more traditional/second-wave forms of CBT, ACT decreases the believability of a negative thought instead of changing its content. In essence, ACT is an intervention that applies acceptance and mindfulness processes as well as commitment and behavior change processes to generate a flexible frame of thinking or psychological flexibility.

The underlying theory of ACT is relational frame theory (RFT; Hayes, Barnes-Holmes, & Roche, 2001). According to RFT, people live in a world whose functions are verbally acquired and not a result of direct experience; hence, literal language leads to a series of additional issues, all therapeutically addressed by ACT.

The purpose of this chapter is to describe in detail these core concepts of ACT and its theoretical tenets as well as to provide practical guidelines for counseling or therapy. Aspects such as the therapeutic process and stages of ACT, as well as its specific techniques, are addressed throughout the chapter. Moreover, the current status of research in the field, as well as evidence-based results regarding ACT's efficacy, is discussed.

Steven C. Hayes and Dermot Barnes-Holmes: Key Theorists

The basic foundation of ACT, as mentioned previously, is RFT. This theory, as well as ACT per se, is connected to the work of Steven C. Hayes and Dermot Barnes-Holmes.

Steven C. Hayes, PhD, is currently a Foundation Professor at the University of Nevada, Reno. He studied at Loyola Marymount University in Los Angeles and finished the doctoral program in clinical psychology at West Virginia University in 1977. He is a former president of Division 25 (behavior analysis) of the American Psychological Association (APA), the American Association of Applied and Preventive Psychology, the Association for Behavioral and Cognitive Therapies, and the Association for Contextual Behavioral Science. Moreover, he was the first secretary-treasurer of the American Psychological Society (now known as the Association for Psychological Science) and worked at the National Institutes of Health in the National Advisory Council on Drug Abuse (Hayes, Follette, & Linehan, 2004). Dr. Hayes was listed by the Institute for Scientific Information as the 30th highest impact psychologist in the world from 1986 to 1990.

Dr. Hayes has focused on researching human language and cognition in order to better understand psychopathology, with his research being dedicated to the role of emotional acceptance in psychotherapy. His work has been influenced by personalities such as B. F. Skinner, Irving Kessler, John D. Cone, David Barlow, and Dermot Barnes-Holmes.

Dr. Hayes's most important books are *Acceptance and Commitment Therapy* (Hayes, Strosahl, & Wilson, 1999), *Relational Frame Theory: A Post-Skinnerian Account of Human Language and Cognition* (Hayes et al., 2001), *Mindfulness and Acceptance: Expanding the Cognitive-Behavioral Tradition* (Hayes et al., 2004), and *A Practical Guide to Acceptance and Commitment Therapy* (Hayes & Strosahl, 2004). More about Steven C. Hayes and his work can be found at www.unr.edu/psychology/faculty/steven-hayes.

Dermot Barnes-Holmes, PhD, is a professor of psychology at the National University of Ireland, Maynooth, and was head of the Department of Psychology from 1999 to 2008. He studied at the University of Ulster with Professor Julian Leslie and founded the Behavior Analysis and Cognitive Science Research Unit at the University College Cork. Dr. Barnes-Holmes has published more than 200 scientific articles, books, and book chapters and was recently ranked as the most prolific author in the world in the experimental analysis of human behavior from 1980 to 1999. Dr. Barnes-Holmes was on the Health Research Board from 2002 to 2005 and the Council of the Psychological Society of Ireland from 2004 to 2007. His most important work includes research on human language and cognition, research that contributed significantly to the development of RFT and ACT.

Dr. Barnes-Holmes is currently a member of the editorial boards of several journals. His most important books are published in collaboration with Steven C. Hayes. More information about Dr. Barnes-Holmes and his work can be found at https://www.newharbinger.com/author/dermot-barnes-holmes.

Theoretical Overview of ACT

As noted previously, ACT is based on RFT, which is a post-Skinnerian approach to language and cognition (Hayes et al., 2001). According to RFT, the essence of human cognition and language is the ability to learn not only from direct experiences (e.g., the shape of the coin and the dime) but also from the relationship between two or more events (e.g., that a dime is greater in value than a coin). Thus, relational or associative learning is governed by arbitrary *contextual control* (e.g., a coin could be labeled as being worth more than a dime or vice versa) and based on the relation of one event to another rather than on their physical characteristics. According to RFT, people live in a world whose functions are verbally acquired and not a result of direct experience. RFT approaches the downside of living in a world with verbally acquired functions by evidencing the harmful effects of *experiential avoidance* and *cognitive fusion* on mental health. Both concepts are detailed as follows.

Experiential Avoidance

This concept represents the attempt to avoid or to escape internal events such as thoughts, feelings, memories, or behavioral responses, even when this causes psychological harm (Wilson, Hayes, Gregg, & Zettle, 2001). As research on suppression has shown, efforts to suppress unwanted internal events by not thinking about them may essentially increase emotional distress (Hayes & Gifford, 1997; Wegner, Schneider, Carter, & White, 1987). Therefore, according to RFT, when an internal event is no longer a signal for avoidance or suppression, its significance progressively dissipates and it becomes less frequent, less salient, and less distressing (Hayes & Wilson, 1994).

Cognitive Fusion

The process of experiencing thoughts as reality rather than as the result of a process of thinking is called *cognitive fusion* (Hayes, Luoma, Bond, Masuda, & Lillis, 2006). Cognitive fusion stands for an association between language labels, internal events, and self. For example, when one says, "I am depressed," and believes in it, there is a fusion between the verbal label, the emotion elicited by the thought, and an alteration in the sense of self. In other words, cognitive fusion indicates that the client has fused with the verbal label and perceives it as a matter of identity and not merely as an emotion.

Although experiential avoidance and cognitive fusion are central to RFT, literal language leads to a series of additional issues, all therapeutically addressed by ACT. These additional issues include (a) loss of contact with the present moment, (b) a distorted conceptualization of self, (c) lack of values clarity or values in the service of avoidance, and (d) undermined committed action to life goals and values. These four issues, together with cognitive fusion and experiential avoidance, form the so-called hexagonal model of psychopathology.

The Hexagonal Model of Psychopathology

In addition to the previously described concepts of experiential avoidance and cognitive fusion, the hexagonal model contains the four components introduced in the preceding paragraph, described more fully here. More detail can be found in Luoma, Hayes, and Walser (2007).

Loss of Contact With the Present Moment

In particular, fusion with language leads to loss of contact with the present moment. Being aware of one's feelings, thoughts, and senses is sometimes not a pleasant experience and will lead to emotions of anger, fear, sadness (Hayes et al., 2004; Luoma et al., 2007). Take for instance the experience of a claustrophobic person in a small space. Right at that moment the experience seems unbearable, and being attuned to one's present-moment experience seems too painful to tolerate. However, when one loses contact with the present moment, thinking about another place or moment in time, preprogrammed reactions start to kick in (Luoma et al., 2007). In essence, no new learning takes place, and fear continues to dominate one's existence.

A Distorted Conceptualization of Self

This component of the hexagonal model embodies a narrow and inflexible sense of identity that results in equally narrow and inflexible behavioral and cognitive repertoires. An example of this is when the client begins to identify with a diagnosis (e.g., "I am an agoraphobic") instead of referring to it in terms of behavior or emotions ("I feel fear"). Hence, all behavioral repertoires will be narrowed by this new identity (e.g., not going outside). According to RFT, language is the main reason why the sense of self overlaps with a mere verbal label (Luoma et al., 2007).

Lack of Values Clarity or Values in the Service of Avoidance

Values imply living in a chosen and meaningful way as well as reflecting and choosing life goals. However, people do not typically set life goals in a reflective, planned manner. Instead, they establish goals mindlessly or create a list of pros and cons and then select the so-called best options. Consequently, people will have a hard time being in touch with what really matters to them (Luoma et al., 2007).

Undermined Committed Action to Life Goals and Values

Committed action is a process of acting in a value-congruent manner in order to create a wholesome life of integrity, wishes, values, and longings. Being committed to goals implies being persistent in change (Luoma et al., 2007). However, the biggest obstacle to healthy, functional life goals is dysfunctional habits (e.g., thoughts, emotions, behaviors), which narrow one's opportunities and development because of their resistance to change. Hence, committed action to life goals becomes undermined by these dysfunctional habits, which are targeted by ACT.

The six elements of the hexagonal model are seen as explanatory causes of human suffering and psychopathology. At the center of the model of psychopathology lies *psychological inflexibility*, which refers to the interaction of all six elements that narrows behavior and patterns of thinking. Because of their presumed etiological importance, these elements are primordially tackled by ACT.

The Therapeutic Process in ACT

As noted, ACT is part of the third wave of CBT interventions (Hayes et al., 2006). The essence of ACT is summed up by its acronym: A = Accept, C = Choose, and T = Take action. ACT endeavors to help clients accept life's difficulties and to move in a committed manner in the direction of their chosen values. The obstacles to doing this are the components of the hexagonal model of psychopathology, especially experiential avoidance and cognitive fusion. These prevent a behavioral commitment to living a valued life. The sources of those obstacles are in essence language related, and to a large extent the goal of ACT is to create a new dictionary that will help clients reach their life goals.

The core differences between ACT and second-wave CBT forms are the following. First, the goal of traditional CBT is to dispute, change, and re-structure thoughts, whereas ACT changes how one reacts or responds to one's difficult environment by altering the function of a belief without ac-tually modifying its content. The result is a decrease in the believability of negative thoughts (L. A. Brown, Gaudiano, & Miller, 2011; Hayes, 2004).

Second, ACT does not focus on the reduction or elimination of unwant-ed internal events. Instead, it acknowledges their existence and, most im-portant, teaches individuals how to live a rewarding life in the presence of undesirable thoughts and emotions (L. A. Brown et al., 2011; Hayes, 2004).

Third, ACT's therapeutic stance inspired by RFT gives a unique expla-nation of the source of psychopathology. Therefore, altering the way one expresses thoughts in language can make a difference between "what I am" and "what thought I have about myself," between mental health and psy-chopathology. Thus, most of the techniques used in ACT deal with lan-guage and ways of expressing oneself in a healthy/functional manner (L. A. Brown et al., 2011; Hayes, 2004).

Fourth, compared to the second wave of CBT, ACT uses more mindfulness and acceptance techniques. In addition, ACT focuses on the clarification of values, uses more existential/humanistic techniques, and tends to take a more contextual approach to behavior change (L. A. Brown et al., 2011).

Fifth, in contrast to second-wave CBTs, symptom reduction in ACT is not an explicit aim; instead, the focus is on psychological flexibility and value-consistent behavior (O'Donohue & Fisher, 2009). Hence, improvements in quality of life (e.g., "How much did this thought disturb you?") and general functioning (e.g., "Were you able to do what you valued even if you had a specific symptom?") are closely followed in ACT.

Psychological Flexibility: Therapeutic Goals and Mechanisms of Change

The main goal of ACT is to foster *psychological flexibility*, which is the ability to remain attuned to the present moment and to persist in a value-consis-tent behavior change that will lead to the desired outcomes. Psychological flexibility is also the mechanism of change in ACT. Through psychological flexibility the client learns to alter the function of a belief without actually modifying its content. Most important, through psychological flexibility, ACT teaches clients how to live a rewarding life in the presence of undesirable thoughts and emotions (Gross & Fox, 2009; Hayes & Strosahl, 2004).

Psychological flexibility can be attained in counseling/therapy via six core ACT processes that are the functional alternatives to the repertoire-narrowing effects of the hexagonal model of psychopathology emphasized by RFT. These are detailed here.

Acceptance and Willingness

This process is considered a functional alternative to experiential avoidance. Acceptance entails embracing one's life events, good or bad. In this respect, for example, a client with anxiety is encouraged to fully experience the anxiety as a feeling without any defense. He or she would be encouraged to think in the following manner: "I am experiencing *x* level of anxiety, which is more (or less) than I experienced before" (Hayes, 2004; Ruiz, 2010). Practice putting the concept of acceptance to work with yourself and your clients by following the directions in Sidebar 1.

Cognitive Defusion

This ACT process is meant to neutralize undesired thoughts without actually changing their frequency or content and is a functional alternative to cognitive fusion. For example, a negative thought could be repeated out loud and rapidly until it loses its meaning. The result of the defusion is usually a decrease in the believability of a thought rather than an immediate change in its frequency (Hayes, 2004; Ruiz, 2010).

Values

An ACT definition of *values* is "verbally construed global desired life consequences" (Hayes et al., 1999, p. 206). In ACT values are typically approached as a desired way of behaving rather than a desired life consequence, which

Sidebar 1
Understanding Acceptance

In order to better understand acceptance, do the following exercise with a client or a partner. First ask the client or partner to identify a thought that he or she is avoiding. Then, before he or she writes this thought on paper, place an obstacle in front of the paper. Then instruct the client or partner to think of a solution and still look at the sheet of paper, all within a limit of a few seconds. In the next part of the exercise, instruct the client or partner to accept that the obstacle is there and try not to avoid the obstacle, but instead just focus on writing the thought he or she is avoiding. You can do this exercise yourself. What do you notice when you focus on the obstacle and when you do not?

will most of the time lead to desired outcomes. For instance, the counselor/therapist can ask the client questions that are in essence philosophical, such as "What do you want your life to symbolize?" The client is then asked to list his or her core values in various domains of life, such as family or health (Hayes, 2004; Ruiz, 2010).

Contact With the Present Moment

Being present is a core ACT process that allows a direct experience of an event as it is happening, so a person can be more flexible and can choose to respond in congruence with his or her values. An example of being in the moment is the following: "Now I am feeling distressed and I am thinking that I can't finish my research project" (Hayes & Strosahl, 2004; Ruiz, 2010).

Self-as-Context

In simple terms, this process defines a stable and present-aware person who notices the transiency of thoughts, emotions, and sensations, which flow in and out of awareness. In other words, internal events change, and because clients can notice this change, they themselves are more stable than the shifting internal states they experience. For instance, in the case of a client who thinks that he or she is a bad parent, a helpful exercise would be to instruct the client to look at the items in the room, noting that the lamp or the table the client is looking at are mere objects. However, these objects, very much like internal states, do not alter who he or she is (e.g., "Is that table you or something that you are noticing?"). The client is not his or her internal states. Self-as-context is fostered in ACT by mindfulness exercises, metaphors, and experiential processes, and it is a good starting point in counseling/therapy sessions (Hayes, 2004; Ruiz, 2010).

Committed Action

This core ACT process reminds clients of the importance of being committed to act according to a personal value. Change is a long-term process, and an attempt to act according to a value may sometimes fail. Thus, one must remember that the next moment is an opportunity to get back on track and act in a manner consistent with one's values. In other words, commitment entails having more value-consistent behaviors and less value-inconsistent behaviors, even if this means experiencing distressing thoughts and emotions at certain times (Hayes, 2004; Ruiz, 2010).

The six core processes can be clustered into two groups: (a) *mindfulness and acceptance processes* and (b) *commitment and behavior change processes*. Acceptance, cognitive defusion, self-as-context, and contact with the present moment are thought to be part of mindfulness and acceptance processes; committed action, self-as-context, values, and contact with the present moment are part of the behavior change processes (Hayes, 2004; Ruiz, 2010). The overlap between mindfulness/acceptance processes and commitment and behavior change processes, such that self-as-context and contact with the present moment are found in both categories, is intended to highlight the interrelated nature of ACT's processes. In other words, targeting one process can activate the others, and each of these processes supports psychological flexibility (Luoma et al., 2007). The order in which the six psychological processes are targeted depends on what problem is identified in the hexagonal model of psychopathology. Most of the time, interventions are introduced alongside one another because they often address overlapping processes.

The Therapeutic Alliance

The therapeutic alliance can be a very important tool in the service of cultivating greater psychological flexibility. ACT focuses on a therapeutic alliance that is "equal, compassionate, and connected" (Flaxman, Blackledge, & Bond, 2011, p. 151), and in this respect several core competencies are necessary for an optimal therapeutic alliance, detailed here.

Manner of Addressing the Client

The counselor or therapist addresses the client in an equal, vulnerable, genuine manner, acknowledging the client's ability to naturally evolve to the desired outcomes. Vulnerability can be reflected in self-disclosure of difficult moments. Thus, the counselor's willingness to use self-disclosure when needed is a pathway to a better therapeutic alliance. In addition, skills in intercultural communication are also very important in ACT and ease communication with the client. Hence, the manner of addressing the client should very much reflect knowledge and respect for the client's cultural background.

Acceptance of Contradictory Views

The counselor or therapist accepts the possibility that the client may hold contradictory ideas and does not try to argue or coerce the client into his or her point of view. The counselor or therapist should remain neutral about the client's life choices, and an observer perspective helps in this respect. Consequently, ACT is very culturally sensitive in that the counselor communicates respect and accepts cultural differences between his or her own values and those of the client.

Facilitation of Exposure to Unpleasant Experiences

The counselor or therapist encourages contact with present-moment experiences and discourages avoidance of painful experiences, thoughts, or feelings. In return, the counselor or therapist encourages acceptance of experiences, thoughts, and feelings and helps the client find a secure and safe place to confront feared emotions, thoughts, and sensations (Luoma et al., 2007).

Tailored Language and Techniques

The therapist uses appropriate experiential exercises, paradoxes, and metaphors, respecting the client's language, experience, and culture. An effective ACT counselor or therapist is able to approach obstacles that arise in therapy, as well as his or her personal setbacks, to grow and develop through experience, having a great tolerance for ambiguity, irony, confusion, and paradox.

In addition, Hayes et al. (1999) emphasized several additional particularities of the therapeutic alliance in ACT. First, it is important for the client to be open and to accept the ACT principles and strategies. Second, an important feature of an effective therapeutic alliance is the ability to foster commitment to therapeutic goals, values, and choices in clients. Third, the counselor or therapist should clarify that a value-consistent behavior change will usually result in the desired outcomes, although there is no guarantee in this respect.

Furthermore, in order for there to be a good therapeutic alliance, client–therapist communication needs to avoid the traps of literal language. Verbal modalities that are less literal help in this respect. Therefore, metaphors, therapeutic paradoxes, and experiential exercises are used, as detailed here, to strengthen the therapeutic alliance.

Use of Metaphors

Numerous ACT strategies use metaphorical language, which has several advantages (McCurry & Hayes, 1992). First, metaphors are literal and prescriptive. Hence, it is more difficult for clients to show compliance to them. Second, metaphors are more descriptive, sometimes more informative, and easy to imagine. Therefore, the essence of a metaphor is hard to capture in literal language, so clients are able to make analogies and draw their own conclusions. Third, metaphors are easily remembered and therefore much more likely to be used in other settings, which fosters behavior change. For example, take the metaphor "Your life as a movie." This metaphor is frequently used as a cognitive defusion exercise. The metaphor requires a client to imagine that he or she is a movie director with limited power and another actor is cast to play his or her life. *Limited power* refers to the fact that the client is able to make decisions only for the actor who is playing his or her role and cannot influence how the other characters act. Keeping in mind his or her life goals, the client is asked to direct the movie and his or her character according to a desired life. Important lessons here twofold: that one is in control of one's life and not the responses of others, and that paying attention to the desired end result of an action helps the client reach his or her goals instead of paying too much attention to the obstacles (e.g., avoidance of unwanted feelings). More examples of the most recent metaphors used by ACT therapists can be found at www.contextualscience.org.

Therapeutic Paradox

The use of paradox is an important feature of ACT. According to ACT principles, language traps clients in their disorders. The paradox stems from the fact that language can also be a tool to help clients. Inherent paradox is the most frequently used paradoxical mode in ACT and embodies a contradiction between literal language and the functional properties of a verbal event. One example of this is when someone plans to be spontaneous. More specifically, planned spontaneity is an inherent paradox, as by definition spontaneity rules out planning.

Experiential Exercises

ACT uses experiential exercises to expose clients to thoughts, feelings, memories, and physical sensations they fear and/or avoid. Exposure is frequently used in ACT because it is much more intuitive for clients to take part in exercises that evidence traps and issues in human language than to simply discuss them.

Overall, the therapeutic alliance helps clients identify and reduce cognitive fusion, contact a sense of self, identify valued life directions and goals, and engage in committed action toward these goals. All of this is achieved with the purpose of facilitating psychological flexibility.

The Therapeutic Stages

ACT is usually delivered in 10 or 12 sessions. However, depending on the problem it can be delivered over a shorter time period. There are five therapeutic stages in ACT. However, these do not have a fixed order, and depending on what problem in the hexagonal model of psychopathology is identified, a counselor or therapist may feel that it is necessary to omit or revisit certain stages of ACT (Hayes & Strosahl, 2004). Each stage can have one or more sessions, depending on the problem. Usually one session per stage is used in short-term interventions. The main objectives of each of these five stages of ACT are presented here.

The First Stage

The focus of the first session is usually oriented toward assessing the client's history of struggling with psychopathology and creative hopelessness. *Creative hopelessness* is an ACT intervention that challenges what the client has done so far to counteract and respond to the presenting problem. Mainly, it emphasizes that what has been done so far evidently was not the solution and new strategies should be applied. Metaphors and experiential exercises are a good pathway to awareness in the first stage (Hayes & Strosahl, 2004).

The Second Stage

Whereas the first stage of ACT is focused on making clients aware that something in the current state of affairs needs to be changed, the second stage emphasizes that attempting to control internal experiences, such as trying to avoid sadness, is the main cause of current dysfunctional emotions and behavioral responses. Clients come to counseling thinking that some of their internal experiences are harmful, and therefore their goal is to get rid of them. However, according to ACT philosophy, avoiding unwanted thoughts and emotions prevents the client from experiencing the moment, hence living his or her life (Hayes & Strosahl, 2004). Therefore, in this second stage the counselor points out that the control/avoidance strategies used so far by the client were ineffective and did not enhance his or her development. If avoidance of unwanted experiences had been effective, the client would not be seeking counseling (e.g., "Did the things you've tried before work so far?").

The Third Stage

This stage of ACT builds on the second stage in that it emphasizes that control of unwanted emotions and feelings is the main cause of emotional and behavioral problems. It introduces cognitive defusion exercises as a main buffer against control of internal experiences. The therapeutic task undermines cognitive fusion by creating distance between the thought/emotion and the client's thinking/feeling it (e.g., "This is a thought, this is a feeling, and you are thinking these thoughts and feeling these emotions, but you are not these thoughts and emotions"; Hayes & Strosahl, 2004). Another example is the passengers on the bus analogy. The driver can still drive the bus even if the passengers are shouting out directions. Moreover, the driver can allow them to shout and still be attentive to the road. By creating distance between thoughts and the person's experiencing of them it is much easier to pursue life goals.

The Fourth Stage

The fourth stage of ACT continues to focus on cognitive defusion but also introduces mindfulness in order to foster a sense of self-as-context. The purpose of mindfulness is for clients to be aware of the here and now without expressing evaluative judgments in language. In addition to cognitive defusion and mindfulness, this stage of ACT also introduces experiential exercises to address unwanted thoughts and feelings (Blackledge, 2007; Hayes & Strosahl, 2004). In ACT the primary intent of exposure is not to reduce anxiety, although this is a byproduct. Rather, exposure is intended to enable the client to engage in valued activities, such as continuing to teach despite being fearful of public speaking.

The Fifth Stage

This final stage prepares clients to deal with barriers that may come with change and to publicly commit to those efforts of change. Briefly, clients are taught that even if at times they return to the repertoire-narrowing effects of cognitive fusion and experiential avoidance, each moment is an opportunity to go back to what was learned during ACT sessions. This stage also focuses on further solidifying the relationship between goals and valued actions fostered by cognitive defusion, mindfulness, and willingness to change (Gross & Fox, 2009; Hayes & Strosahl, 2004).

Each stage of ACT follows a standard timeline during counseling or therapy sessions, including (a) engaging in a brief update and internal experiences check, especially from the second session onward; (b) debriefing the previous session; (c) setting the agenda for the current session and which of the six processes it will focus on; (d) checking homework progress; (e) supporting exercises of one or more core ACT processes; (f) assigning new homework; and (f) debriefing the current session (Hayes & Strosahl, 2004). These stages are further clarified in the verbatim transcript at the end of this chapter and in the discussion about the case of Marcos in Chapter 9.

ACT Interventions

It is beyond the scope of this chapter to present a comprehensive list of ACT strategies, but here we describe some of those that are most frequently used, grouped according to the six core processes of ACT. A more detailed set of strategies is described in Hayes and Strosahl (2004).

Developing Acceptance

Some of the most popular interventions that counteract the negative effects of experiential avoidance through acceptance are the following.

The Tin Can Monster Exercise

This teaches clients to explore the dimensions of an unpleasant event and let go of the struggle in order to accept the unpleasant experience. Through this exercise, the counselor encourages the client to explore the unpleasant feeling, event, or memory as if it were a tin can monster that can be defeated more easily if it is dismantled and each piece is dealt with individually (Hayes et al., 1999; Orsillo & Roemer, 2007). This intervention has been used with panic attack sensations, in which the client is taught to treat the symptom (e.g., a tight chest) as a mere physical sensation.

The Serenity Prayer

The implicit message in this exercise is that one should attempt to change something that can be changed while accepting something that cannot be changed. For instance, grief after losing someone is natural and should be accepted as such. The same principles are applicable to traumatic events that happened and cannot be altered (Hayes & Strosahl, 2004).

Undermining Cognitive Fusion Through Cognitive Defusion

Undesired thoughts and experiences stemming from the fusion between language and cognition are neutralized through cognitive defusion strategies such as the ones described here (Hayes & Strosahl, 2004).

Titchener's Milk, Milk, Milk Repetition

This exercise undermines the fusion between language and self through fast and repetitive utterances of a unpleasant thought (e.g., "I am a fool") until the thought is no longer seen as a reflection of self but as a mere word. It is routinely used in treating depression and anxiety (Hayes & Strosahl, 2004; Orsillo & Roemer, 2007).

Sound It Out/Sing It Out or Silly Voices (e.g., Donald Duck)

Similar to the milk, milk, milk repetition and to several other cognitive defusion exercises, the sound it out/sing it out or silly voices exercises require clients to speak very differently than usual. In this case, unpleasant thoughts are verbalized and repeated very slowly while singing or mimicking funny voices (Hayes & Strosahl, 2004). Thoughts expressed in language in this manner lose their negative meaning, which helps clients detach from the negative content of their thoughts. Learn more about cognitive defusion by following the instructions in Sidebar 2.

Increasing Present-Moment Awareness

When individuals are present-moment aware, they can be more flexible and choose to respond in congruence with their values. Some of the most often used ACT strategies for increasing contact with the present moment are the following.

Mindfulness Exercises

These types of exercises are useful to bring present-moment focus into counseling or therapy sessions through techniques such as visualization exercises (e.g., "See this pencil from all its sides. When you have a clear image of this object, focus on the details like color, surface, shape"; Hayes et al., 2004; Hofmann & Asmundson, 2008).

The Future–Past–Now Exercise

Psychological flexibility is best manifested in the present. One exercise that can train clients to remain in the present is to voluntarily pull their attention back in the present moment when the dialogue between the client and the counselor shifts into the past or into the future (Hayes & Strosahl, 2004). Specifically, the questions asked by the therapist can deliberately lead to a discussion about the past or the future. However, the client needs to pay attention to this shift in the discussion and keep talking about present-moment experiences.

Developing a Sense of Self-as-Context

Awareness of self-as-context, also known as the observing self, is achieved when a client realizes that an instance of the self is constant and is different from his or her inner experiences. In other words, self-as-context is the "I"

Sidebar 2
Experiencing Cognitive Defusion

Experience the milk, milk, milk cognitive defusion technique. Identify a short phrase that you think describes you and is currently disturbing you (e.g., "I'm stupid" or "I'm too fat"). Write this phrase on a piece of paper, and then read it out loud in a detached manner. Then read it out loud as fast as you can for 45 seconds or more, until the phrase becomes meaningless. What did you notice as you did the exercise? To better notice the changes, before and after the exercises rate on a scale from 0 (*not at all*) to 10 (*extremely*) how believable this phrase is to you and how much discomfort is associated with it. Keep practicing this exercise until the believability of this phrase, rather than just emotional distress, diminishes.

that was and has always been there, and this notion of self is different from the content of the experience. Clients are taught to get in touch with an observant self, the one that watches and experiences yet is distinct from their inner experiences. The chessboard and furniture in the house metaphors illustrate effectively the notion of self-as-context.

The Chessboard Metaphor

This metaphor shows clients that good and bad private events are just components of the self, and when they struggle to eliminate one of these components, clients enter into a self-absorbed state, fighting with themselves. Through the chessboard metaphor, a client is asked to imagine that thoughts and feelings are like pieces on a chessboard: Black pieces are the bad thoughts, and white pieces are the good and desirable thoughts. When the client knocks off the black or white pieces, he or she knocks off pieces of the self. Thus, a war between those pieces is a war against the self, and one can become so self-absorbed that it is difficult to see the outside world (Hayes & Strosahl, 2004).

The Furniture in the House Metaphor

Similar in essence to the chessboard metaphor is the furniture in the house metaphor:

> Suppose you build a billion dollar house but filled it with furniture you found at the dump or at a thrift shop. Would such furniture in any way reduce the value of the house?. . . What if you are like the house and your thoughts and feelings are like the pieces of furniture?. . . The furniture is not the house and you are not your thoughts and feelings. . . . The furniture neither adds [to] nor takes anything away from the value of the house. (Zettle, 2007, p. 182)

Identifying Valued Life Directions and Goals

Goals such as identifying one's life values without fear or avoidance, as well as approaching desired life values despite possible barriers, are dealt with using the following strategies.

The Tombstone Exercise and the
Two Sides of the Same Coin Exercise

Another common exercise encourages finding values in the presence of pain and distress. In the tombstone exercise, the counselor asks clients to imagine what values they would write on their tombstone. This metaphor stimulates clients to think about their life values in the absence of fear and avoidance (Hayes & Strosahl, 2004). The two sides of the same coin exercise reinforces the idea that a person cannot achieve valued life goals without some amount of pain or distress. Practice it in Sidebar 3.

Sidebar 3

Understanding the Relationship Between Pain and Values

Together with a partner, use this exercise to understand the two sides of the same coin metaphor. Take a sheet a paper, and have your partner fill out his or her top five most painful experiences on one side and his or her top five most significant values on the other side. Discuss the connection between the two sides and how he or she cannot have one without the other. Ask your partner to try to eliminate the unpleasant and painful side by hiding it or pushing it away. Then use this metaphor to discuss how pushing away one's pain results in pushing away one's values. With the help of your partner practice this exercise on yourself.

The What if No One Could Know Exercise

The counselor asks the client, "Imagine no one could know of your achievements: Then what would you value?" (Hayes & Strosahl, 2004, p. 48). This technique helps the client think about his or her life values independent of other persons' life values.

Developing Patterns of Committed Action

Strategies that reflect the committed action core process emphasize that change is a long-term process and that an attempt to act according to a value may sometimes fail. Therefore, clients must remember that the next moment is an opportunity to get back on track and act in a manner consistent with their values. The following strategies can enhance committed action toward life values.

The Choosing Not to Choose Exercise

The counselor explains to clients that they cannot avoid a choice because even no choice is actually a choice. Therefore, choosing one type of action is inevitable in every situation. Hence, why not choose a value-congruent action (Hayes & Strosahl, 2004)?

The Taking Responsibility for Each Act Exercise

The counselor or therapist contrasts clients' successes and failures by asking them to write a narrative self-description. An example looks like this: "I chose to stop eating junk food, but I just couldn't. What is the point of continuing if I failed in my commitment?" Finding arguments in favor of persevering toward change helps clients to better commit to action despite barriers (Hayes & Strosahl, 2004).

Applications of ACT

Since it was developed in the late 1980s, a growing number of randomized controlled trials (RCTs) have investigated the efficacy and effectiveness of

ACT (A-Tjak et al., 2014; Powers, Zum Vorde Sive Vording, & Emmelkamp, 2009). More specifically, in the past two decades, ACT has been used in the treatment of anxiety and depression (Arch et al., 2012; England et al., 2012; Folke, Parling, & Melin, 2012; Forman et al., 2012); other mental health disorders, such as psychosis, borderline personality disorder, and trichotillomania (Morton, Snowdon, Gopold, & Guymer, 2012; Shawyer et al., 2012; White et al., 2011; Woods, Wetterneck, & Flessner, 2006); addiction (Hayes et al., 2004; Luoma, Kohlenberg, Hayes, & Fletcher, 2012; Petersen & Zettle, 2009; Smout et al., 2010; Stotts et al., 2012); and somatic health problems (Gregg, Callaghan, Hayes, & Glenn-Lawson, 2007; Hesser et al., 2012; Jensen et al., 2012; Wicksell, Melin, Lekander, & Olsson, 2009). Despite its multiple applications, ACT's therapeutic stance is largely used to treat posttraumatic stress disorder (PTSD) and chronic pain. With respect to the targeted populations, ACT has also recently been used in work with children and adolescents. These applications are described here.

ACT Applications With PTSD

In ACT clients are taught that they do not necessarily need to accept each and every situation. For example, some situations are not acceptable even in the short term, such as domestic violence or child abuse. But other situations, such as physical reality or historical events, should be ultimately accepted in the present or should be accepted with the expectation of eventual change (Mattaini, 1997). A good example of something that should be ultimately accepted is the experience of certain traumatic events. The event already happened; it is in the past, so the client has the option to accept it as he or she would accept any historical event. PTSD sufferers can accept the experience(s) they have had without fusing with the thoughts and emotional pain associated with that experience(s), thus paving the way for a reduced intensity in overall reaction to the negative events.

More specifically, ACT asserts that trauma survivors often try to imagine a past that could have been radically different. This focus on the past is not helpful. Instead, trauma survivors should focus on building a positive history from the present moment forward, including all of the past experiences associated with it. In this way they accept all instances of the self, good and bad. Under these conditions, trauma survivors can begin to live a valued life, incorporating the past in it instead of living a life driven by the past (Walser & Hayes, 2006).

ACT's approach to PTSD is very different from cognitive therapy's approach, for instance. The differences between these approaches become quite apparent when one thinks of their therapeutic goals. In ACT symptom reduction per se is not an explicit aim (O'Donohue & Fisher, 2009). Consequently, ACT does not directly target symptom reduction in PTSD but rather aims for psychological flexibility and value-consistent behaviors. Symptom reduction is a byproduct of this goal.

Moreover, whereas cognitive therapy's challenging thoughts strategy may be more suited to certain types of adverse experiences, ACT can be more suited to others. For example, it would not be very helpful to tell someone who was sexually abused in childhood that the disturbing thoughts that arise in sexually intimate situations are irrational. Instead, ACT focuses on helping the client come to terms with what happened, exposing the client to the thoughts and feelings retrieved by the event, and eventually helping the client to accept the traumatic experience. In the process, the client becomes aware that previous strategies of avoidance did not work. Moreover, in his or her attempt to control the negative thoughts and feelings, the client lost control over life in general. The client is taught to observe and learn to be distinct from his or her inner experiences. Eventually the client can regain control by being willing to experience, accept, and face negative thoughts and emotions.

ACT Applications With Chronic Pain

According to ACT, clients dealing with chronic pain need to learn to accept their reality for now. That is to say, through medical treatment and/or pain management, improvement will come gradually, so clients would benefit significantly from learning to accept the situation they find themselves in for now or accept the situation and expect eventual change. As in the case of the PTSD example, it would not be very helpful to ask chronic pain sufferers to challenge the logical and/or empirical evidence supporting their thoughts about the intense pain they feel almost constantly (Dahl, Wilson, & Nilsson, 2004). Instead, mindfulness helps them accept the pain but not identify with it or let it present a serious obstacle to their life goals, as in the following example: "Notice that you are not just your body, your feelings, and your pain. These are fragments of your life. No matter what happens, you remain the same, noticing the pain, but not being the pain."

ACT Applications With Children and Adolescents

The literature on ACT for children and adolescents is still in the early stages of development. However, ACT's philosophy is considered to be successfully adapted for this age range (Baer, 2015; Greco & Hayes, 2008; Hayes & Strosahl, 2004).

The case conceptualization in ACT is a little different for children than it is for adults. According to Hayes (2004), it should focus on cores areas such as (a) assessment of the frequency, intensity, and type of the difficult behavior; (b) identification of the triggers of such behavior, including internal and external events; (c) identification of the distressing thoughts, feelings, memories that the child avoids; (d) the strategies of experiential avoidance/control that the child uses to keep these experiences in check; (e) identification of the short-term reinforcers (e.g., feeling less anxious) that maintain these counterproductive strategies; (f) assessment of the client's valued directions in school, recreation, friendships, and family; and (g) assessment of the extent to which difficult behaviors are interfering with the desired life outcomes.

Another characteristic of ACT with children is represented by the different gradation and mode of application of the therapeutic components. For example, developing a sense of self-as-context and making contact with the present moment may be too abstract for children, especially young children, to grasp (Murrell & Scherbarth, 2006). To overcome this and increase the effectiveness of treatment, the use of metaphors such as mud in a glass has been suggested (Murrell, Coyne, & Wilson, 2004). The mud in a glass metaphor alludes to a painful treatment process that is like a glass of muddy water. In order to solve the problems embodied by the mud, one has to first make a mess in order for the glass to be clean again. This metaphor is quite frequently used, as it can be easily visualized with the help of an actual muddy glass whose water becomes dirtier in the process of trying to extract the mud.

The primary particularity of ACT with children and adolescents is the use of metaphors. In essence, metaphors are used to help explain the core concepts of ACT (e.g., cognitive defusion), which can be difficult for children to grasp if explained directly (Murrell et al., 2004). Given the relative lack of data on the time spent on the specific components of the intervention or their order, it is recommended that the ACT counseling process with children and adolescents be client driven and session specific (Murrell et al., 2004).

Efficacy of ACT

In order to assess the evidence-based efficacy of the theory and practice, it is important to look at some of the meta-analyses published so far, all targeting adults. We identified four meta-analyses that assessed whether ACT is superior to placebo, treatment as usual (TAU), or established psychotherapeutic interventions (e.g., cognitive therapy, CBT; A-Tjak et al., 2014; Öst, 2008, 2014; Powers et al., 2009). However, relatively few studies included in these meta-analyses included RCTs, especially when separated by disorder. For instance, the Öst (2014) meta-analysis included five RCTs on depression, four on psychotic symptoms, two on math/test anxiety, three on generalized anxiety disorder, two on social anxiety, eight on addiction/drug abuse/nicotine dependence, one on trichotillomania, two on borderline personality disorder, nine on pain, and seven on stress (see Öst, 2014, for a complete list). Another recent meta-analysis (A-Tjak et al., 2014) included eight RCTs on anxiety/depression, eight on other mental health disorders (e.g., psychosis, borderline personality disorder, and trichotillomania), eight on addiction, and 16 on somatic health problems. These results of these meta-analyses were as follows.

The Öst (2008) meta-analysis revealed an overall medium and large significant effect size (ES) when ACT was compared to waitlist and a medium significant ES when ACT was compared with TAU or an active treatment for the primary treatment of disorders such as depression, anxiety, psychotic symptoms, or eating disorders.

The Powers and colleagues (2009) meta-analysis yielded an overall small significant ES in favor of ACT compared to control conditions for mental disorders (e.g., psychosis, anxiety, depression, diabetes) and physical health. ACT was superior to waitlist and psychological placebos with a medium ES and to TAU with a small ES. However, ACT was not significantly more effective than established treatments. It is also surprising that ACT was not superior to control conditions for anxiety/depression.

The Öst (2014) meta-analysis revealed an overall small significant ES in favor of ACT for psychiatric disorders (e.g., anxiety disorders, depression, borderline personality disorder), somatic disorders (e.g., pain of various types, headache, epilepsy, cancer), and work stress. Compared to waitlist or TAU, ACT was superior, with a medium ES. It is interesting that ACT was not significantly superior to placebo. Compared to active treatment (e.g., medication), ACT was marginally superior. A comparison between ACT and CBT/behavior therapy revealed that ACT was not significantly superior to established treatments. These results were maintained at follow-up.

The A-Tjak et al. (2014) meta-analysis revealed that ACT was overall significantly superior to control conditions, with a medium ES at posttreatment and follow-up for mental and physical health problems. ACT was also significantly superior to waitlist, with a large ES, and to psychological placebo and TAU, with a medium ES. However, compared to established treatments (e.g., CBT), ACT was not significantly different, rendering a small, nonsignificant ES.

From these data, we can safely assume that ACT is (a) superior to waitlist, yielding large ESs; and (b) superior to placebo and TAU, yielding moderate ESs. However, it is not superior to established psychological interventions such as CBT, cognitive therapy, behavior therapy, and so forth.

The issue of the small number of RCTs has a direct bearing on the current evidence-based status of ACT. Öst (2014) further illustrated this problem in his meta-analysis. Using the criteria developed by the APA Division 12 Task Force (Chambless et al., 1996, 1998) and later modified by Silverman and Hinshaw (2008), Öst (2014) split the available ACT studies into (a) well-established treatment, (b) probably efficacious treatment, (c) possibly efficacious treatment, and (d) experimental treatment. Based on these criteria, the conclusions of this meta-analysis are were follows.

First, ACT was not deemed a well-established treatment for any of the disorders investigated (including somatic conditions). Second, ACT was deemed probably efficacious for chronic pain and tinnitus. Third, ACT was deemed possibly efficacious for depression, psychotic symptoms, obsessive-compulsive disorder, mixed anxiety, drug abuse, and work stress. Fourth, ACT was deemed experimental for nicotine dependence, borderline personality disorder, trichotillomania, epilepsy, obesity, diabetes, multiple sclerosis, and ovarian cancer.

Despite the fact that the same criteria were used, there are differences between the conclusions of the Öst (2014) meta-analysis and those of the

APA Division 12 Task Force. The latter evaluated the efficacy of ACT for chronic pain, depression, psychotic symptoms, obsessive-compulsive disorder, and mixed anxiety one step higher than the rankings made by Öst (2014). According to Öst (2014), the discrepancy stems from the different interpretation of the term *good group-design studies*. Another discrepancy stems from the fact that "the Division 12 website has only one or two section authors for each of the various disorders and there is no information about any committee discussion before decisions are made concerning the empirical support of the treatments" (Öst, 2014, p. 118). Another meta-analysis by Öst pointed out the worrisome fact that "third wave treatment RCTs used a research methodology that was significantly less stringent than CBT studies . . . and that none of the third wave therapies fulfilled the criteria for empirically supported treatments" (Öst, 2008, p. 296). Reflect on some of the research by discussing with a partner the questions posed in Sidebar 4.

Besides the aforementioned issues raised by Öst (2008, 2014) and backed up by data, there are also a number of different views regarding ACT. For example, Corrigan (2002) argued that the optimism regarding the third wave of CBT was ahead of the data because of the ratio of nonempirical to empirical articles, a situation that is still currently very much true. Furthermore, Corrigan argued that disseminating a therapy before its empirical findings are obtained is too liberal a view and that "therapies and data are co-synchronous; one should not precede the other" (p. 140). Another line of criticism implies that ACT and CBT, despite the fundamental differences in philosophical foundation, are the same (Hofmann & Asmundson, 2008). Especially regarding the viewpoints expressed by Corrigan and by Hofmann (2008), you should also read Hayes's replies to Corrigan (Hayes, 2002) and Hofmann (Hayes, 2008) for another perspective.

A few other recent meta-analyses and systematic reviews worth mentioning are those of Hacker, Stone, and MacBeth (2016), M. Brown, Glenden-

Sidebar 4
Research Reflections
With a partner, discuss the following:

1. Based on the information you read in "Efficacy of ACT," would you give more credit to the conclusions drawn by Öst (2014) or those of the APA Division 12 Task Force, and why?
2. In which areas was ACT deemed only experimental? How significant (or not) do you think this is?
3. Why do you think that Öst (2008, 2014) emphasized the importance of RCTs and especially RCTs with second-wave CBT control groups?

ning, Hoon, and John (2016), and Veehof, Trompetter, Bohlmeijer, and Schreurs (2016). All three meta-analyses included only RCTs. The conclusion by Hacker and collaborators was that standard in-person treatment renders no differential efficacy of ACT in the treatment of anxiety compared to active control conditions, nor can ACT be considered a primary treatment for anxiety up to now. Similarly, Veehof et al. remarked that ACT and mindfulness-based interventions may be superior to waitlist, (medical) TAU, and education or support control groups. However, no such investigation was made in comparison to active control groups (i.e., traditional CBT). Recently, ACT started to be delivered in a Web-based format (M. Brown et al., 2016). However, with only 10 RCTs on ACT's relationship to mental health and well-being, it is premature to draw firm conclusions on its efficacy. More research is needed.

In conclusion, ACT has been used to treat a plethora of health problems, but despite the existing studies, some questions still require answers. What specific type of problem and/or population does this form of therapy best address? Do clients have to accept every unpleasant situation or internal event? Should some situations or internal events be accepted and some changed? How do experts discriminate between them? What can and cannot be changed? The responses to these essential questions will help guide and customize current ACT interventions in order to optimally suit them for the problems and populations ACT addresses. Given the trend of increased ACT research, it is likely that these questions will be answered in the near future.

Verbatim Transcript: ACT

The following verbatim transcript of a fourth session is presented in order to illustrate the information about the principles and practice of ACT as described in this chapter. We provide a brief overview of the case, the actual transcript, a short critique of the session, and an explanation as to why we think this theory effectively addressed the problem.

Overview

Ethan was a 45-year-old Caucasian male who referred himself for therapy to help himself deal with couple problems and difficulties in social interactions, especially small talk and everyday social conversations. Ethan had been married for 10 years, and he and his wife had no children. He was a competent and well-respected professional who had a relatively stable and well-paying job as an information technology engineer at a software company. Ethan described his main problem as marital dissatisfaction characterized by masked conflict and anxiety about his wife finding another partner. According to the client, his anxiety was triggered by his wife's high degree of comfort in social situations in contrast to his "pronounced social clumsiness," as he saw it. During the assessment phase in the initial session, it became clear that Ethan was obsessed with controlling events, thoughts, and feelings and believed he had done whatever he could to resolve their couple problems and improve his social abilities. Some of his efforts had apparently paid off, at least temporarily, but now he thought things were not good and said there was nothing else that he could try to fix things.

Following the assessment phase, it became evident that Ethan was struggling with anxiety and depressive symptoms triggered by experiential avoidance, lack of contact with the present moment, cognitive fusion, inaction, and lack of clarity about his values. During the first three sessions the therapist (Cristina Mogoașe) focused on building rapport with Ethan and coming to an agreement about the therapeutic goals and methods of achieving them. In addition, a good deal of time was dedicated to acquainting the client with the ACT philosophy. During the first two sessions, the therapist spent most of the time discussing the ubiquity of suffering and the normality (even necessity) of (psychological) pain for the human life. The client partially agreed with that view but seemed unwilling to accept pain without trying to minimize it. The next session focused on explaining how language leads to suffering: Psychological pain automatically accompanies the verbal system all normal humans acquire because, once acquired, language makes it impossible for normal humans to escape the experience of thinking and generating thoughts. Therefore, agreeing with or challenging thoughts is equally unproductive, as they are not true or false in and of themselves but rather describe a dynamic interrelated system. In other words, they *are* *thoughts*. Nothing more, nothing less. This seemed to resonate with Ethan, but he still expressed doubts related to the potential utility of stopping trying to eliminate his negative, distorted thinking. This following transcript of the fourth session focuses on control strategies, which are an "unworkable system."

Transcript of the Fourth Session

Therapist: Hi, Ethan! How are you doing?

Client: Hi! I'm still struggling, but this seems to make no noticeable difference. On the contrary . . . I really need some help—something else to try to get out of this mess.

Therapist: So you experienced some difficulties during the last week. Can you offer me some more details? What do you mean?

Client: Hmmm, yes . . . we, I mean me and my wife, we went out to dinner several days ago. Two other couples—friends of ours—joined us . . . [pause]

Therapist: Okay . . . and what happened?

Client: Well . . . hmmm . . . my wife was very social, as she's always. She was in the spotlight all night.

Therapist: Okay . . . and what was wrong with that?

Client: Nothing was wrong with that, except for the fact that I felt like a loser. I was unable to enjoy the night because I was seeing my wife laughing and joking with others. She wasn't paying too much attention to me. Moreover, she seemed very involved with one man there—Joshua, the husband of her friend.

Therapist: Do you mean she paid special attention to him, like she was possibly romantically interested in him?

Client: Well, hmmm . . . yes, something like that. At least this is what I was thinking. Now, looking back, I'm not very sure I was right . . . I mean, I hope I wasn't. I cannot imagine my wife leaving me . . . what am I going to do? However, I cannot stop myself thinking about that when I see her so easy, smiling and talkative in the presence of other men, or when I hear her speaking admiringly about other men. On the other hand, it's true I don't have any concrete proof to distrust her . . . My thoughts could be true or not. Sometimes I come to the conclusion that my thinking is just distorted. How can I be sure about that? And if it is my biased thinking, how can I fix it? It's just overwhelming . . .

Therapist: I see . . . well, let's see what you tried so far to test these thoughts or to get rid of them.

Client: Oh, I tried everything I thought it might work . . .

Therapist: Like? Let's speak specifically about this incident: What did you try?

Client: First of all, I tried not thinking any more about the possibility that my wife could be interested in anyone else. That simple thought just paralyzed me: My mind was fully absorbed by this thought to such an extent that I was unable to attend to or participate in the ongoing conversation.

Therapist: Do you mean you became very nervous, anxious?

Client: Yes, exactly. And when anxious, it was even more difficult for me to be socially active. Actually, I couldn't help myself observing how awkward I was, especially in contrast with the other guy: No wonder that my wife seemed more interested in him. If only I could stop those thoughts and just relax, at least for the moment!

Therapist: So, you wanted to stop the disturbing thoughts in order to lower your anxiety, because you became aware that your anxiety interfered with your social skills on that specific occasion.

Client: Exactly. And that's a typical scenario—I found myself in similar circumstances several times. Actually, I think my social awkwardness could be explained specifically by the high level of anxiety I feel in social situations. When anxious, I'm feeling out of control; I can't control my anxiety and, even worse, I can't control other reactions that I usually manage to control. That's terrible!

Therapist: So, you think that your thoughts make you anxious, and your anxiety interferes with your ability to function normally . . .

Client: Yes, exactly . . .

Therapist: Well, that could be a possibility. But let's go back to what happened last week. Was there anything else that you tried to lower the anxiety that was triggered by the thought that your wife could be interested in someone else?

Client: Hmmm, yes. While we were going home that night I was thinking that maybe I should speak to my wife, to tell her how I feel and that I don't like her to be so easy with other men, while almost ignoring me at the same time. I was thinking about that all night. In the end, she could confirm or invalidate my thoughts. At that point I felt that even if she confirmed my thoughts, that would have been better than struggling with doubts.

Therapist: And what did you do?

Client: Well, I was afraid to talk to her that night. However, I couldn't help myself to think about all these things. I guess I was a little bit "absent"— she remarked at a certain point that I was behaving strangely and asked what the problem was.

Therapist: And?

Client: Well, I told her that night that there was no problem. But the next day I decided it would be better to have a discussion with her. And I told her about my experience.

Therapist: And?

Client: Well, that didn't work very well. She was initially very surprised, then she was angry with me. She said it is only in my mind and I am not entitled to accuse her only because I am socially awkward, and that it would be better to try to be more friendly and talkative. Then . . . she was distant with me. I think she still is . . . And I don't know what to do next.

Therapist: So, to summarize: You tried to manage anxiety, right? And you told me about two strategies you tried: Stop thinking negatively and talk to your wife. Neither seemed to have worked . . .

Client: Unfortunately . . . [sigh]

Therapist: Moreover, you tell me that you have no more strategies to try . . . and everything else you have tried failed to work.

Client: You're right.

Therapist: It seems to me that every effort you made to lower your anxiety actually resulted in making you even more anxious . . .

Client: That could be true. What am I doing wrong? And how can I do things differently?

Therapist: Maybe it's not about what you're doing and the point it's not to do things differently or to try other problem-solving strategies . . .

Client: What do you mean?

Therapist: Well, do you remember our discussion about how our mind continuously and dynamically creates relationship between concepts?

Client: Yes, I do . . .

Therapist: What if your efforts to lower anxiety are thwarted by the incredible ability of the mind to create new ways of making you anxious?

Client: Hmmm . . . I didn't think about that. But doesn't that imply that the harder I try to get rid of anxiety, the more anxious I will be?

Therapist: It seems so . . .

Client: This . . . this can't be true. This sounds like there is nothing that I can do to make a change. It's crazy.

Therapist: Maybe it is not about doing something . . .

Client: What do you mean?

Therapist: If the harder you try to control your thoughts and feelings, the more anxious you become, what about trying the other way around?

Client: Namely? Trying to be anxious in order to lower anxiety?

Therapist: Something like this. What do you think?

Client: It's . . . crazy. Do you think it will work?

Therapist: What do you mean by "work"?

Client: Will this strategy help me in lowering my anxiety?

Therapist: I'm not sure.

Client: And then? What's the point in trying it?

Therapist: Listen, the point is not to lower anxiety. I know, it sounds paradoxical, but please hear me out: If you try to be anxious in order to become less anxious, don't you actually try to become less anxious?

Client: Of course . . .

Therapist: You see; you'd get to the same point where you started. Does it make sense to rely on the same old strategies that prove themselves wrong? You would find yourself trapped in anxiety again.

Client: Hmmm . . . you're right. But then . . . What's the point? Should I embrace anxiety and discomfort genuinely? Sincerely, I'm afraid I cannot do that . . . I don't want to make suffering the purpose of my life.

Therapist: It's not about making suffering the purpose of your life. But I can see your point. However, remember that suffering *is* an integral part of the human existence. It's inevitable. It's even necessary.

Client: Yes, I remember our discussion . . . but if this is not about making suffering the purpose of my life, then what is?

Therapist: Let's say it's about opening up yourself to the vitality of the moment and fully living in accordance to your genuine values. It's about allowing yourself to thoroughly feel anxiety as you feel the texture of a cashmere sweater. Fully feel the present moment and move more effectively toward what you value.

Client: Sounds interesting, but . . . very complicated. How will I be able to achieve that?

Therapist: Yes, you're right: You cannot achieve that overnight. But you can achieve it! All you need is practice. And let me suggest a starting point.

Client: Please . . .

Therapist: I want you to keep a diary for the next week. At the end of each day please write down if you faced any notable struggling over the day. If yes, please indicate how much distress you experienced, on a scale where 1 means no distress and 100 means extreme distress. Next, please rate how much effort you put in managing the distress, using a scale where 0 means no effort and 100 means extreme effort. Finally, please rate how well did your efforts worked: How much overall vitality and aliveness would characterize your life for that day? Again, use a 0 to 100 scale. I'm expecting this exercise will help you be more aware about your distress and your struggles to alleviate it, as well the strategies you use to that end. That's enough for now. Just observe your experience. What do you think?

Client: Well, I could do that. It doesn't seem complicated. I'm curious where it can lead me [smile].

Therapist: By the way, did you fill in that list of what you used to do to feel better when you're down?

Client: Yes, I did it. Here is it.

Therapist: Aah . . . [reading from the list]: "Trying to stay calm," "Trying to stop thinking about the disturbing thing," "Trying to avoid situations where I feel uncomfortable," "Trying to get clues that are supporting the accuracy/inaccuracy of my thoughts," "Distracting myself." That's all you remembered?

Client: Yes . . . maybe there are also other things, but I don't remember them . . .

Therapist: It's all right. It seems you used some of these strategies last week, too [smile]. Probably you're used to relying heavily on them.

Client: Yes, kind of . . . [smile]

Therapist: Notwithstanding, they seem to be an unworkable system [smile].

Client: Yes . . . and we shouldn't try to fix it, but just to observe it, should we? [smile]

Therapist: Exactly [smile]. Let's do that and see what's happening. We have a deal for next week: Don't forget about the diary!

Client: Okay. Thank you! And see you next week!

Therapist: See you!

Session Critique

This session demonstrates a typical ACT approach to working with anxious adults. The therapeutic style was adapted for working with this solution-focused information technology engineer, who seemed determined to apply a problem-solving approach to his inner events in the same way he used problem-solving strategies to resolve a software bug. I (Cristina) used practical issues and logical debate instead of metaphors in this relatively early stage of the therapy because the client seemed to be technically oriented. The approach was gradual. A considerable amount of the session was dedicated to discussing a recent incident that the client had experienced during the previous week. I intentionally fed this discussion in order to use the occasion to introduce the idea of an "unworkable system." At the same time, discussing something problematic for the client was a good opportunity to consolidate the therapeutic alliance. However, this was done at the cost of discussing homework, which was briefly mentioned only at the end of the session. I integrated it with the rest of the session but could have allocated some more time to discussing it in greater detail. Similarly, I should have summarized the main point that arose from the session before the session's end.

Effectiveness of the Theory Relative to This Case

One of the key issues that Ethan was facing was a tendency toward experiential avoidance and cognitive fusion. According to RFT, experiential avoidance and cognitive fusion are triggering and maintaining Ethan's anxiety and related issues by impeding him from having direct experiences that could change his frame of mind and allow him to have new learning experiences. Hence, this approach is extremely effective in Ethan's case, as ACT would increase his psychological flexibility, helping him to remain attuned to the present moment and to persist in a value-consistent behavior change that would lead to the desired outcomes.

Summary

RFT (Hayes et al., 2001) is considered the theory underlying ACT. According to RFT, people live in a world whose functions are verbally acquired and where literal language leads to experiential avoidance and cognitive fusion, all therapeutically addressed by ACT.

ACT is part of the third wave of CBT interventions (Hayes et al., 2006). ACT helps clients accept life's difficulties and move in a committed manner in the direction of their chosen values despite obstacles. The sources of those obstacles are in essence language related, and to a large extent ACT creates a new dictionary that will help clients reach their life goals. The main goal of ACT is to foster psychological flexibility. Through psychological flexibility the client learns to alter the function of a belief without actually modifying its content.

ACT has been used to treat a plethora of physical and mental health problems, especially PTSD and chronic pain. Up to now, ACT was not more efficacious than second-wave forms of CBT, and in some cases it was evaluated as having an experimental status. Many books have been written on ACT and RFT, some of them including step-by-step guidelines for implementing ACT. However, there needs to be more emphasis on rigorous scientific papers that include more RCTs, especially RCTs in comparison to second-wave forms of CBT. The responses to these issues will help guide and customize current ACT interventions.

Suggested Resources and Websites

For more information on the theory and practice of ACT, please refer to the following resources and websites (see the References for detailed information).

1. A step-by-step guide to ACT and a comprehensive list of strategies can be found in Hayes and Strosahl (2004) and Hayes, Strosahl, and Wilson (2012).

2. Clinician's guides to using ACT to treat two of the most pervasive mental disorders, depression and anxiety, can be found in Zettle (2007) and Eifert and Forsyth (2005).
3. A clinician's guide for ACT across disorders can be found in Ciarrochi and Bailey (2008).
4. One of the first books in the field that provides excellent background was written by Hayes et al. (1999). Another must-have for beginners was written by Luoma et al. (2007).
5. Transcripts are always useful when one is trying to master a new form of therapy. Thus, we recommend Twohig and Hayes (2008).
6. Törneke's (2010) book is a helpful introduction to RFT.

Also check the following websites:

- ACT Mindfully
  www.actmindfully.com.au
- ACT Online Training
  www.actmadesimple.com
- Association for Contextual Behavioral Science
  www.contextualscience.org
- I'm Learning ACT With Dr. Russ Harris
  www.imlearningact.com

References

Arch, J. J., Eifert, G. H., Davies, C., Vilardaga, J. C. P., Rose, R. D., & Craske, M. G. (2012). Randomized clinical trial of cognitive behavioral therapy (CBT) versus acceptance and commitment therapy (ACT) for mixed anxiety disorders. *Journal of Consulting and Clinical Psychology, 80,* 750–765.

A-Tjak J. G. L., Davis, M. L., Morina, N., Powers, M. B., Smits, J. A. J., & Emmelkamp, P. M. G. (2014). A meta-analysis of the efficacy of acceptance and commitment therapy for clinically relevant mental and physical health problems. *Psychotherapy and Psychosomatics, 84*(1), 30–36.

Baer, R. A. (2015). *Mindfulness-based treatment approaches: Clinician's guide to evidence base and applications.* Cambridge, MA: Academic Press.

Blackledge, J. T. (2007). Disrupting verbal processes: Cognitive defusion in acceptance and commitment therapy and other mindfulness-based psychotherapies. *The Psychological Record, 57,* 555–577.

Brown, L. A., Gaudiano, B. A., & Miller, I. W. (2011). Investigating the similarities and differences between practitioners of second-and third-wave cognitive-behavioral therapies. *Behavior Modification, 35*(2), 187–200.

Brown, M., Glendenning, A., Hoon, A. E., & John, A. (2016). Effectiveness of Web-delivered acceptance and commitment therapy in relation to mental health and well-being: A systematic review and meta-analysis. *Journal of Medical Internet Research, 18,* e221.

Chambless, D. L., Baker, M. J., Baucom, D. H., Beutler, L. E., Calhoun, K. S., Crits-Christoph, P., . . . Johnson, S. B. (1998). Update on empirically validated therapies, II. *The Clinical Psychologist, 51*(1), 3–16.

Chambless, D. L., Sanderson, W. C., Shoham, V., Johnson, S. B., Pope, K. S., CritsChristoph, P., et al. (1996). An update on empirically validated therapies. *The Clinical Psychologist, 49,* 5e18.

Ciarrochi, J., & Bailey, A. (2008). *A CBT-practitioner's guide to ACT: How to bridge the gap between cognitive behavioral therapy and acceptance and commitment therapy.* Oakland CA: New Harbinger.

Corrigan, P. (2002). The data is still the thing: A reply to Gaynor and Hayes. *Behavior Therapist, 25*(7/8), 140.

Dahl, J., Wilson, K. G., & Nilsson, A. (2004). Acceptance and commitment therapy and the treatment of persons at risk for long-term disability resulting from stress and pain symptoms: A preliminary randomized trial. *Behavior Therapy, 35,* 785–801.

Eifert, G. H., & Forsyth, J. P. (2005). *Acceptance and commitment therapy for anxiety disorders: A practitioner's treatment guide to using mindfulness, acceptance, and values-based behavior change.* Oakland, CA: New Harbinger.

England, E. L., Herbert, J. D., Forman, E. M., Rabin, S. J., Juarascio, A., & Goldstein, S. P. (2012). Acceptance-based exposure therapy for public speaking anxiety. *Journal of Contextual Behavioral Science, 1*(1), 66–72.

Flaxman, P. E., Blackledge, J. T., & Bond, F. W. (2011). *Acceptance and commitment therapy: Distinctive features.* New York, NY: Routledge.

Folke, F., Parling, T., & Melin, L. (2012). Acceptance and commitment therapy for depression: A preliminary randomized clinical trial for unemployed on long-term sick leave. *Cognitive and Behavioral Practice, 19,* 583–594.

Forman, E. M., Chapman, J. E., Herbert, J. D., Goetter, E. M., Yuen, E. K., & Moitra, E. (2012). Using session-by-session measurement to compare mechanisms of action for acceptance and commitment therapy and cognitive therapy. *Behavior Therapy, 43*(2), 341–354.

Greco, L. A., & Hayes, S. C. (2008). *Acceptance and mindfulness treatments for children and adolescents: A practitioner's guide.* Oakland, CA: New Harbinger.

Gregg, J. A., Callaghan, G. M., Hayes, S. C., & Glenn-Lawson, J. L. (2007). Improving diabetes self-management through acceptance, mindfulness, and values: A randomized controlled trial. *Journal of Consulting and Clinical Psychology, 75*(2), 336–343.

Gross, A. C., & Fox, E. J. (2009). Relational frame theory: An overview of the controversy. *The Analysis of Verbal Behavior, 25*(1), 87–98.

Hacker, T., Stone, P., & MacBeth, A. (2016). Acceptance and commitment therapy—Do we know enough? Cumulative and sequential meta-analyses of randomized controlled trials. *Journal of Affective Disorders, 190,* 551–565.

Hayes, S. C. (2002). On being visited by the vita police: A reply to Corrigan. *The Behavior Therapist, 25*(7/8), 134–137.

Hayes, S. C. (2004). Acceptance and commitment therapy, relational frame theory, and the third wave of behavioral and cognitive therapies. *Behavior Therapy, 35,* 639–665.

Hayes, S. C. (2008). *Criticism: "ACT is outright taken from Morita therapy."* Retrieved from https://contextualscience.org/node/3303

Hayes, S. C., Barnes-Holmes, D., & Roche, B. (Eds.). (2001). *Relational frame theory: A post-Skinnerian account of human language and cognition.* New York, NY: Springer.

Hayes, S. C., Follette, V. M., & Linehan, M. (Eds.). (2004). *Mindfulness and acceptance: Expanding the cognitive-behavioral tradition.* New York, NY: Guilford Press.

Hayes, S. C., & Gifford, E. V. (1997). The trouble with language: Experiential avoidance, rules, and the nature of verbal events. *Psychological Science, 8*(3), 170–173.

Hayes, S. C., Luoma, J. B., Bond, F. W., Masuda, A., & Lillis, J. (2006). Acceptance and commitment therapy: Model, processes and outcomes. *Behaviour Research and Therapy, 44*(1), 1–25.

Hayes, S. C., & Strosahl, K. D. (Eds.). (2004). *A practical guide to acceptance and commitment therapy.* New York, NY: Springer.

Hayes, S. C., Strosahl, K. D., & Wilson, K. G. (1999). *Acceptance and commitment therapy.* New York, NY: Guilford Press.

Hayes, S. C., Strosahl, K. D., & Wilson, K. G. (2012). *Acceptance and commitment therapy: The process and practice of mindful change* (2nd ed.). New York, NY: Guilford Press.

Hayes, S. C., & Wilson, K. G. (1994). Acceptance and commitment therapy: Altering the verbal support for experiential avoidance. *The Behavior Analyst, 17*(2), 289–303.

Hesser, H., Gustafsson, T., Lundén, C., Henrikson, O., Fattahi, K., Johnsson, E., . . . Andersson, G. (2012). A randomized controlled trial of Internet-delivered cognitive behavior therapy and acceptance and commitment therapy in the treatment of tinnitus. *Journal of Consulting and Clinical Psychology, 80,* 649–661.

Hofmann, S. G. (2008). Acceptance and commitment therapy: New wave or Morita therapy? *Clinical Psychology: Science and Practice, 15*(4), 280–285.

Hofmann, S. G., & Asmundson, G. J. (2008). Acceptance and mindfulness-based therapy: New wave or old hat? *Clinical Psychology Review, 28*(1), 1–16.

Jensen, K. B., Kosek, E., Wicksell, R., Kemani, M., Olsson, G., Merle, J. V., . . . Ingvar, M. (2012). Cognitive behavioral therapy increases pain-evoked activation of the prefrontal cortex in patients with fibromyalgia. *Pain, 153,* 1495–1503.

Luoma, J. B., Hayes, S. C., & Walser, R. D. (2007). *Learning ACT: An acceptance and commitment therapy skills-training manual for therapists.* Oakland, CA: New Harbinger.

Luoma, J. B., Kohlenberg, B. S., Hayes, S. C., & Fletcher, L. (2012). Slow and steady wins the race: A randomized clinical trial of acceptance and commitment therapy targeting shame in substance use disorders. *Journal of Consulting and Clinical Psychology, 80*(1), 43–53.

Mattaini, M. A. (1997). *Clinical practice with individuals.* Washington, DC: NASW Press.

McCurry, S. M., & Hayes, S. C. (1992). Clinical and experimental perspectives on metaphorical talk. *Clinical Psychology Review, 12,* 763–785.

Morton, J., Snowdon, S., Gopold, M., & Guymer, E. (2012). Acceptance and commitment therapy group treatment for symptoms of borderline personality disorder: A public sector pilot study. *Cognitive and Behavioral Practice, 19,* 527–544.

Murrell, A. R., Coyne, L. W., & Wilson, K. G. (2004). ACT with children, adolescents, and their parents. In S. C. Hayes & K. D. Strosahl (Eds.), *A practical guide to acceptance and commitment therapy* (pp. 249–273). New York, NY: Springer.

Murrell, A. R., & Scherbarth, A. J. (2006). State of the research and literature address: ACT with children, adolescents and parents. *International Journal of Behavioral Consultation and Therapy, 2,* 531–543.

O'Donohue, W. T., & Fisher, J. E. (Eds.). (2009). *General principles and empirically supported techniques of cognitive behavior therapy.* New York, NY: Wiley.

Orsillo, S. M., & Roemer, L. (Eds.). (2007). *Acceptance and mindfulness-based approaches to anxiety: Conceptualization and treatment.* New York, NY: Springer.

Öst, L. G. (2008). Efficacy of the third wave of behavioral therapies: A systematic review and meta-analysis. *Behaviour Research and Therapy, 46*(3), 296–321.

Öst, L. G. (2014). The efficacy of acceptance and commitment therapy: An updated systematic review and meta-analysis. *Behaviour Research and Therapy, 61,* 105–121.

Petersen, C. L., & Zettle, R. D. (2009). Treating inpatients with comorbid depression and alcohol use disorders: A comparison of acceptance and commitment therapy versus treatment as usual. *The Psychological Record, 59,* 521–536.

Powers, M. B., Zum Vorde Sive Vording, M. B., & Emmelkamp, P. M. G. (2009). Acceptance and commitment therapy: A meta-analytic review. *Psychotherapy and Psychosomatics, 78*(2), 73–80.

Ruiz, F. J. (2010). A review of acceptance and commitment therapy (ACT) empirical evidence: Correlational, experimental psychopathology, component and outcome studies. *International Journal of Psychology and Psychological Therapy, 10*(1), 125–162.

Shawyer, F., Farhall, J., Mackinnon, A., Trauer, T., Sims, E., Ratcliff, K., . . . Copolov, D. (2012). A randomised controlled trial of acceptance-based cognitive behavioural therapy for command hallucinations in psychotic disorders. *Behaviour Research and Therapy, 50*(2), 110–121.

Silverman, W. K., & Hinshaw, S. P. (2008). The second special issue on evidence-based psychosocial treatments for children and adolescents: A 10-year update. *Journal of Clinical Child & Adolescent Psychology, 37*(1), 1–7.

Smout, M. F., Longo, M., Harrison, S., Minniti, R., Wickes, W., & White, J. M. (2010). Psychosocial treatment for methamphetamine use disorders: A preliminary randomized controlled trial of cognitive behavior therapy and acceptance and commitment therapy. *Substance Abuse, 31*(2), 98–107.

Stotts, A. L., Green, C., Masuda, A., Grabowski, J., Wilson, K., Northrup, T. F., . . . Schmitz, J. M. (2012). A stage I pilot study of acceptance and commitment therapy for methadone detoxification. *Drug and Alcohol Dependence, 125*(3), 215–222.

Törneke, N. (2010). *Learning RFT: An introduction to relational frame theory and its clinical application.* Oakland, CA: New Harbinger.

Twohig, M., & Hayes, S. C. (2008). *ACT verbatim for depression and anxiety: Annotated transcripts for learning acceptance and commitment therapy.* Oakland, CA: New Harbinger.

Veehof, M. M., Trompetter, H. R., Bohlmeijer, E. T., & Schreurs, K. M. G. (2016). Acceptance- and mindfulness-based interventions for the treatment of chronic pain: A meta-analytic review. *Cognitive Behaviour Therapy, 45,* 5–31.

Walser, R. D., & Hayes, S. C. (2006). Acceptance and commitment therapy in the treatment of PTSD: Theoretical and applied issues. In V. M. Follette & J. I. Ruzek (Eds.), *Cognitive behavioral therapies for trauma* (pp. 146–173). New York, NY: Guilford Press.

Wegner, D. M., Schneider, D. J., Carter, S. R., & White, T. L. (1987). Paradoxical effects of thought suppression. *Journal of Personality and Social Psychology, 53*(1), 5–13.

White, R., Gumley, A., McTaggart, J., Rattrie, L., McConville, D., Cleare, S., & Mitchell, G. (2011). A feasibility study of acceptance and commitment therapy for emotional dysfunction following psychosis. *Behaviour Research and Therapy, 49,* 901–907.

Wicksell, R. K., Melin, L., Lekander, M., & Olsson, G. L. (2009). Evaluating the effectiveness of exposure and acceptance strategies to improve functioning and quality of life in longstanding pediatric pain—A randomized controlled trial. *Pain, 141*(3), 248–257.

Wilson, K. G., Hayes, S. C., Gregg, J., & Zettle, R. D. (2001). Psychopathology and psychotherapy. In S. C. Hayes, D. Barnes-Holmes, & B. Roche (Eds.), *Relational frame theory: A post-Skinnerian account of human language and cognition* (pp. 211–237). New York, NY: Plenum Press.

Woods, D. W., Wetterneck, C. T., & Flessner, C. A. (2006). A controlled evaluation of acceptance and commitment therapy plus habit reversal for trichotillomania. *Behaviour Research and Therapy, 44,* 639–656.

Zettle, R. (2007). *ACT for depression: A clinician's guide to using acceptance and commitment therapy in treating depression.* Oakland, CA: New Harbinger.

Chapter 7

Dialectical Behavior Therapy

Chris Kelly and Diana M. Robinson
Case study contributed by
Nora Gerardi

Dialectical behavior therapy (DBT) is a comprehensive and collaborative therapeutic approach that emphasizes the importance of the counselor–client relationship and validation of the client. Marsha Linehan, PhD, began developing DBT in the late 1970s for clients struggling with suicidal and self-harm behaviors. DBT integrates cognitive–behavioral techniques with acceptance-based "Eastern psychological and spiritual practices" (Linehan, 1993, p. 6) and balances striving to make behavior changes with learning acceptance.

The purpose of this chapter is to present relevant information about DBT, including how and why Dr. Linehan developed this approach. Major constructs of the theory, the process, and interventions are addressed, as are supporting research and limitations.

Marsha Linehan: Key Theorist

Marsha Linehan, PhD, was born in Tulsa, Oklahoma, and graduated from Loyola University in Chicago. At the beginning of her career as a psychologist in the 1970s, Linehan worked primarily with suicidal clients and those diagnosed with borderline personality disorder (BPD), clients who faced insurmountable problems and whose lives were full of pain and hopelessness (Haddock, 2016). BPD is a *Diagnostic and Statistical Manual of Mental Disorders, Fifth Edition*, personality disorder characterized by a longstanding, pervasive pattern of emotional lability, unstable sense of self, unstable personal relationships. Clients with BPD often struggle with fears of abandonment, feelings of emptiness, impulsive acts in relation to stressors (including but not limited to self-harm acts like cutting), and paranoia.

Her mission was to develop a successful treatment approach that gave these clients a reason to live. From her own personal experiences and her clinical work, she concluded that individuals with BPD would require a therapeutic program that taught acceptance as much as change. Inspired by Eastern philosophies and her Catholic faith, Linehan incorporated mindfulness and other Zen practices and concepts as a basis for acceptance. As a behaviorist, she embraced the idea that changes in behavior would lead to changes in mental state and, as a basis for change, included explicit training in behavioral skills. Over the past 30 years, DBT has become the gold standard for treating individuals with BPD, and it continues to be modified for use in other populations such as those with treatment-resistant depression, bipolar disorder, anxiety, substance abuse, posttraumatic stress disorder, and eating disorders (Bedics, Atkins, Harned, & Linehan, 2015). It can be used in a variety of settings such as inpatient treatment centers, intensive outpatient settings, or community settings.

In 2011 Linehan first publicly acknowledged her own struggles with mental illness in a speech at the Institute of Living, a clinic where she had received psychiatric treatment in her late teens. Later sharing her story in a *New York Times* interview (Carey, 2011), she revealed the background to what the faded scars on her arms hinted at: Linehan herself had struggled with BPD, suicidal behavior, and self-harm. She had spent more than 2 years institutionalized for psychiatric care and was treated with antipsychotic medication, Freudian analysis, and electroshock therapy. It was largely in response to what she saw as inappropriate treatment for her own mental illness that she began her studies in psychology at Loyola University, from which she eventually received her doctorate in social and experimental psychology.

In her professional life, Linehan sought out clients battling the most severe symptoms of BPD, such as self-harm and suicidal behavior (Linehan, 1993). Although she acknowledged the reality that a person struggling with suicidal behavior must change his or her life, she saw from her own experiences and her clinical work the necessity of completely accepting oneself as is, an idea she referred to as *radical acceptance* (Shearin & Linehan, 1992). These seemingly conflicting ideas formed the dialectical backbone in DBT of fully embracing both acceptance and change. With Linehan's insights, DBT evolved from standard cognitive behavior therapy (CBT) into a treatment that has proven successful in addressing the particular vulnerabilities of clients with BPD as well as clients with other disorders.

Linehan is the founder of the nonprofit The Linehan Institute, which further supports and researches mental health treatment, and Behavioral Tech, which trains providers of DBT (The Linehan Institute, n.d.). Currently she is a professor of psychology, adjunct professor of psychiatry and behavioral sciences, and director of the Behavioral Research and Therapy Clinics at the University of Washington. Linehan has served as past president of the Association for the Advancement of Behavior Therapy and has received numerous awards for her research and clinical work, including several lifetime and career achievement awards.

Theoretical Overview of DBT

In her postdoctoral studies at the Suicide Prevention and Crisis Service in Buffalo, New York, Linehan saw that traditional CBT was failing clients with BPD (Linehan, 1993). She first observed that to clients in the midst of overwhelming pain, CBT's constant focus on change felt invalidating. Among individuals already sensitive to rejection and blame, a strong focus on cognitive distortions can send the message that problems are all in one's head. Clients felt misunderstood and even blamed by their therapists, who sometimes dismissed clients as unmotivated to change. As a result, the client dropout rate was high, the client–therapist relationship was strained, and at times clients engaged in acts of self-harm in response to perceived slights by the therapist (Linehan, 1997). Although she acknowledged the reality that a person struggling with suicidal behavior must change his or her life, Linehan saw the necessity of completely accepting oneself as is, an idea she referred to as *radical acceptance* (Shearin & Linehan, 1992). This concept became a fundamental aspect of DBT.

Linehan further noted that clients' frequent suicidal gestures and non-suicidal self-injury (NSSI) created a situation in which therapists spent most of their therapy sessions focused on reducing harm rather than addressing the underlying cause, which was that these clients lacked effective coping behaviors for their intense emotionality (Lynch, Chapman, Rosenthal, Kuo, & Linehan, 2006). In response to this concern, Linehan ensured that DBT would include explicit training in behavioral skills by way of weekly skills groups dedicated solely to learning and strengthening behavioral skills.

Another variable that Linehan discovered in working with high-risk, so-called unmotivated clients who were desperate for warmth but at the same time rejected it was that therapists often experienced burnout and sometimes themselves withdrew from therapy or acted in punitive ways toward clients (Koerner & Linehan, 1997). Linehan concluded that therapists working with chronically suicidal clients needed support of their own. Thus, the consultation team was born to help keep therapists motivated and capable of providing effective treatment.

Biosocial Theory

Linehan began seeing BPD as primarily a problem of emotion dysregulation. As she developed DBT, she also developed a transactional model of BPD wherein a biological predisposition to emotional vulnerability is reinforced in and exacerbated through an invalidating social environment (Crowell, Beauchaine, & Linehan, 2009; Linehan, 1993). People with this vulnerability are born with a heightened sensitivity and reactivity to emotional stimuli and return more slowly to an emotional baseline than others do. As a result, they find it more difficult to tolerate distress and to focus attention away from emotional stimuli, therefore reacting intensely to emotional stimuli, which sometimes results in impulsive and risky acts. In turn, dysregulated emotional expression pulls for invalidating behavior from parents (and others) who themselves either are unable to regulate their own emotions, do not understand why the person is so upset, or lack the skills to teach the person how to manage overwhelming emotions. The vulnerable individual's reactions are punished in any number of ways (e.g., trivializing, ignoring, or criticizing). In some cases, invalidating behavior may take the form of abuse (Hernandez, Arntz, Gaviria, Labad, & Gutiérrez-Zotes, 2012; Wagner & Linehan, 1997). The invalidating environment also intermittently reinforces expressions of emotional displays that are out of control by giving them more attention than normal emotional expression.

The individual eventually learns to mistrust his or her emotions and never learns how to manage them, resulting in ever-escalating emotion dysregulation. He or she enters into cycles of inhibiting emotions followed by bouts of extreme emotional outbursts that contribute to difficult social and disciplinary conflicts, further exacerbating the biological predisposition to emotional vulnerability (Fruzzetti, Shenk, & Hoffman, 2005). Empirical support for the biosocial model and its related constructs has grown in the past decade, particularly for the negative effects of an invalidating childhood environment and in the transaction between environment and emotional vulnerability (Arens, Grabe, Spitzer, & Barnow, 2011; Kuo, Khoury, Metcalfe, Fitzpatrick, & Goodwill, 2015; Sturrock, Francis, & Carr, 2009).

Influences

DBT is unique in many ways but nevertheless shares commonalities with various psychotherapeutic paradigms (for a review, see Neacsiu & Linehan, 2014). In the psychodynamic paradigm, for example, transference and its examination are essential for therapeutic progress. Similarly, in DBT a positive and genuine therapeutic relationship is vital to client change. Both psychodynamic treatments and DBT involve transference analysis in some sense, such as focusing on relationship patterns, increasing the capacity for recognizing emotions, and controlling impulses and anxiety. Client-centered approaches also share various essentials, in particular unconditional positive regard and the emphasis on warmth and empathy. In DBT these are best mirrored in radical acceptance and in validation skills (Linehan, 1993, 1997).

The influence of Zen practice is woven throughout DBT, not only in its guiding principle of balance but also in therapeutic techniques such as entering the paradox and extending as well as in client behavioral skills like acceptance and mindfulness (Heard & Linehan, 1994). As one of the four sets of behavioral skills, mindfulness has a particularly prominent role, just as it does in other CBTs such as acceptance and commitment therapy (Hayes, Strosahl, & Wilson, 1999) and mindfulness-based cognitive therapy (Segal, Teasdale, & Williams, 2002). However, whereas acceptance and commitment therapy and mindfulness-based cognitive therapy conceptualize mindfulness as a tool for distancing oneself from the present moment, DBT conceptualizes mindfulness in the style of Thích Nhất Hạnh—as a way to fully engage with the present moment (as cited by Lynch et al., 2006, p. 463).

Cultural Responsiveness

DBT has been shown to work in a variety of Western cultures outside of the United States, including Germany (Stiglmayr et al., 2014) and Norway (Torgersen, Kringlen, & Cramer, 2001). DBT has also been adapted for primary language (e.g., DBT for use with deaf clients; O'Hearn, Pollard, & Haynes, 2010) and for use with specific populations like American Indians/Alaska Natives and Latina adolescents (Beckstead, Lambert, DuBose, & Linehan, 2015; Germán et al., 2015). However, similar to other therapies, DBT methods are nested in culturally specific understandings of communication between client and therapist. For example, in DBT therapists are encouraged to use irreverent communication when client progress stalls; yet what one culture finds irreverent may simply be impolite in another. It is important to emphasize that a treatment is not culturally responsive by virtue of the fact that it has roots in Eastern philosophy. In fact, it could be argued that all newer mindfulness-based approaches still firmly reside in Western conceptualizations of mental health (Hall, Hong, Zane, & Meyer, 2011).

DBT was developed in response to the specific needs of individuals with BPD. Although BPD has been subject to more research attention than other personality disorders, it still cannot escape the cultural underpinnings that inform how a society conceptualizes personality and personality disorders. Personality disorders as a category have been widely criticized as culturally biased, especially given the obvious gender differences in their diagnosis (Bhugra & Bhui, 2001). BPD tends to be diagnosed most often in Caucasian females, with males making up only 30% of those diagnosed with BPD (Simmons, 1992). Some research suggests that the same underlying psychopathology evinced in men is more often diagnosed as antisocial personality disorder instead of BPD because of gender stereotypes and related gender differences in the expression of emotion (Nehls, 1998; Paris & Lis, 2013).

Although not all countries include BPD in their diagnostic systems, studies from around the globe support the presence of BPD in both Western and Eastern societies (Distel et al., 2008; Ono & Okonogi, 1988; Pinto, Dhavale, Nair, Patil, & Dewan, 2000; Wang & Xiao, 2012). Until DBT is tested empirically in those societies beginning to study BPD in their populations, generalizations cannot be made about the efficacy of DBT for those cultures.

The Therapeutic Process in DBT

Four Treatment Stages

Despite targeting high-lethality behaviors, DBT is not a suicide prevention program. Even when not actively suicidal or engaging in self-harm, clients with BPD still experience extreme emotion dysregulation and remain severely dysfunctional in their daily lives (Linehan, Bohus, & Lynch, 2007). DBT aims to reduce emotion dysregulation and the attendant ineffective coping behaviors, but the superordinate goal is to help a client attain a life from which he or she does not desire to escape—a *life worth living* (Dimeff & Linehan, 2001). When a client commits to treatment in DBT, he or she is asked to name specific goals in life that would make life worth living to him or her. The subordinate goals of behavior control, skills acquisition and generalization, self-management, achieving ordinary happiness and unhappiness, and transcendence all serve to make a life worth living. Each of these goals is addressed in stages.

Prior to treatment, the goals are contracting and committing to this very intensive and time-consuming therapy. The Stage 1 goals are stability, connection, and safety. In order to engage in therapy, clients have to stay in therapy, which means staying alive and staying out of the hospital. Therapy in Stages 2 through 4 becomes less structured (e.g., no behavioral skills group) as the client progresses through processing an emotionally painful past in order to be able to experience feelings without dissociating or avoiding (Stage 2), increasing self-respect and a positive self-image and beginning to focus on problems involved with daily living (Stage 3), and finding meaning and a higher purpose in life in order to feel more complete and connected (Stage 4; Haddock, 2016). Most of the research focus in DBT has been on Stage 1, which is the major focus of this chapter.

In Stage 1, clients and therapists use the following hierarchy of treatment targets to determine the order in which problems should be addressed (from most to least urgent):

1. Eliminate *life-threatening behaviors,* including suicidal threats, gestures, attempts; homicidal behavior; and NSSI.
2. Eliminate *therapy-interfering behaviors,* such as missing sessions, not doing homework, disrupting group sessions, or not taking meds as prescribed.
3. Decrease *quality-of-life-interfering behaviors.* These issues will be customized to the client's dysfunction behavior and life goals but may include issues such as drug and alcohol use, fighting with others, financial trouble, depression, and binge eating.
4. Increase *behavioral skills* in the four domains of core mindfulness (controlling concentration in order to focus on the present instead of worrying about the past or future), distress tolerance (experiencing emotional pain without self-harming), interpersonal effectiveness (initiating new relationships or ending unhealthy ones), and emotion regulation (understanding emotions and how to handle them; Haddock, 2016).
5. Increase *self-management.* Help clients move from acting in their lives in a mood-dependent way to instead acting in a goal-directed way, from a place of intuitive wisdom (Linehan, 1993).

Therapy-interfering behaviors take secondary prominence to ensure that the client receives the full dose of DBT. Anything that gets in the way of the therapist and client working together effectively is considered a therapy-interfering behavior and must be resolved prior to moving forward. In many cases, therapy-interfering behaviors are behaviors the client also engages in outside of therapy (Swales & Heard, 2007). In terms of resolving conflicts, DBT is unique in emphasizing a therapeutic dialectical stance in which the therapist actively searches for the wisdom in the client's position or behavior and does not insist on being right, which enhances the therapeutic alliance (Linehan, 1993).

Actively resolving client–therapist conflicts is beneficial for several reasons. It normalizes difficulties in interpersonal relationships and acts as a good model for how to use effective means of resolving them; it builds a client's confidence in his or her ability to manage interpersonal stress in a constructive way; and it helps both client and therapist to feel good about the team relationship (Lynch et al., 2006).

Comprehensive Structure

At its core, DBT is a principle-driven therapy, which allows for great flexibility. It is also highly structured. Therapeutic procedures are tailored to an individual client's needs based on the risk, severity, and complexity of the disorder (Van Nuys & Linehan, 2007). Although client needs determine at what stage and where on the hierarchy a client begins, all clients participate in the skills training curriculum. The four components in Stage 1 of standard DBT are the *skills training group, individual treatment, coaching calls,* and the *therapist consultation team* (Linehan, 1993).

In standard DBT, clients attend two sessions each week: one individual session for addressing specific behavior targets relevant to them and one group session for skills training (Linehan, 1993). The skills training group is nonprocess and structured like a class, with a group leader or leaders who instruct on the four sets of DBT behavioral skills. Personal discussions are kept brief so that all group members can benefit from the learning experience. Homework is assigned to promote skills acquisition and strengthening. Groups occur weekly for 2 to 2.5 hours over 24 weeks, with each of the four sets spanning a 6-week period. Many clients repeat the full module twice, back to back.

Individual treatment is required for at least as long as a client remains in the skills training group. The client and therapist meet once a week, with a focus on maintaining client commitment, motivation, and application of behavioral skills in daily life (Linehan & Dexter-Mazza, 2008). Over the week, clients fill out a diary card daily to track their emotions, urges, and ineffective and effective coping behaviors as well as their specific quality-of-life behaviors. Problem behaviors are then addressed according to the target hierarchy. Counselors and therapists use of a wide range of strategies, like behavior chain analysis, in vivo coaching, exposure and response prevention, and dialectical dialogue, to help the clients reach their stated goals (Linehan, 1993). This kind of focus can feel unusual to those clients who have had therapy in the past, but it is effective in maximizing the use of session time and helping clients learn how to apply behavioral skills.

As clients with BPD have a strong need for contact and often face difficulties in daily life, they need frequent guidance to stay stable throughout the week. To facilitate proper application and generalization of behavioral skills, clients are expected to make coaching calls to their individual therapist in between sessions. Clients call when they need help with group training homework, are having difficulty applying a skill or knowing which skill to use, or want to use skills to avoid crisis behaviors like self-harm or drug abuse (Linehan & Dexter-Mazza, 2008). Clients may even call to address the therapeutic alliance or to share good news. If clients are unwilling to use skills or have engaged in self-harm, they are not allowed to make a coaching call for 24 hours (because self-harm has solved their problem, just in an ineffective way; Ben-Porath, 2015). (See Ben-Porath, 2015, to learn more on dealing with suicidal ideation and self-harm with coaching calls.)

Hours on call vary by program and individual therapist, and therapists are encouraged to consider their own boundaries and also the specific reinforcement contingencies per client. Nevertheless, this level of contact can feel unusual to counselors or therapists accustomed to infrequent contact between therapy sessions or contact only in emergencies. However, coaching calls hasten skills generalization and progress toward client goals (Lynch et al., 2006). Coaching calls can also strengthen the therapeutic alliance, as most clients appreciate the benefits of having a stable source of cheerleading and coaching to help them through difficult times. When the alliance is strong, contact can become a powerful tool for reinforcing or discouraging specific behaviors (Linehan, 1993).

Therapeutic work with clients who have a high number and severity of problem behaviors is difficult for clients and therapists alike (Koerner & Linehan, 1997). Therapists need support to prevent burnout and to stay effective in their therapeutic approach. The therapist consultation team is like therapy for the therapists who share responsibility for client care, including individual therapists and group leaders. Required to meet once a week, the consultation team discusses cases, practices DBT skills (e.g., mindfulness), cheerleads and praises one another, promotes maintenance of the dialectical stance with clients, and role-plays dialectical dialogues. Reflect more on the advantages and disadvantages of the consultation team as directed in Sidebar 1.

Sidebar 1
The Consultation Team

Most health care settings have some form of case conference, but few match the form and function of the DBT therapist consultation team. With a partner or in a group, come up with parts of the consultation team (e.g., treatment assumptions, therapist skills practice, therapist cheerleading) that appeal to you. Are there disadvantages to the consultation team? If so, how would you address them?

Contracting

After the counselor/therapist orients the client to the structure of DBT and gauges interest, the counselor/therapist and client construct a treatment contract that stipulates the client's goals. Establishing explicit goals with the client provides several benefits during the treatment program (Linehan, 1993). The first benefit is that by explicitly asking the client to identify goals, the therapist ensures that both are working on improving the aspects of life that the client values most, not what the therapist thinks is a life worth living (Ben-Porath, 2004). A second benefit is that it establishes the client–therapist relationship as an equal partnership. For optimal success, the client and therapist must both feel like members of a team working toward the same goals. Finally, the client and therapist will be able to monitor whether progress is being made. Objective progress can help motivate the client and therapist during stressful periods. If the treatment is not working, the client and therapist may have to investigate what aspects are impeding progress.

After explicit goals have been set, the therapist must get the client to commit to the goals and to the treatment plan, including full participation for the entire 24 weeks of skills training. It is important to realize that no person's commitment is perfect (Linehan, 1993). No one can perfectly predict the future or exhibit perfect self-control. Therefore, a commitment is merely the intention—not a promise—to take specific actions toward a goal. Motivation in DBT is a state (not a trait) of being directed toward a choice of greater benefit and lower cost in a specific context (McMain, Sayrs, Dimeff, & Linehan, 2007). Many DBT clients have been through previous therapies and in and out of hospital settings with little to no positive results. Thus, it is important for the therapist to generate hope and enthusiasm for treatment, and tying client goals to treatment targets works well to increase motivation and also strengthen the therapeutic alliance (Hawkins, 1986).

DBT offers no guarantee of success and may fail the client (i.e., the client does not fail the treatment). Therapists need to be able to recognize when a treatment contract is not serving the client and be open to the possibility that change is needed, either by adjusting the level of treatment or trying a different therapeutic approach altogether (Linehan, 1993). Treatment failure need not be completely negative; any so-called failure can be viewed as a learning experience that informs future treatment.

The Termination Process

By the end of the first session, a contract between the therapist and the client should be created that states the expectations and specific end date of the skills training portion (Ben-Porath, 2004). Because many clients benefit from a second round of skills training, the therapist and client should jointly reach a decision as to whether the client would benefit from and is able to commit to a second round as the end date approaches (Linehan, 1993). If a client does not need or is unable to commit to a second round of group skills training, the client and therapist may decide to continue therapy on an individual basis (moving on to Stage 2 DBT), or, depending on the setting, the therapist may refer the client to a lower intensity program to continue working on Stage 1 targets.

Dialectical Thought

To fully appreciate DBT methods, one must understand the dialectical approach to reality itself: Reality is dynamic and always changing; any whole is composed of dynamic, interrelated parts; and any dynamic whole is greater than the sum of its parts (Bopp & Weeks, 1984; Houlgate, 1991). (In DBT any *whole* might be defined as a system, a person, or even some phenomenon about a person [e.g., a disorder like BPD].) This nonreductionist perspective holds that any phenomenon can only be understood as part of a whole, and any whole can only be understood by knowing its discrete parts. It is from this line of logic that DBT treats not a disorder but the whole client (Linehan, 1993; Linehan & Schmidt, 1995). People, their environments, their personalities, and their symptoms are always changing as they influence others and as others influence them. One cannot effectively treat a client's symptoms without understanding the client and the context in which the client is behaving.

Dialectical philosophy also contends that life is full of contradictions that are equally valid and nonmutually exclusive (Lynch et al., 2006). In DBT, for example, clients are asked to fully accept the nature of their dysregulated emotions as part of life and to fully embrace the need to learn new ways to regulate their emotions. Life progresses by reconciling these contradictions into higher truths or levels of understanding. However, reality is ever changing, and as old contradictions are reconciled, new contradictions are formed and the cycle begins again.

Dialectical Methods

DBT uses the dialectical method refined by German philosopher Georg Hegel at the end of the 18th century (Linehan & Schmidt, 1995). The method provides a three-step process for reasoning often simply referred to by its three steps: *thesis–antithesis–synthesis*. With the thesis, one begins with an intellectual proposition. Next one examines the negative of that proposition, which is the antithesis. Finally, one searches for the higher truth— the synthesis—that reconciles the truths of both the thesis and antithesis. In DBT one will frequently come across dialectics of theses and opposing antitheses in which both are held to be equally valid.

To facilitate therapeutic progress, therapists use the dialectic method to challenge a client's thinking. For example, a client may oscillate between thinking that he or she should not need help handling problems in life and blaming others for not helping him or her handle those problems. The dialectical idea of thesis–antithesis–synthesis provides a tool for dislodging such thinking and finding a transcendent middle ground between the two extremes. In this example, one synthesis may be that the client sometimes needs to ask for help from others in order to become more self-reliant.

Three Dialectical Dilemmas

Dialectical thought helps therapists conceptualize a client's dysfunctional behaviors as a result of oscillating between opposing extremes of a dialectical pair. Linehan refers to these dialectical pairs as *dialectical dilemmas* and identified three common to individuals with BPD (Linehan, 1993; Linehan & Schmidt, 1995). The first dilemma is *emotional vulnerability* versus *self-invalidation*. When in an emotionally vulnerable state, clients are extremely sensitive and are therefore prone to emotional outbursts, which may include aggression. Clients may then swing to the opposite pole of self-invalidation by disparaging themselves for an outburst, furthering eroding self-confidence and conception of identity. Clients distrust their emotional intuition and look to others to determine how to respond to situations.

The second dilemma that Linehan identifies is *active passivity* versus *apparent competence*. When experiencing a problem, sometimes clients respond with active passivity by expressing incapability and demanding that others fix their problem. At other times, they may respond with apparent competence by expressing confidence and capability in applying problem-solving skills themselves. However, levels of competence vary and can be particularly dependent on mood and situation for the client with BPD (Linehan & Schmidt, 1995). In this dilemma, clients alternate between demanding help from others and exuding competence, which makes their reactions to stressful situations difficult to predict.

The third common dilemma is *unrelenting crisis* versus *inhibited grieving*. *Unrelenting crisis* refers to the tendency of clients with BPD to lurch from one crisis to another without enough time to ever return to an emotional baseline between events. Spending extended time in a continuously emotionally aroused state is emotionally exhausting and can give rise to inhibited grieving. Clients then purposefully avoid experiencing negative emotions, which results in dysfunctional behaviors like self-harm or even suicide attempts.

When therapists recognize that a client is operating within a dilemma, they are better able to predict client behavior and avoid therapeutic traps (Koerner & Linehan, 1997). Therapeutic traps are common responses that stall progress or worsen a situation (e.g., invalidating the client or insufficiently planning for predictable roadblocks). Therapists can avoid these traps by pushing for synthesis via the dialectical method and by taking specific therapeutic positions in response to these dialectical dilemmas. Learn more about dialectical dilemmas in Sidebar 2.

Sidebar 2

Dialectical Dilemmas

Have you noticed dialectical dilemmas in clients without a BPD diagnosis? Discuss with a partner how these dilemmas could help you predict the behavior of those clients and how you might respond.

Three Dialectical Therapeutic Positions

To facilitate synthesis and therapeutic progression, therapists alternate between the opposite poles of dialectical positions in response to dilemmas presented by the client. DBT identifies three pairs of dialectical positions that therapists will need to use during sessions (Linehan, 1993; Linehan & Schmidt, 1995). The first pair is *orientation to acceptance* versus *orientation to change*. In this pair, the therapist oscillates between radical acceptance of the client and pushing for changes in the client's behavior. The second pair is the dialectic of *compassionate flexibility* versus *unwavering centeredness*. When taking a position of compassionate flexibility, the therapist is willing to take in new information about a client or situation and update his or her position accordingly. By contrast, when the therapist takes the position of unwavering centeredness, he or she looks toward the long term and maintains his or her belief in the treatment in spite of difficulties or arguments otherwise. The third dialectical pair is *nurturing* versus *benevolently demanding*. While in a nurturing position, the therapist acts as a coach and cheerleader for the client. When switching to a benevolently demanding position, the therapist makes demands on the client with mindful attention to the client's ability to meet such demands.

Interactions can be extremely complicated, but knowing these dilemmas and therapeutic positions can help the therapist maintain course and keep the therapy moving (Koerner & Linehan, 1997). For example, if a client presents in an emotionally vulnerable state, the therapist would know to meet the client with an orientation to acceptance of the emotion first before pushing for a change skill. The therapist also should be prepared for the possibility of the client swinging to self-invalidation, to which the therapist would react with an orientation for change (e.g., suggesting a self-validation skill). This quick responding to a client's state helps maintain movement, speed, and the flow of the session.

DBT Interventions

DBT is principle based but also has clearly delineated protocols for use in treatment. Most strategies exist in the dialectical framework, with some strategies particularly reflective of acceptance (e.g., validation and reciprocal communication style) and of change (e.g., shaping and irreverent communication style).

The Therapeutic Alliance

In DBT the role of the counselor or therapist is that of motivator, cheerleader, guide, and, most important, equal partner on a team (Swales & Heard, 2007). Thus, when working with clients, therapists adopt language that reinforces that they are a member of a team rather than an authority figure, using pronouns such as *we* rather than *you*. Therapists adopt a familiar tone with clients and encourage the same tone from them. DBT encourages genuine relationships, so therapists must be able to both cheerlead and speak frankly to clients, not shying away from pointing out self-destructive behavior (Linehan, 1997).

Building a strong therapeutic alliance is key to the effectiveness of DBT, but this can be difficult with clients who not only lack skills in interpersonal effectiveness but also suffer from severe emotion dysregulation (Ben-Porath, 2004). Clients with BPD and borderline features have long been maligned in therapy settings, unfairly disparaged as unmotivated and manipulative (Aviram, Brodsky, & Stanley, 2006). (It is rarely the case that a client with BPD is being purposefully manipulative as opposed to responding to conflict with crisis behaviors because of severe emotion dysregulation.) Such clients—already naturally sensitive to interpersonal rejection—will be even more sensitive to rejection and pretense and easily prone to invalidation.

Communication Strategies

Communication styles exist as a dialectical pair reflecting acceptance and change: *reciprocal* versus *irreverent* communication, respectively (Linehan, 1993). Reciprocal communication is characterized by a responsive, warm, engaging, and friendly style that may even include self-disclosure. Irreverent communication is characterized by a matter-of-fact, deadpan style that is jarring and often incorporates humor. Irreverence is helpful when a therapist wishes to change a client's affective response, reorient the client to a new point of view, or invalidate the invalid. Alternating these styles in response to client dilemmas keeps therapy flowing and the client moving toward synthesis (Dimeff & Linehan, 2001). As clients often oscillate between dialectical extremes, the therapist must maintain the ability to respond in kind. Moving between therapeutic positions and communication styles in response to a client's oscillations is like a dance, and therapists must be quick on their feet to keep the client from falling too far in one direction or the other (Linehan, 1993).

Commitment Strategies

Prior to beginning therapy or asking a person to attempt a skill, the therapist must check for commitment. If it is absent or disappears, the therapist retreats to orientation and commitment strategies to increase motivation and obtain commitment to act in effective ways. These strategies include, but are not limited to, the following: evaluating pros and cons, devil's advocate, foot-in-the-door and door-in-the-face, freedom to choose and absence of alternatives, behavioral shaping, and generating hope (Ben-Porath, 2004). It is important to remember that a client's lack of skill use does not indicate a lack of motivation. The client may lack ability, have a weak ability, or be unable to apply a skill in different contexts. There may also be thoughts, emotions, or environments preventing skill use that need to be addressed first.

Dialectical Strategies

To find synthesis, therapists engage clients in dialectical argumentation (Linehan, 1993). One benefit of this approach is that clients often find themselves arguing for the antithesis of their initial belief (Lynch et al.,

2006). This practice helps clients see alternatives to dysfunctional beliefs and increases flexibility of thinking in general. Dialectical discourse is very engaging conversationally, and the therapist can use a number of strategies to encourage a client to find synthesis. For example, *metaphor* uses a story with a parallel moral but a nonthreatening context, illustrating the client's reluctance and need for change. *Activating wise mind* develops statements that honor both the rational mind and the emotion mind. *Entering the paradox* identifies and embraces the equally valid truths of contradictory statements, and *devil's advocate* argues on the side of the client's implied or voiced reluctance. *Dialectical assessment* actively seeks the wisdom in the client's position, particularly when the therapist and the client are at odds, and looks for a synthesis of the two positions (Linehan, 1993).

Acceptance Strategies

Mindfulness

Contrary to popular myth, mindfulness is not emptying the mind of all thought. *Mindfulness* is defined as "paying attention in a particular way: on purpose, in the present moment, and nonjudgmentally" (Kabat-Zinn, 1994, p. 4). Practicing mindfulness in DBT is not the same as mindfulness meditation, nor does it necessitate formal meditation training. Instead, DBT breaks mindfulness practice into discrete skills of "what" (observing, describing, and participating) and "how" (nonjudgmentally, one mindfully, and effectively). Many DBT settings encourage short practices of these skills prior to beginning sessions as a way to have clients practice and strengthen the skill and to help clients focus on the session at hand (Linehan, 1993).

Mindfulness practice can facilitate client progress in many ways. Mindfulness encourages the client to accept and experience emotions as they are rather than attempting to change them. This practice can defuse situations in which clients find themselves growing increasingly frustrated to the point that they are unable to change their emotional state (Lynch, Robins, Morse, & Krause, 2001). Mindfulness also emphasizes observing thoughts as just thoughts rather than literal truths or good or bad thoughts (Kabat-Zinn, 1990). Thus, mindfulness can reduce the anxiety and discomfort one experiences when having a negative thought. In addition, mindfulness strengthens a client's ability to control his or her focus, including the ability to shift focus away from emotionally distressing thoughts, which is particularly helpful during therapy sessions (Linehan, 1993). Mindfulness also teaches the client to live with and experience strong emotions and impulses without losing control or worsening the situation (Swales & Heard, 2007).

Radical Acceptance

Sometimes life presents obstacles that cannot be immediately remedied (e.g., the bank does not open until 9 a.m.) or ever remedied (e.g., the loss of a loved one). Radical acceptance is accepting—not approving of or liking—the present reality, including painful thoughts, emotions, and experiences (Heard & Linehan, 1994). It is acknowledging that pain is part of life and sometimes must be endured until it dissipates. Resignation or toler-ance, by contrast, implies rejecting pain as part of life (e.g., "Life *should not* be this way but I can't do anything about it"; Hayes et al., 2004). Combined with mindfulness, acceptance exercises facilitate patient progress by allow-ing the client to simply be in the present moment as opposed to being stuck thinking about a painful past or worrying about the future.

A Nonjudgmental Stance

In order to be truly mindful, one must take a nonjudgmental stance to the present moment. Taking a nonjudgmental stance means removing evalu-ations or judgments (e.g., right/wrong, good/bad, fair/not fair, should/ should not) from our experience and simply observing the experience as it is, not how we wish it were (Linehan, 2015). For clients, a nonjudgmental stance promotes objectivity (Lynch et al., 2006); for therapists, it promotes empathy (Heard & Linehan, 1994).

It is critical that therapists view their clients nonpejoratively, as doing so will improve the results of therapy and even reduce client suicidality (Shea-rin & Linehan, 1992). Working with individuals who have severe emotion dysregulation is stressful, and although establishing limits can aid in pre-venting professional burnout, therapists are nevertheless at risk for devel-oping resentment when attending to frequent crises (Gunderson, 1996). As a preventive measure, consultation teams regularly review DBT treatment assumptions (e.g., clients are doing the best they can; clients want to im-prove; clients may not have caused all of their own problems, but they have to solve them anyway; clients need to do better, try harder, and be more mo-tivated to change) that remind therapists to seek synthesis and to maintain a nonjudgmental stance with their clients (Linehan, 1993).

Validation Strategies

Validation is a central therapeutic tool in DBT. By validating early and of-ten, a therapist can build a genuine relationship based on trust without necessarily agreeing with all of the client's thoughts or actions (Linehan, 1993). Validation is particularly helpful when the therapist and client are stuck or at odds. Validation skills help the therapist understand the client's point of view without making pathologizing assumptions about his or her thoughts, emotions, or experiences. For the client, validation reduces nega-tive emotions and feelings of aggression and fosters feelings of belonging-ness (Shenk & Fruzzetti, 2011), creating emotional space to resume con-structive activities during a session. Receiving validation per se can serve as a motivating force for the client to attend therapy (Linehan, 1997).

As a behavioral skill, validation helps the client construct a stable self-view, which enhances the ability to function in social interactions (Swann, 1983). As a therapeutic strategy, validation communicates to the client that some part of his or her behavior or experience makes sense or is understandable in the context of that person's life (Linehan, 1993). Specifically, validation is not praise, positive feedback, or even positive reinforcement. It is also not cheerleading (e.g., "We can do this!"), although all of these strategies are important in DBT as well. Dialectically speaking, the therapist must acknowledge that some part of that client's behavior or experience holds validity or wisdom and must therefore look for the synthesis between positions.

One must learn how to validate, what and when to validate, what not to validate, and how to bounce back from accidental invalidations. Crucial as it is, validation is a difficult skill to apply, and at times it may seem difficult to find anything to validate. Fortunately, there are many sources for possible validation: emotions, legitimacy in desires, opinions, values, priorities, the difficulty of tasks, the effort made toward a goal, or actions to enhance a relationship (Axelrod & Lee, 2013). The therapist also makes sure to match the tone of his or her voice, his or her body language, and his or her facial expression to the content of the validating statements. DBT outlines six levels of validation to aid the therapist and client, with each level being a higher degree of validation (Linehan, 1997). During therapy, the therapist actively searches for validation opportunities and applies the highest possible level at each turn.

The basis of the next five levels, the first level of validation is the act of attentively listening and being fully present mentally. When listening, one should not appear distracted or as if one is formulating responses or judgments rather than actively focusing full attention on the speaker. The second level of validation involves being able to accurately reflect what the client has said without any added judgment. It is important not to mimic the exact words of the client but rather to reiterate the statement in a way that demonstrates listening and understanding. The third level of validation is *mind reading*, which refers to the therapist verbalizing what he or she believes are the client's unspoken emotions and thoughts. Although the therapist will at times be wrong, when he or she is right, it is powerful tool demonstrating attention and understanding. The fourth level of validation involves validating, on the basis of the client's past history or psychological predispositions, that his or her actions are understandable in the given context. The fifth level of validation involves comparing a client's thoughts and actions to those of people in general. It is extremely validating to hear that one's actions are similar to how most people would respond. The sixth and final level of validation is referred to as *radical genuineness*. Radical genuineness refers to breaking down the artificial distance that can occur between therapists and clients. The therapist strives to make the client feel like an equal by communicating in the way that one would with a friend, speaking naturally and showing interest, sincerity, and respect (Robins & Koons, 2000). As an equal, the client is free to ask what the therapist is thinking or experiencing.

Radical genuineness is the highest level of validation and is vitally important to maintaining a genuine relationship with a client. It encourages the purposeful use of therapist self-disclosure, which is often discouraged in other approaches. To benefit the client, a therapist may share a situation in which he or she solved a problem successfully using the behavioral skills taught in DBT. In this way, therapists convey that they too are human and are capable of making mistakes (Linehan, 1993). Learn more about validation by referring to Sidebar 3.

Change Strategies

Many of the change strategies in DBT mirror those used in other CBTs, such as behavior analysis/chain analysis, thought records, exposure, operant conditioning, shaping, and extinction (Linehan, 1993). Some methods, like cognitive modification, are deemphasized because of the vulnerabilities of clients with BPD, who are exquisitely sensitive to blame (Lynch et al., 2006). In DBT the therapist avoids conveying the idea that the problem is all in the client's head by avoiding language like *distorted* or *irrational* in favor of language like *ineffective* and *nondialectical*. Emphasis is placed on contingency clarifications, such as mood effects on cognition and behavior (Linehan & Dexter-Mazza, 2008). Much time is spent on clarifying the short- and long-term effects of specific behaviors and on making the effective or wise mind decision even when under duress. Should a client feel out of control, instead of evaluating thoughts for thinking errors or cognitive distortions, he or she is encouraged to use specific behavioral skills that will first help him or her tolerate distress, change the intensity of the emotion, or change the emotion itself. Once the client is regulated, the therapist may proceed with modification with the caution that DBT therapists use validation more than modification.

Chain Analysis

Chain analysis is a particularly important mechanism of change (Lynch et al., 2006). During a chain analysis, a client recounts the details of the events and emotions that led to dysfunctional behaviors over the past week as indicated on the diary card (Rizvi & Ritschel, 2014). The most obvious benefit is the chance to turn a negative incident into an opportunity for troubleshooting problems in the application of effective behavioral skills. Therapists may then provide in vivo coaching, which may include exposure and response prevention, or perform role plays in preparation for the next week (Linehan, 1993). Another benefit is that by working through a minutely detailed chain analysis, the client becomes better aware of what vulnerabilities and situations precede dysfunctional behaviors, which makes

Sidebar 3
Validation Strategies

Reflect back on a specific interpersonal interaction that went poorly despite your best efforts. Briefly describe points of intervention for validation in the dispute, and come up with several examples of validating statements and their levels (Levels 1–6). Do you think the interaction would have gone differently had you used these validations? Discuss with a partner or in a small group why or why not.

it easier for him or her to spot and avoid similar situations in the future (Lynch et al., 2006). In addition, given that chain analysis requires the client to thoroughly discuss a dysfunctional and therefore likely shame-inducing behavior, the requirement of performing chain analysis in itself can serve as a deterrent to dysfunctional behavior.

Skills Training

One of the main goals of DBT is to decrease ineffective coping behaviors and increase effective ones through acquisition, strengthening, and generalization (Linehan, 1993). To accomplish this goal, DBT teaches four sets of skills in the group skills training classes: core mindfulness, distress tolerance, emotion regulation, and interpersonal effectiveness. These skills are also balanced in the fundamental dialectic of acceptance (mindfulness and distress tolerance) and change (emotion regulation and interpersonal effectiveness). In core mindfulness, clients learn how to stay fully awake and aware in the present moment. Distress tolerance teaches the ability to tolerate distress without trying to change it or wallow in it. In emotion regulation, clients learn how to increase or decrease the intensity of an emotion or how to change it altogether. In interpersonal effectiveness, clients develop skills for communicating with others in ways that are maximally effective, maintain relationships, and preserve and build self-respect. Clients also learn self-management, which is the overarching skill of knowing when to deploy a skill from each of the four sets.

Problem-Solving Method

The term *skills* can actually refer to any behaviors that are needed to effect desired outcomes and minimize undesirable ones (Linehan, 1993). Clients can use their skills to address any problem that may occur by following the stepwise problem-solving method in DBT, as reflected here. There are four ways to respond to any problem, but one must be mindful to be able to make the choice (which is why the module is called *core mindfulness*). One may choose to *solve the problem* (using interpersonal effectiveness), *change how one feels about the problem* (emotion regulation), *accept or tolerate the problem and how one feels* (distress tolerance), or *stay miserable and/or make things worse* (anything that is not one of the previous choices; Linehan & Dexter-Mazza, 2008, p. 396). Think critically about skills training and problem solving by referring to Sidebar 4.

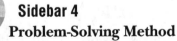

Sidebar 4
Problem-Solving Method

One of the main goals of DBT is to decrease ineffective coping behaviors and increase effective ones. Read about the four sets of skills. How do you think the problem-solving method could help clients in moments of high urge for suicide or self-harm? How would you help a client who called you but reported feeling incapable of using any skill to avoid self-harming? Discuss with a partner or in a small group.

Case Management Strategies

Case management strategies also reflect the fundamental dialectic of balancing *intervention on the client's behalf* (acceptance) and *consultation to the client* (change; Linehan & Schmidt, 1995). Because the therapist and client are a team, the client is included in case management issues, and DBT is heavily weighted toward consultation to the client. This means that the therapist consults with the client rather than with the client's other treatment providers alone and tries to get the client to set up meetings regarding his or her own treatment. Conference calls are made with the client in the room. This teaches clients how to effectively care for themselves and manage their affairs. It also decreases staff splitting because all treaters are involved in the decision-making process (Linehan, 1993). The therapist will only intervene on the client's behalf if the short-term gains outweigh the long-term gains as a learning situation (e.g., to save the client's life, when it is the humane thing to do, when the issue is very minor, or when the client is unable to make contact with his or her providers).

Family and Support Systems

Clients with BPD need a strong support system. Unfortunately, even when clients with BPD possess good interpersonal skills, they may have difficulty applying them appropriately because of interfering high emotions (Linehan & Schmidt, 1995). Difficulties with emotion regulation and with applying interpersonal effectiveness skills can contribute to strain in family relationships. Furthermore, given that the biosocial model contends that clients with BPD grew up in an invalidating environment, it may be the case that some family members have a past or current role in perpetuating clients' dysfunctional behaviors (Sturrock & Mellor, 2014). Several skills normally taught during the group skills training sessions are particularly helpful for interacting with family members. For example, reality acceptance can help a client accept that sometimes family members will continue to be invalidating and view those situations as learning opportunities.

It is often beneficial for families and loved ones of clients to learn what DBT is and to see what the client is doing to achieve a life worth living (Rathus & Miller, 2014). Family sessions can reduce family members' anxiety by showing that progress is being made and that family members are not being blamed. In addition, it can be constructive to invite family members to a group skills training session to learn DBT skills for themselves (Fruzzetti, Santisteban, & Hoffman, 2007). For example, radical acceptance can help family members come to terms with a client's mental illness. Instructing family members in validation and limit setting can reduce the number and severity of conflicts during interactions with the client.

Applications of DBT

As the most researched and effective approach for the treatment of BPD, DBT has evolved from a treatment for suicidality and NSSI into the gold-standard treatment for adult clients with BPD, reducing multiple associated problems, including suicide attempts, NSSI, suicidal ideation, inpatient psychiatric days, treatment attrition, and hopelessness (Lynch, Trost, Salsman, & Linehan, 2007; Robins & Chapman, 2004). Thus far, DBT has been found effective for adults who suffer jointly from BPD and other conditions, such as substance use disorders (SUDs; Chen, Matthews, Allen, Kuo, & Linehan, 2008). For stand-alone diagnoses, DBT has applications for depression in older adults with mixed personality features (Lynch, Morse, Mendelson, & Robins, 2003), for posttraumatic stress disorder and complex trauma (Bohus et al., 2013), for adult attention-deficit/hyperactivity disorder (Philipsen et al., 2010), and for binge-eating disorder (Telch, Agras, & Linehan, 2001). DBT has been adapted successfully for use with adolescent populations (Rathus & Miller, 2002) and adolescents with eating disorders (Fischer & Peterson, 2014). Three specific applications are described in greater detail here. It is important to note that until efficacy has been rigorously tested, DBT should not be used with different populations.

DBT Applications With Children and Adolescents

DBT has been adapted successfully for use with adolescent populations (Rathus & Miller, 2002), including multidisordered suicidal adolescents (Mehlum et al., 2016) and adolescents with eating disorders (Fischer & Peterson, 2014). It has been developed for a variety of settings, such as residential care and foster care (Groves, Backer, van den Bosch, & Miller, 2012; Perepletchikova et al., 2011).

Although idiographic modifications of DBT should be used with caution when one is treating younger clients with mental disorders (Linehan & Dexter-Mazza, 2008), certain elements of DBT, like validation skills or behavioral skills training, have broad appeal for this population. Skills training is particularly appealing for child and adolescent populations at large (Rathus & Miller, 2014). Depending on risk level and current functioning, teaching DBT skills to all children and adolescents could avert future problems in these behavioral domains, protect against the full blossoming of a mental disorder, or treat a disorder and improve functioning.

DBT Applications With Eating Disorders

Anywhere from a quarter to a half of all those diagnosed with an eating disorder also meet criteria for BPD (Sansone, Levitt, & Sansone, 2006). Furthermore, when an eating disorder is comorbid with BPD, it is more difficult to treat (Federici & Wisniewski, 2013). DBT is an effective treatment for stand-alone eating disorders like binge-eating disorder (Telch et al., 2001) and for those comorbid with BPD like bulimia nervosa and binge-eating disorder (Bankoff, Karpel, Forbes, & Pantalone, 2012; Chen et al., 2008).

In DBT eating disorders are primarily conceptualized as disorders of emotion regulation. Bingeing, for example, is thought to function as a way of regulating intolerable and out-of-control emotions (Linehan & Chen, 2005). Dietary restriction in anorexia nervosa, however, is a form of overcontrol. Similar to the biosocial model of BPD, restriction in anorexia nervosa may develop over time from the transaction between biological sensitivities (e.g., sensitivity to threat) and environmental reinforcement of overcontrolled behaviors (Chen et al., 2015). In the DBT hierarchical system of targets, disordered eating behaviors of both types fall under quality-of-life-interfering behaviors.

Multidiagnostic eating disorder–DBT (MED–DBT) is a newer form of DBT specifically tailored to address eating disorders—including both subtypes of anorexia nervosa—comorbid with BPD (Federici, Wisniewski, & Ben-Porath, 2012). MED–DBT follows a group therapy format for 6 months of intensive outpatient or day treatment and weaves well-established eating disorder interventions in with standard DBT protocols. In addition to being effective in ameliorating under- and overcontrolled eating behaviors, MED–DBT has been helpful for achieving weight gain in underweight patients, a reduction in suicidal/NSSI behaviors, medical stabilization, and treatment retention. Note that both MED–DBT and standard DBT may be helpful in particular because of high treatment retention. MED–DBT was originally tested in patients who had already attempted standard treatment for an eating disorder without success. Other studies show that in head-to-head comparisons with effective treatments, individuals in a DBT group often have lower dropout rates (Courbasson, Nishikawa, & Dixon, 2012).

DBT Applications With SUDs

Roughly three quarters of individuals with BPD will have a comorbid SUD in their lifetime (Tomko, Trull, Wood, & Sher, 2014). It is especially difficult to treat patients who have BPD comorbid with SUDs, and such cases present even higher rates of suicidal behaviors and poorer treatment outcomes than either disorder alone (Dimeff & Linehan, 2008; Zanarini, Frankenburg, Hennen, Reich, & Silk, 2004). Fortunately, DBT is effective for adults who suffer jointly from SUDs and BPD (Linehan et al., 1999; van den Bosch, Verheul, Schippers, & van den Brink, 2002). With its high treatment retention rates, DBT helps clients reduce use, maintain abstinence, and better regulate emotion. One study investigating a smartphone application for comorbid SUD/BPD ("DBT coach") showed that participants had a significant reduction in substance cravings and emotion intensity (Rizvi, Dimeff, Skutch, Carroll, & Linehan, 2011).

DBT modified for treating SUDs (DBT–SUD) balances the goal of total abstinence with strong elements of relapse prevention, such as coping ahead (e.g., taking proactive steps to prevent future use) and burning bridges (e.g., removing cues to substance use). For the duration of treatment, clients commit to abstinence while they work on a path to *clear mind*, which is the DBT–SUD synthesis between the *addict mind* (i.e., a focus on substance use) and the *clean mind* (i.e., a focus on abstinence). Throughout treatment, clients work on building an environment conducive to clean living for themselves balanced with gaining mindful awareness of threats to recovery. Clients learn through chain analysis when and how urges have led to use, and they develop problem-solving skills to predict and prevent future use. Many DBT–SUD programs use urinalysis to aid in tracking client progress, and some include concurrent opiate agonist treatment (Linehan et al., 2002).

Thus far, there are few studies of DBT–SUD among those with SUD without comorbid BPD, and it is therefore possible that DBT–SUD may not generalize to populations with primary SUD alone. However, as DBT was originally developed for patients with multiple Axis I and II disorders, DBT–SUD reasonably might be used to treat SUDs with psychiatric comorbidities other than BPD, particularly when the substance use is associated with emotion dysregulation (Dimeff & Linehan, 2008).

Efficacy of DBT

The first randomized clinical trial using DBT to treat patients with BPD found a statistically significant decrease in parasuicidal behavior (26% DBT vs. 60% treatment as usual) and the number of inpatient treatment days 1 year after treatment (Linehan, Armstrong, Suarez, Allmon, & Heard, 1991). These results were subsequently replicated across multiple independent research teams and multiple randomized clinical trials (Koons et al., 2001; McQuillan et al., 2005; Verheul et al., 2003). Most efficacy studies of DBT have investigated standard DBT, which is comprehensive and includes the skills training group, individual sessions, coaching calls, and the consultation team. Modifications from standard protocol continue to be studied for efficacy with specific populations, settings, and disorders.

Although DBT in its many forms has promising results, it nevertheless has limitations important to consider when evaluating which psychotherapy modality is optimal for a client. General limitations include small sample sizes and methodological heterogeneity in meta-analyses. A review by Chapman (2008) found that there was better evidence at the time for non-DBT types of therapy in adult patients with major depressive disorder (with the earlier noted exception of major depressive disorder in older adults), panic disorders, posttraumatic stress disorder, bulimia nervosa, primary SUDs, and psychotic disorders. DBT is still a relatively new therapy, and many research teams continue to explore its use for other indications, including bipolar disorder (Van Dijk, Jeffrey, & Katz, 2013) and treatment-resistant depression (Harley, Sprich, Safren, Jacobo, & Fava, 2008).

Verbatim Transcript: DBT

The following verbatim transcript of a fourth session is presented in order to illustrate information about the principles and practice of DBT as described in this chapter. We provide a brief overview of the case, the actual transcript, a short critique of the session, and an explanation as to why we think this theory effectively addressed the problem.

Overview

Cara was a 16-year-old Hispanic female referred by her psychiatrist to a comprehensive DBT program. The psychiatrist recommended DBT in response to a suicide attempt earlier in the year as well as a pattern of disordered eating. Cara presented with significant emotion dysregulation as well as a lack of skills for coping with negative affect. She reported needing help with problems in all five of the DBT problem areas (i.e., inattention, poor dysregulation of sadness and anxiety, feelings of being overwhelmed, communication difficulties with her family members, and binge/purge behaviors). Cara reportedly had attempted suicide by cutting her wrist, which was her first self-injurious and suicidal act. In the intake interview, Cara presented with a euthymic affect and reportedly did not think DBT was needed at this time, as she was not currently in a crisis. Cara's apparent competence persisted through the first several sessions of pretreatment, which focused on providing psychoeducation about biosocial theory and the structure, modes, and functions of DBT. Commitment was obtained during pretreatment, and Cara began comprehensive DBT including individual therapy, a multifamily skills group (with her parents), and phone coaching. As per the fourth mode of treatment, the therapist (Nora Girardi) participated in a DBT consultation team in order to receive help with problem assessment and address any skill deficits. The following transcript reflects the fourth treatment session with the client.

Transcript of the Fourth Session

Therapist: Hi Cara! I'm so happy to see you are on time and that we can have our full 45 minutes together. On my agenda, I have reviewing your diary card and checking in on how group has been going. What is on your agenda?

Client: Nothing. I don't think you will be happy when you see my diary card.

Therapist: Oh, that makes me feel anxious. Let's see it. [Therapist reviews diary card] Okay, so to summarize—it looks like you were thinking about suicide throughout the week with low to moderate intensity. Is that right?

Client: Yeah. But I am over it now, it's fine.

Therapist: And you engaged in self-harm on Monday. Cara! I am so disappointed that you did not call me for coaching prior to cutting. I would have loved the opportunity to coach you through this moment of distress. Not calling for coaching is a therapy-interfering behavior, a Target II, that we will also have to address, okay?

Client: Yeah, I get it. I just didn't want to bother you.

Therapist: Cutting yourself bothers me a lot more than you calling for coaching ever will. We are going to have to chain out this behavior. Before we do that let me finish reviewing the card. So I see no urges to binge, no urges to purge, and no binge/purge behaviors. That's awesome! It looks like we are getting some of this disordered eating under control.

Client: Yep.

Therapist: Now we just have to build up your skill set to continue building a life worth living, including not cutting or thinking about suicide. Okay, so it also looks like you took your medication as prescribed, great. So Cara before we start chaining out what happened on Monday, I want to ask what your urge was from zero to five to quit therapy when you let my office last week.

Client: About a one. I wasn't really thinking about it at all.

Therapist: And what about your urge to quit therapy today, walking into my office? Again on a scale from zero to five.

Client: About a one. I figured you would be pissed about me cutting but didn't necessarily want to quit because of that.

Therapist: Good, I am so glad to hear that. And no, I am not pissed off. I just wish I had been given the opportunity to coach you on using skills before you cut. Now we need to use quite a bit of our session to chain through what happened and see where we can take a different and skillful path. Before we do that, tell me—where did you cut?

Client: On my wrist.

Therapist: How long was the cut?

Client: I don't know, less than an inch.

Therapist: And how deep?

Client: Not very deep.

Therapist: You mean a superficial cut?

Client: Yeah. It bled for like a minute but wasn't like dripping or anything and stopped pretty quickly.

Therapist: Okay. So let's start this chain. [Therapist takes out whiteboard and marker] Let's first think about any vulnerabilities that were going on that day. Can you think of any?

Client: I didn't sleep that great the night before. I had a lot of trouble falling asleep and then had to wake up early for school. I was exhausted and just did not feel like going to school or doing anything at all.

Therapist: What time do you think you fell asleep?

Client: I don't know . . . probably not 'til like one or something.

Therapist: And remind me what time you have to get up for school?

Client: Five.

Therapist: Whoa! So you really did not get much sleep. It sounds like sleep was a huge vulnerability.

Client: Yeah, I guess so.

Therapist: What else?

Client: I'm not sure.

Therapist: Well let's think of other vulnerabilities and refer to the PLEASE [(treat) PhysicaL illness, (balance) Eating, Avoid mood-altering alcohol/drugs, (balance) Sleep, (get) Exercise] skill. How was your physical health that day? Were you feeling under the weather at all?

Client: I was feeling fine, nothing out of the ordinary.

Therapist: Eating? How was your eating on Monday?

Client: I didn't eat a ton. Skipped breakfast, had pizza for lunch and really can't remember if I had dinner. The end of the day is kind of a blur.

Therapist: Luckily we have a whole skills module to help you with that inattention to the present moment. So you didn't quite have balanced meals and your food choices may have had negative impacts on your mood as well. Any alcohol or drugs?

Client: Nope.

Therapist: We already talked about sleep and how that was certainly a vulnerability factor on this day. What about exercise?

Client: No, I didn't exercise either. This is making me feel really shitty. I didn't try to let all of these things happen and I feel like you're just pointing out all the crap that I should have done but didn't.

Therapist: I hear that you are feeling frustrated and kind of defeated right now, and it is so important to go over the events leading up to and immediately following your self-harm in order to decrease your urges and actions. That is a goal you still have, right? To stop cutting?

Client: Yeah. I just feel like there is nothing I can do about it.

Therapist: In this first part of the chain it actually does look like there are some things you can do to decrease your vulnerability to negative emotions. Continuing to work on your sleep hygiene and patterns will be something we work on. Anything else that you see here that you think you could do differently in the future?

Client: I've been meaning to start going for walks again after school to clear my head.

Therapist: I love that! Maybe we can add that to your diary card. So yes, there are a number of things you can do to decrease these vulnerabilities. I will print out a copy of the PLEASE skills worksheet for you before you leave so that you can reference that throughout the week. So we have gone through the vulnerabilities, and now I am wondering what time of the day on Monday did you cut yourself?

Client: It was pretty much right after school. Maybe like 4:00.

Therapist: So what happened? What was the precipitating event that made you feel like you needed to cut?

Client: I just had a stressful day overall.

Therapist: How so?

Client: It's just about to be midterms, which is already a time that stresses me out a lot. It's just so much going on at once and teachers expect so much from us! I have to study and then they just load on additional assignments and act as if their class is the only class that matters.

Therapist: You must be really strapped for time. It makes sense that you were feeling overwhelmed with so much on your plate.

Client: Yeah. So I had so much shit to do that by the time I got home my anxiety was like a 10 because I knew I was going to be up all night studying and doing work.

Therapist: So I am adding to the chain this buildup of school stress. Possibly another vulnerability. Walk me through when you get home. You said your anxiety was at a 10, was it this high the moment you walked through the door at home?

Client: Yeah. Maybe like an eight on the drive home and then I pulled into the driveway and just felt sick.

Therapist: What was going through your head?

Client: I was thinking that my mom was going to be on my back and that no one would understand or get why I was feeling so stressed.

Therapist: I know that we have talked about you getting stomachaches and feelings of nausea when feeling super anxious—were these symptoms some of what were making you feel sick?

Client: Yeah definitely.

Therapist: And your mind was sort of thinking about a lot of stressful things including how much school work you needed to do and then being even more stressed from your parents not getting it.

Client: Yeah exactly.

Therapist: At what point did you start thinking about self-harm?

Client: Well when I pulled into the driveway I remember thinking that I was better off killing myself right there in the car than going inside and dealing with my parents.

Therapist: Well yes, it is true that if you were dead you wouldn't have to deal with them. And we have no evidence that it would in fact be better than dealing with them.

Client: [Smirks] Yeah, whatever. That is what I was thinking.

Therapist: So you have this thought that you would be better off dead. You're feeling physically sick from your anxiety. What happens next?

Client: Well I walked inside anyway.

Therapist: That was a great use of your opposite action. I'm sure your emotions were telling you to do a lot of other things like maybe drive away, stay in the car, or hurt yourself.

Client: Right. So I walked inside and just as I had thought, a shitstorm is brewing. The absolute second that I walk in I can hear my little brother Ryan crying, my mom like throws a dishrag at me and tells me to clean the dishes so she can take care of him. This is literally all before I even put down my backpack, books, or anything!

Therapist: You must have been so annoyed that exactly what you expected was accurate. So I am adding all of these things you are mentioning as links in our chain.

Client: So then I throw the dishrag down and I just scream that I am absolutely not doing the dishes. My anger was about a 1,000 out of 10.

Therapist: And so I am wondering here is this could have been another place to use a skill. It sounds like you wanted to communicate with your mother that you were feeling overwhelmed and that you needed to spend the evening studying and doing your schoolwork.

Client: Yeah but I just couldn't right then!

Therapist: I think that it would have been possible to use the DEAR MAN [Describe, Express, Assert, Reinforce Mindful, Appear confident, Negotiate] and GIVE [Gentle, Interested, Validate, Easy manner] skills. We can review those later.

Client: I guess I could have if I had remembered.

Therapist: And since we know that going home after school tends to be stressful and overwhelming, it may be important for us to make a cope-ahead plan. So this is possibly an alternate route that the chain could take. Walk me through what else happened that day.

Client: I screamed at my mom and then she just looks at me with such an evil eye and basically says that I am the laziest person she ever met, that I have no responsibilities at all and that if I don't start contributing to the household that she will kick me out.

Therapist: And that completely invalidated how you were feeling.

Client: Yep, typical. I didn't even say anything back. I ran into my room, threw my books and backpack at the wall, grabbed the pocket knife I have hidden in my drawer, and cut myself.

Therapist: So the prompting event, it sounds like, was going into your bedroom where you knew your knife was. Shit was totally hitting the fan for you and you were getting angrier, more upset, and more anxious. Those emotions were too difficult to cope with and so you went into your room with the intention of hurting yourself.

Client: Pretty much.

Therapist: Now what could you have done instead?

Client: I could have called you.

Therapist: Yes, I love that! If you walked into your room and noticed your urge to cut, you could have and should have called me for coaching, yes. So that is an alternate direction for this chain of events.

Client: True.

Therapist: What else? I am thinking that we need to get rid of this knife so that you don't have the option to cut with it. I know mom doesn't keep any sharp knives in the house and she probably doesn't know that you have this one hidden, right?

Client: Right. But like what do you want me to do with it? Throw it out?

Therapist: I would love if you threw it out, yes. Threw it out somewhere where you wouldn't be able to retrieve it.

Client: It's an old knife that a friend gave to me, it means a lot.

Therapist: So it sounds like you are not on board for getting rid of it completely?

Client: Yeah, I'd rather not.

Therapist: I still want to do something that will slow you down when you go to reach for the knife. Do you have duct tape in the house?

Client: Yes.

Therapist: I want you to put about 15 layers of duct tape on and around the knife. Tape it so that you cannot easily flip the blade up.

Client: Seriously?

Therapist: Seriously. That way, you cannot cut impulsively with the knife. You will have no choice but to slow down and think of something else you can do, such as call me.

Client: [Laughs] I mean I guess if you really want me to I will.

Therapist: Great. What other things could have gone differently?

Client: I don't know.

Therapist: I am thinking that you could have used your TIPP [Temperature, Intense exercise, Paced breathing, Progressive muscle relaxation] skills here. You could go into the bathroom and splash some cold water on your face or use an ice pack. Or practice some of the paced breathing I taught you last week.

Client: That's true, I could. I mean I guess I would be more likely to think of it if I had to stop and slow down because of the duct tape on my knife.

Therapist: Exactly! That is the idea. So it looks like we have identified a number of missing links in this chain and have brainstormed some really great things you can do differently next time. That includes decreasing your vulnerabilities and increasing skills use and phone coaching. So here is your diary card for this week. Let's add in going for a walk as a behavior to monitor. That would be great to get outside and get some fresh air and a little exercise on your own.

Client: Okay, I will.

Therapist: Can you take a picture of this chain with your phone? So you can remind yourself of the other options you have besides cutting yourself?

Client: Yes.

Therapist: And I'd like you to duct tape your knife tonight. That would be great news to hear so please give me a call to let me know when you have done it. If I don't hear from you by 8 p.m., I will check in, okay?

Client: Okay.

Therapist: Okay, great. So I will hear from you later tonight and see you next week.

Critique of the Session

This session demonstrates a standard DBT for adolescents individual therapy session. In individual sessions, one of the primary agenda items is a review of the diary card. Clients are provided with a diary card that monitors suicidal and self-harm urges and actions and general emotionality on a daily basis. Diary cards are tailored to also monitor behaviors relevant to the patient; in this case, binge/purge behaviors were added to Cara's diary card. When Target I behaviors (life-threatening behaviors, including suicidal, homicidal, and self-harm thoughts, urges, and actions) are indicated on the diary card, a chain analysis is utilized to assess vulnerabilities, precipitating events, links, and consequences. One of the purposes of the chain analysis is to identify where more skillful behavior can replace unskillful behavior. In this session, I (Nora) went through an entire chain analysis with Cara following indication of self-harm behavior. I balanced change strategies (e.g., irreverence) with acceptance-based strategies, including validation. I adequately allocated most of the session to assessing and problem-solving the patient's self-harm.

Why the Theory Is Effective Relative to This Problem

DBT is specifically indicated for the treatment of suicidal behaviors, and DBT views suicidality as the patient's approach to problem solving. Thus, skills are taught to replace these unskillful behaviors; this is part of the process of building a life worth living for the patient. DBT balances acceptance and change while maintaining movement, speed, and flow to optimize session content and process. In the session, suicidal and life-threatening Target I behaviors are targeted directly as the key problems to be solved. In addition, DBT is specifically indicated for individuals for whom emotion dysregulation is at the core of their problems. Thus, a teen presenting with ineffective responses to emotional affectivity (e.g., binge/purge behaviors) would particularly benefit from the skills modules of DBT, which each target specific problem behaviors. With the dialectical philosophy at its core, DBT radically accepts the patient as he or she is and believes that each patient is trying as hard as he or she can and at the same time try harder to build a life worth living.

Summary

Since its inception in the late 1970s, DBT has earned a reputation as the definitive treatment for difficult-to-treat, severely disordered clients. Originally developed by Marsha Linehan to treat women with chronic suicidality and self-harm behaviors, it evolved from its cognitive–behavioral roots into a comprehensive therapeutic program that balances behaviorist principles with Zen practices and dialectical philosophy. It is the gold-standard treatment for adults with BPD, which is primarily characterized by severe emotion dysregulation. For clients suffering from severe emotion dysregulation, DBT offers a highly structured and supportive framework within which clients can work toward making a life worth living. Once admitted to a DBT program, clients engage in weekly individual therapy sessions; telephone coaching calls; and intensive skills training in mindfulness, distress tolerance, emotion regulation, and interpersonal effectiveness. DBT therapists engage in their own version of therapy—the therapist consultation team—to help them maintain effective therapeutic behaviors with clients. Researchers have found DBT to be efficacious for treating several other disorders and populations (like adolescents with suicidality), but because it is a relatively new treatment, more high-quality, controlled studies are warranted.

Suggested Resources and Websites

For more information about DBT theory and practice, please refer to the following resources and websites:

Jobes, D. A. (2006). *Managing suicidal risk: A collaborative approach.* New York, NY: Guilford Press.

Koerner, K. (2012). *Doing dialectical behavior therapy: A practical guide.* New York, NY: Guilford Press.

Linehan, M. M. (2014). *DBT® skills training handouts and worksheets.* New York, NY: Guilford Press.

Linehan, M. M. (2014). *DBT® skills training manual.* New York, NY: Guilford Press.

Linehan, M. M., & Dawkins, K. (2003). *From suffering to freedom: Practicing reality acceptance.* Seattle, WA: Behavioral Tech.

Martin, G., & Pear, J. (1998). *Behavior modification: What it is and how to do it* (Part 3, 6th ed.). Englewood Cliffs, NJ: Prentice Hall.

Nhât, H., & Vo-Dinh, M. (1987). *The miracle of mindfulness: A manual on meditation.* Boston, MA: Beacon Press.

- Cornell University, What Is Self-Injury?
  www.selfinjury.bctr.cornell.edu/index.html
- National Education Alliance for Borderline Personality Disorder
  www.borderlinepersonalitydisorder.com/
- National Institute of Mental Health, Borderline Personality Disorder
  https://www.nimh.nih.gov/health/topics/borderline-personality-disorder/index.shtml
- New York-Presbyterian Weill Cornell Medical Center, Borderline Personality Disorder Resource Center
  www.nyp.org/bpdresourcecenter
- The Linehan Institute, Behavioral Tech
  www.behavioraltech.org

References

Arens, E. A., Grabe, H. J., Spitzer, C., & Barnow, S. (2011). Testing the biosocial model of borderline personality disorder: Results of a prospective 5-year longitudinal study. *Personality and Mental Health, 5*(1), 29–42.

Aviram, R. B., Brodsky, B. S., & Stanley, B. (2006). Borderline personality disorder, stigma, and treatment implications. *Harvard Review of Psychiatry, 14*(5), 249–256.

Axelrod, S. R., & Lee, J. (2013). Applying dialectical behavior therapy methods to personality disorder patients in healthcare settings. *Asia Health Care Journal, 1,* 5–10.

Bankoff, S. M., Karpel, M. G., Forbes, H. E., & Pantalone, D. W. (2012). A systematic review of dialectical behavior therapy for the treatment of eating disorders. *Eating Disorders, 20*(3), 196–215.

Beckstead, D. J., Lambert, M. J., DuBose, A. P., & Linehan, M. M. (2015). Dialectical behavior therapy with American Indian/Alaska Native adolescents diagnosed with substance use disorders: Combining an evidence based treatment with cultural, traditional, and spiritual beliefs. *Addictive Behaviors, 51,* 84–87.

Bedics, J., Atkins, D., Harned, M., & Linehan, M. (2015). The therapeutic alliance as a predictor of outcome in dialectical behavior therapy versus nonbehavioral psychotherapy by experts for borderline personality disorder. *Psychotherapy, 51,* 67–77.

Ben-Porath, D. D. (2004). Strategies for securing commitment to treatment from individuals diagnosed with borderline personality disorder. *Journal of Contemporary Psychotherapy, 34*(3), 247–263.

Ben-Porath, D. D. (2015). Orienting clients to telephone coaching in dialectical behavior therapy. *Cognitive and Behavioral Practice, 22,* 407–414.

Bhugra, D., & Bhui, K. (2001). *Cross-cultural psychiatry: A practical guide.* London, UK: Arnold.

Bohus, M., Dyer, A. S., Priebe, K., Krüger, A., Kleindienst, N., Schmahl, C., . . . Steil, R. (2013). Dialectical behaviour therapy for post-traumatic stress disorder after childhood sexual abuse in patients with and without borderline personality disorder: A randomised controlled trial. *Psychotherapy and Psychosomatics, 82*(4), 221–233.

Bopp, M. J., & Weeks, G. R. (1984). Dialectical metatheory in family therapy. *Family Process, 23*(1), 49–61.

Carey, B. (2011, June 23). *Expert on mental illness reveals her own fight.* Retrieved from the *New York Times* website: http://www.nytimes. com/2011/06/23/health/23lives.html?pagewanted=all&_r=0

Chapman, A. (2008). Is dialectical behavior therapy the right "fit" for your patient? *Current Psychiatry, 7*(12), 60–66.

Chen, E. Y., Matthews, L., Allen, C., Kuo, J. R., & Linehan, M. M. (2008). Dialectical behavior therapy for clients with binge-eating disorder or bulimia nervosa and borderline personality disorder. *International Journal of Eating Disorders, 41,* 505–512.

Chen, E. Y., Segal, K., Weissman, J., Zeffiro, T. A., Gallop, R., Linehan, M. M., . . . Lynch, T. R. (2015). Adapting dialectical behavior therapy for outpatient adult anorexia nervosa: A pilot study. *International Journal of Eating Disorders, 48*(1), 123–132.

Courbasson, C., Nishikawa, Y., & Dixon, L. (2012). Outcome of dialectical behaviour therapy for concurrent eating and substance use disorders. *Clinical Psychology & Psychotherapy, 19,* 434–449.

Crowell, S. E., Beauchaine, T. P., & Linehan, M. M. (2009). A biosocial developmental model of borderline personality: Elaborating and extending Linehan's theory. *Psychological Bulletin, 135,* 495–510.

Dimeff, L. A., & Linehan, M. M. (2001). Dialectical behavior therapy in a nutshell. *The California Psychologist, 34*(3), 10–13.

Dimeff, L. A., & Linehan, M. M. (2008). Dialectical behavior therapy for substance abusers. *Addiction Science & Clinical Practice, 4*(2), 39–47.

Distel, M. A., Trull, T. J., Derom, C. A., Thiery, E. W., Grimmer, M. A., Martin, N. G., . . . Boomsma, D. I. (2008). Heritability of borderline personality disorder features is similar across three countries. *Psychological Medicine, 38,* 1219–1229.

Federici, A., & Wisniewski, L. (2013). An intensive DBT program for patients with multidiagnostic eating disorder presentations: A case series analysis. *International Journal of Eating Disorders, 46*(4), 322–331.

Federici, A., Wisniewski, L., & Ben-Porath, D. (2012). Description of an intensive dialectical behavior therapy program for multidiagnostic clients with eating disorders. *Journal of Counseling & Development, 90,* 330–338.

Fischer, S., & Peterson, C. (2014). Dialectical behavior therapy for adolescent binge eating, purging, suicidal behavior, and non-suicidal self-injury: A pilot study. *Psychotherapy, 52,* 78–92.

Fruzzetti, A. E., Santisteban, D. A., & Hoffman, P. D. (2007). Dialectical behavior therapy with families. In L. A. Dimeff & K. Koerner (Eds.), *Dialectical behavior therapy in clinical practice* (pp. 222–244). New York, NY: Guilford Press.

Fruzzetti, A. E., Shenk, C., & Hoffman, P. D. (2005). Family interaction and the development of borderline personality disorder: A transactional model. *Development and Psychopathology, 17,* 1007–1030.

Germán, M., Smith, H. L., Rivera-Morales, C., González, G., Haliczer, L. A., Haaz, C., & Miller, A. L. (2015). Dialectical behavior therapy for suicidal Latina adolescents: Supplemental dialectical corollaries and treatment targets. *American Journal of Psychotherapy, 69*(2), 179–197.

Groves, S., Backer, H. S., van den Bosch, W., & Miller, A. L. (2012). Dialectical behaviour therapy with adolescents. *Child and Adolescent Mental Health, 17*(2), 65–75.

Gunderson, J. G. (1996). The borderline patient's intolerance of aloneness: Insecure attachments and therapist availability. *American Journal of Psychiatry, 164,* 1637–1640.

Haddock, L. R. (2016). Dialectical behavior therapy. In D. Capuzzi & M. D. Stauffer (Eds.), *Counseling and psychotherapy: Theories and interventions* (6th ed., pp. 253–281). Alexandria, VA: American Counseling Association.

Hall, G. C. N., Hong, J. J., Zane, N. W., & Meyer, O. L. (2011). Culturally-competent treatments for Asian Americans: The relevance of mindfulness and acceptance-based therapies. *Clinical Psychology: Science and Practice, 18*(3), 215–231.

Harley, R., Sprich, S., Safren, S., Jacobo, M., & Fava, M. (2008). Adaptation of dialectical behavior therapy skills training group for treatment-resistant depression. *Journal of Nervous and Mental Disease, 196*(2), 136–143.

Hawkins, R. P. (1986). Selection of target behaviors. In R. O. Nelson & S. C. Hayes (Eds.), *Conceptual foundations of behavioral assessment* (pp. 331–385). New York, NY: Guilford Press.

Hayes, S. C., Strosahl, K., & Wilson, K. G. (1999). *Acceptance and commitment therapy: An experiential approach to behavior change.* New York, NY: Guilford Press.

Hayes, S. C., Strosahl, K. D., Wilson, K. G., Bissett, R. C., Pistorello, J., Toarmino, D., . . . McCurry, S. M. (2004). Measuring experiential avoidance: A preliminary test of a working model. *The Psychological Record, 54,* 553–578.

Heard, H. L., & Linehan, M. M. (1994). Dialectical behavior therapy: An integrative approach to the treatment of borderline personality disorder. *Journal of Psychotherapy Integration, 4*(1), 55–82.

Hernandez, A., Arntz, A., Gaviria, A. M., Labad, A., & Gutiérrez-Zotes, J. A. (2012). Relationships between childhood maltreatment, parenting style, and borderline personality disorder criteria. *Journal of Personality Disorders, 26,* 727–736.

Houlgate, S. (1991). *Freedom, truth and history: An introduction to Hegel's philosophy.* London, UK: Routledge.

Kabat-Zinn, J. (1990). *Full catastrophe living: The program of the Stress Reduction Clinic at the University of Massachusetts Medical Center.* New York, NY: Delta.

Kabat-Zinn, J. (1994). *Wherever you go, there you are: Mindfulness meditation in everyday life.* New York, NY: Hyperion Books.

Koerner, K., & Linehan, M. M. (1997). Case formulation in dialectical behavior therapy for borderline personality disorder. In E. Eells (Ed.), *Handbook of psychotherapy case formulation* (pp. 340–367). New York, NY: Guilford Press.

Koons, C., Robins, C., Tweed, J., Lynch, T., Gonzalez, A., Morse, J., . . . Bastian, L. (2001). Efficacy of dialectical behavior therapy in women veterans with borderline personality disorder. *Behavior Therapy, 32*(2), 371–390.

Kuo, J. R., Khoury, J. E., Metcalfe, R., Fitzpatrick, S., & Goodwill, A. (2015). An examination of the relationship between emotional abuse and borderline personality disorder features: The role of difficulties with emotion regulation. *Child Abuse & Neglect, 39,* 147–155.

Linehan, M. M. (1993). *Cognitive-behavioral treatment of borderline personality disorder.* New York, NY: Guilford Press.

Linehan, M. M. (1997). Validation and psychotherapy. In A. Bohart & L. Greenberg (Eds.), *Empathy reconsidered: New directions in psychotherapy* (pp. 353–392). Washington, DC: American Psychological Association.

Linehan, M. M. (2015). *DBT® skills training manual* (2nd ed.). New York, NY: Guilford Press.

Linehan, M. M., Armstrong, H. E., Suarez, A., Allmon, D., & Heard, H. L. (1991). Cognitive-behavioral treatment of chronically parasuicidal borderline patients. *Archives of General Psychiatry, 48,* 1060–1064.

Linehan, M. M., Bohus, M., & Lynch, T. R. (2007). Dialectical behavior therapy for pervasive emotion dysregulation. In J. J. Gross (Ed.), *Handbook of emotion regulation* (pp. 581–605). New York, NY: Guilford Press.

Linehan, M. M., & Chen, E. Y. (2005). Dialectical behavior therapy for eating disorders. *Encyclopedia of Cognitive Behavior Therapy, 4,* 168–171.

Linehan, M. M., & Dexter-Mazza, E. (2008). Dialectical behavior therapy for borderline personality disorder. In D. H. Barlow (Ed.), *Clinical handbook of psychological disorders* (pp. 365–420). New York, NY: Guilford Press.

Linehan, M. M., Dimeff, L. A., Reynolds, S. K., Comtois, K. A., Welch, S. S., Heagerty, P., & Kivlahan, D. R. (2002). Dialectical behavior therapy versus comprehensive validation therapy plus 12-step for the treatment of opioid dependent women meeting criteria for borderline personality disorder. *Drug and Alcohol Dependence, 67*(1), 13–26.

Linehan, M. M., & Schmidt, H. III. (1995). The dialectics of effective treatment of borderline personality disorder. In W. O. O'Donohue & L. Krasner (Eds.), *Theories of behavior therapy: Exploring behavior change* (pp. 553–584). Washington, DC: American Psychological Association.

Linehan, M. M., Schmidt, H., Dimeff, L. A., Craft, J. C., Kanter, J., & Comtois, K. A. (1999). Dialectical behavior therapy for patients with borderline personality disorder and drug-dependence. *American Journal on Addictions, 8*(4), 279–292.

Lynch, T. R., Chapman, A. L., Rosenthal, M. Z., Kuo, J. R., & Linehan, M. M. (2006). Mechanisms of change in dialectical behavior therapy: Theoretical and empirical observations. *Journal of Clinical Psychology, 62,* 459–480.

Lynch, T. R., Morse, J. Q., Mendelson, T., & Robins, C. J. (2003). Dialectical behavior therapy for depressed older adults: A randomized pilot study. *American Journal of Geriatric Psychiatry, 11*(1), 33–45.

Lynch, T. R., Robins, C. J., Morse, J. Q., & Krause, E. D. (2001). A mediational model relating affect intensity, emotion inhibition, and psychological distress. *Behavior Therapy, 32,* 519–536.

Lynch, T. R., Trost, W. T., Salsman, N., & Linehan, M. M. (2007). Dialectical behavior therapy for borderline personality disorder. *Annual Review of Clinical Psychology, 3,* 181–205.

McMain, S., Sayrs, J. H. R., Dimeff, L. A., & Linehan, M. M. (2007). Dialectical behavior therapy for individuals with borderline personality disorder and substance dependence. In L. A. Dimeff & K. Koerner (Eds.), *Dialectical behavior therapy in clinical practice: Applications across disorders and settings* (pp. 145–173). New York, NY: Guilford Press.

McQuillan, A., Nicastro, R., Guenot, F., Girard, M., Lissner, C., & Ferrero, F. (2005). Intensive dialectical behavior therapy for outpatients with borderline personality disorder who are in crisis. *Psychiatric Services, 56*(2), 193–197.

Mehlum, L., Ramberg, M., Tørmoen, A. J., Haga, E., Diep, L. M., Stanley, B. H., . . . Grøholt, B. (2016). Dialectical behavior therapy compared with enhanced usual care for adolescents with repeated suicidal and self-harming behavior: Outcomes over a one-year follow-up. *Journal of the American Academy of Child and Adolescent Psychiatry, 55*(4), 295–300.

Neacsiu, A. D., & Linehan, M. M. (2014). Dialectical behavior therapy for borderline personality disorder. In D. H. Barlow (Ed.), *Clinical handbook of psychological disorders* (5th ed., pp. 394–461). New York, NY: Guilford Press.

Nehls, N. (1998). Borderline personality disorder: Gender stereotypes, stigma, and limited system of care. *Issues in Mental Health Nursing, 19*(2), 97–112.

O'Hearn, A., Pollard, R., & Haynes, S. (2010). Dialectical behavior therapy for deaf clients: Cultural and linguistic modifications for outpatient mental health settings. In I. Leigh (Ed.), *Psychotherapy with deaf clients from diverse groups* (2nd ed., pp. 372–392). Washington, DC: Gallaudet University Press.

Ono, Y., & Okonogi, K. (1988). Borderline personality disorder in Japan: A comparative study of three diagnostic criteria. *Journal of Personality Disorders, 2*(3), 212–220.

Paris, J., & Lis, E. (2013). Can sociocultural and historical mechanisms influence the development of borderline personality disorder? *Transcultural Psychiatry, 50*(1), 140–151.

Perepletchikova, F., Axelrod, S. R., Kaufman, J., Rounsaville, B. J., Douglas-Palumberi, H., & Miller, A. L. (2011). Adapting dialectical behavior therapy for children: Towards a new research agenda for pediatric suicidal and non-suicidal self-injurious behaviors. *Child and Adolescent Mental Health, 16,* 116–121.

Philipsen, A., Graf, E., van Elst, L. T., Jans, T., Warnke, A., Hesslinger, B., . . . Jacob, C. (2010). Evaluation of the efficacy and effectiveness of a structured disorder tailored psychotherapy in ADHD in adults: Study protocol of a randomized controlled multicentre trial. *ADHD Attention Deficit and Hyperactivity Disorders, 2*(4), 203–212.

Pinto, C., Dhavale, H. S., Nair, S., Patil, B., & Dewan, M. (2000). Borderline personality disorder exists in India. *Journal of Nervous and Mental Disease, 188*(6), 386–388.

Rathus, J. H., & Miller, A. L. (2002). Dialectical behavior therapy adapted for suicidal adolescents. *Suicide & Life-threatening Behavior, 32*(2), 146–157.

Rathus, J. H., & Miller, A. L. (2014). *DBT® skills manual for adolescents.* New York, NY: Guilford Press.

Rizvi, S., Dimeff, L., Skutch, J., Carroll, D., & Linehan, M. (2011). A pilot study of the DBT coach: An interactive mobile phone application for individuals with borderline personality disorder and substance use disorder. *Behavior Therapy, 42,* 589–600.

Rizvi, S. L., & Ritschel, L. A. (2014). Mastering the art of chain analysis in dialectical behavior therapy. *Cognitive and Behavioral Practice, 21*(3), 335–349.

Robins, C. J., & Chapman, A. (2004). Dialectical behavior therapy: Current status, recent developments, and future directions. *Journal of Personality Disorders, 18*(1), 73–89.

Robins, C. J., & Koons, C. R. (2000). The therapeutic relationship in dialectical behavior therapy. In A. N. Sabo & L. Havens (Eds.), *The real world guide to psychotherapy practice* (pp. 237–266). Cambridge, MA: Harvard Press.

Sansone, R. A., Levitt, J. L., & Sansone, L. A. (2006). The prevalence of personality disorders in those with eating disorders. In R. A. Sansone & J. L. Levitt (Eds.), *Personality disorders and eating disorders: Exploring the frontier* (pp. 23–39). New York, NY: Routledge.

Segal, Z., Teasdale, J., & Williams, M. (2002). *Mindfulness-based cognitive therapy for depression.* New York, NY: Guilford Press.

Shearin, E., & Linehan, M. (1992). Patient–therapist ratings and relationship to progress in DBT for BPD. *Behavior Therapy, 23,* 730–741.

Shenk, C. E., & Fruzzetti, A. E. (2011). The impact of validating and invalidating responses on emotional reactivity. *Journal of Social and Clinical Psychology, 30*(2), 163–183.

Simmons, D. (1992). Gender issues and borderline personality disorder: Why do females dominate the diagnosis? *Archives of Psychiatric Nursing, 6*(4), 219–223.

Stiglmayr, C., Stecher-Mohr, J., Wagner, T., Meißner, J., Spretz, D., Steffens, C., . . . Renneberg, B. (2014). Effectiveness of dialectic behavioral therapy in routine outpatient care: The Berlin Borderline Study. *Borderline Personality Disorder and Emotion Dysregulation, 1*(1), 20. doi:10.1186/2051-6673-1-20

Sturrock, B. A., Francis, A., & Carr, S. (2009). Avoidance of affect mediates the effect of invalidating childhood environments on borderline personality symptomatology in a non-clinical sample. *Clinical Psychologist, 13*(2), 41–51.

Sturrock, B. A., & Mellor, D. (2014). Perceived emotional invalidation and borderline personality disorder features: A test of theory. *Personality and Mental Health, 8,* 128–142.

Swales, M. A., & Heard, H. L. (2007). The therapy relationship in dialectical behaviour therapy. In P. Gilbert & R. L. Leahy (Eds.), *The therapeutic relationship in the cognitive behavioral psychotherapies* (pp. 185–204). New York, NY: Routledge.

Swann, W. B., Jr. (1983). Self-verification: Bringing social reality into harmony with the self. In J. Suls & A. G. Greenwald (Eds.), *Psychological perspectives on the self* (pp. 33–66). Hillsdale, NJ: Erlbaum.

Telch, C., Agras, W., & Linehan, M. (2001). Dialectical behavior therapy for binge eating disorder. *Journal of Consulting and Clinical Psychology, 69,* 1061–1065.

The Linehan Institute. (n.d.). *Dr. Marsha Linehan, founder.* Retrieved from http://www.linehaninstitute.org/about-Linehan.php

Tomko, R. L., Trull, T. J., Wood, P. K., & Sher, K. J. (2014). Characteristics of borderline personality disorder in a community sample: Comorbidity, treatment utilization, and general functioning. *Journal of Personality Disorders, 28,* 734–750.

Torgersen, S., Kringlen, E., & Cramer, V. (2001). The prevalence of personality disorders in a community sample. *Archives of General Psychiatry, 58,* 590–596.

van den Bosch, L. M. C., Verheul, R., Schippers, G. M., & van den Brink, W. (2002). Dialectical behavior therapy of borderline patients with and without substance use problems: Implementation and long-term effects. *Addictive Behaviors, 27,* 911–923.

Van Dijk, S., Jeffrey, J., & Katz, M. R. (2013). A randomized, controlled, pilot study of dialectical behavior therapy skills in a psychoeducational group for individuals with bipolar disorder. *Journal of Affective Disorders, 145*(3), 386–393.

Van Nuys, D. (Interviewer) & Linehan, M. M. (Interviewee). (2007). *Wise counsel interview transcript: An interview with Marsha Linehan, Ph.D. on dialectical behavior therapy* [Interview transcript]. Retrieved from the Gulf Bend Center website: http://gulfbend.org/poc/view_doc.php?type=doc&id=13825

Verheul, R., Van Den Bosch, L. M. C., Koeter, M. W. J., De Ridder, M. A. J., Stijnen, T., & Van Den Brink, W. (2003). Dialectical behaviour therapy for women with borderline personality disorder: 12-month, randomised clinical trial in The Netherlands. *British Journal of Psychiatry: The Journal of Mental Science, 182,* 135–140.

Wagner, A., & Linehan, M. (1997). Biosocial perspective on the relationship of childhood sexual abuse, suicidal behavior, and borderline personality disorder. In M. Zanarini (Ed.), *The role of sexual abuse in the etiology of borderline personality disorder* (pp. 203–223). Washington, DC: American Psychiatric Association.

Wang, L., & Xiao, Z. (2012). The need to establish diagnostic criteria for borderline personality disorder in China. *Shanghai Archives of Psychiatry, 24*(4), 231–232.

Zanarini, M. C., Frankenburg, F. R., Hennen, J., Reich, D. B., & Silk, K. R. (2004). Axis I comorbidity in patients with borderline personality disorder: 6-year follow-up and prediction of time to remission. *American Journal of Psychiatry, 161,* 2108–2114.

Chapter 8

Mindfulness

Anthony Pantaleno and Mark Sisti

Mindfulness is a form of being that is rooted in awareness and careful attention to the present. Predominantly influenced by Buddhist traditions, it has been increasing in popularity in recent decades. Although all human beings have the inherent ability to be mindful, practicing mindfulness may need to be enhanced through training because the skill of staying present in the moment and practicing intentional attending may not come easily. The benefits of mindfulness are supported by research that confirms that it enhances psychological well-being not only by reducing negative functioning but also by enhancing the positive. A review of the contents of the University of California at Los Angeles Mindful Awareness Research Center website (www.marc.ucla.edu) can inform you about how far this field has come in its short history.

The purpose of this chapter is to introduce you to the significant contributions of Jon Kabat-Zinn, who pioneered this approach, and to the theory and practice of mindfulness. Theoretical constructs, practical applications, and specific interventions are addressed.

Jon Kabat-Zinn: Key Theorist

The long and honorable history of what we study as mindfulness today would likely not have even been placed on the map of human history without the creative lifetime work of its most often quoted American scientist, Jon Kabat-Zinn. The start of this very personal journey, like most great human achievements, was very much shaped by family history as it was by global events of the time. Jon Kabat-Zinn was born in the Washington Heights neighborhood of New York City on June 5, 1944, the day before D-Day. His father, Elvin Kabat, was a molecular immunologist at Columbia University, and his mother, Sally Kabat, was a painter who sent her young son to art school at the Museum of Modern Art as a preschooler. Kabat-Zinn and his mother painted together until she was into her 90s.

Kabat-Zinn was born Jewish but is often cited in interviews as holding beliefs representing more of a fusion of art and science. "Science gave me a cosmic religious feeling and I would get that same feeling when I was dragged to the Met and the Museum of Modern Art," Kabat-Zinn said (Cochran, 2004, p. 1). He attended Stuyvesant High School in Manhattan, then Haverford College, finally earning a doctorate in molecular biology from MIT in 1971, where he studied medicine under Nobel Laureate Salvatore Luria.

Influenced by Huston Smith, a professor of philosophy and religion, Kabat-Zinn started meditating when he was a 22-year-old graduate student at MIT in 1966. Kabat-Zinn confessed that "almost no one knew that I was meditating back then and anyone who was, was considered to be somewhat beyond the lunatic fringe, a drug-crazed hippy communist" (Szalavitz, 2012, p. 1). It was on a retreat led in the United States by the revered Buddhist monk Thích Nhât Hạnh that Jon Kabat-Zinn first realized the applicability of mindfulness in the treatment of chronic medical conditions.

You are referred to the October 2015 issue of *The American Psychologist,* and specifically to the article by Anne Harrington of Harvard University and John D. Dunne of Emory University, for an excellent review of the history of contemplative practices in the West. This article tracks the historical interchange between the psychoanalysts of the 1950s and the rise of Zen in Japan, the historical work of Herbert Benson's relaxation response of the 1960s, and the introduction of transcendental meditation to pop culture by the Beatles. It was within this theoretical cross-pollination of therapeutic interventions that Jon Kabat-Zinn persuaded officials at the University of Massachusetts Medical Center to let him establish his Stress Reduction and Relaxation Program, not as a trained therapist but as a trained Dharma teacher who felt that the greatest impact for self-care in medicine should be located in no less a setting than a major medical center in which people were suffering from all brands of human misery and whose own physicians had reached the end of their treatment interventions.

He called this new 8-week experiential course, much of which was taught on yoga mats, *mindfulness-based stress reduction* (MBSR). However, he sought far more than stress reduction in the clinical sense. Kabat-Zinn had to be mindful that any serious treatment program that evoked images of monks or mysticism or New Age anything would doom the program to failure before it was even off the ground. He carefully defined *mindfulness* as paying attention in a particular way, on purpose, in the present moment, without judgment, and proceeded to develop a standardized curriculum that sought not to change or modify physical or psychological symptoms themselves but to change a practitioner's *relationship* to these same symptoms, nurturing themes of acceptance, heartfulness, and a gentle kindness toward oneself. He has stressed from his early writings to the current day that practicing mindfulness is not about getting anywhere or achieving anything as much as it is becoming intimately familiar with the present moment, a novel approach in the least to a Western culture that is preoccupied with the past and the future (Kabat-Zinn, 2005).

With the 1990 publication of his book *Full Catastrophe Living: Using the Wisdom of Your Body and Mind to Face Stress, Pain, and Illness,* Jon Kabat-Zinn laid the cornerstone of what has become the integration of Western and Eastern mind/body arts in the service of human suffering. It is no surprise that what followed in the professions of mental health and school counseling was the next wave of mindfulness-based approaches: dialectical behavior therapy (DBT), mindfulness-based cognitive therapy (MBCT), and acceptance and commitment therapy (ACT), to name a few. Each of these approaches has mindfulness carefully woven in as the core, and each has a long and rich empirically based research tradition of positive outcomes.

Today, Kabat-Zinn is celebrated as the founding executive director of the Center for Mindfulness in Medicine, Health Care, and Society at the University of Massachusetts Medical School. He has authored numerous textbooks on the theory and practice of mindfulness, has received countless awards over the years, and continues to lead retreats throughout the world to diverse audiences of professionals and laypeople. Jon Kabat-Zinn's work has inspired notables such as neuroscientist Richard Davidson at the University of Wisconsin and the Center for Investigating Healthy Minds (Davidson & Kaszniak, 2015) as well as Ohio Congressman Tim Ryan, author of *A Mindful Nation: How a Simple Practice Can Help Us Reduce Stress, Improve Performance, and Recapture the American Dream* (Ryan, 2012). Kabat-Zinn has witnessed the creation of diverse mindfulness workshops and curriculums in health care, corporate America and the workplace, the prison system, the military, and kindergarten–Grade 12 educational arenas, to name a few. He has also celebrated the creation of *Mindful,* a monthly magazine that seeks to promote the most current and creative applications of mindfulness around the world. In the media, Dan Harris's (2014) *New York Times* bestseller *10% Happier* has introduced a nation to the power and accessibility of mindfulness practice.

Theoretical Overview of Mindfulness

General meditative theories and practices can be traced back to India for many millennia, and something resembling modern mindfulness specifically reaches back to a particular branch of Buddhist Theravada contemplative philosophy and methodologies known as *vipassana* ("insight meditation"). Vipassana meditation aims to cultivate nonconceptual direct experiential perception through practicing a type of open monitoring of one's stream of consciousness. A broader theoretical and historical purpose for mindfulness traditions is the cultivation of the following resilient psychological states: equanimity (*upekkha*), compassion (*karuna*), kindness (*metta*), empathic joy (*mudita*), and the general actualization of ourselves and others in the here and now (the four immeasurables or four *brahma viharas;* Germer & Siegel, 2012).

The contemporary Buddhist leaders the Dalai Lama and Thích Nhất Hạnh are two of the most influential Buddhist teachers of this generation and have been largely responsible for disseminating these philosophies, particularly in the Western world. Contemporary scientific and secularized mindfulness has often stripped mindfulness down to its largely nonconceptual equanimity elements, including sensory focus, nonjudgment, and a here-and-now focus. Many believe that modern secularized mindfulness practices would offer even more impact if they retained more of this broader theoretical context, much of which is the universal principles found underlying all religions: compassion; empathy for suffering; kindness; an interdependent self-concept; transcendence of ego and self; altruism; an appreciation of joy, beauty, and the accomplishments of others; and ethical and existential reasoning (Garland, Farb, Goldin, & Fredrickson, 2015; Tirch, Silberstein, & Kolts, 2015).

Modern Mindfulness

Particularly relevant to the mental health challenges in the United States are the exponential spikes in depression, anxiety, loneliness, suicide, and mass murder rates. Mindful pauses and practices are meant to remind us of the importance of the simplest things, such as pausing, listening, silence, nature, our senses, our choices, our mutual vulnerabilities, and our needs. Contemplative traditions such as mindfulness offer a counterpoint to our fast-paced culture in this consumer-driven, socially competitive, virtual, overstimulating, multitasking, and ironically isolated world. A mindfulness Eastern philosophical context can act as a counterbalancing alternative: the Western emphasis on control, mastery, and change of one's environment versus acceptance and appreciation of things as they naturally are, Western individuality versus self as community, and Western analytical problem solving versus nonconceptual contemplation.

Essential Dimensions and Constructs of Mindfulness

Although an ongoing debate continues as to what the essential mechanisms of action may be in achieving a state of present-moment mindful awareness, most mindfulness researchers would cite these four fundamental processes: *equanimity* or *openness* instead of impulsive emotional avoidance and impulsive behavioral reactions; *nonjudgmental awareness,* which is flexible perspective taking versus dichotomous thinking as well as decentering/ defusion thinking rather than evaluative thinking; *intentional singular attention* as opposed to multitasking and other forms of unconsciousness and defensive enactments; and a *here-and-now orientation* versus fusion with future or past ruminations (Kabat-Zinn, 2003).

A broader conceptualization of mindfulness reaches beyond these primarily nonconceptual elements of mindfulness and would also include an expanded mindful appreciation of additional life-enhancing domains such as values, ethics, love, prosociality, and gratitude (Garland et al., 2015). Perhaps one of the best representatives of this expanded form of mindfulness is mindful compassion, which emphasizes a triumvirate of overlapping processes that includes equanimity, empathic common humanity, and kindness (Neff, 2011).

Compassionate mindfulness is based on developing the classical mindful quality of equanimity (nonjudgmental open awareness) but alongside a more prosocial caretaking repertoire (the so-called tend-and-befriend reflexes). Mindful compassion for our common needs and vulnerabilities comes in particularly handy at moments when we fall short or fail, publicly or privately. It is ironic that these threatening, stressful moments are the exact moments when the supposed resilience of accomplishment-based self-esteem often fails us. In contrast, compassion-based resilience is based on our common vulnerabilities and can therefore withstand losses and setbacks. Here suffering and vulnerabilities are not hidden away as the exception but are seen as an essential part of what it means to be courageous and human. Compassionate mindfulness may be a superior alternative to potentially narcissistic achievement-based self-esteem. Rather than promoting a sense of self, which asks "Am I good enough?" it prompts us to ask "Have I cared for myself and others?" (Neff, 2011). Learn more about compassionate mindfulness by referring to Sidebar 1.

Sidebar 1
Three Core Compassion Principles and Poisons

Consider and discuss with a partner how fear and other emotions evoke automatic, sometimes self-defeating (poisonous) fight and flight responses that are related to the following compassion principles. How do you see the poisonous behaviors manifested in yourself and/or your clients or students?

1. *Common humanity:* We all suffer, we all want happiness, we achieve more together than apart.

   Poison: Various forms of isolation and separateness (e.g., I don't belong, why me, why only me, I should avoid/hide/withdraw/attack).

2. Equanimity: Neutral, descriptive, and sensory observation.

   Poison: Various forms of judgment and evaluation (e.g., egocentric, fused, inflexible perspective taking).

3. *Kindness:* The intention to alleviate suffering, tend and befriend, care-take, love, forgive, and empathize with the joy and suffering of others.

   Poison: Various forms of fight or flight (e.g., aggression, superiority-narcissism, indifference, hopelessness, and nihilism).

Unique Features of Mindfulness

Both traditional cognitive restructuring therapies and mindfulness-informed therapies acknowledge the importance of cognitions in the quality of our lives. However, unlike more traditional cognitive restructuring therapies, which emphasize coping with stressful cognitions by altering their *content*, mindfulness targets the cognitive *context*. By developing mindful open attention, mindfulness targets the struggle with our cognitions (the struggle to debate, assess, avoid, reframe, reappraise, and so forth). Mindful attention helps us to change our relationship with our inner lives, which is sometimes described as shifting over to a neutral or compassionate observer viewpoint. Teaching us to mindfully pause rather than to automatically react or rigidly defend our thoughts and emotions, mindfulness is aimed at noticing the difference between seeing our thoughts and seeing through our thoughts and noticing the crucial importance of our behavioral choices. A mindful pause highlights personal responsibility for being open and aware of our own needs and the needs of others as well as responsibility for how our choices cocreate ourselves, our situations, and our relationship with others. It raises awareness of the fact that we often have multiple opportunities each day to pause and consciously choose to make stressful situations either better or worse for ourselves, for others, and for the world (Hayes, Follette, & Linehan, 2004).

Mindfulness-Based Theory of Personality and Human Nature

Mindfulness philosophies tends to see humans as thriving best when they strike a less dichotomized and pragmatic middle path, perhaps the most fundamental example of which would be balancing acceptance and change in our lives—accepting in ourselves and others what we cannot change while simultaneously committing to taking responsibility for optimizing our mutual welfare when we can. This is consistent with much of postmodern contextualist thought and with contemporary biology; that is, we are not entirely separate individuals but intricately part of others and our environments. Mindfulness philosophies tend to suggest that such isolated individuality may be the most fundamental of all illusions and comes from overidentifying with parts and narratives rather than wholes and contexts. Mindfulness philosophies are also amazingly consistent with much of contemporary evolutionary thinking in proposing that humanity is fundamentally prosocial, if not outright altruistic. A mindful theory or self would encourage us to be open and aware of what we feel and need not only so we can care for ourselves as individuals but additionally so we can optimally adapt and care for ourselves when we mindfully transcend our own limited individual identities and coordinate with others and our environment. Interdependency with others and our environment is ultimately in our own mutual best adaptive interest (Barash, 2014).

Mindfulness philosophies assume that a certain fundamental level of suffering is irreducible and ubiquitous to human nature. However, we have an immense role in cultivating an awareness of how our choices have the power to multiply that suffering or have compassion for it. Ontologically mindfulness philosophies propose that we reciprocally cocreate ourselves and our environment in an ongoing, reciprocally causal way. This is an empowering philosophy and is also consistent with cultivating an increasing sense of responsibility for self, others, and the environment, a useful and relevant perspective for developing responsible children, adolescents, and young adult men and women. Mindful neurophysiology suggests that such a reciprocally causal and interdependent sense of self is even consistent with the emerging science of epigenetics, in which it seems we have more power than we thought to shape not only external environments and the wiring in our brains but even our genetic makeup based on how we choose to behave (Barash, 2014).

The Therapeutic Process in Mindfulness

The goals of mindfulness-based interventions (MBIs) include enhanced concentration, a greater sense of executive control, awareness of valued choices, decreased control by arbitrary thoughts/emotions/urges, and general emotional resilience. Compassionate aspects of mindful goals include enhanced empathy and increased awareness of self and others' emotional needs, an interconnected and interpersonal sense of self, self-worth based on compassion for life's inevitable failures, the development of courage as a form of openness to meet common needs and vulnerabilities, and mutual caretaking.

Mindfulness practices are didactically introduced alongside a set of experiential methods for exploring and practicing those principles. Engaging the commitment required could be facilitated by promoting the extra edge that someone with mindfulness skills can cultivate. The learnable skill of social-emotional competence has been shown to predict success in a wide variety of life endeavors (health, academics, occupations, relationships, athletics), but that skill requires intentional practice to develop. If a mindfulness program is time limited (e.g., 8 weeks), then in order to generalize and maintain these new skills consideration should be given to cultivating these skills in some extended form through ongoing practice groups with counselors, teachers, and/or parents, whether individually and/or in groups. If mindful therapy is being used in a counseling center or other outpatient facility, it is essential that mindful homework be assigned in order to ensure that these mindfulness practices generalize into a person's day-to-day life (Germer & Siegel, 2012; Hayes et al., 2004).

The Role of the Counselor or Therapist

A counselor or therapist who has some mindfulness experience and/or history of mindfulness training is a key element in the success of both solo practitioner and prepackaged MBI programs. For educators or counselors with little to no experience who wish to bring mindfulness methods into their schools or clinical settings, mindfulness organizations abound to provide mindfulness trainings specifically tailored to complement individual educator and/or counselor skill sets. Such mindfulness training can be individually and invisibly integrated into complementing preexisting educator/counselor roles and goals (e.g., mindful classroom management for teachers or mindful listening and communicating for counselors). A more ambitious plan is for a school or mental health organization or other agency to hire a professional mindfulness trainer to work with staff on site or for therapists to refer clients to existing local MBSR courses as an adjunct to treatment.

In order for counselors to support others through such an ongoing endeavor it would be very helpful for them to have a personal commitment to developing a personal mindfulness practice for themselves. This is largely a body knowledge or experiential practice, and without such a commitment to personal experience it is difficult to guide others.

The Mindful Therapeutic Stance and Alliance

A common stance for the mindfulness-based counselor is that of a coach or helper explicitly committed to creating a safe and accepting place to discuss, explore, and practice mindfulness. Ideally the counselor would be personally experienced with mindfulness and would also model not having to be an expert to help oneself and others. The helper is a stance of mutuality, a fellow traveler or fellow explorer. These are good metaphors because they imply two central principles: (a) that life is to be lived as a moment-to-moment journey, not a destination; and (b) that we are all interconnected fellow helpers experiencing universal human joys, needs, and losses (Hayes et al., 2004). This all-in-the-same-existential-emotional-boat stance is an essential part of emotional and social resilience and is a model of compassionate vulnerable courage. The ability to open up, accept, and share the fact that we all experience suffering, uncertainty, imperfections, failures, and vulnerabilities is the modeling of compassionate courage, as opposed to the many ways we can avoid or otherwise defend against it.

This is also a great stance from which counselors can model and evoke not only openness and courage but also descriptive functional language ("When I do *x, y* happens," "I value *z* outcome") rather than judgmental, evaluative language. This mindful nonevaluative/descriptive observation also emphasizes the importance and opportunity for social cooperation and mutual care with ourselves as well as with others, particularly when we encounter stressful moments.

Termination and Generalization in Mindfulness Practice

As noted previously, mindfulness practices would ideally be maintained beyond the end of an introductory program in some extended form. Extension and maintenance could be practiced individually or in small groups by counselors in a multitude of settings, by teachers in schools, and even by parents if they have been included in the school trainings. Having a weekly practice group and establishing short periods of time (even just a minute) at certain times of the day for quiet reflection would be helpful. A mindful minute can become the most generalized and ongoing part of a mindful lifestyle if it is highlighted from the outset (*minute* is not to be taken too literally—15 seconds to a minute is fine).

For mindfulness to generalize beyond the classroom, counseling office, hospital, or other setting, the experiential practices must become integrated into day-to-day, minute-to-minute life. The supportive context of an institutionally based MBI can introduce and then support such practices with varying degrees of follow-through. The more integrated such practices become, the more powerful and long lasting the outcome. Highlighting reminder prompts that evoke a mindful pause throughout the day is very helpful for maintenance (daily repetitive tasks, such as brushing teeth, walking, stopping for red lights, and so forth, make great prompts). If mindful exercises are only recalled when they are integrated into formal meditative exercises and environments, they are much less likely to be maintained or have a lasting impact. However, if formal mindfulness practices are complemented with both mindfulness-in-motion exercises (while showering or walking) and mindful minutes purposefully distributed throughout the day, the effects of mindful generalization are much more likely to have a deeper and longer-term impact.

Targeted Processes of Change in Mindfulness

References to the underlying mechanisms of change in mindfulness can be described as occurring on three reciprocally causal and interactive levels: psychological, social, and neurophysiological. Each level of explanation can be equally valid, offering valuable insights into clinical application, goals, and rationale.

Psychological

The executive cognitive and particularly metacognitive processes inherent in cultivating reflective functions are central to mindfulness. Engaging in metacognitive processing likely affects our ability to engage in less rigid, more flexible perspective taking—that is, perspective taking that is more descriptive, dialectical, and mutual and less egocentric, with fewer dichotomized viewpoints. This reflective type of processing also improves attention, concentration, and follow-through by continually refocusing on the here-and-now environment and on our own needs and values as well as those of others. It is also metacognitive in the sense that we learn to see our thoughts as thoughts, not just see through our thoughts (defused, mentalized, or decentered processing). The emphasis here is not necessarily on changing the content, form, or frequency of our thoughts but on having a more flexible relationship regarding our thoughts and feelings. Such metacognitive flexibility also manifests as equanimity as well as courage and openness to emotions, which enhances our ability to be aware of and reflectively act on our own and others' long-term needs. Mindful openness of this sort reduces impulsive emotional avoidance and rigid automatic defenses, enabling mindful awareness of our priorities and hence wiser behavioral choices (Hayes et al., 2004).

Social

The practice of mindfulness affects not only executive cognitive processes regarding our internal world but also our awareness of the feelings, thoughts, and needs of others, which is often referred to as *mentalization*. Compassionate mindfulness practices also highlight interpersonal mindfulness alongside the caretaking repertoire. Compassionate mindfulness not only activates the essential openness and emotional equanimity of mindfulness but takes the additional step of practicing intentional acts of kindness. This so-called tend-and-befriend mindset is a fundamental aspect of a social-emotional system, hardwired by evolution into our makeup and ready to activate caretaking, mutual coordination, and the soothing of distress in others and ourselves. Finally, compassionate mindfulness also encourages a sense of self-transcendence, a perspective on the self that looks beyond our own limited thoughts, egocentrism, and stories about ourselves. It imagines a sense of self that is interconnected and interdependent with others (Germer & Siegel, 2012).

In our global, 21st-century America, contemporary challenges and opportunities impact our sense of compassionate common humanity. With freedom and diversity also come complexities and opportunities, such as in gender and sexual identities, new challenges among our diverse religious communities, racial and ethnic objectification, xenophobia and prejudice, and so forth. Our nearly daily school massacres seem to be a collective cry for help among our youth. Perhaps particularly with our developing young men, we must mindfully redefine the concept of courage as kindness and openness to vulnerability, as a particularly important antidote to the cultural stereotype of hypermasculine power through dominance, violence, invulnerability, and imperviousness to hurt. Our schools and therapy offices are ideal places in which to respond to this renewed need for a mindful, peaceful, compassionate dialogue among our increasingly diverse racial, religious, and gender communities. Although mindfulness and compassion are insufficient to solve all of the complex socioeconomic challenges impacting our youth and society in general, compassionate mindfulness can be one among many solutions (Neff, 2011). Experience what compassionate mindfulness is like by participating in the exercise described in Sidebar 2.

Neurophysiological

The evolutionary imperative of developing a secure attachment system was introduced long ago in classic attachment studies of Harry Harlow's monkeys and John Bowlby's orphaned infants (Wallin, 2015). Mindful

Sidebar 2
Compassion Imagery Exercise

Practice (with eyes closed for 2–5 minutes) the mindset of mindful compassion by imagining and directing (repeating) the following phrases, ideas, and feelings toward someone you really love, bodily calling up the feelings involved, and then replacing the image with yourself:

"May I/they be safe."
"May I/they be happy."
"May I/they be healthy."

Then try this extended version. Imagine a series of people with whom you have some level of personal relationship. Start first with someone from whom you would receive unconditional love, perhaps a trusted partner or a personal wisdom figure. Bring that person's image to mind as you repeat the above phrases softly to yourself. Now select someone with whom you have a less personal relationship—perhaps a colleague or a neighbor. Again, repeat the phrases several times as you bring his or her image to mind. To challenge your own ability to extend compassion even to those with whom you struggle, consider bringing an image to mind of someone who strongly dislikes you or perhaps even someone who has betrayed you in some way. Make your best effort to repeat these phrases as softly and gently as you can in the spirit of healing yourself, the individual, and the world.

equanimity and mindful compassion seem to activate and develop this secure attachment safety system in our parasympathetic autonomic nervous system. Compassion repertoires have been shown to activate the vagus nerve (a unique cranial nerve that is known to influence various basic bodily functions, such as speech, posture, heart rate, digestion, and so forth). This domino-like cascade of effects in the central nervous system activates the so-called love neurotransmitter, oxytocin, which reciprocally turns on the rest-and-digest response (oxytocin is classically produced during, e.g., touch, hugs, breast feeding, or lovemaking). This safety system can be activated through a variety of mindful compassion practices and can help people face distressing emotions rather than avoid them or aggressively overcompensate during times of emotional distress. Instead, they can pause, act more adaptively, and rebound more resiliently (Barash, 2014; Davidson & Kaszniak, 2015).

MBIs

When counselors and therapists embark on a course of locating mindfulness practices and dabbling with the experience of mindfulness meditation, they will find numerous resources online, in professional books and journals, and in formal courses and retreat trainings. There are several distinctions to keep in mind as a new practitioner. The first of these involves the distinction between formal and informal meditation practices. Formal practice is typically scheduled at the same time(s) each day; in the same location; and with the specific intention of being on the cushion, chair, or bench for a specific amount of time. New practitioners may find that a 10- to 15-minute practice period once or twice a day resonates with their lifestyle and their time framework. More experienced meditators may sit for an hour or more, up to and including full-day, weekend, week-long, or monthly meditation retreats. Informal meditation practice refers to a slowing and a deliberate focus of attention on everyday tasks such as showering, eating, walking, and virtually any other daily routine.

The second distinction found in the literature involves the style of meditation that one attempts to practice, from focused attention to open monitoring (Davidson & Kaszniak, 2015). The former seeks to direct and sustain attention on a selected object (such as one's breath) or some specified focal point (such as a candle) and to be aware of the mind wandering from that focal point to any number of other physical or mental phenomena. Open monitoring, which often follows a period of stabilizing one's attention, involves the attainment of a mind-state in which there is no focus on any type of object. One's task is to maintain vigilance and be present for whatever manifests itself in the moment with a calm, nonreactive type of awareness and a willingness to let any experience come and go as if on a conveyor belt, with a sense of curiosity and acceptance, but not necessarily agreement, with what is already here. Another kind of meditative practice postulated by advocates of transcendental meditation referred to as *automatic self-transcending* prescribes the use of a word vibration (mantra) to bring the brain into a state of silence in which brain-wave synchronicity is maximized. This is the experience of transcendence, or pure awareness (Rosenthal, 2012).

What follows is a description of some of the most common formal and informal mindfulness exercises with some brief instructions, along with an Internet resource for locating some of the audio-guided versions of these practices free of charge. Bear in mind that becoming culturally sensitive in implementing mindfulness interventions is critical (Jinich, 2015). Also note that these practices may be facilitated in individual or group settings.

Interventions for Children and Adolescents

Relaxing Sighs

The counselor or therapist begins by saying the following:

> Let's begin by finding a comfortable position—with your eyes closed if you wish, or letting your gaze fall softly in front of you. You'll be taking a relaxing breath, in through the nose and out through the mouth. Now inhale through your nose and exhale through your mouth, making a soft, relaxing sigh as you exhale. Notice how this long, slow, gentle breath raises and lowers your

abdomen as you inhale and exhale. Take another relaxing breath, focusing on the sound and feeling of the breath as you inhale through your nose and exhale out through the mouth in a soft sigh. Now let's try it silently. Inhale through the nose and exhale out through the mouth in a long, gentle breath. Take a moment to notice how your body is feeling right now. (Pantaleno, 2015)

Simply Listening

The counselor or therapist asks the young client to start by sitting comfortably, eyes either slightly open or gently closed, and then reads the following script:

Allow yourself to simply listen to the sounds around you. Notice the sounds of the traffic, the wind, the rain, the birds, or the air conditioner. There is no need to name the sounds, to grasp or hold on to them, or to push them away. Just allow yourself to listen to the sounds as they are. Imagine that your body is a gigantic ear, or if you prefer, a satellite dish, picking up 360 degrees of sound—above, below, in front, behind—all around you. Listen with your entire being. Notice that each sound has a beginning, middle, and end. If your mind wanders, no problem. Just bring it back to the present moment. Let yourself rest in the sounds of the moment, knowing that this moment is unique and that this constellation of sounds will never be repeated. Take a deep breath, wiggle your fingers and toes, stretch, and open your eyes if they have been closed. Try to extend focused attention into your next activity. (Pollack, Pedulla, & Siegel, 2014, "Simply Listening")

Hershey's Kiss (an Eating Meditation)

Ask the young client to close his or her eyes. Place a Hershey's kiss in his or her hand. Ask the client the following:

What comes to mind? How does your body feel? What do you notice happening in your mouth? Now open your eyes and observe the shiny silver shape, the tag of white paper with blue writing, the way the light dances off the object, the feeling of its weight in your hand. What does it feel like? What does it look like? Does it bring back any special memories of earlier times in your childhood?

Slowly open the kiss. Listen to how it sounds as you open it. Bring the kiss to your nose and smell it. What does it smell like? Place the kiss on your tongue. Before biting into it, let it sit on your tongue. What does it taste like? What happens in your mind and your body? Do you feel relaxed, excited, satisfied? What thoughts come into your mind? Just notice them all— liking, disliking, the urge to bite into it. Let it slowly melt in your mouth and observe the sensations, thoughts, feelings, images. (Pantaleno, 2015)

Flower Meditation

Invite the client to look at a vase of flowers in front of him or her and to choose a single flower that he or she thinks is the most beautiful. Ask the client to sit comfortably, either in a chair or on a cushion on the floor, with the flower at eye level. Say the following:

> Now, allow your gaze to rest on the flower in front of you. Smile gently, as though saying hello to a friend. Direct your attention to the color, shape, scent, and healing energy of the flower and allow this healing energy to flow into your eyes and from your eyes into every cell of your body. Appreciate the gifts of healing and beauty being so generously offered by the flower. Allow your eyes to close gently. See if you can still feel the presence of the flower in front of you. Then take a couple of deep, slow breaths, bringing your attention fully back into your own body. Sit quietly for a minute or two, noticing the effects of the practice, and then open your eyes. (Pantaleno, 2015)

Brief Mountain Meditation

Invite the young client to find a chair where he or she can comfortably sit upright, with his or her back supported by the chair, feet resting firmly on the floor, and an imaginary string pulling his or her head slowly upward. Then ask the client to slowly visualize himself or herself as the most beautiful mountain imaginable in a favorite season of the year. Invite the client to take in all of the colors, fragrances if any, the sky, the temperature, and the surrounding activity. Ask the client to become the mountain! Allow the seasons to very slowly move forward through a full cycle of one year—summer, fall, winter, and spring. Tell the client that his or her mountain will experience many changes as the year and the weather progresses but that he or she will always retain the essence of the mountain-hood and can return to this image during times of stress (Pantaleno, 2015).

Interventions for Adults

Soles of the Feet

Meditating on the soles of the feet is a simple way of moving attention away from emotionally arousing thoughts and feelings to a neutral place, the soles of the feet. Invite the client to stand or sit in a comfortable position while reading the following script:

> Rest the soles of your feet on the floor and close your eyes. Breathe normally for a minute or two. Now, think of a situation when you were angry, or verbally and/or physically aggressive. Visualize the situation in your mind. Attend to the anger, verbal aggression, or physical aggression. Now, refocus all your attention on the soles of your feet. Move your toes, feel your shoes covering your feet, feel the texture of your socks or hose, the curve of your arch, and the heels of your feet against the back of your shoes. If you

do not have shoes on, feel the floor or carpet with the soles of your feet and when your attention is totally on the soles of your feet, gently open your eyes. Practice this procedure until you are able to automatically focus your attention on the soles of your feet whenever you feel a strong negative emotion or behavior, such as angry, anxious, or acting aggressively. (Singh, Singh, Singh, Singh, & Winston, 2011, pp. 9–26)

Touch Points

Invite the client to begin by sitting comfortably, assuming a posture of dignity with the spine erect and the feet touching the ground. Eyes can be slightly open with a soft gaze or gently closed. Say the following:

Take three or four breaths to let the mind and body settle and come into the present moment. Notice the places where your body is "touching"—the eyelids touching, the lips touching, the hands touching, the sitting bones touching, the backs of the knees touching the chair, and the feet touching the ground. Repeat the sequence, finding a comfortable rhythm—attending to your eyes touching, lips touching, hands touching, sitting bones touching, knees touching, feet touching. Note these touch points silently to yourself if it helps you focus. If you get distracted, no problem, no blame—just start again. When you are ready, take a deep breath, stretch, wiggle your fingers and toes, rotate your wrists and ankles, and open your eyes if they have been closed. Try to extend focused attention into your next activity. (Pollack et al., 2014, "Touch Points")

Anchor at the Bottom of a Stormy Sea

Invite the client to sit comfortably, taking a few breaths to ground and center, using the practices of sound, touch points, the breath, or loving-kindness phrases. Next say the following:

Visualize a boat anchored in a deep harbor. It is a tranquil, sunny day, and the water is still. But then the wind shifts suddenly. Dark clouds roll in, and the wind and waves start to batter the boat. Watch as the storm intensifies, bringing high winds, driving rain, hail, and enormous waves. Now imagine that you can drop below the waves, perhaps in a diving bell or in scuba gear, and bring your attention to the boat's anchor at the bottom of the ocean. Allow yourself to rest here, seeing the storm and wind and waves high above you. Even though the storm is raging, see if you can find some spaciousness and stillness at the bottom of the ocean. Allow yourself to rest here, finding a quiet, still point in the midst of the storm. When you are ready, take a few deep breaths, stretch, and slowly open your eyes. As you return to the stormy surface, remember that you can return to the stillness whenever you need to. (Pollack et al., 2014, "Anchor at the Bottom of a Stormy Sea")

Mindfulness of Thoughts and Emotions
Say the following to the client:

> Allow your body to come into a comfortable position, whether
> sitting or lying down. You may choose to close your eyes if it feels
> right for you, or allow your gaze to fall downward to the floor with
> your eyes open but not on anything in particular. Simply begin
> to observe your in-breaths and your out-breaths as they occur
> naturally. No need to alter your breathing in any way. Sooner or
> later, your attention is likely to wander . . . it happens to all of us.
> You are not doing anything wrong, this is just what our minds have
> a tendency to do. Imagine that all of the thoughts, feelings, or
> sensations that may show up are like a set of objects on a conveyor
> belt. Label thoughts, no matter what they are, as "thinking,"
> pleasant or even very difficult emotions as "feeling," pleasant or
> unpleasant recollections of the past as "memory," and perhaps
> any recognizable body discomfort as "sensation." Our tendency as
> humans has perhaps been to push away what we don't like and hold
> on to what we like. In mindfulness practice, we allow these all to be
> here in this moment without doing much of anything at all. Try to
> stay in this moment for a time without trying to change anything.
> What does this feel like for you? When you are ready, slowly open
> your eyes, take a gentle stretch, and congratulate yourself for taking
> the time to enjoy a few mindful moments. (Pantaleno, 2015)

Person Just Like Me
Invite the client to find a comfortable sitting posture with his or her feet flat
on the floor and hands in the lap. Then say the following:

> If you're comfortable with this, close your eyes or allow your gaze to
> fall softly in front of you. Just take a moment to check in with your
> breath [pause]. Now bring to mind the image of a person in this
> room. It could be someone who is a friend or someone you don't
> know at all. Hold the image of this person, a fellow human being
> just like you, as vividly as possible in your mind. Now let's consider
> a few things: This person has, from time to time, felt distracted,
> mindless, and has been on "automatic pilot" in day-to-day life, just
> like me. This person has, like me, felt off-balance and unprepared
> for the challenges in life, just like me. This person has, at some
> time, felt tension, fatigue, restlessness, and bodily discomfort, just
> like me. Remember that this person wishes to feel empowered and
> better able to handle the ups and downs that come up in everyday
> life, just like me. So now let's allow some wishes to arise: I wish for
> this person to be mindful of the simple things in life that can bring
> joy. I wish for him or her to be strong and balanced so as to better
> handle life's ups and downs. I wish for him or her to feel safe and
> at ease in his or her body and be free of physical discomfort as
> much as possible. I wish for him or her to treat his or her body with
> kindness and to listen to what it needs, because this person is a
> fellow human being, just like me. (Broderick, 2015)

Mindful Check-In

Say the following to the client:

> Take a few moments to be still . . . congratulate yourself for tak-
> ing this time for meditation practice. Begin this mindful check-
> in by feeling into your body and mind and simply allowing any
> waves of thought, emotion, or physical sensation to just be . .
> . perhaps this is the first break you've taken amidst a busy day.
> As you begin to enter the world of being rather than doing,
> you may notice the trajectory of the feelings that you've been
> carrying within yourself . . . there is no need to judge, analyze,
> or figure things out . . . just allow yourself to be in the here and
> now, amidst everything that is present in this moment. Spend
> about three minutes simply checking in with yourself in this
> way . . . as you come to the end of this mindful check-in, again
> congratulate yourself for doing this practice and directly con-
> tributing to your health and well-being. (Stahl & Goldstein,
> 2010, p. 21)

Informal Practice: STOP

An informal way of using mindfulness to decrease stress and anxiety in daily life is encapsulated in the acronym STOP, which outlines a very simple and effective method for bringing the body and mind back into balance: Stop, Take a breath, Observe, Proceed (Stahl & Goldstein, 2010, p. 60).

After having read the mindfulness practices just described, refer to Side-bar 3, which directs you to practice several scripts and debrief the experi-ence according to the questions provided.

As is often the case in the counseling field, there is no universal means or technique of teaching these practices. The prevailing wisdom would speak to the following points:

Sidebar 3

Practicing Mindfulness

After reading the sampling of mindfulness practices described here, have your classmates or clients practice them with you—perhaps one at the start of each of your next 12 classes or counseling sessions—using the sample scripts provided. If you are reading this chapter for personal growth, please consider following each mindfulness script yourself as best you can. Consider the following questions following each practice:

1. What was that experience like for you?
2. On a scale from 1 (low) to 10 (high), how much of a challenge was it for you to maintain focus on the present moment?
3. If your attention drifted, where did it go? Were you able to return to the present moment, and if so, how?

1. Before introducing mindfulness practice to clients, take the time to establish a daily sitting practice of your own. A wonderful way to develop and nurture your own practice is to take an 8-week MBSR course yourself with a local teacher or online (Salzberg, 2011).
2. It is not a necessary prerequisite to use the term *mindfulness,* the term *meditation,* or any other such language. Local norms and administrative support are the keys to introducing mindfulness in the classroom or a counseling session.
3. A good counselor is a good listener and a good role model. Perhaps sit in silence for the first 3 or 4 minutes of each session to let go of the day's busy-ness and come into the present moment with your student(s) or counselee(s) (Pantaleno, 2008).
4. Join a regular sitting group and encourage your colleagues to do the same. Stick with your daily practice and become intimate with your own struggles (Pantaleno, 2009).

Applications of Mindfulness

MBIs is often the term reserved for protocol-based packages, particularly those delivered as turnkey institutional rollouts, such as Calm Classroom. Mindfulness-based therapies have both a rationale and conceptualizations built around mindful relations with our inner lives and one or more mindfulness interventions, such as MBCT. Mindfully informed therapies may or may not use formal mindfulness interventions such as the body scan but are guided and theoretically based on a group of underlying and overlapping psychological mindful processes (e.g., nonjudgmental thinking/defusion, a here-and-now orientation, the nonconceptualized self). These processes may be elicited through any number of interventions and then practiced as stand-alone or integrated packages such as ACT or DBT. Whether as stand-alone MBI packages or as broader mindfully informed therapies, all aim to strengthen agency, psychological flexibility, and adaptability toward our thoughts and emotions. This psychological flexibility is often described as changing our relationship to our thinking and emotions (reshaping meta-emotions or secondary emotions) as opposed to changing the content of our thinking (Zenner, Herrnleben-Kurz, & Walach, 2014).

The question of which populations and which clinical presenting problems may be effectively addressed in a framework of MBIs is often raised. With the growing interest in mindfulness since the late 1970s, and the diversity in its applications, this has become an even more important question. Note that the number of research studies in 1980 targeting mindfulness is an easy number to remember. It is zero. The American Mindfulness Research Association listed a total of 674 mindfulness journal publications in their database (https://goamra.org/resources) as of 2015. A 2017 search of the National Institutes of Health's PubMed database (https://www.ncbi.nlm.nih.gov/pubmed) using the search term *mindfulness meditation* yields 1,340 research citations. This has prompted some conflict in the field, with some critics raising the banner that mindfulness is being oversimplified and moving out of its original venue of therapeutic practice, touted as the new snake oil for what ails you, and is being paired with improved functioning in sports, sexual satisfaction, and keeping cool while playing the stock market (Harrington & Dunne, 2015).

The contemporary wave of secular scientific interest in mindfulness was introduced and is currently maintained by a variety of modern scientists, from the previously mentioned seminal MBSR researcher Jon Kabat-Zinn, to DBT therapist Marsha Linehan, to a reinvented third-generation form of Steven Hayes's ACT (Hayes et al., 2004). These mindfulness-informed therapies utilize many of the elements of cognitive behavior therapies (CBTs) but tend to emphasize mindful acceptance of internal experience. Mindfully informed therapies have integrated the multiple underlying processes inherent in mindfulness into the fundamental fabric of therapy, which includes openness, a here-and-now perspective, equanimity, being nonjudgmental and compassionate, and so forth. In contrast, formal mindfulness-based therapies, such as MBSR, MBCT, and school-based mindfulness intervention programs (MBIs), more narrowly focus on teaching limited specific mindfulness practices such as breath watching, body scanning, thought naming/labeling, and walking meditation exercises.

CBT itself has been transformed by the addition of mindful elements as to how cognitive restructuring and exposure are conceptualized and executed. Entirely new generations of CBT (e.g., DBT and ACT) have seamlessly incorporated these changes to treat a wide variety of common psychological problems, such as personality disorders, anxiety disorders, mood disorders, and addictive disorders (Hayes et al., 2004). There are also several programs and therapies that are based on explicitly incorporating mindfulness philosophies and practices to specifically target various populations and problems. We discuss some of these now.

Mindfulness Applications With Stress Reduction

This is the original 8-week course first piloted by Jon Kabat-Zinn at the University of Massachusetts Stress Reduction Center in 1979 (MBSR; www.mindfullivingprograms.com). More than 20,000 people have completed the MBSR course at the University of Massachusetts alone. Furthermore, the Oasis Institute has trained more than 12,000 health care professionals worldwide, and an additional 740 MBSR programs have been created globally. Mindfulness practice is ideal for cultivating greater awareness of the unity of mind and body as well as the tendency of unconscious thoughts, feelings, and behaviors to undermine emotional, physical, and spiritual health. In addition to mindfulness practices, MBSR uses yoga to help reverse the tendency of Western cultures' sedentary lifestyle, especially for those with pain and chronic illnesses. Originally created to treat physical syndromes, pain, and skin disorders, its initial empirical success has expanded to other stress- and mood-related disorders (Kabat-Zinn,

2003). *Time* magazine acknowledged the growing force of mindfulness in Western culture in its cover story "The Mindful Revolution" (Pickert, 2014).

Mindfulness Applications With Depression and Other Disorders

MBCT is designed to help people who suffer repeated bouts of depression and chronic unhappiness as well as a host of other clinical problems such as addictive behaviors and eating disorders (*Your Guide to Mindfulness-Based Cognitive Therapy*, n.d.). It combines some of the core concepts of cognitive therapy with meditative practices and attitudes based on the cultivation of mindfulness. The heart of this work lies in becoming acquainted with the modes of mind that often characterize mood dysregulation while simultaneously learning to develop a new relationship to them. MBCT for depression was developed by Mark Williams, John Teasdale, Zindel Segal, and Jon Kabat-Zinn (2007) based on Kabat-Zinn's MBSR program.

Mindfulness Applications With Chronic Pain

Mindfulness-based chronic pain management is a program developed by Dr. Jackie Gardner-Nix (2009), a physician and chronic pain consultant at St. Michael's Hospital in Toronto, Ontario, Canada (www.neuronovacentre.com). It is based on the famous MBSR program originated by Jon Kabat-Zinn and has been developed into a program more customized to the needs of those dealing with chronic pain. Mindfulness assists clients in remaining calmer and better able to control their pain despite the challenges of everyday life, such as when interacting with family, friends, colleagues, and employers. Mindfulness can change the intensity of pain and disability suffering, both emotional and physical, in a very positive way.

Mindfulness Applications With Substance Abuse

Mindfulness-based relapse prevention for substance abuse was pioneered by Alan Marlatt (www.mindfulrp.com), whose research focused on managing relapses in alcohol and substance abuse. In fact, an extensive body of empirical work exists demonstrating the effectiveness of mindfulness-informed/-based treatments for treating substance and alcohol abuse. Specifically, Marlatt found that practicing mindfulness meditation increased activity in the prefrontal cortex, a sign of greater self-control, and that practicing mindfulness meditation reduced cravings for substances (Bowen, Chawla, & Marlatt, 2011).

Other researchers have expanded this work into many other programs for treating abuse and other forms of impulsivity and self-harm (Bowen et al., 2011; Hayes et al., 2004). In the *Mind-Body Workbook for Addiction*, Stanley Block, Carolyn Bryant Block, and Guy du Plessis (2016), founder of the popular Integrated Recovery Program, described an innovative and clinically proven mind–body bridging technique to help individuals stay sober, manage emotions and stress, and ultimately build a better life. They presented a series of exercises to help substance abusers uncover addiction triggers, stay grounded, and prevent future relapses. In addition, mind–body bridging is a proven-effective method of self-help that teaches clients how to regulate strong emotions such as anxiety, anger, worry, and stress—all emotions that lie at the core of addiction issues. Participants become aware of their negative thoughts, experience them without pushing them away, and then use the physical senses to become more grounded and relaxed rather than turning to alcohol or drugs for relief.

Mindfulness Applications With Couples

According to O'Kelly and Collard (2012), relationships are subjected to different stressors throughout their life span. Therefore, it makes sense that reducing stress and increasing emotional functioning is important in working with couples to enhance relationship well-being. Mindfulness techniques have been found to help couples by increasing their ability to cope with stress in their lives as well as in their relationships. Techniques such as breathing exercises and walking meditations can help couples develop an awareness of the present and develop a noncritical attitude. Burpee and Langer (2005) reported findings from a study that supported the contention that there is strong relationship between mindfulness and marital satisfaction, so counselors and therapists would be advised to use this approach not only with distressed couples but also as a preventive approach to enhance a couple's relationship.

Further support for applications of mindfulness in working with couples comes from Kazdin (as cited by O'Kelly & Collard, 2012), who found that intimate partner violence was reduced in a program that included mindfulness as well as skills to improve interpersonal effectiveness and emotional regulation (as in DBT). Obviously further research in this area is needed, but initial results seem promising, as there was a reduction in physical, emotional, and verbal abuse in posttreatment studies.

Mindfulness-informed interpersonally focused third-generation CBTs such as functional analytic therapy and compassion-based therapies such as compassion-focused therapy have been designed to elicit altruistic social behavior, the so-called mutual caretaking or tend-and-befriend repertoires. These are core aspects of our prosocial repertoires, and increasing these compassionate prosocial processes has also been shown to activate the rest-and-digest parasympathetic system, along with flexible perspective taking, empathy, and decreased shame, all of which can enhance couple relationships (Hayes et al., 2004). These therapies also elicit wellness-oriented emotions, thoughts, and behaviors (Germer & Siegel, 2012). DBT has also been effective in treating high-conflict couples by reducing the level of conflict inherent in working with stressed couples (Fruzzetti, 2006). In this DBT framework, high emotional arousal, emotional reactivity, and judgmental thinking are tempered by a faster return to baseline through the promotion of active instruction in mindfulness and mutual validation of each partner.

Mindfulness Applications With Children and Adolescents in School Settings

A brief overview of several elementary and school-based mindfulness/contemplative education programs follows as an example of applied mindfulness in the classroom. The preferred model is typically a turnkey method of training, in which classroom teachers and other support staff are introduced to the model and taught the basics of the techniques associated with each program. A significant buy-in from those who will implement the program, whether via classroom lessons or in an individual or small-group counseling contexts, is imperative. As Rechtschaffen (2014) noted, "If a classroom teacher is not supportive of mindfulness, then the outside provider's lessons may be directly contrary to the way the teacher directs the class" (p. 21).

The costs associated with rolling out mindfulness successfully in schools is proportionally related to the financial commitment that the district is willing to put into professional development for its staff. There is no quality or sustainable mindfulness program without teacher education.

Calm Classroom (*www.calmclassroom.com*)
Calm Classroom is a social-emotional learning program that uses simple research-based mindfulness techniques to help students and teachers develop self-awareness, mental focus, and inner calm. When it is implemented with fidelity, numerous positive outcomes are attributed to Calm Classroom. Because the program supports the reduction of stress and anxiety in students by teaching them self-regulation skills, students develop the ability to be more relaxed, focused, and emotionally resilient (Luster, 2013).

The Learning to Breathe Curriculum (*www.learning2breathe.org*)
This curriculum provides an introduction to and foundation in mindfulness for students at the secondary level. Learning to Breathe introduces mindfulness as a universal intervention that builds on many of the themes and practices derived from MBSR (Kabat-Zinn, 1990). Unlike content-specific curriculums that might focus on friendship skills, decision making, or conflict resolution, in this program attention is the curriculum. Learning to Breathe can be taught in a variety of ways (e.g., in 6, 12, or 18 classes or more) to general education populations (Broderick, 2013).

The Quiet Time Program (*www.davidlynchfoundation.org/schools.html*)
This school-based curriculum from the David Lynch Foundation is a student program that is designed to enhance learning, reduce violence, and improve emotional and physical health along with a teacher program designed to reduce burnout and improve teacher effectiveness. The key component of Quiet Time is an evidence-based, nonreligious, stress reduction and cognitive development technique known as transcendental meditation. The goal of this method is to arrive at a fourth state of consciousness and brain synchronicity described as pure awareness (Rosenthal, 2012).

An excellent review of the relationship between mindfulness programs and wellness in a typical university setting may be found in K. A. Williams, Kolar, Reger, and Pearson (2001). Renshaw (2012) and Renshaw and O'Malley (2014) have also provided comprehensive overviews of cultivating mindfulness in students. To learn more about mindfulness-based curriculums or treatments, follow the instructions in Sidebar 4.

Multicultural Social Relations

With the rollout of mindfulness practices across this global domain of educational and clinical interventions, the matching of strategies in various cultural settings has been embraced by organizations such as Mindfulness Without Borders (www.mindfulnesswithoutborders.org). Since 2007, they have served more than 4,000 youth in more than 60 schools, with professional development workshops reaching more than 1,500 educators crossing eight international borders: Canada, the United States, Rwanda, Uganda, Nigeria, Israel, Jamaica, and Botswana. Their key mission is to introduce mindfulness within the cultural boundaries of international consumers so as not to offer mindfulness as a practice that seeks to challenge, compete with, or supplant traditional belief systems. In addition, mindfulness has historical roots in numerous faith traditions but also may be embraced by those with no particular faith affiliation (Kabat-Zinn, 2003; Rudell-Beach, 2014). Clearly, mindfulness has great potential for multicultural applications.

Efficacy of Mindfulness

It has been the experience of researchers worldwide that the treatment of almost all clinical presentations may be enhanced by the introduction of some form of mindfulness practice. Clinical depression, anxiety, eating disorders, pain management, and student stress are but a few of the applied fields of research

Sidebar 4
Curriculum and Treatment Paradigm Review

Review several of the mindfulness-based curriculum and/or treatment paradigms discussed in this chapter. Describe how they are similar or different. Discuss the following with a partner or in a small group:

1. Did each curriculum/treatment paradigm present its research in a manner that supported mindfulness practice?
2. Which programs could you see implementing in your school or clinical setting?
3. What challenges do you see for yourself and your students/ clients in introducing mindfulness work?

in which mindfulness has found a home (Goyal et al., 2014). In a similar vein, cutting-edge university and college counseling centers have followed suit and now offer regular introductory mindfulness and more extensive courses of study to their general student bodies. It has been proposed that quieting the mind may be the prerequisite universal foundation on which all other forms of effective learning are based. A brief sampling of several clinical research–based mindfulness interventions is presented here.

Since 1980 there has been an exponential increase in mindfulness research, which now averages hundreds of studies per year. In 2014 alone there were a total of 535 publications documenting the effectiveness of this method (Boyce, 2014). The National Institutes of Health has invested millions of dollars investigating a wide variety of mindfulness benefits, from mindfulness as a social-emotional performance enhancer to mindfulness as a preventive technology against skyrocketing child and adolescent mental disorders. Similarly, the United Kingdom has approved mindfulness treatments among its other empirically approved mental health treatments. Given the increasingly competitive global culture of multinational, multiskilled, multitasked, overbooked, and overachieving individuals, therapeutic mindfulness programs are proving to be an ideal way to introduce the prioritization of quiet reflective practices.

MBIs are plagued by the typical empirical challenges encountered by any therapy when attempting to specify their precise mechanisms and preferred methodology. These empirical limitations are due to the multifaceted fundamental nature of mindfulness and further complicated by the multiple formats and methods in which varying MBIs are typically delivered, such as formal/informal mindfulness practices, concentration methods versus open-monitoring mindfulness methods, varying didactic and experiential methodology, varying duration of the MBI, outside trainers versus in-house MBI trainers, or the level of experience of the trainers, for example (Khoury et al., 2013).

In spite of these methodological limitations, empirical research with children and adolescents has been accumulating and demonstrating that mindfulness can bring a wide variety of benefits with moderate effect sizes. Perhaps some of the strongest outcomes are in cognitive functioning: improved attention, decreased impulsivity, and improvements in delayed gratification as well as mood regulation and resilience to stress (Zenner et al., 2014; Zoogman, Goldberg, Hoyt, & Miller, 2015). Also showing promise are improved social competencies such as increased kindness, empathy, compassion, forgiveness, altruism, mutual perspective taking, mentalization, and skills in conflict resolution (Seppala, Rossomando, & Doty, 2013). The increasingly multiculturally diverse communities that make up today's society have made mastering such social skills challenging and increasingly crucial. Empirical evidence is slowly accumulating that among the varied forms of mindful social competence, compassion-oriented mindfulness interventions have had the strongest influence on social competence (Leiberg, Klimecki, & Singer, 2011).

Finally, empirical evidence is also accumulating regarding the neuropsychological benefits of mindfulness. Childhood and adolescence may be an ideal time to capitalize on the plasticity of the brain. Neurological studies have begun to document how mindfulness can slowly rewire the various areas of the brain involved in a variety of essential psychological and social functions, from changes in the amygdala and mood regulation to alterations in attention and impulse control via changes in the frontal cortex (Marchand, 2014). Perhaps most astounding is that the emerging science of epigenetics is showing us that practices like mindfulness can alter the molecular structure of our DNA, influencing which genetic predispositions may get turned on and therefore expressed (or not; Kabat-Zinn & Davidson, 2013).

Verbatim Transcript: Mindfulness

The following verbatim transcript of a fourth session is presented in order to illustrate information about the principles and practice of mindfulness as described in this chapter. We provide a brief overview of the case, the actual transcript, a short critique of the session, and an explanation as to why we think this theory effectively addressed the problem.

Overview

Monique, a 19-year-old, was a junior at an out-of-state college. She lived in an off-campus apartment with several close friends. Her presenting problem was a recent episode of severe anxiety and depressed mood lasting several weeks subsequent to her first exposure to marijuana 6 weeks ago. Monique reported that she had not felt like herself since this experience, slipping into these moods randomly and experiencing a loss of interest in sports and social activities, often downing herself for loss of what she described as a previously high functioning level. Prior to this episode, academic and social relatedness were excellent. She was enjoying academic life at college and thinking about pursuing a career in broadcasting or sports management. She denied any other activating events at home or in her peer group.

During summer and winter breaks, Monique resided with parents and younger sister. She presented in counseling during winter break and planned to return to school in a few weeks. In the first session, we engaged in some psychoeducation regarding marijuana use and discussed the fact that marijuana in 2016 was often not just the dried, crushed leaves of a marijuana plant. We discussed how various chemical additives could occasionally produce some very unusual, even hallucinogenic, effects, but that the good news was that lingering physiological effects should dissipate with time, given that this was a single episode. We also discussed the fact that trying to "reset" the mind and body's behavioral activation programming since this event would be important and that resuming normal activities would be a vital task over the next few weeks of her recess before she resumed the next semester of study.

In the second session, Monique reported no additional symptoms but expressed feeling "stuck" in ruminating about whether this episode would impact the upcoming semester. We reviewed the antecedent situation–beliefs–consequences of rational emotive behavior therapy and spent some time uncovering problematic beliefs that would not be very workable moving forward, such as "I messed up my brain and will never be the same again," "What if my therapist is missing something that could have catastrophic health consequences for me?" and "What if my friends notice something different about me?" We brainstormed how she could become more aware of these intrusive thought processes as well as the rational response to them using a simple journaling diary and noted the self-downing tendencies that people experience when they are not "on their game" as a part of restoring therapeutic wellness.

In the third session, Monique was introduced to a short video about stress, a 13-minute segment that had originally aired on the weekly CBS news program *60 Minutes* in December 2014 and featured an interview with Jon Kabat-Zinn about mindfulness and the events surrounding a weekend mindfulness retreat. After watching the video, we did an introductory mindfulness exercise called the *body scan* together, and for homework Monique was instructed to practice an online, audio-guided version of the same exercise and to suspend judgment about how this may help her to transition back to her regular daily routines with less anxiety and depression. I (Tony) provided her with the specific website (www.mindfulness-solution. com) where she could gain access to the body scan practice.

At the beginning of the fourth session, Monique explained that she had just returned from a very brief vacation with family and friends. She reported having a great time and remaining symptom free while she was away. However, when she returned home and was watching a televised football game with her family, her symptoms started to reoccur. She noticed that it was late afternoon and getting dark. She sensed that as the daylight was receding, her vision was somehow being compromised. She told me, "I started thinking again . . . oh my God, what is this? I can't make it stop. Pretty soon, my knees are shaking and I'm pounding my couch. I try to play with the dog, but this shaking keeps ongoing. My mom walks in and finds me crying. I think I just had my first panic attack." What follows is the transcript of the fourth session, in which Tony was the therapist.

Transcript of the Fourth Session

Therapist: So what feeling were you most aware of as this was happening?
Client: I was scared out of my mind and wondering if this was some kind of breakdown.
Therapist: Was anything else happening that day?
Client: Friends were leaving to go back to college, but that would not cause me to react like that.
Therapist: Was there anything else that seemed to make this worse?
Client: That I was not in control of my body and did not know what to do.

Therapist: We have been talking about how our thinking plays a huge role in how our emotions and behaviors then play out. Would you be willing to learn how to approach this experience from the perspective of using the mindfulness skills we started to learn in our last session?

Client: Sure, anything that would help.

Therapist: Do you remember when you were in a high school or college biology or psychology class and studied the fight-or-flight response?

Client: Yes, something about bracing to fight a danger or running away from it.

Therapist: Exactly. Other than the central nervous system—our brain and spinal cord—there is a structure deep in the brain called the limbic system which regulates fight or flight. It's deep within the skull because it was a primitive part of our early brains. It has always functioned very automatically and without thinking involved at all.

Client: Okay, and what does that have to do with me?

Therapist: Suppose you came out of your prehistoric cave one day around noon and saw what looked like a sweet bush of fresh blueberries. What would you do?

Client: Head straight for it.

Therapist: Yes you would. Lunch is served, but what if, as you approached the bush, it looked like it moved? Now what?

Client: Get out of there ASAP.

Therapist: And when you were back in your cave, how would you feel?

Client: Probably hungry, but at least safe.

Therapist: That's right. So when faced with a real and present danger, your limbic system fires automatically and keeps you safe. Adrenaline pumps into your system, blood rushes to your legs to prime the muscles to run, and all other activity like digestion and thinking about the weather and other unnecessary activities in that moment slow down or stop altogether. So here is the thing. In 2016 you're not likely to encounter a large animal that could pose a threat to your life, but what if some completely unrelated experience seemed to produce that same response of fear?

Client: Like being afraid that I was losing my sight?

Therapist: Right, and since the limbic system is a sort of "switch on/switch off" system, what if it could not differentiate between real and present danger and let's say indigestion, stomach cramps, or something it had never experienced before?

Client: You're saying that once I experience something uncomfortable physically that my mind does not recognize, that the danger switch flips on anyway?

Therapist: Precisely. And once this happens, your brain and thought stream become aware that something unwanted is happening.

Client: That is pretty much what happened. When my mom came home, I was in tears.

Therapist: So what did you do then?

Client: She and I sat down on the couch and practiced the body scan together.

Therapist: What then?

Client: About 30 or 40 minutes later, everything had passed.

Therapist: So we could call this a panic attack if we like, but that might send your brain in search of all kinds of information. Suppose we reframed this into what may be thought of as a sensitive limbic system firing occasionally and without any outside stressor setting it off at all?

Client: That would make me feel better.

Therapist: I would think so. But the question remains about what you should do if another one of these comes along. By the way, it's possible that you could have this experience tomorrow late afternoon, or maybe not, or maybe next week, or maybe next month, or not at all, but let's be prepared with a plan. Why don't you do a Google search for the "ten commandments of a panic attack" on your phone and we can review each of the steps at our next session. This "ten commandments" worksheet is one of the best reminder lists for clients with panic-like symptoms. I suggest that it be used when bodily sensations start to fire off that old limbic system. Since we're dealing with real physical symptoms, we want to take care of and soothe our bodies. If we get good at that, two things happen: We send a silent message to the limbic system that "all is well and I have this covered," and at the same time our mind and thoughts get the picture and typically follow suit.

Client: So will it eventually stop?

Therapist: Every single time. We just need to accept that for the time it takes for our body to return to baseline, we are going to ride out the storm. What would be about the worst thing you could do if discomfort calls in whatever form?

Client: Start to think about how crappy and out of control I feel?

Therapist: Bingo! To think about this another way, did you ever take care of a baby?

Client: Not really!

Therapist: What would you do if the baby started crying very loudly?

Client: Maybe pick it up and cradle it, walk it around?

Therapist: You will be a good mom one day . . . but what if that didn't work and the crying just got louder?

Client: I don't know. Take his temperature.

Therapist: Good idea! What about checking his diaper, maybe feed him that bottle in the fridge?

Client: Yes, sure.

Therapist: Would you just put him down and let him cry it out? No way! You would try all things to soothe him until you hit upon what worked! People have that tendency to catastrophize when they can't find an immediate solution. We are going to take care of your discomfort in the same way as we would soothe that crying baby.

Client: When I'm stressed, I listen to music, go outside for some fresh air, take a hot shower, eat some ice cream, sip on some chai tea.

Therapist: Fantastic! I don't want you to think of meditation as just a bunch of audio tracks that have some magical power. It's more about paying attention to the moment you are in, allowing it to be just as it is—including being very uncomfortable at times, and returning to our senses at those times.

Client: So you want me to make a list of sensory things that soothe me and do one of those things?

Therapist: I do. And I took the liberty of checking your college's counseling Web page. They offer free mindfulness meditation sessions for all students at various locations and times during the week. Could you see yourself attending one of these?

Client: Yes, sure.

Session Critique

Monique was a highly motivated client, primarily because of the physiological experience of what seemed like a postdrug reaction. While I tried to monitor her cognitive content and doing appropriate disputing and problem solving where appropriate, a typical psychoeducational review of the fight-or-flight response set the stage for the use of mindfulness as the natural response to her body's overreactivity. The notion of caring for one's anxiety and strong emotional response introduced a new style of personal management as opposed to merely pushing away what is uncomfortable. I could have arranged for a more specific follow-up when Monique returned to her campus to ensure that she had in fact located a mindfulness sitting group, which would have increased the likelihood of continued practice and skill generalization.

Effectiveness of the Theory Relative to This Case

With all cases of anxiety management, it is essential to teach the power of challenging the content of irrational thoughts, but it is also advised that for periods of intense emotional dysregulation the process of mindfully relating to thoughts, emotions, and sensory experiences be incorporated into the treatment approach to soothe the body and mind and create some distance from these experiences as feared entities in themselves. Monique was able to blend mindfulness as a management tool into her behavioral repertoire to sooth her physical state of arousal, to anchor herself in present-moment sensory awareness, and to allow the experience to pass in its own time without reinforcing the more typical fear–avoidance–fear cycle. Mindfulness was also conceptualized not just as a series of mechanical exercises but as a means of creating greater self-compassion for the more challenging moments of our lives.

Summary

A variety of MBIs were described in this chapter. Some stand-alone MBIs described herein are protocol packages that are delivered as turnkey rollouts in schools and other institutional settings. Non-prepackaged mindfulness-informed interventions were also described as a group of psychological processes often utilized to optimize other preexisting social-emotional learning programs and CBTs, whether in group or individual formats. The four core processes of mindfulness were explored both in theory and in application: experiential openness (acceptance), nonjudgmental awareness (decentered/defused or mentalized thinking), intentional singular awareness, and here-and-now perspective taking. A fifth and broader form of mindfulness (compassionate mindfulness) that emphasizes more social perspective taking was also addressed.

Mindfulness and acceptance-based strategies are key elements in many so-called third-generation CBTs such as ACT and DBT that promote mood regulation and distress tolerance. Research is accumulating that demonstrates that mindful acceptance, descriptive observation, and nonjudgmental openness to experience, rather than cognitive restructuring emphasizing cognitive realism and accuracy, may be an expedient alternative to traditional cognitive restructuring. In this way, metacognitive change, altering our reactions to and relationship with our thinking, is seen as an alternative to restructuring the content of our thinking. For a more thorough understanding of how mindfulness works, read the case of Marcos in Chapter 9.

Suggested Resources and Websites

For more information on mindfulness theory and practice, please refer to the following resources and websites.

Books

Biegel, G. (2009). *The stress reduction workbook for teens.* Oakland, CA: New Harbinger.

Brantley, J. (2003). *Calming your anxious mind.* Oakland, CA: New Harbinger.

Brantley, J. (2014). *Calming your angry mind.* Oakland, CA: New Harbinger.

Goldstein, E. (2015). *Uncovering happiness: Overcoming depression with mindfulness and self-compassion.* New York, NY: Atria Books.

Greco, L. A., & Hayes, S. C. (Eds.). (2008). *Acceptance and mindfulness treatments for children and adolescents: A practitioner's guide.* Oakland, CA: New Harbinger.

Siegel, R. (2010). *The mindfulness solution: Everyday practices for everyday problems.* New York, NY: Guilford Press.

Compact Discs

- www.mindfulnesscds.com

Mindfulness Conferences

- Wisdom 2.0
  www.wisdom2summit.com

Online Mindfulness Apps

Companies like Apple offer dozens of apps, some for free, but most with a cost. Simply search for "mindfulness meditation" in your app store. A critical review of mindfulness apps, Stephany Tlalka's "The Trouble With Mindfulness Apps," appears in the August 10, 2016, *Mindful* magazine (www.mindful.org/trouble-mindfulness-apps). We highly recommend that you read this review before investing your time and funds.

Recommended Research-Based School Curriculums

- Calm Classroom
  www.calmclassroom.org
- Learning to Breathe
  www.learning2breathe.org
- Mindfulness in Schools Project
  www.mindfulnessinschools.org
- Mindful Schools
  www.mindfulschools.org
- Mission Be
  www.missionbe.org
- Quiet Time
  www.davidlynchfoundation.org

Websites

- American Mindfulness Research Association
  www.goamra.org
- *Mindful* magazine
  www.mindful.org
- University of Massachusetts Medical School, Center for Mindfulness in Medicine, Health Care, and Society
  www.umassmed.edu/cfm
- University of Wisconsin–Madison, Center for Healthy Minds
  www.centerhealthyminds.org

YouTube Videos

- *60 Minutes* Special on Mindfulness With Anderson Cooper
  https://www.youtube.com/watch?v=vBhimxmhCpI&t=6s
- Bill Moyers's *Healing and the Mind*
  https://www.mindfulnesscds.com/pages/bill-moyers-special
- Mindfulness With Jon Kabat-Zinn
  https://www.youtube.com/watch?v=3nwwKbM_vJc&t=2s

References

Barash, P. D. (2014). *Buddhist biology: Eastern wisdom meets modern Western science.* New York, NY: Oxford University Press.

Block, S. H., Block, C. B., & du Plessis, G. (2016). *Mind-body workbook for addiction: Effective tools for substance abuse recovery and relapse prevention.* Oakland, CA: New Harbinger.

Bowen, S., Chawla, N., & Marlatt, G. A. (2011). *Mindfulness-based stress reduction for addictive behaviors: A clinician's guide.* New York, NY: Guilford Press.

Boyce, B. (2014, February). No blueprint: Just love. *Mindful,* pp. 35–41.

Broderick, B.. & Reibel, D. (2014, June). *Relaxing sighs: A mindfulness practice.* Handout presented at conference "Mindfulness for YOU and Mindfulness for YOUth," Wheatley Heights, NY: Western Suffolk BOCES.

Broderick, P.(2013). *Learning to Breathe: A mindfulness curriculum for adolescents to cultivate emotion regulation, attention and performance.* Oakland, CA: New Harbinger.

Broderick, P. C. (2015). *A person just like me (a mindfulness exercise).* Unpublished training material available from the author at pcb13@psu.edu

Burpee, L., & Langer, E. (2005). Mindfulness and marital satisfaction. *Journal of Adult Development, 12*(1), 43–51.

Cochran, T. (2004, December 6). *Mindful writing: Jon Kabat-Zinn asks us to come to our senses.* Retrieved from http://www.publishersweekly.com/pw/print/20041206/27421-mindful-writing.html

Davidson, R. J., & Kaszniak, A. W. (2015). Conceptual and methodological issues in research on mindfulness and meditation. *The American Psychologist, 70,* 581–592.

Fruzzetti, A. E. (2006). *The high conflict couple: A dialectical behavior therapy guide to finding peace, intimacy, and validation.* Oakland, CA: New Harbinger.

Gardner-Nix, J. (2009). *The mindfulness solution to pain.* Oakland, CA: New Harbinger.

Garland, E. L., Farb, N. A., Goldin, P. R., & Fredrickson, B. L. (2015). The mindfulness-to-meaning theory: Extensions, applications, and challenges at the attention-appraisal-emotion interface. *Psychological Inquiry, 26*(4), 377–387.

Germer, C., & Siegel, R. (2012). *Wisdom and compassion in psychotherapy: Deepening mindfulness in clinical practice.* New York, NY: Guilford Press,

Goyal, M., Singh, S., Gould, N., Rowland-Seymour, A., Berger, Z., Sleicher, D., . . . Haythornthwaite, J. (2014). Meditation programs for psychological stress and well-being: A systematic review and meta-analysis. *Journal of the American Medical Association, 174*(3), 357–368.

Harrington, A., & Dunne, J. D. (2015). When mindfulness is therapy: Ethical qualms, historical perspectives. *The American Psychologist, 70,* 621–631.

Harris, D. (2014). *10% happier.* New York, NY: HarperCollins.

Hayes, S., Follette, V., & Linehan, M. (2004). *Mindfulness and acceptance: Expanding the cognitive-behavioral tradition.* New York, NY: Guilford Press.

Jinich, R. (2015, April 12). *Teaching mindfulness across cultures* (interview). Retrieved from http://www.mindfulteachers.org/2015/04/teaching-mindfulness-across-cultures.html

Kabat-Zinn, J. (1990). *Full catastrophe living: Using the wisdom of your body and mind to face stress, pain, and illness.* New York, NY: Delacorte.

Kabat-Zinn, J. (2003). Mindfulness-based interventions in context: Past, present, and future. *Clinical Psychology: Science and Practice, 10*(2), 144–156.

Kabat-Zinn, J. (2005). *Coming to our senses: Healing ourselves and the world through mindfulness.* New York, NY: Hyperion Books.

Kabat-Zinn, J., & Davidson, R. (2013). *The mind's own physician: A scientific dialogue with the Dalai Lama on the healing power of meditation.* Oakland, CA: New Harbinger.

Khoury, B., Lecomte, T., Fortin, G., Therien, P., Bouchard, V., Chapleau, M. A., & Hofmann, S. G. (2013). Mindfulness-based therapy: A comprehensive meta-analysis. *Clinical Psychology Review, 33,* 764–770.

Leiberg, S., Klimecki, O., & Singer, T. (2011). Short-term compassion training increases prosocial behavior in a newly developed prosocial game. *PLoS ONE, 6*(3). Retrieved from http://journals.plos.org/plosone/article?id=10.1371/journal.pone.0017798

Luster, J. (2013). *Calm Classroom case studies.* Retrieved from http://www.calmclassroom.com/wp-content/uploads/2011/06/Sample-Research-Reports-6-20-2013.pdf 3–26

Marchand, W. (2014). Neural mechanisms of mindfulness an meditation: Evidence from neuroimaging studies. *World Journal of Radiology, 6,* 471–479.

Neff, C. (2011). *Self-compassion: The proven power of being kind to yourself.* New York, NY: William Morrow.

O'Kelly, M., & Collard, J. (2012). Using mindfulness with couples: Theory and practice. In A. Vernon (Ed.), *Cognitive and rational-emotive behavior therapy with couples: Theory and practice* (pp. 17–32). New York, NY: Springer.

Pantaleno, A. (2008, Fall). *On becoming more compassionate therapists, teachers, students, parents, humans: The path to mindfulness-based stress reduction.* Retrieved from the Suffolk County Psychological Association website: http://www.suffolkpsych.org/pdfs/newsletters/SCPA_Newsletter_Fall_2008.pdf

Pantaleno, A. (2009, Fall). *Why we meditate: Seeking the path to silence, stillness, gratitude, and finding out who we really are.* Retrieved from the Suffolk County Psychological Association website: http://www.suffolkpsych.org/pdfs/newsletters/SCPA_Newsletter_Fall_2009.pdf

Pickert, K. (2014, February). The mindful revolution. *Time, 183*(4), 40–46.

Pollack, S. M., Pedulla, T., & Siegel, R. D. (2014). *Download meditations.* Retrieved from http://sittingtogether.com/meditations.php

Rechtschaffen, D. (2014). *The way of mindful education: Cultivating well-being in teachers and students.* New York, NY: Norton.

Renshaw, T. L. (2012). *Crisis prevention and intervention tools.* Retrieved from http://smhp.psych.ucla.edu/pdfdocs/wheresithappening/stpaul/A-19-34.pdf

Renshaw, T. L., & O'Malley, M. D. (2014). Cultivating mindfulness in students. In M. J. Furlong, R. Gilman, & E. S. Huebner (Eds.), *Handbook of positive psychology in the schools* (pp. 245–259). New York, NY: Routledge.

Rosenthal, N. (2012). *Transcendence: Healing and transformation through transcendental meditation.* New York, NY: Penguin Group.

Rudell-Beach, S. (2014). *Is mindfulness a religion?* Retrieved from http://www.huffingtonpost.com/sarah-rudell-beach-/is-mindfulness-a-religion_b_6136612.html

Ryan, T. (2012). *A mindful nation: How a simple practice can help us reduce stress, improve performance, and recapture the American dream.* Carlsbad, CA: Hay House.

Salzberg, S. (2011, Spring). Sticking with it: How to sustain your meditation practice. *Tricycle,* pp. 77–79, 110–112.

Seppala, E., Rossomando, T., & Doty, J. R. (2013). Social research: Social connection and compassion: Important predictors of health and well-being. *Social Research Quarterly, 80,* 411–430.

Singh, N. N., Singh, J., Singh, A. D. A., Singh, A. N. A., & Winston, A. S. W. (2011). *Meditation on the soles of the feet for anger management: A trainer's manual.* Raleigh, NC: Fernleaf.

Stahl, B., & Goldstein, E. (2010). *A mindfulness-based stress reduction workbook.* Oakland, CA: New Harbinger.

Szalavitz, M. (2012, January 11). *Q&A: Jon Kabat-Zinn talks about bringing mindfulness meditation to medicine.* Retrieved from http://healthland.time.com/2012/01/11/mind-reading-jon-kabat-zinn-talks-about-bringing-mindfulness-meditation-to-medicine/

Tirch, D., Silberstein, L., & Kolts, R. (2015). *Buddhist psychology and cognitive-behavioral therapy.* New York, NY: Guilford Press.

Wallin, D. (2015). *Attachment in psychotherapy.* New York, NY: Guilford Press.

Williams, K. A., Kolar, M. M., Reger, B. E., & Pearson, J. C. (2001). Evaluation of a wellness-based mindfulness stress reduction intervention: A controlled trial. *American Journal of Health Promotion, 15,* 422–432.

Williams, M., Teasdale, J., Segal, Z., & Kabat-Zinn, J. (2007). *The mindful way through depression: Freeing yourself from chronic unhappiness.* New York, NY: Guilford Press.

Your guide to mindfulness-based cognitive therapy. (n.d.). Retrieved from http://mbct.com/

Zenner, C., Herrnleben-Kurz, S., & Walach, H. (2014). Mindfulness-based interventions in schools: A systematic review and meta-analysis. *Frontiers in Psychology, 5.* Retrieved from https://www.ncbi.nlm.nih.gov/pmc/articles/PMC4075476/

Zoogman, S., Goldberg, S. B., Hoyt, W. T., & Miller, L. (2015). Mindfulness interventions with youth: A meta-analysis. *Mindfulness, 6*(2), 290–302.

Chapter 9

The Case of Marcos From Each Theoretical Perspective

In this chapter, the authors of Chapters 2–8 respond to a case study from their theoretical perspectives in order to provide you with a specific example of how the theories are applied. This real case (name changed to protect the identity of the client) was contributed by author Anthony Pantaleno and is described first, followed by discussion from the perspective of each of the theories in the order in which they are presented in the book: behavior therapy (BT), cognitive therapy (CT), rational emotive behavior therapy (REBT), multimodal therapy, acceptance and commitment therapy (ACT), dialectical behavior therapy (DBT), and mindfulness. We hope that this practical application is helpful in understanding the way in which the same case is conceptualized and addressed by the different theories under the cognitive–behavioral umbrella.

The Case of Marcos

Background

Marcos is a 22-year-old male, the younger of two brothers. He grew up in a suburban New York community, where he currently lives with his father and older brother. Marcos and his brother were raised in an intact nuclear Hispanic family, and they have always spent extended time once or twice a year visiting family members in Colombia. His mother served as the matriarch and the role model for a large extended Catholic family, many of whom still reside in South America. Last year Marcos's mother died unexpectedly in a freak automobile accident on her way to work. The loss has been very traumatic for Marcos and his family, but they receive a lot of support from the extended family, and this network of love and support has allowed them to move on with their lives.

Marcos's brother attended college out of state, but Marcos chose to remain at home and take classes at the local community college, majoring in music. Marcos described having a very close relationship with his mother and father but a more conflicted relationship with his older brother. According to Marcos, his brother was the extrovert of the family and he (Marcos) was the introvert, the tag-along. His perception was that he grew up in his brother's shadow—that his brother received all of the accolades because he was smart and funny. Despite their differences, the two brothers were taught to be loyal to each other.

The loss of Marcos's mother triggered self-examination about his future and what he wanted it to look like. Whereas his older brother had always been independent and an adventurer of sorts, Marcos never strayed too far from home. He was comfortable living at home, had some friends, and even had experienced several relationships with women. However, he doubted that he would actually be successful in forming a romantic, intimate relationship and said that he missed his mother's support and guidance in this area. She had assured him that he would eventually find his "true love" but stressed that he must not have sexual relationships prior to marriage. Because of his affection and loyalty to his mother, he intends to honor her beliefs regarding premarital sex.

Marcos had a friendship with a female student in his freshman year. He had made it clear to her that he was not looking for an exclusive girlfriend, as he believed that it could become a distraction from his studies. Unfortunately, as their friendship continued, this woman began to share stories with him about her history of self-injurious behavior. This progressed to her sharing sexual fantasies, including the request that he and another mutual male friend experiment with a ménage-a-trois. Realizing that he was in way over his head, Marcos sought his father's advice, which was to end this relationship. Marcos did so rather abruptly, and the fallout from this was that Marcos's male friends began to question his sexuality and began to tease him about being gay. His embarrassment and shame quickly propelled him to find another female friend, but he ended this relationship when the young woman disclosed her love for Marcos. It was at this time that he and his father decided it might be helpful to seek help. Despite the fact that he had never been in counseling before, he wanted to see whether this would help.

Presenting Problem

Marcos came to his first and all other subsequent appointments on his own, expressing that it was his problem and he wanted to work on it without any family involvement. He was a friendly, soft-spoken, handsome young man. He stated at the outset, "I'm tired of being the social misfit with my friends. I want to be true to my mom's wishes, but it is so hard in New York culture to find a girl who wants the same companionship that I do without the whole sexual relationship thing. My friends think I'm gay, but I'm not. Is it a crime to just be an old-fashioned kind of guy?"

Marcos made it clear that he did not want a girlfriend right now. He just wanted to feel more comfortable in his own skin and learn to socialize with people in general with the ease and wit of his older brother. He knew he sometimes came across as shy and unassertive, but he did not want this to prevent him from being more sociable, especially with women. Marcos said he felt relaxed and enjoyed himself in the company of his extended family but knew that in other contexts he presented as "stiff, serious, and sad." Because many of his male friends were now in exclusive relationships, he did not want his social world to shrink more than it already had. He had also recently shared with a friend in his group that he was a virgin, not realizing that this news would travel around campus like wildfire, making him feel like more of a social isolate than ever before.

As treatment began, Marcos's tendency to self-down and to be his own worst critic quickly emerged. He had always taken solace in his music; however, now he was beginning to question his talent and skills in this area as well. If his self-confidence with interpersonal relationships was so limited, he reasoned, maybe his skills in music were also mediocre. Marcos began to dread his senior year and the expectation that he had to plan and execute a major musical performance in order to graduate. He worried that others would think he was incapable of fulfilling this major requirement because of his lack of skill, and he also was concerned that others might not want to work with him on this project because he was shy and unassertive and not as confident as they were.

Although he had some limited insight into the futile comparisons to his older brother, Marcos expressed that maybe life had already passed him by and that he had somehow let his mother down by not doing something about all of this sooner. Although he never missed a therapy session except for conflicts with school assignments, Marcos was doubtful that therapy could serve much of a purpose for him except to provide him with a place to vent his feelings. "So maybe being the quiet one will be all I will ever be." Marcos clearly recognized the anxiety that he carried into so many areas of his life. What he was seeking was the hope that he could complete college, decide on a future career path, and find that one true love that his mother had promised him would come one day.

BT

Case Conceptualization

The case of Marcos presents a number of important variables to consider in developing a behavioral treatment plan to best help him meet his treatment goals. These include, but are not limited to, issues of culture and religion, family history, maintaining factors for some of his socializing behaviors, along with coping with the recent sudden death of his mother. These mediating factors could all have a potential impact on Marcos's ability to achieve his goals.

The information provided about Marcos offers a fairly detailed history as well as presents some themes and behaviors that may reflect certain personality traits of Marcos. An example of this may be seen in Marcos's relationship with his older brother and the history of reinforcement of his behavior as an introvert. That is, with his brother being described as the more outgoing of the two and Marcos considering himself to be the tag-along, Marcos has not had to develop his interpersonal relationships and receive feedback on them until he has become more independent in college. In addition, the fact that Marcos identifies as Hispanic and Catholic may be an area that the counselor would want to explore and consider in developing a conceptualization of this case. More specifically, his loyalty to his family, his commitment to his mother, his abstention from sexual intercourse until marriage, and his belief that therapy may not be helpful may also be variables to consider in a case conceptualization and treatment plan.

From a behavioral perspective, additional information could be gathered during the assessment procedures to help understand Marcos's behaviors better as well as to set treatment goals. More specifically, examining Marcos's behaviors from a functional standpoint may be helpful in understanding *why* he does or does not engage in certain behaviors. Looking at the learned history of the behavior as well as the contexts that may be currently maintaining it will assist in identifying which of these variables can be targeted for change. Examining the functional relationship between the presenting problems is also important when planning treatment goals and clinical strategies. For Marcos, it appears that his interpersonal difficulties, along with a number of cognitions, relate to anxiety. In his case, his anxiety may be a consequence of his perceived lack of interpersonal skills, and the combination of the two may impact his ability to work toward specific behavioral outcomes (e.g., complete a major requirement and graduate).

It would be important to try and gather some additional behavioral data from Marcos to fully understand his perception of his difficulties. For example, Marcos describes himself as having anxiety and poor interpersonal skills. Behaviorally speaking it would be important to understand any stimulus variables (e.g., specific individuals, social evaluative situations) that may exacerbate his experience of anxiety. Furthermore, it would be important to know just how debilitating his anxiety is and what the consequences are when he experiences it. Gaining an accurate evaluation of his interpersonal skills would also be helpful. Perhaps Marcos is not as deficient in his interpersonal skills as he thinks he is and holds himself to a higher standard of effective social skills (i.e., his brother). If he does in fact have poor interpersonal skills, having clear behavioral examples of which skills he is deficient in may be important so that these skills can be targeted for behavior change. Integrating the information gathered from a clinical interview, behavioral observations, and a functional analysis of his behavior will assist in case formulation, treatment selection, and evaluation.

In sum, Marcos presents with both anxiety and interpersonal difficulties that may have a history of reinforcement that maintains these behaviors currently and has led to avoidant behaviors, interfering with his ability to achieve specific objectives. The role of cognitions and personal and familial values may also be a factor in maintaining these behaviors. The recent death of his mother has removed an effective support system for him, and he has now extended his concerns about his interpersonal skills to his academic performance.

Establishing the Therapeutic Alliance and Goals

Before any interventions are implemented, it would be important for the counselor to develop a good therapeutic alliance. Balancing a warm and empathic approach toward counseling with a behavioral conceptualization of the problem would be important in order to keep Marcos coming to counseling, as he has expressed doubts as to its effectiveness. Furthermore, this approach may also help him to follow through on behavioral assignments between sessions, which are a common hallmark of BT and are discussed here.

Given Marcos's reported interpersonal difficulties, the therapeutic relationship may also provide another opportunity for the counselor to observe his social skills. That is, Marcos may demonstrate his interpersonal skills in the context of counseling and provide the behavior therapist with the opportunity to model effective behaviors and offer feedback on these behaviors. Given the recent death of his mother and his reported loss of social support, the therapeutic relationship may provide some support for Marcos. Expressing concern for his welfare and reinforcing his insight as to some of the negative behaviors that he would like to change may also assist in developing the therapeutic relationship. Fostering a positive working alliance can greatly assist Marcos in working on behavioral goals both in the counseling session as well as in the real world.

It would be important for the counselor to acknowledge that behavior change is not easy and that other variables in Marcos's life may undermine efforts to change. Working collaboratively with Marcos in establishing counseling goals and discussing practical as well as self-created barriers toward achieving them may also have a significant impact on the therapeutic alliance. Agreeing on the initial goals of counseling would be important in establishing a good relationship. The counselor would also work with Marcos to develop behavioral goals to target for change.

It would also be important for the counselor to learn about Marcos's expectations for counseling as well as continue to discuss with him his view on the counseling process. Finally, it would also be important for the therapeutic relationship to discuss the specific behavioral techniques that may be implemented. If Marcos does not think that a specific technique will be effective, or if he considers the process of change to be too difficult, he may not actively engage in efforts to change the behavior, and that may impact the therapeutic relationship and eventual outcome of therapy.

We also think that it would be important for Marcos and his counselor to regularly evaluate progress toward goals. There will be occasions when the priorities of goals may need to shift because of new situations in Marcos's life as well as the counselor's reconceptualization of his case.

The Therapeutic Process and Interventions to Achieve Change

A number of interventions would be considered in the treatment of Marcos, and it would be important for the practitioner to assess which are the most effective relative to the behaviors targeted for change. Each of these interventions would involve a psychoeducational component, and it would be important to make sure that Marcos understands the theoretical rationale for the intervention as well as any risks or discomfort involved. Consistent with the goal of establishing the therapeutic alliance, it would also be important to determine the acceptability of the intervention for Marcos. The *reinforcing procedures* discussed in Chapter 2 would be a regular part of counseling sessions for Marcos and for the interventions listed here. Identifying positive reinforcers for Marcos can motivate him to engage in specific therapeutic activities as well as to implement some of the behavioral strategies in vivo.

To address any physiological symptoms that Marcos may be reporting, the counselor would use relaxation training. The practice of relaxation training has an extensive history in counseling, as clients are taught to systematically relax their muscles as a means of reducing physiological arousal and anxiety. It would be important to prepare Marcos for relaxation training and increase his awareness of his physiological arousal when he experiences anxiety. Marcos would be informed that just as people may learn to create anxiety and tension, they also can be taught to relax. Simply speaking, Marcos can learn to gain control over his anxiety. Prior to engaging in relaxation training, Marcos would be instructed on how some of the more general procedures work. Upon completion of the relaxation training session, the counselor would ask Marcos about his thoughts during the process, how helpful he thought this was, and whether this would be something that he would want to practice independently. If Marcos is motivated to practice this, he and the counselor would collaboratively develop a schedule of relaxation and also work on considering some images of situations (e.g., interpersonal, academic) that may put him at higher risk for experiencing anxiety, practicing relaxation in that context before attempting to transfer these skills to the real-life situation.

Given Marcos's self-reported difficulties in interpersonal relations, this would be an important area to target for behavior change. Simulating interpersonal situations in the context of counseling can provide both an opportunity for an assessment of these skills as well as modeling and corrective feedback when needed. The concept of behavioral rehearsal is not unique to BT, but it can provide Marcos with the opportunity to simulate real-life situations that he reports difficulty with in the counseling setting.

It would be important to behaviorally define the difficulties that he is reporting and determine whether they are more skill deficits or performance deficits. If Marcos has a skill deficit, the counselor would develop a behavioral hierarchy that uses interpersonal situations that Marcos may have experienced or could imagine doing and then structure these situations for behavioral rehearsal or feedback. If Marcos has the interpersonal skills but does not present them effectively, the factors that may be interfering with his performance will need to be assessed and targeted for change.

Prior to implementing behavioral rehearsal, it would be important for Marcos to understand that the rationale for this approach is to have him learn a new behavioral pattern, one that may increase the likelihood of success in social situations. During this period, determining whether Marcos has any concerns about the behavioral rehearsal process would help avoid any uneasiness and promote his performance of these behaviors in a real-world setting.

During the behavioral rehearsal sessions, Marcos may be asked to start with a situation that he has a significant amount of difficulty with, which can be seen as a type of icebreaker activity in counseling as well as help the counselor learn the degree to which Marcos understands what he is supposed to do. Once it is clear that Marcos can stay in the role, the counselor would work with him through the hierarchy, providing feedback as needed about his performance. It may also be desirable to have a recording of his behavior and then review it together and determine Marcos's ability to identify interpersonal strengths and weaknesses. When Marcos has difficulty with certain behaviors, the counselor may model these behaviors or look for other examples of effective behaviors but not necessarily expect mastery.

When Marcos and the counselor agree that he has been able to perform some of these behaviors at a desirable level, the counselor would work with him to identify situations in which he can try out these behaviors in the real world. Working together, they would identify situations over the course of the week that would provide an opportunity to practice these skills. Marcos would be encouraged to briefly practice relaxation training prior to attempting these behaviors and then to take notes on how the interaction went, what behaviors he performed well, and what behaviors he would have liked to have performed better. All of this would be reviewed with the counselor during the subsequent session, and any unhelpful thinking patterns would be addressed through cognitive–behavioral approaches in support of behavioral rehearsal.

Marcos reports anxiety related to his interpersonal challenges and concerns about his academic progress and graduation. It appears that he is ineffective in coping with these situations and thus may experience additional anxiety and struggle even more going forward. Thus, Marcos may benefit from a problem-solving approach related to his challenges in handling a number of different situations. From a behavioral viewpoint, Marcos would be taught a variety of potentially effective responses that would allow him to handle these situations more effectively in the future. Marcos and his counselor would define the problem and situation specifically and then brainstorm alternative solutions to the problem. After generating a number of potential solutions, Marcos would be taught how to select which strategy *may* be most effective in resolving the presenting problem. It would be important for Marcos to understand that just because he may choose a solution that increases the probability of success, it does not necessarily guarantee success. Marcos and the counselor would periodically review the problem-solving approach, examine the effectiveness of its implementation in real-world settings, and discuss strategies for improvement as needed.

Termination Considerations

The decision to terminate counseling is best done collaboratively with Marcos and supported by objective data regarding behavior change. Throughout the therapeutic process, Marcos would continually be reminded that the goal of BT is to have him learn a number of behavioral strategies that he can apply outside of counseling sessions to assist in reducing his anxiety and meeting his behavioral goals. The importance of practicing these behaviors in real-world settings during the process of counseling further supports this notion. Decisions as to how and when to terminate counseling sessions should be arrived at by evaluating the degree to which Marcos has attained his predetermined counseling goals and his ability to apply newly learned strategies and behaviors in a variety of contexts.

CT

Case Conceptualization

Marcos presents with symptoms of anxiety and depression. His anxiety appears to be related mainly to social situations, as he repeatedly reports difficulties interacting with others and reports feelings of shyness and shame. His depression relates to his difficulties in friendships and romantic relationships as well as to his career path and the challenges posed by college graduation. To some extent, dependent and avoidant personality traits might be present, although they might not reach a clinical diagnosis.

From a CT perspective, the working hypothesis is that Marcos holds dysfunctional schemas that he is socially unfit and inferior to others, that others' disapproval is unbearable, that he must appear confident and competent, and that he must not show emotions and characteristics that make him look vulnerable. These schemas are common among people with social anxiety disorder, and their content seems to be consonant with recent events and his emotional and behavioral reactions to these events. He felt embarrassment and shame when friends teased him about being gay and immediately engaged in a new romantic relationship to avoid negative social appraisals. He felt socially isolated after others found out that he has not had any sexual relationships.

The personal history of the case also offers some clues about the development of such schemas. Marcos's older brother always had good social skills, and Marcos feels like he has been overshadowed by him. It is possible that Marcos's childhood experiences in his family have shaped the belief that he is inferior and incapable of presenting in a socially desirable way. Marcos describes himself as shy, unassertive, stiff, serious, and sad in social situations. Such reports are also common among individuals suffering from social anxiety. According to the cognitive model, these reports can be conceptualized as consequences of schema activation in social contexts.

On the one hand, the individual focuses his or her attention on internal and external reactions that might be indicative of inappropriateness. On the other hand, schema activation leads to behavioral inhibition, which becomes again the object of self-focused attention, making the individual think that he or she is acting strangely and that other people will observe this and probably appraise this behavior in a negative manner. In addition, socially anxious individuals engage in safety behaviors (e.g., trying to control themselves) that again lead to behaviors and reactions that they fear that others will observe (e.g., being tense).

Although it is not stated explicitly, Marcos's description of himself seems to fit other characteristics of dysfunctional schema activation. He sees and thinks about himself through the eyes of others. In the first session, he describes his problems by stating, "I'm tired of being the social misfit with my friends" and "Is it a crime to just be an old-fashioned kind of guy?" Both statements reflect the idea that his problems stem from how others perceive him. Moreover, he expresses concerns that others think that he will fail and that he is shy, unassertive, and lacking confidence and that they will decline to work with him for these reasons. Finally, he seems to be unaware of any signs of social approval and acceptance, and this is also congruent with the idea that he holds a schema of being socially unfit. The fact that he managed to easily find a new romantic partner who fell in love with him is a reasonable argument that he may have some socially desirable characteristics, although Marcos seems to ignore these facts.

Depression appears to be a secondary problem that developed as a consequence of Marcos's failures to address interpersonal problems. The full cognitive triad of beliefs specific to depression seems to be present in Marcos's case. He has a negative view of himself that was triggered initially in relation to social situations but now seems to be extended to other domains of life, such as his academic performance. This negative perspective is also reflected in his self-criticism and the idea that he has disappointed his mother. He sees his current situation as harsh, with people judging him for his wish to stay true to religious and traditional values and for his lack of social skills. He also sees his future in a negative manner, thinking that life has passed him by.

His dependent traits, reflected in the great extent to which he relies on his mother's and father's advice for making important life decisions, are likely based on schemas containing beliefs of inadequacy and vulnerability of the self and a belief that he must seek the help of others to handle life problems. For example, he expresses these beliefs when saying that he does not think he will be able to find a romantic partner and that he relied on his mother's advice on how to proceed. Avoidant traits are reflected in the general pattern of avoiding others' rejection, especially in romantic relationships. He engaged in a romantic relationship in the first year of college but did not want an exclusive girlfriend, despite the fact that his model of relationships contains deep involvement. He also ended the relationship with the young woman just after she expressed her love for him. Marcos's avoidant traits might rely on beliefs like "If I get too close to a partner she might discover how defective I am." Marcos's personal recall about his childhood of feeling less appreciated by his parents because he was not as smart and funny as his brother is also consistent with this idea. He might hold some assumptions like "If my parents do not like me, nobody will ever like me."

Marcos's dysfunctional beliefs, shaped by his life history, have been activated by the recent stressors in his life: the death of his mother, the fact that friends and colleagues made fun of him about being gay, and the fact that graduation is approaching. The activation of the schemas has generated negative automatic thoughts (e.g., life has passed away, he let his mother down, others think he is incapable) and dysfunctional emotional experiences (e.g., shame, anxiety) and behaviors (jumping into a new relationship to prove to others that he is not gay, leaving the relationship just after the partner declares her love for him).

Establishing the Therapeutic Alliance and Goals

The therapeutic relationship would be built on an agreement between the counselor and Marcos to work together toward achieving some realistic goals that are important to him. The counselor would show genuine empathy and consideration for Marcos's problems and distress. As a key feature of CT, the counselor would actively engage Marcos in the process of therapy, in setting goals and agendas for sessions, and by testing his beliefs.

Counseling should begin by establishing the priorities for problems to work on and setting realistic goals. Marcos has mentioned that he would like to socialize more easily with other people (including women) and that he would like to complete college and decide on a career as well as find a romantic partner who complements his cultural values. These goals should be openly discussed in the first session and formulated in a realistic and achievable manner. It is important to manage Marcos's expectations for counseling in that it most likely will not bring him his one true love, for example. The counselor can, however, help him alleviate the distress related to graduation and choosing a career, which should enable him to do well in school and have a clearer mind when making big decisions, such as choosing a career. Counseling can help reduce Marcos's distress in social interactions and improve his social skills, which may help his interactions with potential romantic partners as well as friends. Collaboratively formulating realistic goals is important, because otherwise Marcos could feel disappointed that counseling is not effective.

When starting to work on the presenting problems, the counselor should keep in mind that it is better to focus in the beginning on those that are easier to overcome. This will help Marcos acknowledge the usefulness of coming to counseling sessions and will increase his willingness to participate actively in the process. This is an important issue for Marcos, given that he seems quite doubtful about what counseling can do for him. For example, the counselor might suggest starting with working on a plan for graduation and managing the distress of asking others to get involved in the musical performance. This approach could also improve Marcos's self-efficacy and enhance the therapeutic alliance.

The counselor should offer Marcos a brief introduction to the CT model and discuss the relationship of his beliefs and thinking patterns to his current problems. The counselor could present an initial cognitive conceptualization of his problems, with some hypotheses about the cognitive distortions that might contribute to his current problems. Later in counseling, when working on core beliefs, the counselor should take a collaborative empiricism approach and engage Marcos in the process of testing the functionality of his beliefs, rules, assumptions, and attitudes. It is recommended that the counselor frequently ask Marcos for feedback about the evolving conceptualization and progress in counseling to ensure that they are on the right track and that Marcos believes that his goals are being addressed. When formulating the case conceptualization, the counselor should also take into account Marcos's strengths and resources that might be useful in counseling.

The Therapeutic Process and Interventions to Achieve Change

The work with Marcos would begin by clarifying what kind of social interactions he views as being most distressful and whether he engages in any form of avoidance. The counselor would ask Marcos to fill out a daily record of situations in which he feels anxiety over interacting with others, the thoughts that go through his mind in those moments, and what emotional and behavioral responses he experiences. Working on social anxiety problems would require presenting the cognitive model of this problem, taking into account the three phases of social encounters: anticipatory (before getting into a social interaction), situational exposure (while in a feared social situation), and postsituation (after the social interaction has ended). Monitoring daily life situations can be coupled with the use of imagery techniques and role plays to elicit relevant automatic thoughts, emotions, and behaviors. To ensure that Marcos feels that counseling is addressing his most important problems, the focus of these exercises could be to ask colleagues to get involved in the musical performance that is required for graduation. Role-play exercises might simulate how he would do that. If depressive symptoms turn out to be clinically relevant, then a behavioral activation component would be introduced in the early phase of therapy. Behavioral activation can also be used toward the goal of graduation as well as used to gather relevant information for making a decision about a future career. For example, using Marcos's input, the counselor might explore what steps should be taken to address these issues in the immediate future and together with Marcos begin to schedule them. Engagement in pleasurable activities might also be addressed and, if needed, such activities might be added to the schedule. Ratings of mastery and pleasure when planning and after performing these activities can be requested.

In the next phase, counseling could move to challenging and restructuring dysfunctional automatic thoughts that arise before Marcos engages in a social interaction. Unrealistic and catastrophic scenarios about the consequences of a social encounter can be restructured using Socratic questioning and balancing the evidence for such a scenario. This could be used to teach Marcos how to modify his thoughts before entering social situations. In the cognitive model, heightened anticipatory anxiety facilitates the appraisal of vulnerability, and the resulting anxiety and nervousness become inputs for the self-focused attention in the situation. This in turn facilitates the activation of an inadequacy schema. Teaching Marcos to adopt a more realistic pattern of thinking before engaging in social interactions might reduce the negative input in the social encounter and reduce the frequency of avoidance behaviors. Meanwhile, progress in behavioral activation could be monitored and might offer additional information about negative automatic thoughts that Marcos experiences in the face of more difficult activities. The counselor can help Marcos replace dysfunctional thoughts such as "I won't be able to do it" with more adaptive ones such as "I might not do it perfectly on the first try, but exercises will help me improve."

Role-play and video feedback techniques might be used to help Marcos reduce his exacerbated self-focused attention during social interactions. Such techniques, especially videotaping and rewatching a simulated interaction, might also show Marcos that the reactions and behaviors that he believes make him look "stiff, serious, and sad" might not be as obvious as he thinks.

In the next phases of the treatment the counselor might start testing and challenging dysfunctional thoughts that appear during social interactions and perform real-life exposure exercises. Emotional thinking (e.g., "Because I feel like this others must see me as anxious") is a frequent bias that appears while one is being exposed to a social interaction, and such bias should be approached during this cognitive change. Exposure can follow a hierarchy from moderately feared situations to those that generate the most anxiety. Exposure should be conceptualized using the cognitive model to test the beliefs and assumptions that Marcos holds about social interactions (e.g., "People don't like me and don't want to work with me because I am shy").

Cognitive restructuring techniques would also be used for engaging in postevent processing, correcting distorted interpretation about previous interactions, and reducing rumination. Cognitive restructuring strategies might move from addressing automatic thoughts to intermediate beliefs (the assumptions, rules, and attitudes he holds about social relationships).

Toward the final phases of therapy, the counselor would start working on core beliefs. The collection of information from previous exercises should offer sufficient input for the counselor and Marcos to have a more precise hypothesis about his schemas and start working on them. The general beliefs of being unlovable and defective should be defined in Marcos's terms and tailored to his life experience. Other schemas that emerge that are relevant to his depressive and dependent symptoms should also be addressed. Avoidant traits are likely to relate to the same schemas as the previous ones, especially those relevant for social anxiety, and increasing the flexibility of those should also reduce avoidant symptoms. If, however, these symptoms prove to be more relevant and more persistent, then the counselor might explore additional hypotheses and develop a more complex conceptualization of Marcos's problems, perhaps focusing more on romantic relationships. Ultimately, the counselor might engage Marcos in a problem-solving process focused on finding circles and people who share his values and among whom he is more likely to find a partner.

Termination Considerations

A well-performed CT treatment should equip Marcos with useful tools to identify, test, and correct dysfunctional thinking and beliefs. These tools will help him further in preventing possible relapses, managing daily stressors, and developing mastery over his own life. The counselor will openly discuss the possible obstacles and problems that might emerge in the long run and ways to manage them. Two booster sessions might be suggested in the next year, a few months apart, in order to maintain treatment gains and reduce the risk of relapse.

REBT

Case Conceptualization

Marcos chooses to follow the expectations and values set forth by his Colombian Catholic family, in particular his mother, whom he was very close to. Marcos's values regarding premarital sex differ from those of his peers, which leads to being teased and ridiculed. Marcos experiences several unhealthy negative emotions and maladaptive behaviors, specifically shame and anxiety as well as being shy and unassertive. REBT views shame as resulting from the perception or reality of others looking down on one or having something unfavorable about oneself exposed to others. Marcos reports feeling shame when his male friends questioned his sexuality and teased him. Cognitive processes associated with shame include "I have made a mistake/acted stupidly/failed/been rejected/been thought of negatively; it's terrible this has happened to me; this means I am a weak, stupid, inadequate person." The behavioral responses associated with shame include defending threatened self-esteem in self-defeating ways. In Marcos's case, he sought out a relationship with the goal of proving his worth to his friends rather than out of having a genuine interest in a relationship.

From an REBT perspective, anxiety is the result of asking oneself "what if" questions and answering such questions with a catastrophic response. Marcos is likely telling himself that it is awful, terrible, and horrible that he let his life pass him by and perhaps he let his mother down. Avoidance behaviors are typically experienced with anxiety. Marcos indicates that he is shy and unassertive. Specifically, his anxiety has interfered with his goal of graduating because he has avoided the required musical performance. The healthy alternative to anxiety is concern, in which he would be thinking it is bad, perhaps very bad, *possibly* to have let his life pass him by and *possibly* to have let his mother down. If Marcos believed these statements, he would be more likely to engage in the behaviors necessary to graduate.

Establishing the Therapeutic Alliance and Goals

Although Marcos is attending therapy willingly, it is important to obtain agreement on the goals and tasks of therapy, which will aid in the development of the therapeutic alliance. Without such agreement, it is quite possible that the counselor and client would be working on different goals and the therapeutic relationship would be affected. Marcos presents with several activating events and unhealthy negative emotions and maladaptive behaviors. The counselor would ask Marcos to identify one particular emotional or behavioral goal to work through. This sets the stage for the collaborative work that will occur throughout the therapeutic process. As Marcos doubts the efficacy of therapy and instead sees therapy as a place to vent his feelings, the counselor would discuss the concepts of *feeling better* versus *getting better.* Venting his feelings every week may provide temporary relief for Marcos, but he will continue to experience the same problems. Getting better is the result of changing one's cognitive (and therefore emotive and behavioral) reactions to events. Once Marcos identifies a specific emotion or behavior to address, the counselor would use motivational syllogism to obtain agreement on the goals and tasks of therapy for this particular problem. The use of motivational syllogism not only helps motivate a client to change but also provides education about the theory and process of REBT. There are four steps in motivational syllogism:

Step 1. Marcos's present emotion is dysfunctional. The counselor would use Socratic questioning to help Marcos see that his present emotion is dysfunctional for him and focus on identifying and discussing the negative consequences he experiences as a result of the negative emotion.

Step 2. An alternative acceptable emotional goal exists for this particular activating event. The counselor would teach Marcos that there is an alternative emotion that is more adaptive for him by identifying and discussing the consequences of the new emotion. This establishes the goal of therapy.

Step 3. Teach the B (beliefs) → C (feelings and behaviors) connection. It is important that Marcos understand and buy into the concept that beliefs, rather than events themselves, largely lead to emotions and behaviors.

Step 4. Change beliefs to change the dysfunctional emotion. This establishes the tasks of therapy.

The Therapeutic Process and Interventions to Achieve Change

To maximize therapeutic efficiency, REBT addresses one unhealthy negative emotion or maladaptive behavior at a time. For illustrative purposes, we have chosen to address Marcos's shame.

REBT sessions typically begin with a review of how clients did on the homework that was assigned in the previous session. Following this, the counselor would ask Marcos for a specific example of when he experienced shame during the week to obtain a specific activating event. The counselor then would establish an emotional goal for that activating event, such as working on sadness, disappointment, or regret. Together they would explore the consequences of the healthier, negative emotion. In this case, let us suppose for demonstration purposes that it is sadness. The counselor would identify, through inference chaining, Marcos's irrational beliefs leading to shame. Once this is accomplished, the counselor would reinforce the irrational B–C connection (e.g., "Do you see how telling yourself, 'I've been thought of negatively; it's terrible this has happened to me; this means I am an inadequate person' results in feeling shame?"). Once Marcos sees the B–C connection, the counselor would challenge his irrational beliefs. Beginning with the *functional dispute,* the counselor would ask Marcos the following: "How does holding the belief 'Because I have been thought of negatively, I am an inadequate person' help you to achieve your goal of sadness? How does holding the belief 'Because I have been thought of negatively, I am an inadequate person' get in the way of you achieving your goal of feeling sad rather than shame?" The *empirical dispute* would be used to ask Marcos for evidence that the opinions of others determine his overall worth as a person. The *logical dispute* would involve asking Marcos whether it is logical to base one's *entire* value as a person on the opinions of others. The *friend dispute* can be very helpful for clients who globally rate themselves negatively. The counselor would ask Marcos whether his best friend would be *inadequate* if other people thought negatively of him or her. The *circle exercise* described in Chapter 4 is a helpful way of visually highlighting the various disputes in an interactive format.

Following disputation, the counselor would collaborate with Marcos to generate the rational alternative "Even though I have been thought of negatively, that does not make me an inadequate person." Following this, the counselor would negotiate a homework assignment based on what was discussed in session and identify any barriers (practical or emotional) to completing the homework. Specifically, the counselor would introduce a self-help form and explain the rationale for completing it (see the Chapter 4 Appendix). The goal of self-help forms is to have clients practice what they learned in counseling, specifically identifying and challenging irrational beliefs leading to unhealthy negative emotions. In addition, it would be important for Marcos to strengthen his conviction in the rational beliefs. This would occur through repeated rehearsal. The counselor would also ask Marcos whether he would be willing to carry out a shame attack exercise by telling his peers that he is a virgin while rehearsing a coping statement. The counselor would address any obstacles to completing each homework assignment and work with Marcos to overcome them prior to attempting the homework.

Termination Considerations

Termination would be addressed when Marcos has achieved all of his stated goals for therapy and demonstrates the ability to become his own counselor. Termination could be done in a fadeout manner, whereby the frequency of sessions is reduced to every other week, and then every 3 weeks, and so forth.

Multimodal Therapy

Case Conceptualization

From the information provided, it would appear that Marcos does not show signs of serious emotional problems. Although there is a great deal of self-doubt as well as self-recrimination, there is no mention of self-harm or suicidal ideation. The precipitating events leading him to seek counseling included ending a relationship with a woman that he initiated for the purpose of altering his standing with his male friends after they questioned his sexuality. His stated goals for treatment include finding that one true love that his mother had promised him would come one day. For Marcos this means being "true to [his] mom's wishes" that he not have sexual relationships prior to marriage. It would appear that a major conflict for Marcos is the bind that he experiences between the traditional values of his Hispanic roots and Catholic background and how his upbringing may differ from the more liberal practices in today's society regarding sexuality, for example. This conflict has led to behaviors that have contributed to a substantial amount of anxiety and self-doubt. However, his difficulties are much more robust, and a variety of BASIC ID modalities are evident in his current life situation. He also is seeking hope for a better future and career path. It appears that Marcos has a variety of personal resources, which suggests that there is hope that his life circumstances can improve.

Multimodal therapy cases are conceptualized using BASIC ID, always keeping in mind the factors that shape and maintain human personality and problems, such as operant and classical conditioning, modeling and imitation, nonconscious processes, defensive reactions, private events (including expectancies and selective attention), and internal metacommunications. This case is a good example of the typical client presenting for counseling. He comes for treatment with a plethora of mild to moderate problems that are plaguing him. He is therapy naïve and has doubts that therapy will be of much help. He views counseling as a place to vent his feelings. Nonetheless, he wants to see whether counseling will help him. Thus, after reinforcing his self-efficacy and his ability to act on his decisions to obtain assistance to improve his life, the multimodal therapist would immediately begin to engage in psychoeducation about the therapeutic process, goal setting, and the therapeutic relationship. It might sound something like this: "Marcos, I'd like to congratulate you on your ability to assess how your life is progressing and the decision to seek assistance. Because you've never been in counseling before, it might be helpful for us to have a brief discussion regarding what happens in counseling. Doing so is likely to help you sharpen your expectations as well as improve your ability to benefit from our joint efforts."

Establishing the Therapeutic Alliance and Goals

A discussion of the need for the relationship between Marcos and the counselor to be different from most other relationships seems necessary. The inner circle strategy may prove to be helpful. This is a concrete procedure that orients the client to the intimate nature of the therapeutic relationship. Five concentric circles are drawn on a sheet of paper with the letter *A* drawn in the center and the letters *B, C, D,* and *E* labeled and placed between subsequent circles. The counselor would explain that circle *A* indicates a person's most private thoughts and feelings, those that he or she generally does not share or reveal to others except perhaps to the most trusted friends or family members. Other friends and acquaintances who are less emotionally close or not part of the private inner circle (*A*) of friends tend to have information that is more on the periphery, such as in the *C, D,* and *E* circles. The relationship between the counselor and counselee works best when they are engaging in discussions concerning information (thoughts, feelings, sensations, images, behaviors, relationships, etc.) from the *B* area, which would be private information such as in the *A* circle. Although initially the client may not feel comfortable sharing *A*-level information, this would be the ultimate goal.

This kind of discussion frequently leads to more fruitful dialogue and understanding between the counselor and counselee. Similar psychoeducational discussions regarding the development and selection of goals, together with regular assessment of progress, also assist in developing trust and increase the likelihood that the client will self-disclose at the most significant level. Also, sharing specific examples of how people have resolved problems by going to counseling might help relieve some of the client's doubts about it. A concrete metaphor such as going to the dentist for a root canal, consulting a computer specialist when there is a glitch, or taking a car that continues to stall to an auto mechanic might help the client understand that counseling is about more than just venting feelings.

The Therapeutic Process and Interventions to Achieve Change

At this point it would be helpful for Marcos to complete the Multimodal Life History Inventory. It would provide substantial information that would amplify and perhaps clarify Marcos's thinking as well as delineate issues and expectations surrounding goal setting and treatment planning. From a multimodal perspective, a problem list and BASIC ID profile from the information provided would look like this:

Behavior: Being shy and unassertive; wanting to find a companion without the sexual component before marriage; wanting to be more sociable, especially with women, but currently not having a girlfriend.

Affect: Unresolved grief over the mother's death; feeling uncomfortable in his own skin; being "stiff, serious, and sad" away from his extended family; anxiety about his skill level and music; anxiety about others not wanting to work with him on his senior project; anxiety in many areas.

Sensation: [Some therapists would place anxiety here; however, information coming in directly from the senses belongs here. Sensory information is frequently uncovered in the Second Order BASIC ID.]

Imagery/Image of Self: Limited self-confidence in interpersonal situations, image of mother continues as a role model and family matriarch.

Cognition: Believes he might let his mother down, questions his music ability, thinks life may have passed him by, discounts himself—his own worst enemy, conflict regarding family (Catholic, Hispanic) values and current-day morals.

Interpersonal Relationships: Conflict with brother, socially isolated and a social misfit.

Drugs/Basic Biological Processes: No issues presented at this time.

After reviewing the BASIC ID with Marcos, the counselor could ask him which of the various issues from the list of problem areas he deems most urgent or immediate to him. This would be followed by a discussion of the problems or concerns that he chooses to work on first. When a selection is finally determined, intervention may be very direct, such as implementing an assertiveness training program to help him overcome his shyness and feelings of social inadequacy. A Second Order BASIC ID may be necessary in order to gain more insight into how Marcos experiences this particular problem. Should he choose to work on the issue of believing that he has let his mother down, which could easily be seen as a central aspect of his situation, the technique of an imaginary reflecting team may be helpful.

An imaginary reflecting team is a technique similar to the Gestalt empty chair technique. Marcos could identify individuals he respects (the individuals need not be living) and invite them into the counseling session. This would allow Marcos to concretely incorporate into his processing of issues perspectives that represent not only his cultural heritage but also his religious affiliation. Hispanics historically value community and church. Allowing for the inclusion of representatives of both areas on his imaginary reflecting team ensures that these important life components will be available to him as he goes through this process. If desired or required for greater effect, chairs and name tags for the team members can be provided. These imaginary team members can be used in a variety of ways. They may be asked for suggestions to resolve the current problem or perhaps to amplify how Marcos might view his situation in the future. They may be asked how he will be different when the problem is resolved. The team members might reinterpret his mother's message or the intention of her message. They could possibly place his mother's instructions in a specific time for when they were meant for him, such as when he was younger as opposed to an adult. Marcos would provide the input as he sees it from the viewpoint of each of the team members. Multiple possibilities in Marcos's situation could be addressed from the perspective of each member of the team. In fact, suggestions to address each problem in the Second Order BASIC ID profile could be accomplished with the imaginary reflecting team. Of course, all of this is done by Marcos collaborating with the counselor, who would guide Marcos through the process.

Another method that might be helpful to Marcos would be to conceptualize the seven BASIC ID modalities as themes, asking "Is it what you are doing or feeling that is creating the most discomfort? Or perhaps it's the way you are thinking or relating to people that is of the highest concern. What piece or aspect of your current experiences is causing you the greatest degree of distress?" Once identified, the various problems or issues surrounding that theme from each of the modalities could be examined and a set of goals could be delineated.

Once the goals of treatment were determined, specific interventions would be selected and discussed with Marcos. Helping Marcos to understand the intervention strategies selected and the anticipated outcomes is likely to result in cooperation and therapeutic progress. Care would need to be taken to ensure that language issues do not interfere with treatment. Because Marcos already has a sense of inferiority, reducing an authoritative stance and affording him measured respect would be necessary. Providing concrete, direct interventions should be considered. The counselor would need to be careful to avoid coming from a position of power or superiority, as Marcos is already sensitized to ridicule. In investigating his mother's place in Marcos's life, it would be essential to avoid disparaging her in any way. Any hint of disrespect toward his mother could easily be misinterpreted and contribute to an adversarial/defensive stance that could adversely affect rapport.

Termination Considerations

In general, termination is considered when the client assesses that his or her situation has sufficiently improved and his or her problems are substantially resolved. For Marcos, this would likely include resolution of his conflict related to his mother's teachings and modern dating practices. In addition, numerous issues may well require attention. These would include his introversion, conflict with his brother, lack of a career path, and sense of personal doubt and inadequacy. Ultimately, Marcos will have to decide when he is feeling confident enough to begin handling issues with less assistance from the counselor. Titration in terms of the frequency of counseling sessions would likely be the most reasonable approach in this situation given the number of problems presented.

ACT

Case Conceptualization

Most probably, Marcos is struggling with anxiety and depression. His symptoms are explained by *experiential avoidance*, as illustrated by his tendency to avoid uncomfortable relationships and experiences. His pattern of experiential avoidance is reflected in his tendency to be introverted and avoid new experiences (e.g., he chose to remain at home, he never strayed too far from home) and also in how he faces uncomfortable situations and feelings (e.g., he did not want to get emotionally involved with a girlfriend because he assumed that this would affect his performance in school, he turned to his father for help when in a problematic situation with his former girlfriend and leaned exclusively on his advice in resolving the situation, he sought the friendship of another female because of embarrassment and shame). Experiential avoidance (as opposed to acceptance) is demonstrated as well in the manner in which Marcos expresses his problem at the outset of therapy: He does not want a girlfriend, he wants to be more comfortable in his own skin, and he wants to be more assertive and popular.

Cognitive fusion also contributes to his symptoms: He describes himself as being shy and unassertive and "stiff, serious, and sad" and seems to behave accordingly. In addition, he seems to believe that he will find "true love" if he does not have sex until marriage, only because his mother told him so; therefore, he confounds words with reality. *Attachment to the conceptualized self* is demonstrated by his self-description as an "old-fashioned kind of guy" along with his wish to be more comfortable in his own skin (which implies that he wants to change things in his life so that he can get along in various circumstances without changing the kind of guy he is) and his hope that he can complete college, decide on a future career path, and find that one true love. His hope for the future, along with his constant worries regarding his (cap) abilities as well as his constant preoccupation with letting his mother down by not fulfilling her wishes, illustrates his *lack of contact with the present moment*.

Maybe one of the most salient processes underlying his symptoms is the *lack of values clarity*. Marcos's behavior seems to be directed by momentary emotions and thoughts and by desirable rules rather than personal values. For example, not having sex before marriage seems to be one of his mother's values rather than his own. In addition, his behavior seems to be characterized by *inaction* (e.g., he does not seem to have any initiative to implement actions congruent with his goals outside the therapy sessions and believes that therapy is at most a place to vent his feelings), *impulsivity* (e.g., he felt the need to immediately find another female friend in order to escape shame and embarrassment), and *avoidant persistence* (e.g., he explicitly states that he does not want a girlfriend at the moment).

Overall, Marcos seems to have been using relationships to help avoid making contact with negative self-evaluations or a sense of social alienation. It is important to note that all of the processes promoting psychological inflexibility interact to potentiate Marcos's emotional problems. All of these processes should be targeted in concert in therapy in order to increase Marcos's psychological flexibility.

Beyond processes that promote psychological inflexibility and thus sustain symptoms, there are also *factors that promote psychological flexibility* in Marcos's case—and these should be considered as well, as it is the unique constellation of factors promoting psychological (in)flexibility that particularizes the case of every client. In Marcos's case, he has chosen to be in counseling, and despite thinking that it will not do much for him, he attends the therapy sessions (*acceptance*). It is also possible that certain values he holds could be used to promote psychological flexibility. For example, he seems to value family, he seems to want meaningful social relationships, and he wants to make a contribution in the world as a musician (*values*).

Establishing the Therapeutic Alliance and Goals

To establish the therapeutic relationship and agreement on goals for counseling, the counselor can capitalize on client factors that are related to psychological flexibility. In Marcos's case, the main factors that can be built on are acceptance of the therapeutic context and his potential values. Starting with his presenting problem, the counselor can help Marcos to see the link between anxiety symptoms ("Marcos clearly recognized the anxiety that he carried into so many areas of his life") and difficulties related to interpersonal relationships. The counselor can show Marcos how his attempts at controlling anxiety are interfering with his ability to establish and maintain meaningful relationships (one of his goals). Then the counselor can explore with Marcos alternative ways of managing anxiety by pointing out the advantages of doing so. It is important to note that throughout the initial discussion and always after that, the counselor will carefully model processes that promote psychological flexibility. For example, the counselor can model acceptance and defusion by not changing the possible negative evaluative statements Marcos may make about the possibility of accepting anxiety or the discomfort that these statements could cause him.

Regarding the main goals for counseling, in Marcos's case the counselor would consider assisting him (a) to be in contact with his worry and self-criticism, (b) to be in contact with his anxiety and depression, and (c) to be able to identify his values and the subordinated goals and acting congruent with these. At a more specific level, the counseling goals should include the following: (a) to fully understand the nature of Marcos's anxiety and depressive symptoms as well as previous coping strategies that he has used to overcome these symptoms; (b) to assist Marcos in seeing that his attempt at controlling thoughts and feelings is an unworkable system; (c) to introduce and explain the ACT conceptualization as it pertains to Marcos's problems; (d) to build up a list of problems and to approach each of them from an ACT viewpoint; (e) to develop alternative coping skills (i.e., nurturing psychological flexibility) in contrast to worry, self-criticism, and avoidance; (f) to introduce the concept (and importance) of values and the distinction between goals and values; (g) to establish behavioral goals and introduce and promote commitment; and (h) to prepare Marcos for the termination of the therapy and to develop a posttreatment plan.

The Therapeutic Process and Interventions to Achieve Change

The first step of the intervention would consist of establishing the therapeutic relationship and negotiating therapy goals. Related to this, case conceptualization plays a key role: The counselor should aim to fully understand Marcos's problems and the specific modalities of coping that he tried previously and then introduce the ACT conceptualization. To illustrate the idea that trying to control thoughts and feelings is an unworkable system, the counselor could ask Marcos to do simple experiential exercises that demonstrate the paradoxical effect of intentional control of private experience. For example, the counselor could ask Marcos how frequently during the past few days he has thought about a white tiger. After writing down his answer, the counselor could ask him to think about whatever he wants for the next 5 minutes with the exception of a white tiger. Most probably, Marcos would report a significant increase in thoughts about a white tiger. The counselor could explain to him that when told "Do not think of a white tiger," his mind created a rule that included "white tiger"— this is why it is so difficult to respect the rule. The counselor could make use of concrete worries relevant to Marcos to help him understand that the mechanism is the same when Marcos worries, and it is of no use to attempt to control the worries, especially in the long term.

Imaginative exercises and metaphors can be used to illustrate that the paradoxical effect of intentional control applies to emotions too. For example, the counselor could ask Marcos to imagine that he is suspended above the cage of a hungry lion while being wired to a sensitive device capable of detecting any small change in his physiological parameters. While suspended there, Marcos's task is not to get anxious at all. If he does, then he will be thrown in the cage. What is the probability he will manage not to get anxious? Using such scenarios, the counselor could show Marcos that when he is trying not to get anxious, the most probable outcome is that he will get anxious (i.e., trying to minimize works the other way around, in most cases).

To illustrate the uselessness of struggling with suffering or gaining control of things, the counselor could use other metaphors, like the metaphor of the drowning man: The more the man struggles, the greater the chance that he will drown.

After Marcos understands the general ACT conceptualization, specific treatment goals could be collaboratively devised. To that end, the counselor could ask Marcos to list how his life would be different if he gave up his anxiety. Based on this list, specific therapeutic goals could be established.

After Marcos agrees with the therapeutic goals, most of the therapy would be dedicated to increasing psychological flexibility while working on specific problems. For example, to teach Marcos alternatives to cognitive fusion and the contextualized self, the counselor could challenge him to do simple experiential exercises aimed at helping him understand the distinction between language and reality and the distinction between being and doing. For example, the counselor could ask Marcos to write down two unrelated words, then try to relate them (i.e., elaborate an explanation about how the words can be related). Then the counselor could provide Marcos with a third word invented on the spot and ask him to relate it to the previous two. With this exercise, the counselor could demonstrate the human mind's incredible capacity to build hypothetical meanings and relations that are profoundly subjective and that are subsequently used in guiding interactions with the world as if they were valid. The idea is that language is not reality.

To illustrate that there is a clear distinction between person and act/behavior, the counselor could ask Marcos to drink a cup of tea and then ask him whether he is tea. With this experience, the counselor could show Marcos that there is a difference between having misfit social behaviors (something he *does*) and being a social misfit (something he *is*) and that nothing he does defines who he is. Further on, the counselor could ask Marcos to imagine that he has the thought that drinking tea is going to make him tea. Is the experience of having that thought really transforming him into tea? A thought is a thought and nothing else. Although he could have thoughts that he might fear more than others, thoughts are thoughts and should be seen like that. That is, the challenge for Marcos is to look *at* his thoughts, not *from* his thoughts.

To help Marcos clarify his own values, the counselor could ask him to list the things that are most important for him in life. Then the counselor could ask him to rank them, and then gradually restrict the list to only three things, and then only to one. Based on Marcos's list, the counselor would then introduce the distinction between values and goals and ask Marcos what he would do differently today if he were going to die the next day. The purpose is to link specific behavioral goals to valued domains.

Because of space limitations, we do not discuss here the specific strategies for addressing *every* psychological process that could interfere with psychological flexibility. The counselor could creatively try any strategy— experiential exercises, metaphors, paradoxical approaches, and so on— that fits the ACT conceptualization, is insightful for Marcos, and serves the purpose of increasing psychological flexibility.

Termination Considerations

Termination consideration would be based on changes indicative of progress in increasing psychological flexibility. Mindfulness and acceptance processes, as reflected in higher levels of self-acceptance and eradication of the need to change thoughts and emotions, as well as commitment and behavior change processes, as reflected in regular and successful engagement in behaviors congruent with Marcos's goals and values, are factors that suggest consideration of termination.

DBT

Case Conceptualization

DBT conceptualizes problematic behaviors from a biosocial theory. According to this biosocial model, individuals exhibit difficulties in emotional dysregulation as a result of a transaction between a biological predisposition to emotional vulnerability and an invalidating environment. The biological vulnerability includes three components: (a) a higher reactivity, (b) a higher sensitivity, and (c) a slower return to baseline. The biosocial theory conceptualizes an invalidating environment as one in which skills for managing intense emotional responses were not taught and emotionality may have been made worse through trauma, neglect, abuse, or invalidation.

It is possible that Marcos exhibits a biological vulnerability to emotional dysregulation; there is a pattern of emotion suppression such that Marcos avoids negative affectivity despite traumatic events (e.g., his mother's death). Marcos is different from his more outgoing brother, in whose shadow he perceives having grown up. It is possible that his more extroverted brother obtained positive attention and validation, whereas Marcos's more introverted expression was overlooked or invalidated. For example, when he requested advice from his father regarding his friendship with a female, Marcos's father problem-solved the issue by suggesting that Marcos end the friendship; no validation of Marcos's emotional distress was reported. Furthermore, a significant pattern of self-invalidation has emerged in which Marcos interprets his emotional experiences, thoughts, and opinions as invalid, incorrect, or unimportant. For example, Marcos doubts ever having success in romantic relationships, perceives himself as a misfit, and is concerned with his ability to complete college. His lifelong pattern of self-invalidation and overpleasing of his family members has prevented him from developing a set of personal values. Instead, Marcos has embodied the values of his parents and thus has inhibited his behaviors based on their values and ethical code.

Overall, Marcos presents with anxiety, sadness, and an incomplete sense of self. He exhibits emotional dysregulation (e.g., affective lability), interpersonal dysregulation (e.g., unstable relationships), self-dysregulation (e.g., difficulties with sense of self, a sense of emptiness), and cognitive dysregulation (e.g., anxiety and ruminative ideation). These patterns of dysregulation would be replaced in DBT with more skillful responses. Mindfulness, interpersonal effectiveness, distress tolerance, and emotional regulation strategies would be taught to Marcos so that he could notice his experiences of negative affectivity (e.g., shame, sadness, anxiety) and regulate these experiences to effectively move him toward his short- and long-term goals.

Establishing the Therapeutic Alliance and Goals

It would be important to consider Marcos's level of disorder when planning an effective DBT program. Marcos does not display any Level 1 problems, such as significant behavioral dyscontrol or suicidality. To confirm or disconfirm the presence of Level 1 behaviors, the therapist would conduct a comprehensive assessment during the first session. Marcos exhibits several Level 2 (quiet desperation), Level 3 (problems in living), and Level 4 (incompleteness) problems. The therapist would consider a comprehensive assessment of Marcos's problems in addition to available programs and resources to determine the best DBT program. Comprehensive DBT would include individual therapy for Marcos, a DBT skills training course, phone coaching, and team consultation for the therapist. You are referred to the *DBT Skills Training Manual* (Linehan, 2014) for DBT skills training program schedule options.

Marcos would engage in pretreatment with the therapist. During this time, psychoeducation regarding DBT, the biosocial theory, and Marcos's presenting problems would be provided. In addition, the therapist would discuss the client and therapist agreements for DBT, the group skills training mode of treatment, therapist and client limits, and the diary card. During these pretreatment sessions, the therapist would use several commitment strategies (e.g., pros and cons, devil's advocate) to obtain and strengthen commitment to the DBT program and process. Pretreatment typically lasts approximately four sessions. Following pretreatment and agreement for comprehensive DBT, Marcos would be enrolled in a DBT skills training course in addition to his individual therapy. Marcos would also have the opportunity to utilize phone coaching, in which he could call his therapist any time, 24/7, to receive coaching for generalizing skills in his environment.

The Therapeutic Process and Interventions to Achieve Change

In the DBT skills training group, Marcos would learn skills in four different modules. Mindfulness skills are at the crux of DBT treatment, and Marcos would learn skills including wise mind, "what" skills, and "how" skills. Overall, mindfulness skills are used to increase awareness and focus as well as decrease confusion about the self. Specifically in regard to Marcos, these skills would be effective in increasing his awareness of the present moment, including external and internal experiences. These skills would increase effective decision making as well by discerning reasonable-mind from emotional-mind thoughts and choices. Treatment would emphasize Marcos being attuned to his wise mind, which honors both his emotional experiences and the facts of a given situation.

Emotional regulation skills include the ABC PLEASE (Accumulate positives, Build mastery, Cope ahead; Physical illness, Eating, Avoiding substances, Sleep, Exercise). These skills specifically target vulnerability to emotional experiences and mood regulation. It would be particularly important for Marcos to accumulate positive experiences and build his sense of mastery in a number of areas, possibly including his musical interests and school. Cope-ahead plans would be relevant for moments in which Marcos experiences negative affectivity and is likely to engage in emotion-minded behaviors. It would be important as well for the counselor to work on decreasing Marcos's emotional vulnerabilities by targeting self-care, including engaging in balanced eating, avoiding drugs and alcohol, increasing effective sleep hygiene, and engaging in exercise.

Distress tolerance skills target acting without thinking and escaping or avoiding emotional experiences. These skills include crisis survival strategies (e.g., distract, self-soothe, and IMPROVE [Imagery, create Meaning, Prayer, Relaxation, One thing in the moment, Vacation, Encouragement] the moment) and skills for accepting reality (e.g., willing hands, half-smiling, radical acceptance). It would be important for Marcos to work on radically accepting himself, his emotional experiences, and his similarities to and differences from his family and friends. In moments when Marcos feels overwhelmed with emotion, crisis survival skills can be utilized as short-term solutions. For example, if feeling overwhelmed with shame, Marcos might self-soothe with pleasant stimuli. Marcos and his counselor might create a cope-ahead plan in which Marcos has a self-soothe box with visual images (e.g., pictures of his family), soothing smells (e.g., cologne), soothing sounds (e.g., a favorite song), soothing tastes (e.g., chocolate), and things to touch (e.g., a soft blanket). Marcos would be able to self-soothe with these stimuli in moments of distress and subsequently proceed mindfully.

Finally, interpersonal problems would be targeted with interpersonal effectiveness skills that target effectively getting what one wants (e.g., DEAR MAN [Describe, Express, Assert, Reinforce, stay Mindful, Appear confident, Negotiate]), keeping a relationship (e.g., GIVE [be Gentle, act Interested, Validate, use an Easy manner]), and keeping self-respect (e.g., FAST [Fair on, no Apologies, Stick to values, Truthful communication]). These skills would be essential for Marcos given his interpersonal difficulties and concerns. Marcos, for example, might utilize these skills to assert himself when needed while simultaneously sticking to his own core values. Values work may be conducted in individual therapy to evaluate Marcos's personal values and may subsequently be used to highlight when Marcos acts in accordance with, against, and contrary to his value set.

The skills training group would consist of homework review of practicing a given skill and didactics of learning new skills. Skill generalization is reinforced by phone coaching. The individual counseling sessions would focus on reviewing Marcos's diary card and reviewing behavior chain analyses for Target 1 (or in Marcos's case Target 2 and Target 3) behaviors. Marcos's diary card would monitor suicidal ideation and suicidal urges or actions. These behaviors would be monitored throughout treatment, even if they were not endorsed in the intake or pretreatment sessions. The remainder of the diary card would be tailored for Marcos. His diary card may include monitoring of his self-invalidation and unassertiveness. The diary card also provides a place for Marcos to record his emotionality and skill usage.

Marcos would be required to complete his diary card on a daily basis and bring it with him to individual counseling sessions. The individual therapist may decide to assign additional homework as well that may target generalizing skills in the environment. For example, the individual therapist might assign Marcos a DEAR MAN task in which he must ask a professor for an extension on an assignment. Marcos would also be assigned homework from his skills training group that would include handouts and worksheets aimed at rehearsing skills. If Marcos did not complete his homework or diary card, these behaviors would be directly addressed and targeted as therapy-interfering behaviors.

Termination Considerations

Termination would be considered following completion of the full skills training module. Marcos's goal achievement would be reviewed, and he and his counselor would discuss termination and/or continuation in treatment. Continuation may include a second round of skills training, a DBT skills graduate group, or individual counseling only.

Mindfulness

Case Conceptualization

Marcos's mindset and narrative are primarily reliant on intellectualizing; evaluating; measuring his self-worth through achievements and the evaluation of others; and finally concluding that others are superior, that others know more, and that he is an inadequate man who will never be loved again. In the context of his childhood history, this narrative actually makes some degree of functional sense (and the counselor would indicate such; e.g., as a child and teen he was surrounded by older and wiser family: his mother, father, and outgoing older brother). He learned to respond to his youthful uncertainty with evaluative judgment and eventually self-criticism. His self-doubt and avoidant strategies were further exacerbated by the traumatic loss of his most trusted source of security and guidance, his mother. Through that loss he further learned that loving relationships are dangerous and that letting oneself be vulnerable enough to love leads to terrible emotional pain and loss. The counselor would talk about how this became the story for this young boy and how Marcos came to equate his quietness and feelings of perfectly reasonable vulnerability with being unmanly and unlovable. He learned to cope and protect himself by trying to achieve more, be different, and avoid possible loss and rejection.

Eventually the counselor would begin to question the pros and cons of continuing to cope in these old ways, ways that may have worked and made perfect sense earlier in his life (i.e., the counselor would question the present functionality of Marcos's coping strategies). The counselor would explore whether in the present these strategies of avoiding emotional distress and loss and criticizing his quiet, cautious side are leading him to the life he really wants to live now.

Establishing the Therapeutic Alliance and Goals

A fundamental aspect of a compassionate and mindful alliance is built on establishing both a visceral and a cognitive sense that Marcos feels accurately understood and that together, as a team, he and the counselor will find a way to clarify his priorities and then together work toward them. This is accomplished alongside the previously described historical validation and functional analysis. Thinking mindfully in functional/descriptive terms is modeled during and beyond the early stages of therapy. Compassion and mindfulness are introduced as a flexible form of perspective taking and even as an alternative neurological state of functioning. Mindful compassion is described as an alternative to worry and problem solving from which Marcos can objectively relate to his own thoughts and emotional reactions as well as to the thoughts and emotions of the counselor. Mindfulness would also help Marcos increase his awareness of his adult needs and values, asking him what his feelings are telling him about what is really important to him in life. Mindfulness is learning to live and take valued action in the moment, to learn from the past and plan for the future, but to repeatedly come back to living life more in one's senses and in the here and now, both in and out of session.

The Therapeutic Process and Interventions to Achieve Change

Mindfulness would also be introduced as a set of practices or exercises for living not only in the moment but also nonjudgmentally, being open to all feelings and with compassionate care for self and others. This would be presented as an alternative to trying to rigidly protect and/or motivate Marcos through the acts of self-criticism, self-punishment, isolation, and withdrawal. It would also be an alternative to always intellectualizing and figuring things out and planning. There is a time for planning, but there is also a time for being in the moment, courageously open to one's feelings, and guided by one's values. Marcos would be asked repeatedly how mindfully open he is to being compassionately vulnerable in the moment. The counselor would let him know when he is using a mindfulness (nonjudgmental, descriptive courage) approach to being open to his feelings, to being imperfect and vulnerable in session, behaviors he has been avoiding with others, and the counselor would reinforce him by trying to be mindfully open, genuine, and vulnerable in return.

A variety of experiential methods of practicing open-mindful attention would be explored both in and out of session. There would be discussion of mindfully relating to one's thoughts and feelings by looking to describe thoughts more as thoughts instead of facts and learning to look at thoughts not just from thoughts (one classic exercise for dong this is called *describing and physicalizing thoughts*). For example, the counselor would have Marcos close his eyes and describe the physical properties of his thoughts, asking whether they are sentences, fragments, or pictures and whether he is in the picture or watching the pictures. The counselor would also ask whether he hears the thoughts, and if so, whose voice is it? Is it loud or soft, slow or fast? Do the thoughts have color, and if so, what color? Are they big or small? Another fundamental classic exercise for open-monitoring mindfulness is the *leaves on a stream* exercise (asking Marcos to take a few minutes each day to be totally open to his stream of consciousness). Rather than evaluating and figuring out these thoughts, Marcos would be asked to just watch each thought and feeling go by like a leaf on a stream without trying to change them or evaluate them.

A more fundamental moving-mindful practice is *mindful sensory pauses*. In this exercise, which is practiced throughout the day for 30-second periods, Marcos would be instructed to pause and tune into sensory awareness, naming and describing three sensory experiences he is having in the moment. If thoughts come up, he is to simply label them as thoughts and come back to his senses (DBT refers to this as *mindfully distinguishing between observe and describe*). This type of mindful defusing and decentering from thoughts might also include the more traditional CT labeling of thought patterns (e.g., black-and-white thinking, personalizing, catastrophizing). However, with mindfulness, the emphasis is not on determining how realistic the thoughts are but simply on not allowing thoughts to determine one's valued actions. The counselor might ask Marcos to practice thinking one thing and doing the exact opposite to reinforce this same essential principle. Mindfulness would also ask Marcos to engage in *need or value awareness,* practiced as a pause so as to choose to act on what is really important to him (e.g., being a creative musician, treating people with love, checking with the needs of others).

Regarding self-image or self-concept, it would be important to have Marcos mindfully notice the difference between *thoughts about himself* and *his actual self,* mindfully noticing that these two things are not one and the same. This might be practiced (using the *thought is not the object exercise*) by asking Marcos to describe any object (e.g., a desk), asking him to describe his thoughts about that desk, and asking whether those thoughts about the desk are identical to the actual desk. He would be asked to repeat this with other objects and then finally with himself as the object. This is a mindful discrimination exercise with the goal being to show clients that their story will always be an incomplete story, never the same as their ongoing selves (just like a biography, movie, or book is never the same as the actual person). Furthermore, regardless of the stories about him, thoughts do not determine his choice of values and actions. Mindful awareness is also part of learning nonjudgmental self-acceptance. Mindful self-acceptance would be described to Marcos as having the courage to *compassionately accept all parts* of himself, even the parts he does not always like. Accepting those parts compassionately might at times require being flexible and genuine about those qualities, letting others know that at times he feels anxious and that he needs some time alone.

Termination Considerations

Over the course of months the counselor would look to see that Marcos is becoming aware of and able to declare his values and that he is able to describe and request his needs both in and out of session. Periodic feedback regarding his sense of progress would be elicited from Marcos. Specifically, the counselor would want to know how Marcos gauges his progress as well as when he thinks the right time to taper the work would be. The possibility of booster sessions when needed would also be discussed. Reframing his sense of vulnerability and inferiority at least partly as a universal struggle with evolving into adulthood would also be addressed. As Marcos becomes aware of how his values and needs tie in with living mindfully in the here and now, it would also be important that he recognize that one can never truly finish living according to one's values. The counselor would emphasize that it is one's ongoing values that make life worth living.

Summary

Although each of the authors' approaches have some unique insights into how they would treat Marcos, it is clear that they all emphasize the importance of establishing a therapeutic alliance and are cognizant of potential ruptures to the relationship throughout the course of therapy. All of the therapies respect and work within the bounds of Marcos's cultural and religious values. As was demonstrated in this chapter, there are many different paths counselors can take with their clients, not only with case conceptualization but also with which problems to target first. Obviously the specific therapeutic process is based on the particular therapeutic approach, but as is evident in reading this case study, there are many similarities among the cognitive behavior therapies (CBTs) under the CBT umbrella. Furthermore, many of the interventions overlap and can be used across the individual CBT approaches.

It is our hope that through reading this book and the case studies you have a better understanding of CBT. This is the foundation that will guide you in the direction of a particular approach. As was clearly pointed out throughout the book, CBT has strong empirical support as an efficacious treatment for many mental health problems with a strong bias for prevention as well as intervention.

References

Linehan, M. M. (2014). *DBT® skills training manual*. New York, NY: Guilford Press.

Index

Tables are indicated by "t" following the page number.